LONDON'S IMMORTALS

SAVOY PRESS

LONDON'S IMMORTALS

THE COMPLETE OUTDOOR COMMEMORATIVE STATUES

John Blackwood

Photographs by Caroline Irwin, Richard Cheatle
and Philip Ward-Jackson

SAVOY PRESS

The author would like to thank David Nabarro for having put forward the idea for this book, for having undertaken its publication and for his continuing enthusiasm and support. He would also like to thank all those who have helped him by reading and commenting on various parts of the manuscript: Professor William Blackwood, Professor Brian Bond, Jonathan Boulting, Enid Drury, Martin Ludlow, John Marshall, David Nabarro, Rosie Parsons, Robert Peberdy and Sir David Piper. The mistakes that remain are his own.

Savoy Press Ltd.
Broadlands,
27 Broadlands Rd
Highgate, London N6 4AE
and
104, Ferry Road
Oxford OX30EX

First published 1989

Design and layout by Jerry Burman and John Blackwood

Typeset in Goudy Old Style by PGT Design at Opus, Oxford, and printed by BAS, Over Wallop, Hampshire
Black and white origination by Oxford Litho-Plates

ISBN 0-9514296-0-4

CONTENTS

FOREWORD
by
Sir Hugh Casson

We all accept and most of us welcome the long and noble tradition of enriching our streets and squares with statues of the great and the good. Our eyes need to be engaged by something more permanent and worthy than posters and shop signs. We still need at times to celebrate community pride.

Yet public sculpture is a risky business. The familiar hazards – patronage by committee, an inappropriate site, arrogance from experts and artists – can quickly sharpen public apathy into resentment. When such sculpture is an image of a national figure (in the choice of whom not many of us have had a say) that resentment can turn easily to ridicule. Public art, in other words, is often dismissed as elitist and "imposed". It is thus easy to be funny – or fairly funny – about public portraits on our streets, if only to speculate about how many pairs of clay feet are concealed within those bronze boots or marble robes. Easy certainly, but surely to be avoided.

This fascinating book takes account of these pitfalls but carries us beyond them. Being a comprehensive study, it shows us in full detail what is there and where it can be found: plenty of royalty, more generals and statesmen than artists, poets and scholars – the British are suspicious of ideas and frightened by those who have them – and hardly any women, except of course those portrayed as symbols of virtue. (Courage and Justice, Tolerance and Mercy are seldom depicted by men. As Marina Warner has pointed out, even the figure of Naval Gunnery on the Admiralty Arch is the usual toga'd lady.)

The total number is comparatively small, but growing. There have been few departures – and quite right, too. These men were honoured in their time and who are we to deny them our respect today? Here in these pages you will find all those that survive, the handsome, the dedicated, the pompous, the beloved, the touching and the absurd. You will discover who designed them, how to find them, and why they are there. The descriptions are factual but never pedantic, the illustrations are sensitive and of high quality. Even today when heroes (and heroines) are regarded with scepticism and sculptors seem reluctant to accept the challenge of large-scale portraiture, they make fascinating, worthy company. The author has clearly enjoyed making their acquaintance and he shares his enjoyment effortlessly and sympathetically with all of us.

Hugh Casson

PUBLISHER'S PREFACE

During the summer of 1986 I was lunching in the City with an old friend, Professor William Blackwood, a leader in the field of British neuropathology during the 1960's and 70's. Over a glass of claret the conversation turned to how he might enjoyably occupy himself now that retirement loomed and I disclosed my pet project of publishing a book about the statues of London. In the ensuing discussion I learned to my surprise and delight that his son John had recently published a small work on the gargoyles of Oxford and was looking for a new venture. From that excellent lunch and my subsequent meeting with John Blackwood, a dream has turned into reality and after three years our book *London's Immortals* has emerged. I hope that you, the readers, will gain as much pleasure as we have had fun from its creation, design and development.

With no previous publishing experience, *London's Immortals* was born out of a desire on my part to widen my horizons beyond my usual investment activities in the City. But why statues? Well, something about statues has always fascinated me. Their sense of permanence in a changing world, their strength, beauty and sense of history, a certain solidity ... a world away from the intangible values of the financial markets.

Most men and women, I believe, would like to be remembered, to make their mark against the transience of life and achieve – in a word – immortality. Very few ever attain it. Memories are short even for the most momentous events. How remarkable then were the ancient Pharaohs and their thousands of years old pyramids at Gizeh. In general it seems that leaving a great building or work of art, or being commemorated by a statue is far more likely to fulfil a subject's ambition for immortality than a lifetime of conquests or the creation of cash or concepts. As George Bush said in his presidential inauguration speech, "My friends, we are not the sum of our possessions." Good examples of such fulfilment in the quest for immortality are Louis XIV, the Sun King, commemorated by his magical palace at Versailles, Christopher Wren, immortalised by St Paul's Cathedral, Michaelangelo by the Sistine Chapel, Paul Getty by his museum in Malibu and maybe best of all, Gustave Eiffel by his Tower in Paris.

Good architecture and intense building activity are nearly always a reflection of the self-confidence felt by the city or nation in question. And so it has been with the erection of statues in London. The number raised in the capital reached a peak during the self confident empire building years of Victorian and Edwardian England and then went into a sharp decline during the twentieth century's years of economic slump and post-war austerity. However, a resurgence of British patriotism and self-confidence associated with the Thatcher era of the 1980's seems to be resulting in a significant increase in the number of statues being put up and perhaps we will see a repeat of the pattern of a century ago. Certainly at least seven new statues will have been raised in London during 1988 and 1989.

The outside statues of London add charm and a human dimension to the great streets and towering buildings of our city centre, and I hope that this book will awake in some of you a new interest and awareness of the importance of statues, both as a historical record and a spiritual enhancement of our capital.

Amongst the one hundred and sixty odd statues covered in this book, there is a preponderance of kings, queens, soldiers and politicians. Sadly, our greatest artists, musicians, scholars and, most chauvinistically, women, have been largely ignored. The selection process has in some ways been arbitrary and in certain cases, in terms of the relative contribution to our society, absurd. Therefore, in an effort to redress this imbalance and encourage the raising of new statues, I propose to make a contribution of £1 for every copy of this book sold to a fund for the raising of a new outside statue in London.

On the inside back cover of this book there is a voting slip for each purchaser to return to the publishers with their suggestion of whom they believe to be the most suitable subject for one of the next statues to be put up in London. We have included our own small list of potentially suitable people but the choice is yours. As a general guideline, candidates should be British, posthumous, and famous rather than infamous! There are of course no hard and fast rules but readers may care to reflect that since 1800 only nine subjects have had statues erected during their lifetimes – among them two Queens, Alexandra and Victoria, Fenner Brockway (at the age of 96!), Gladstone, Paolozzi (represented by a self-portrait and poignantly the only sculptor to appear on the streets) and the Duke of Wellington. As stated above, there are too few figures either of women in general or more specifically of our greatest artists, authors, musicians or scientists. Personally, I find it mystifying that Turner does not stand, with Millais, before the Tate Gallery, forever surveying the changing pattern of the Thameside sky.

In due course our "candidate for immortality", the majority choice of you the buyers of this book, will be announced. At that time we will endeavour to raise the balance of funds necessary by corporate donation or public subscription, in order subsequently to have your majority choice immortalised in bronze.

So *London's Immortals* was conceived, a background and pictorial guide to the statues of London, a compendium of remarkable and not so remarkable people who have touched this country of ours and through being commemorated in statue form have left their own footprints in the sands of time.

My sincerest thanks go to John Blackwood, his father William, Lois Heller and Rosie Parsons for their energy, enthusiasm, unfailing patience and sense of humour.

To end, I borrow once again from the words of President Bush who, speaking of ex-President Reagan, said, "There is a man who has earned a lasting place in our hearts and in our history." It is for men and women who merit such a description that statues have and should be raised.

David J.N. Nabarro
Publisher
March 1989

INTRODUCTION

To write an account of commemorative sculpture world-wide – to say which of its fellows the human race has most admired and how it has represented them – would be an immense task and one not yet attempted. This book focuses on a single city in a small country at the edge of the world's major land masses; it confines itself to a particular kind of commemoration and hence to a comparatively brief period of some three hundred years. However, the changes through which that country passed during those years and the effects which it had on the world at large were considerable. All these are represented in the statues in the streets of its capital, which stand as one of the most cogent witnesses of its past.

Let us first define the boundaries of our subject. This book covers all London's outdoor, free-standing, full-length commemorative statues erected up to the year 1988. It does not describe commemorative busts, of which there are a number (the most famous being the vast countenance of Karl Marx in Highgate Cemetery). It does not describe statues on buildings, which are uncountable (there are three hundred and seventy on the Houses of Parliament alone). It does not deal with commemorations of groups, so the many war memorials are mentioned only in passing. It does not deal with general, allegorical or abstract sculptures so, for example, the Monument which commemorates the Great Fire of London, London's oldest and tallest free-standing memorial, is omitted. There is is no account of Dick Whittington's stone or, regretfully, since only human figures are included, of his cat.

Distinctions sometimes blur and the rules have been bent a few times for the sake of completeness or to answer some especially pressing claim. It seemed impossible to have a book on London statues without Peter Pan, who is a real enough character to the many thousands of children who have seen J.M. Barrie's play or walked in Kensington Gardens. Eros and Achilles – two famous symbolic figures which commemorate historical people – have been included. A statue on a building, that of David Livingstone at the Royal Geographical Society, appears as a well-known and striking representation of a significant figure. Statues that were indoors and are now out of doors are included. Statues that were once out of doors and are now indoors are occasionally included; one is the early, epoch-making figure of the philanthropic Captain Maples now at Trinity House. An additional chapter has been given to statues which have been removed from London's streets and have either been broken up, resited elsewhere or kept in store; a few of these vanished statues, for example the gilded equestrian statue of George I once in Leicester Square, have for the sake of continuity been placed in the principal text. The rate of loss has in fact been remarkably low.

This, then, is a book about the British hero and his (or, in a very few cases, her) commemoration. André Malraux once said that a nation should be judged by the statues it erects. If that is so, then what is revealed about the character of the British people over the last three hundred years? They are royalist but like to see their kings as efficient, military leaders rather than figures of luxury and elegance; out of uniform they prefer them on the informal side. They are a male-led society, yet they respond most deeply and in the most complete and complex manner to the rule of Queens. They value individual generosity and benevolence, and respect housing, property and the care of the poor and sick. They honour the arts and sciences to some extent but have never really done collective justice to the creative genius of their race. They are a political people and are justly proud of having given birth to democratic government in the present age. They put up statues to those of all political persuasions and, once up, they do not pull them down again (the one exception, Marochetti's statue of Peel, was removed out of aesthetic, rather than factional, prejudice). They have fought wars and they honour their military men next after their kings and statesmen; nevertheless, they unveil the statues of their generals quietly and without bombast. Commerce and empire have been dominant themes in their history but they have had virtually no admiration for the nuts and bolts of trade. Exploration, even if – particularly if – it ends in tragedy, enthrals them. Religion concerns them less but they respect its ability to reform and underpin society; in recent years their retreat from empire has perhaps been balanced by a greater interest in the religious roots of their past.

The erection of free-standing statues was one of the expressions of the European Renaissance. Since the Renaissance in architecture and the visual arts did not cross the English Channel until encouraged by the Stuart kings in the seventeenth century, so London's first such figure was that of Charles I, erected privately at Roehampton in 1633 and publicly at the top of Whitehall in 1676. In themselves commemorative statues were not new. However, during the Middle Ages such figures were generally to be found on tombs. Statues out of doors were exclusively housed in niches, either on great buildings or on arches, gateways or "crosses". Architecture climbed vertically to Heaven and subsumed the human figure in that ascent. Surrounding streets were narrow and offered no opportunity for free-standing, secular display. With the Renaissance, however, humanity abandoned its safe niche in the tower of eternity and burst out along the horizontal, taking its inspiration from the cultures of ancient Greece and Rome. Eleven of London's outdoor statues wear classical dress, so this link is plain to see. The adoption of Imperial battle-armour as the costume of kings began with Charles II, just as the colonial spirit of the Roman Empire was breaking through again into history. Likewise the first statues of statesmen, which appeared with the growth of parliamentary influence at the beginning of the nineteenth century, were draped in togas; the style may seem incongruous today but every gentleman of the time had had a classical education and looked to the city states of Ancient Greece and to Republican Rome as the fountainhead of oratory and democratic representation. It was not until the middle of the nineteenth century, with the commemoration

Above right. Matthew Cotes Wyatt's original design for the memorial to George III. It continues the classical style, in a highly elaborate way; the King wears a kind of toga and on his brow is the laurel crown of victory. He rides in a triumphal chariot, preceded by Fame (blowing her trumpet) and Victory (waving another crown). The horses are trampling a many-headed monster representing Faction and other evils. The plan proved far too expensive and in the end a much more modest and naturalistic equestrian statue was erected in Cockspur Street (see p48-9).

Below right. George III was the first English monarch to be given a memorial paid for by public subscription. This is the advertisement, showing the names of the patrons and committee. Below are the banks to which subscriptions might be sent. Contributors were asked to write their names and titles carefully, as they were to be recorded in bronze on the pedestal of the monument, another ambitious aspect of the plan which was never carried out.

THE
MONUMENTAL TROPHY
IN HONOR OF
HIS LATE MAJESTY KING GEORGE III.
(DESIGNED, AND TO BE EXECUTED, BY MATTHEW WYATT.)

The Memory of His late Majesty has been endeared to the British Empire, by the firmness, dignity, and purity of his principles.

There exists no Monument to George the Third in any public part of the Metropolis. It is therefore proposed to erect, by General Subscription, a Memorial, which may at once commemorate the splendour of his Reign, and the gratitude of an affectionate People.

The Design (to be executed in Bronze) consists of a Statue of his late Majesty, in a Car drawn by four Horses, with Figures of Fame and Victory: appropriate Bas-reliefs and Decorations will be introduced, upon a massive Pedestal of Granite.

of that great middle-class Prime Minister, Sir Robert Peel, that the statues became completely naturalised and the classical convention was transcended.

For the first hundred or more years, the pattern was essentially one of individual initiative and private gift. All the kings and queens subsequent to Charles I were given outdoor statues. These were erected in the fast growing and picturesque squares of the capital: Soho Square (first called King Square, after its central occupant), Queen Anne Square (now part of Queen Anne's Gate), Grosvenor Square, Golden Square, Leicester Square, Queen Square and St James's Square. The other principal type of commemorative site relates to the British people's prominent concern for the poor and sick. Chelsea and Greenwich Hospitals (magnificently built hostels which cared for retired and destitute soldiers and sailors) saw the erection of two royal statues. So too did St Thomas's, a hospital in the modern sense of the word. Moreover, the only other significant class of person commemorated out of doors during this time was the philanthropist, as statues of merchants and City businessmen were erected outside the buildings which their generosity had endowed or improved.

Public commemoration on an extensive scale began at the beginning of the nineteenth century during and after the wars with France. These called forth a tremendous collective effort from the British people, both militarily and financially. The egalitarianism of the French Revolution had turned sour and collapsed into its opposite, the glamorous imperialism of Napoleon. England was faced with the complete French domination of Europe and the invasion of her shores; she needed to respond in kind, not only with men and arms but also with a corresponding pantheon of national heroes. At first the various military and naval commemorations took place indoors at un-characteristic State expense, as Westminster Abbey and then St Paul's Cathedral were turned into Valhallahs of national bravery and self-sacrifice. It was at this time that the erection of a statue only after the death of its subject became the accepted norm, though the custom has not always been adhered to.

It took a number of years, decades even, for the memorials relating to the Napoleonic period to appear outside, on London's streets. In cities other than London, in Glasgow, Edinburgh, Liverpool and Birmingham, through a more acute sense of civic pride, the outdoor commemorations, paid for by public subscription, went ahead more quickly. One reason for London's slower progress was the magnitude of the tasks being proposed, both indoors and out, and the exhaustion of funds, both State and private. It was a time when impossible schemes were in the air, for example Major John Cartwright's *Heironauticon* or naval temple (see p177) and John Flaxman's plan for a two hundred and thirty foot high statue of Britannia on Greenwich Hill. Another scheme which went astray was Matthew Cotes Wyatt's grandiose plan for a national memorial to George III, who had ruled throughout the French wars; the original design and the advertisement for subscribers are shown on the previous page (p11). Once the outdoor memorials did appear, however, they significantly altered the appearance of the capital, heightening its heroic character. There was the Duke of York's column (the Duke was Commander-in Chief of the army between 1795 and 1827) and Nelson's column. There was Achilles in Hyde Park and the colossal equestrian statue of Wellington on the triumphal arch at Hyde Park Corner (removed in the 1880's).

The Thames Embankment as it was in the 1870's, shortly after its construction. The first of the many statues erected there commemorated the daring and chivalrous Lieutenant General Sir James Outram, who had served for almost all of his life in India (see p262). Note Nelson's column on the right of the picture. The Embankment Gardens offered an ideal site for statues and now has twelve (see map, chapter 11). (Boadicea, on the Embankment by Westminster Bridge, makes up the thirteen.) Whether by design or accident, the statues of Outram and his two closest companions, Bartle Frere (p200) and William Tyndale (p312), fittingly express the three pillars of enlightened rule: the just use of arms, benevolent administration and a religion available to all.

In the same class was the City's great granite statue of William IV by London Bridge (now at Greenwich).

It was at this time that public subscription became the established method of raising funds. Other commemorations, now generally of a political nature, went on as before in London's squares and crescents, but this time the funds were raised collectively among groups of friends and supporters. The statues of the Duke of Bedford, Charles James Fox, the Duke of Kent (as a philanthropist), Major John Cartwright (mentioned above), William Pitt and Lord George Bentinck were paid for in this way. These public statues were in fact considerable items representing a substantial financial commitment by their sponsors. Both Chantrey's statue of Pitt and Westmacott's statue of Canning (erected in 1832 outside the Houses of Parliament) cost their subscribers £7,000. In considering the prices of statues (and also the donations of philanthropists), one must remember how much the value of the pound has changed since the beginning of the Second World War. Between 1660 and 1938 its average purchasing power remained substantially the same. Between 1938 and 1987, however, it declined by a factor of approximately twenty five and £7,000 therefore represents nearly £200,000 in modern terms. This price seems more than somewhat inflated – in keeping, perhaps, with the spirit of the period – and is more or less at the top of the range. (Chantrey's George IV, at £9,450 (£235,000), comes out as the most expensive individual statue of all). Certainly during the eighteenth century sculptors' fees were very much lower. Between 1860 and 1930 the average price for a bronze figure was around £2,500 (or £60,000 – £80,000).

The whole Victorian period has been called an age of hero-worship and the various ways in which this manifested will be illustrated in the following pages. As the century progressed, more and more statues were erected. There was never one, overall strategic plan, though the bureaucracy intervened on various occasions and Trafalgar Square, Waterloo Place and, especially, Parliament Square all developed their particular characters. As we look back on many of those figures, we encounter the British Empire ripening towards its heyday and our feelings about it must inevitably colour our appreciation of the statues of its leaders. By now it should be possible to have a balanced view. Acquired through a mixture of idealism and self-interest, it was, one might say, no worse than the other empires of history; it was in many ways more humane and it was surrendered more or less voluntarily.

What becomes clear is that the individuals who emerged as its heroes were very far from the stereotypes one might imagine.

Let us examine some more statistics. From 1676 until the 1820's the average number of statues erected was one per decade. In the 1830's, 40's and 50's the average rose to five. Then from the 1860's right through to the 1920's the average remained at eleven or twelve per decade. There were two major peaks, with nine statues erected in the years 1880-4 and 1910-4. The decline came in the late 1920's and 1930's; from the 30's until 1987 the rate per decade was down by more than half to four or five. 1930 was of course the time of the depression and a great decline in personal prosperity. However, in another sense the break came sooner and the peak at the end of the Edwardian Age was even more pronounced; of the eight statues erected between 1920 and 1926, no less than four (Edward VII, White, Lincoln and Washington) had been planned before 1914 and two (Wolseley and Roberts) were of men who had died before the First World War or just at its beginning. So, though it produced numerous memorials to the troops who fought in it, the War was clearly a watershed for the self-confident worship of the individual hero.

Since the 1920's and 30's an opposing trend has emerged. There has been a much greater internationalism, as Britain's links, past and present, with other countries and London's character as a world city have emerged out of the decline in individualism. Of the thirty three statues erected between 1920 and 1980, eleven (one third) were either of foreigners or were donated from abroad. With the statue of St Volodymyr erected in 1988 in Holland Park by the Ukranian community in Britain, this internationalism seems to be continuing. On the other hand, 1988 has dramatically reversed the previous decline; with no less than five outdoor statues erected, it has surpassed every other year in London's history (the previous best being 1882, with four). We shall have more to say of this in our penultimate chapter.

The pattern of erecting outdoor statues by public subscription has remained unchanged from the beginning of the nineteenth century until the present day. This may come as a surprise to those who have always thought of them as objects of State, put up as part of a propaganda programme for the inculcation of loyalty. In fact of the one hundred and thirty three or so statues erected since 1800, eleven have been gifts by private individuals, seven have been erected by local government or by institutions, and five have come from abroad. Only seven have been paid for entirely out of British State funds. In the cases of Sir John Franklin, General Gordon, and Field Marshals Kitchener, Haig and Smuts, the money from public memorial appeals had already been put to other uses. The government also paid for the statues of George IV and Field Marshal Roberts, and for three-quarters of the 1888 Wellington replacement memorial at Hyde Park Corner, for half of the Albert Memorial and for the final stages of Nelson's column. All the other hundred or so statues were paid for by the voluntary contributions of well-wishers and admirers (their numbers sometimes running into thousands) and this fact says a great deal for the collective spirit of the British people.

One obvious question arises: if London's statues are financed by individual groups of admirers, then why are there not far more of them? An explosion of this kind occurred in the Roman Empire, where there were reports of many thousands of figures, many of them commemorating people of no particular distinction. The Elder Cato,

The Empire could not last for ever. With some historical license, this cartoon book-cover by Osbert Lancaster shows the reaction of the statue of Lord Roberts (p274) to one of the more unfortunate death-throes of its spirit, the 1956 invasion of Suez.

when his friends expressed surprise that there was no statue of him in the Roman forum, replied, "I would much rather have men ask why I have no statue, than why I have one." In London, however, a tight network of control has been established, beginning with the Public Statues Act of 1854. By this Act, permission was required from the Office of Works (later the Ministry of Works and now the Department of the Environment) before any statue could be erected in a public place. Later the Royal Fine Arts Commission were given an official position as overall adjudicators of artistic quality. Statues erected on public land were generally taken over by the Office of Works, which became responsible for repairing and maintaining them. ("Hero wash-up", *Punch* called the routine of cleaning statues.) Those on ground owned by local authorities (such as the Victoria Embankment Gardens, which have had four different owners) came under those authorities. This places our subject squarely in the world of bureaucracy, with its attendant complexities and conflicts.

The aesthetic qualities of London's statues have been an equally controversial matter. Denigration has been common. Elevated on their pedestals, presumptuous but speechless, they have inevitably been the targets of abuse from the down-to-earth, democratically-minded and somewhat philistine English. An extreme example was *Punch's* 1861 dismissal of Behnes' statue of Havelock as "a short-legged hydro-cephalous abortion" (a comment probably based on an ignorance of the laws of perspective and the need to make the head of an elevated figure proportionally larger than the body). A more common criticism has been dullness. One reason for this is the unfortunate flatness of modern male dress – the "tight-trouser" problem – hence the employment of every kind of ceremonial robe and uniform. Another is the inevitable decay of stone and the darkening of bronze on exposure to the atmosphere. The general gloominess of London's weather does not help. Sometimes the level of craftsmanship has been uninspired, the sculptors failing to "bring out a sharp shadow from every fold and from every border", as the *Art Journal* put it in their review of the somewhat prosaic statue of George Peabody. Fortunately, the climax of national commemoration coincided with a high point in British portrait sculpture. Towards the end of the nineteenth century (inspired, it must be said, principally by Frenchmen like Rodin and Jules Dalou) English sculpture went through a rebirth later known as "the New Sculpture". The public statues of the best sculptors of that movement, Alfred Gilbert, Thomas Brock, Alfred Drury, Onslow Ford, George Frampton and, above all, Hamo Thornycroft, have a liveliness and a humanity which must earn them a more than respectable place as works of art.

This book, then, sets out on a historical and artistic journey of discovery, showing us objects familiar yet largely unknown. It is about attitudes to character and to charisma, and charts the changing ideals and aims of a civilisation. What, finally, do the statues have to say to us? Erected to instruct as well as to inspire, they bring the past to life; their expressions, bearing, dress, the objects they hold and the inscriptions, plaques and supporting figures on their pedestals vividly invoke the occasions which brought them into being. The care that was taken over them and their continuing presence tell us more. Mankind lives by example, they say, and while civilisation lasts the wise, the good, the generous and the brave will, for all their failings, not be forgotten.

Frontispiece, p2. The scene in Old Palace Yard after a bombing raid during September 1940. On the left is the statue of the great warrior and crusader, Richard Coeur de Lion (see p56-7). The raised sword has been bent but remains unbroken. The message contained in the event was soon realised: thus would democracy bend but not break under the attack of tyranny. The sword was left unstraightened until 1947, when it unfortunately became unsafe and had to be replaced.

One of the accompanying themes of this book will be the almost uncanny way in which the physical history of statues comes to reflect those they commemorate, as if they were charged with that person's original *manas*. This seems particularly true of royal statues.

CHAPTER 1
ROYALTY

The statues of England's kings and queens are the most ancient and the most numerous in the streets and squares of London. Every monarch since Charles I has been represented, yet the sequence has grown organically through chance and hazard in a typically English way. Charles I's statue survived the execution of its subject and was erected on the spot where those who had condemned him were themselves put to death. Charles II's statue in Soho Square, like Charles himself, endured a lengthy exile from the capital. William III had to wait a hundred years for his mount in St James's Square. George I no longer rides his gilded horse in Leicester Square; we must look for him in Bloomsbury atop one of the Seven Wonders of the World. George II has two statues; the first was picked up at auction from a bankrupt nobleman, the second was a successful "bribe".

George III was the first monarch to have a national memorial but subscriptions were moderate and the committee had to abandon the by then traditional Roman Imperial style and make do with a plain man on a plain horse, known ever afterwards as "the pigtail and pump-handle". The City of London's great, granite statue of William IV is now at Greenwich, as befits the Sailor-king. With Albert and Victoria we are in the great age of commemoration and their statues far outnumber those of any other royal pair. During this century the progress has been more sedate, though the site of Edward VII's memorial and the design of George V's caused considerable controversy before the final decisions were made.

Ushering in the royal procession is the presence pictured opposite, now the oldest freestanding outdoor statue in London. It was one of a series of fifteen monarchs ordered for Westminster Hall by Richard II in 1385. Its sculptor was Thomas Canon of Corfe and its cost £2-6-8d. In 1822 it was removed from its long concealed place in the outer wall and taken to Trinity House Square, Southwark, where it has been known sometimes as King Alfred and sometimes as Father Trinity. The earliest contemporaneous outdoor royal likeness is the statue of Elisabeth I which was once in a niche on Lud Gate and now adorns the church of St Dunstan-in-the-West, Fleet Street, but not being free-standing it does not qualify for this book. The equestrian statue of Richard I outside the Houses of Parliament was a retrospective commemoration, being the product of the national and technical self-confidence of the nineteenth century. Our story proper therefore begins with that great paradox and patron of the arts, the martyr-king Charles I.

Charles I

Charles I. Born 1600, Dunfermline, second son of James VI of Scotland. Became heir to English throne on death of gifted, intelligent elder brother, Henry, 1612. Became King, 1625. At war with France; failure of expedition to La Rochelle, 1627-30. Dissolved Parliament and ruled without it; raised taxation by personal levy, imposed High Church ritual in England and bishoprics in Scotland, 1629-40. Long Parliament dissolved royal machinery of government, 1640-1. Defeated in First Civil War, 1642-6. Imprisoned but refused to compromise, 1646-8. Aided by navy and by Scots in Second Civil War; defeated and tried for treason, 1648-9. Executed January 30th, 1649.

Statue by Hubert le Sueur. Bronze. First erected 1633 at Lord Weston's estate, Roehampton and re-erected 1676 at the top of Whitehall. Overall height 9ft 3ins, length 7ft 9ins head to tail. Original cost, £600. The pedestal of Portland stone was designed by Sir Christopher Wren and carved by Joshua Marshall, the King's Master Mason.

A medallion of Le Sueur at the age of 59 by his friend Jan Warin, showing an experienced, self-confident man.

At the head of Whitehall, on a pedestal emblazoned with the Stuart arms, rides Charles, King and Martyr. Cast during the king's own lifetime, the statue has the richest and most complex history of any in the capital. Indeed, its story is almost as dramatic as that of its ill-fated subject.

Charles Stuart was not at his best as a king. He pursued useless wars and alliances and he alienated both the men of property and the men of independent conscience. He fended off his opponents with contradictory and impossible promises, yet he never abandoned his belief in himself as a just, divinely appointed ruler. Serious, retiring, delicate in appearance, he could inspire great personal devotion but he lacked that grasp on reality which a ruler needs to survive. He had the soul of a connoisseur rather than a king. He brought England into the European artistic mainstream and he ranks with George IV as England's greatest royal patron of the arts. His interests included sculpture; as a contemporary writer put it, "his royal liking for ancient statues caused a whole army of old foreign emperors, captains and senators all at once to land on his coasts, to come and do him homage and attend him in his palaces."

An important part of Charles's artistic programme was the creation of an image of himself as an absolute ruler along Renaissance lines, the supreme example being found in Inigo Jones' designs for the interior of the Banqueting House. Within the boundaries of Imperial Rome, an equestrian statue was the Emperor's privilege and the kings and dukes of Renaissance Europe revived the image to reinforce their own authority. Thus Inigo Jones designed, though never built, a triumphal arch for Temple Bar crowned by an equestrian statue of his King. The statue now at the top of Whitehall (though originally a private commission) belongs in this tradition and was therefore the first of its kind in Britain since the days of the Romans. It was the work of the French sculptor Hubert le Sueur, one of the many foreign artists attracted by the opportunities at the Stuart court. The technique of bronze casting was hardly known in England at the time and le Sueur was an expert. The royal statue was ordered by the Lord High Commissioner, Lord Weston. According to the terms of the contract the rider was to be a full six foot tall (Charles, though a good horseman, was an unimpressive five foot) and if in doubt over the graceful movement of the mount le Sueur was to consult "His Majesty's riders of great horses". The statue was cast in 1633 and Lord Weston set it up in the garden of his house at Roehampton.

Then came the Civil War. Weston (by then Lord Portland) had died in 1635. By 1644 his estate was in the possession of Sir Thomas Dawes. Probably on the grounds that his father had once loaned money to Charles I, Dawes was adjudged "delinquent" by the Parliamentary authorities; his property was sequestrated, though this was later commuted to a large fine. By order of the House of Commons the statue was sold for £150 to three representatives of the newly formed parish of St Paul's, Covent Garden, who erected it in their churchyard. In 1650, during the Second Civil War, the Council of State ordered the destruction of the royal statues at St Paul's Cathedral and the Exchange. At the same time they made enquiries with the purpose of establishing the ownership of the Covent Garden statue. In 1655 further enquiries were made by General Desborow. In 1660, immediately after the Restoration, the statue was in the possession of a brazier, the appropriately named John Rivett, of the Dial, Holborn.

Rivett was brought before the Court of Exchequer accused of appropriating Crown property. In his defence he stated that he had bought the statue from two members of St Paul's Vestry for £215 (its scrap value) and that he had subsequently been ordered to destroy it by the Puritan authorities. He had, however, concealed it, "with great hazard, charge and care preserving it under ground".

Possession of the statue was awarded to the new Earl of Portland and Rivett was rewarded for his loyalty by the office of King's Brazier. (Later, however, for reasons unknown, he committed suicide.) The story of the burial went down in history and, over the next hundred years or more, details of Roundhead destructiveness and Cavalier cunning proliferated. The statue, it was said, never went to Roehampton. At the outbreak of Civil War it had been concealed in the crypt of St Paul's, Covent Garden, until discovered by Puritan search parties. Rivett had pretended to destroy it and had done a thriving trade in souvenirs supposedly made from its metal; bodkins and thimbles, spoons and pattypans, knife-handles, candlesticks and nutcrackers had been bought by parliamentarians as trophies and by royal sympathisers as relics.

CHARING CROSS,
A COUNTRYMAN STANDING BY THE STATUE.

Cockney: *You have been standing here a long while my lad who are you waiting for?* Countryman: *I ha' gotten a Letter for one Charles Stuart and they tell I thic be he, so I be waiting for'n till he gets off his Horse.*

The statue here features in a traditional country bumpkin story. Cockney: "You have been standing here a long while, my lad; who have you been waiting for?" Countryman: "I ha' gotten a letter for one Charles Stuart and they tell I thic be he, so I be waiting for'n till he gets off his horse." Note the entrance to the Golden Cross coach yard on the right of the picture.

In 1675 Charles II bought the statue of his martyred father from the Duchess of Portland and erected it where it stands today. In choosing that spot Charles was reinforcing his own triumphant return, since some of those who had condemned his father to death were themselves executed close by. He was also filling a void left by Puritan vandalism, for on that spot had stood the greatest of the Eleanor Crosses erected by Edward I to mark the progress of his beloved wife's body from Harby in Lincolnshire to Westminster Abbey. (The version now outside Charing Cross Station was placed there in 1865 by the South Eastern Railway Company (see p56).) During the Commonwealth the Cross had been steadily dismantled and its stone is said to have been used for paving the streets.

The statue itself reveals little of its dramatic origins. Jacob Epstein called it "gay, debonair and charming"; its unpretentiousness, he said, meant that it had no enemies. It soon became one of London's best known landmarks. Coffee houses, where the high financial business of the day was conducted, advertised their proximity to it, and humble street sellers hawked their wares by it:

> I cry my matches at Charing Cross,
> Where sits a black man on a black horse.

A pillory stood beside it and stage coaches left from the yard at nearby Golden Cross for all parts of the kingdom.

Despite its cheerful appearance, the deeper emotions which the Stuarts have always been able to inspire have also swirled around the statue. It is addressed in an old nursery rhyme of revealing poignancy:

This painting shows the statue at a time when the passing of animals through the streets of the capital was still an everyday affair. William IV's monogram on top of the lamps and the presence of the buildings behind – soon to be demolished in the development of Trafalgar Square – indicate a date not long after 1830.

> *As I was passing along Charing Cross*
> *I saw a small man upon a black horse.*
> *And when they said it was Charles the First,*
> *I felt my heart was ready to burst.*

It is also the subject of what is surely the most moving tribute to a statue in the English language. In the 1890's the poet Lionel Johnson, Catholic convert, insomniac, slight of stature like Charles himself, wrote of "the saddest of all kings" as he paced the night streets.

> *Comely and calm he rides*
> *Hard by his own Whitehall:*
> *Only the night wind glides:*
> *No crowds nor rebels, brawl.*

(The full poem is given in the Appendix.) One can see the affinity between the poets of the Rhymers Club, Johnson, Dowson and the young Yeats, who aimed to overcome life through art, and Charles, King and Martyr, whose image was perfected in death.

In Johnson's time the statue also became the focus of a more outward devotion, though not without a struggle. As we shall see, the statues of Disraeli (p197) and of General Gordon (p268) had just then taken on the status of shrines. This prompted a Mr Herbert Vivian of the Jacobite Legitimist League to write to the First Commissioner of Works for permission to lay wreaths around it on January 30th, the anniversary of the King's death. Permission was

Below. In 1917 German zeppelins attacked Charing Cross Station and government buildings in Whitehall, so this ingenious covering was erected. At the beginning of World War Two, a similar corrugated iron shed was provided, but in July 1941 it was decided to take the statue down altogether and remove it by lorry to the safety of Mentmore House.

The laying of wreaths at the foot of the statue as it was carried by the Royal Stuart Society on January 30th, 1988. A chaplain said prayers, soldiers from the Royal Horse Artillery sounded their trumpets and the link with Scotland was confirmed by the presence of a piper.

refused, on grounds of precedent. Other groups, among them the White Cockade Club of Huntingdonshire under the chairmanship of the Marquis de Ruvigny et Rainval, wrote to protest at the decision, threatening – with what surely must have been unconscious irony – to enforce their rights through Parliament and the Law. In 1893 the neo-Jacobins went ahead and laid their wreaths regardless; the police stood by, having been instructed to make arrests only if someone tried to mount the pedestal. Once begun, the observances continued annually and in 1896 the Office of Works finally gave way and announced in the press that wreaths should be sent to them the preceding evening for display. So began a tradition which has lasted in one form or another until the present day.

On at least two occasions urgent repairs have been needed to prevent the royal horseman from crashing to the ground. In 1853 a plaster cast was made of the statue for the Great Exhibition; it was discovered that both back legs were fractured and the bolts holding the plates to the pedestal were rusted through. In 1919, on removing the covering which had kept it safe through the world's first air raids against civilians, several holes were found in the half inch thick metal; the crucial left foreleg was in a particularly dangerous state. Fortunately all these were made good in time.

Horse and rider have been pressing onwards now for over three centuries, no mean achievement if one considers the amount of weight being taken on so slight a support. Together they have endured more changes of weather than any other London statue, yet they remain as fresh and as well groomed as any of their more youthful companions.

Charles II

His tumultuous youth and the years of frustrating continental exile left their mark on Charles II. He believed no less than his father in his right to rule and he was as complex in his political manoeverings. However, where one was rigid and idealistic, the other was cautious, tolerant and shrewd. The father courted death, the son clung to life. Indeed through the medium of his numerous illegitimate children his genes must have survived in an appreciable number of his nation's people – among them the extraordinary Sir Charles Napier, commemorated in Trafalgar Square (p256).

Charles was pleasure loving, worldly wise beyond his years and tempted to *accidie*. He was also a perceptive judge of men and, being a man of science, he made a special study of the technique of assessing character from the face and physical appearance. His statue in Soho Square, with its battered, somewhat cynical air of the survivor, likewise gives us a good opportunity of forming an impression of him. The history of a statue sometimes bears an uncanny resemblance to the life of its subject. This one survived constitutional crisis and penurious exile to make a welcome return to its place of origin. It stands now on its low pedestal, sceptre in hand, clearly royal but easily accessible to any interested passer by.

In its early days Soho Square (built in the 1670's and 80's and originally called King Square) was an elegant, highly fashionable neighbourhood. The Duke of Monmouth, Charles II's eldest illegitimate son, lived there. There were trees and lawns and there was a central fountain upon which the statue of Charles II took pride of place, flanked by classical figures – "old fathers with wette beards" – symbolising the four great royal rivers of Thames, Severn, Tyne and Humber. However, after fifty years or so, administrative problems arose. Who was to govern this fair plot and keep it tidy? Various unsuccessful schemes were tried but by the 1800's the fountains no longer worked and the statues were in a wretched and mutilated state. The Duke of Portland owned the gardens but kept them locked and neglected them. In 1875-6, "improvements" were finally made and the curious ornamental hut now in the centre of the square was erected. At the intervention of a resident, Mr T.Blackwell of Crosse and Blackwell Ltd., the statue of Charles II was rescued and given to his friend, the artist Frederick Goodall R.A., who had just built himself a country house near Harrow Weald. The house was named Graemsdyke after the ditch of an ancient British earthwork which Goodall had dammed to make a lake. In the widest part of it he placed the statue, admiring with a painter's eye its mysterious reflection in the water at twilight.

Graemsdyke later came into the possession of the librettist W.S.Gilbert, that ingenious sorter out of misplaced persons, and in 1938 his widow gave the story a suitably Gilbertian ending by bequeathing the statue back to Soho Square. Tar, cement, paint and water-weed were removed and the statue's remarkable vitality renewed. Alas, this has recently received a severe check. In 1987, like the statue of George II in Golden Square (p41), it was smoothed over with a thick cement wash which has obliterated all the interesting cracks and contours. Fortunately the photograph shows it before this took place. One can only hope that further weathering will undo some of the damage.

The statue of Charles which once stood in the Stocks Market is described in chapter 9. His other surviving outdoor statue is at Chelsea

Charles II. Born 1630, London, son of Charles I. Fought in First Civil War, aged 12, 1642. Second Civil War; sailed for Scotland and made alliance promises (later repudiated) to Presbyterians, 1648. Campaigned in England and was defeated at Battle of Worcester; spent six weeks as fugitive before escaping to France, 1651. Lived in impoverished circumstances in Paris, Cologne, Bruges and Brussels and failed to conclude alliances with France, Holland, Spain and Austria, 1651-60. Restored as King, 1660. Granted Charter to Royal Society, 1662. Dismissed Earl of Clarendon, chief minister, and began attempt to assert absolute rule, 1667. "Popish Plot" against life revealed as extreme Presbyterian hoax; public reaction in favour of monarchy, 1678. Died 1685.

Statue by Caius Gabriel Cibber. Marble. Soho Square. Originally erected 1681. Removed 1876 and re-erected February 22nd, 1938.

Cibber was a Dane who studied in Italy; he probably modelled his Soho Square fountain on Bernini's fountain in the Piazza Navona in Rome. He married an Englishwoman, Jane Colley; their son, Colley Cibber, became Poet Laureate. He carved the magnificent relief for the London Bridge Monument to the Fire of London, but managed his finances so badly that while working on it he had to return each night to a debtor's prison cell. Perhaps his most striking works are the brooding figures of melancholy and madness which he carved for Bethlehem Hospital, London's "Bedlam".

Hospital, the home of the Chelsea Pensioners. He himself founded the Hospital in 1682 as a refuge for the many discharged and disabled soldiers who were wandering the streets in a pitiable state, begging for alms. Tradition says it was Nell Gwynn who touched his heart on their account, but others credit Sir Stephen Fox, paymaster general of the army and grandfather of Charles James Fox (p174). The statue took the classicism introduced by Charles I a stage further and established a new style of royal commemoration. For over a hundred years the kings of England were to be dressed as victorious emperors

The statue of Charles II at Chelsea Hospital (see overleaf) being swathed in oak boughs for the Founders Day Parade.

Statue from the studio of Grinling Gibbons, probably by Arnold Quellin. Bronze. Figure Court, Chelsea Hospital. Erected 1685. Like the statue of James II now outside the National Gallery (p31), it was the gift of the courtier Tobias Rustat; it cost him £500. Rustat was Yeoman of the Robes and Keeper of Hampton Court and his frugal life-style allowed him to make many gifts and benefactions – he also paid for the original "Roman" statue of Charles at Windsor Castle. The diarist John Evelyn somewhat condescendingly called him "a very simple, ignorant but honest and loyal creature."

Gibbons' genius was for carving in wood; for bronze and marble he employed, when possible, those more skilful than himself. Arnold Quellin, the son of the famous Dutch sculptor Artus Quellin, worked with him from 1679. It is recorded that he carved the marble statue of Charles II at the Royal Exchange. He was a tall, handsome man whose hair grew so luxuriously that in that age of pretended finery he had no need of a wig. His death in 1686 at the early age of 33 was a great loss to English sculpture.

of Rome. The attire was originally worn not only by emperors but by other high-ranking Roman military commanders of the Imperial Age. It was authentic enough: the sandals, the short tunic under the *pteruges* or straps of leather, the lappets decorated with lion heads and the *paludamentum* or long cloak fastened at the shoulder. The latter was a sacred emblem of military authority and was put on by a commander at the beginning of his campaign; wearing it, he might not re-enter the City before completing his task. But if successful, he would return with the *corona triumphalis*, the victory crown of laurel or of bay, bound about his brows.

Charles instituted the new style himself. According to the naturalist Dr Martin Lister, who was present on the occasion, three models for his proposed new equestrian statue at Windsor Castle were brought to him, presumably by Grinling Gibbons. He chose the one in Roman dress and also ordered that his marble statue shortly to be erected at the Royal Exchange (and destroyed by fire in 1838) should be carved in the same style. This, the Chelsea figure and the similar statue of James II now outside the National Gallery (p31) were produced together as a group in Gibbons' studio. Some contemporaries, Lister himself for example, disliked the innovation. "Now I appeal to all mankind," he wrote, "whether in representing a living Prince nowadays those naked arms and legs are decent, and whether there is not a barbarity very displeasing in it." Since the French sculptor Desjardins was at the time working on a colossal statue of Louis XIV in a similar classical style, it may have been a case of keeping up with the Bourbons.

The parallel, whether intentional or not, was certainly prophetic, prefiguring the great colonial struggles between the two countries during the next century. Did Charles deserve his imperial accoutrements? As King he continued Cromwell's policy of consolidating England's scattered foreign settlements. He backed the East India Company and he set up the first ever colonial administrative body, the so-called Lords of Trade. And thus were nurtured the seeds of an Empire that would far surpass that of Rome in wealth and extent, if not in duration.

On June 9th, Founder's Day Parade takes place at Chelsea Hospital. Early in the morning, branches cut from an oak tree in the Hospital grounds are brought to swathe the statue. At the parade, as a member of Royalty takes the salute, each pensioner wears a sprig of oak leaves in the third buttonhole of his scarlet jacket. All this commemorates an event which took place when the young Charles was on the run following the Battle of Worcester. Masquerading as Will Jones, farm labourer, his face darkened with walnut juice, he came early one morning to Boscabel House. Its owners took him in and suggested that he would be safer hiding in a tree on their estate. So he climbed into a thick growing oak and slept out the day there, resting his head in the lap of his solitary companion, Colonel Carlis. Later, two days in advance of the Puritan search parties, he continued on his way to Bristol, from where he escaped to France. Charles loved to tell the story over and, when he became King, planned to found an order of chivalry called the Knights of the Royal Oak. The tree itself soon gave its name to a thousand inns and had to be protected from its numerous visitors by a fence. The story is central to Stuart legend. For if Charles I is the divine martyr-victim, then Charles II is the merry, midsummer monarch who succeeds him, the survivor, the oak-god hidden high in the leafy branches.

James II

The statue of James II now outside the National Gallery is the companion piece of that of Charles II at Chelsea (p26). It was commissioned by the same faithful servant of the Stuart Court, Tobias Rustat, and was erected in the year that James became King. As Duke of York and Lord High Admiral of England, he had a fair claim to his imperial, military dress. He was responsible for the establishing of trading posts in West Africa, the Spice Islands and the Malabar Coast of India. He instigated the capture of New Amsterdam and so gave his name to present day New York. If his orders to pursue the Dutch fleet had been carried out, he would have won a decisive victory at the Battle of Lowestoft. Given sufficient funds, he and his chief administrator Samuel Pepys might well have made England's navy invincible. As King, however, he squandered all his natural advantages in a way that bordered on the insane, rapidly making himself the most unpopular ruler in English history. Some have wondered about a medical cause of his imbalance but it seems likely that he had simply inherited his father's fatal weakness for absolutes, in his case for the all pervasive primacy of the Catholic faith.

In the end James became a completely ineffective figure. In 1689, just three years after the statue was erected, he was allowed to flee the country by way of the Thames; humourists said the statue faced the direction of his flight. After the Bloodless and Glorious Revolution of 1688, William III had no need or desire to trouble himself about images of his predecessor, and the statue continued quietly to grace the gardens behind the Banqueting House for over two hundred years. But during this century all sorts of troubles have fallen upon its head, precipitated, as with James's own accession to the throne, by a move to a position of greater prominence. In 1897 the statue was re-erected

James II. Born 1633, London, son of King Charles I. Escaped to Netherlands, 1646. Fought in French and Spanish armies, rising to high rank, 1652-8. Appointed Lord High Admiral, 1660. Became secret Roman Catholic, 1668/9. Commanded fleet in Dutch wars, 1665-7 & 1672-4, but resigned rather than sign Test Act repudiating Catholicism. Survived Parliament's attempt to exclude him from the throne and won general support of conservative, Anglican establishment, 1679-82. Became King, 1685. Put down rebellions of Dukes of Monmouth and Argyll with unexpected ferocity; promoted Catholics to high positions in army and state; dismissed Parliament, 1685-6. Invasion of William of Orange and desertion of Protestant army officers; tried to flee country but was recaptured, 1688. Allowed to escape to France, 1689. Died 1701.

Below. An engraving of the Privy Gardens by J. Maurer, printed in 1741. On the right is the Banqueting House.

Statue from studio of Grinling Gibbons, probably by Arnold Quellin; the Flemings Laurens of Marlines and Dievot of Brussells, and also Thomas Bennier, are recorded as having worked on the modelling and casting. Bronze. First erected December 31st, 1685, in the Privy Gardens, Whitehall. The gift of Tobias Rustat; cost £300. Re-erected in front of Gwydyr House, 1897; in St James's Park, 1903; and in front of the National Gallery, 1948.

in the garden of Gwydyr House which faced directly onto Whitehall. In 1902 the site was required for stands for Edward VII's coronation and for over a year poor James lay in a box in the corner of the garden. Questions were asked in Parliament, some supporting, some hostile to the deposed King, who was eventually found a more appropriate position in St James's Park opposite the Admiralty.

Having spent World War Two and its aftermath immured in Aldwych Underground Station, James' statue once more became the subject of parliamentary controversy. An Ulster Unionist M.P. wanted him erected in St James's Square, where he could gaze forever on the face of his conqueror, William III. A militant backbencher proposed Parliament Square, so that ministers might be daily reminded of the fate of those who tried to limit the rights of Parliament. A plan to pair him with a statue of Samuel Pepys outside the Admiralty failed when the donor of the new figure withdrew. In the end the Ministry of Works seem to have reached a nicely balanced compromise between History and Art by placing him in Trafalgar Square outside the National Gallery. There his statue can be appreciated both as a thing of beauty and also as a tribute to a patriotic and hard working naval commander.

Anne

London had no outdoor statue of William III for over a hundred years (Bristol and Hull honoured him, London either resisted or did not care) and his consort Queen Mary, who played little part in public life, had no outdoor commemorations. Next, therefore, we come to Queen Anne, determined and patriotic like her father James II, but also tolerant, sensible and, above all, Protestant.

St Paul's Cathedral was finished towards the end of Anne's reign and stood as a triumphant symbol of the stability which the country had achieved after the troubles of the previous century. To the west of his great building Sir Christopher Wren wished to build an open piazza and a baptistery tower; however, he was forced to give way over this, as over other aspects of his design. National, Anglican sentiment prevailed and, instead, a statue of the Queen was placed there, surrounded by four figures representing the countries of her dominion. Uniformity is, however, seldom perfect and the new group soon became the butt of satire. The Whig poet-physician Samuel Garth, displeased with Anne's dismissal of Marlborough and the Peace of Utrecht, noted that helmeted France, alone of the four surrounding figures, was looking downwards. Other opponents of the Peace referred more coarsely to the orientation of the Queen's own statue.

Anne. Born 1665, London, second daughter of James, Duke of York (later James II). Brought up as Protestant by direction of Charles II. Married Prince George of Denmark, 1683; during her marriage she suffered 17 difficult pregnancies and her only surviving son died aged 11. Became Queen, 1702. Promoted John Churchill, Duke of Marlborough, as supreme commander in war against France, 1702. France defeated in a series of outstanding victories, 1702-11. Returned revenues to Church in general programme of support for High Anglicanism, 1704. Played important role in bringing about Act of Union between England and Scotland, 1706-7. Dismissed Marlborough and made Peace of Utrecht with France, 1711-3. Died 1714.

Left. The original statues by Francis Bird. Marble. Erected 1712, at the foot of the steps to the west entrance of St Paul's Cathedral. Cost, £1,180 (Anne's statue £250, surrounding figures £220, shield £50).

Sadly, Anne's own appalling health was matched by the damage inflicted on her outdoor statues. At St Paul's, she lost sceptre, orb and both arms in lunatic attacks carried out in 1743 and 1769. For over a hundred years the disfigurements remained and it was left to the Lord Mayor of London, embarrassed by constant complaints from visitors, to take action. In 1884 the whole group was removed and replaced by the orders of the City Corporation. The original figures were rescued from a mason's yard by the travel writer Augustus Hare and taken to his country house, Holmhurst, near St. Leonards, Sussex. This afterwards became a convent school, as can be seen from this photograph taken in 1952.

Right. The statues as replaced by Louis Auguste Malempré under the preliminary supervision of Richard Belt. Belt (see p124) abandoned the job unfinished; according to the overall contractors, he had only directed their men in making good the old figures with plaster to serve as models and the actual carving had been done by Malempré. Erected 1886. The surrounding figures represent Britain, including Scotland, (front, here lacking right hand and trident), North America (left, with Indian bow and quiver of arrows), France (helmeted, right – Anne was still notionally Queen of France) and Ireland (with harp).

Brandy Nan, Brandy Nan,
You're left in the lurch,
Your face to the gin-shop,
Your back to the church.

The allegations of drunkenness were, it must be said, quite unfair.

The other outdoor statue of Anne is to be found in Queen Anne's Gate, south of St. James's Park; it stands half way down, on a pedestal just detached from the wall of number 15. This is not its original position. Queen Anne's Gate was built in 1704-5 at the instigation of Charles Shales, a London goldsmith. At that time a wall divided it into two, with Queen Anne Square to the west and Park Street to the east; in a contemporary engraving one can just see the statue on a pier in the middle of the wall, facing west. It was moved to its present position sometime at the beginning of the nineteenth century.

Statue by an anonymous sculptor. Marble. Queen Anne's Gate. Erected c.1705 and moved to its present position c.1810.

This statue also suffered defamation and attack but survived to tell the tale. In 1861 it found a champion in the Earl of Carnarvon, who wrote to the Office of Works saying that the residents had long been dissatisfied with its wretched condition. The Office sent a representative to investigate this obscure and apparently forgotten figure. His report explained the situation as follows.

'The popular belief among the children who play in the neighbourhood is that the statue represents Queen Mary and their protestant zeal has led them to revile the statue and to call upon Bloody Queen Mary to descend from her pedestal. Upon receiving no reply they have been in the habit of pelting the statue with various missiles and have reduced it to a condition very discreditable to behold. I believe that if the name of Queen Anne be written in legible characters on the pedestal, their puerile outrage will not be repeated... I do not think it desirable that a statue of an illustrious sovereign should be left in a public place without a nose or a right arm.'

The well known architectural sculptor John Thomas (p156) was instructed to make repairs. The statue was transformed and re-erected but local habits died hard; despite a special police watch, the bombardments continued. The inscription ANNA REGINA, as one might have expected, meant little to the local urchins and had no deterrent effect. It took, in fact, a generation before complaints about the stone-throwing ceased.

Left. Had the local children been patient enough to wait until the night of August 1st, the anniversary of Queen Anne's death, their demands would have been met in full, for then, according to local lore, she gets down from her pedestal and walks three times up and down the street. These perambulations must surely have ceased during the Second World War, when total immurement kept her safe from the effects of Hitler's deadlier missiles. Her all clear was finally sounded in April 1947.

Edward VI

As we shall see in chapter two, which describes the statues of philanthropists, the late seventeenth and early eighteenth centuries were a time of great building and rebuilding for London's hospitals and other charitable institutions. Two of the statues put up at this time were of the boy-king Edward VI, who re-founded St Thomas's Hospital. St. Thomas's was originally a monastic almshouse. Being monastic, it was dissolved – in a greatly run down state – by Henry VIII. In 1552 a group of City merchants purchased it from the Crown and rebuilt it as a substantial foundation, Edward having provided it with a Royal Charter the previous year. By 1553 it had 260 patients and supported an additional 500 of London's poor. However, its endowments were quite inadequate for all this activity and the bulk of its income came from private gifts. Edward VI, by now acting on his own personal initiative, made over further endowments worth £600 a year. He was already desperately ill with tuberculosis and after he had signed the necessary documents the members of his Council heard him say out loud, "Lord God, I yield thee most hearty thanks that thou hast given me life this long, to finish this work to the glory of thy name."

Thin-faced, slender, Edward is generally thought of as a pathetic weakling, the inheritor of his father's degenerate state when he at last achieved a male heir. But, though he suffered from occasional colds, he was normally healthy and, as far as can be known, died from a classic case of tuberculosis. Able, cool, controlled, he could have been as outstanding a king as his grandfather Henry VII, whom he closely resembled in character. He seems to have shown little, if any, emotion at the execution of his childhood guardian, the Duke of Somerset, but then he had always resented his domination. His feelings were quite different towards the poor and sick among his subjects. For them he felt a genuine compassion, well demonstrated by one at least of the statues at St Thomas's Hospital.

The first of them was the work of Thomas Cartwright, who was one of Wren's masons at St. Paul's and the Master of the Masons' Company in 1673 and 1694. It stood originally in a curved niche on the western gateway to the old hospital in Southwark, though it was later moved to the far east wall of the western quadrangle and subsequently found a place of its own in the grounds. Perhaps because of its original position it is awkwardly posed and time has not improved the quality of the carving. A much better memorial to Cartwright's skill is now preserved inside the hospital's front entrance hall. These are the four lively and charming figures of patients originally on the same gateway: a woman leaning on a stick, another woman with her arm in a sling, a poor man on crutches and a well dressed man enduring a wooden leg.

The second statue, by Peter Scheemakers, was put up in 1737 in the middle of the hospital's central, administrative quadrangle. It was paid for by the bequest of Charles Joye who, as Treasurer, had lived in a house in that same quadrangle. He was also Treasurer of St Thomas's new sister institution, Guy's Hospital, and would have played a part in commissioning Scheemakers' bronze statue of its founder, Thomas Guy (p84). He must have approved the artistry and felt that, after his death, St Thomas's should have a similar statue. Both are skilful, sensitive works; of Edward VI, a contemporary wrote, "The attitude... and graceful disposition of the limbs is judiciously done and merits great applause."

Edward VI. Born 1537, London, only son of Henry VIII; his mother, Jane Seymour, died the same year. Began thorough education, in classics, astronomy and religious affairs, 1544. Became King, 1547. Downfall of Protector, The Duke of Somerset, 1549. Began to play active part in meetings of Council, 1551-2. Agreed to execution of Somerset, 1552. Deeply impressed by Bishop Ridley's sermon on charity; developed keen interest in care of poor and sick and personally proposed scheme for Bridewell Hospital for poor unemployed, 1552. Became ill with tuberculosis. Made over funds to Royal Hospitals. Tried desperately to exclude his Catholic sister Mary from succession and nominated Lady Jane Grey as Queen, 1553. Died 1553.

Left. Statue by Thomas Cartwright. Stone. St Thomas's Hospital Hospital, Lambeth, north wing terrace, next to the modern, main entrance and in line with the statues of Florence Nightingale (p165) and Sir Thomas Clayton (p82). First erected 1681, in niche on western gateway, St Thomas's Hospital, Southwark. Moved to Lambeth, 1868-70, and erected in present position 1976.

Right. Statue by Peter Scheemakers. Bronze. St Thomas's Hospital, north wing terrace, as above. First erected 1737, in the middle of the central or King Edward Quadrangle, Southwark. Erected in present position 1976. Cost £500.

Peter Scheemakers was yet another foreigner who spent most of his working life in England. He was to become the country's most celebrated sculptor with his memorial to Shakespeare in Westminster Abbey, later reproduced in Leicester Square (p121). He was born in Antwerp, the son of a sculptor. In his youth he studied in Rome, having travelled there on foot. (In this pedestrian feat Francis Bird, the sculptor of Queen Anne (p32) and Scheemakers' one time employer, outdid him, for he is said to have achieved it twice). It seems that, after his success, Scheemakers was inclined to be rude about the work of other sculptors in front of their aristocratic patrons; as the Duke of Portland put it, he was the best in the country for assurance and impertinence. He said of himself, 'I am a little impudent fellow, no matter I can't help it.' He went on producing statues, including one of Robert Clive (p216) dressed as a conquering Roman Emperor, until the age of eighty, when he finally retired to Antwerp.

George I

George I was fifty four years old when he arrived from Hanover to become King of England. A practised soldier, he was brave and honest according to his lights and a shrewd diplomat with wide Continental experience. Like William III, he was not over-fond of the English and his command of their language was rudimentary. Nevertheless, he was still the King and the central focus of his realm. The laying out of London's wide and beautiful squares continued during his reign and provided suitable sites for royal statues. As in William's case, a plan to commemorate him in St James's Square came to nothing when the Chevalier de David (a pupil of Bernini whom William had brought over to England) failed to raise subscriptions. In 1726, however, Sir Richard Grosvenor erected a gilded lead, equestrian statue of him in Grosvenor Square; it came from the Van Nost family's sculpture yard and cost 250 guineas. The following year the horse's leg was torn off by a Jacobite mob and an obscene verse was tied around its neck. It also became the subject of Jacobite song in which King Charles's horse trots over from Whitehall and both animals join in roundly condemning the Hanoverian rider. The statue was still in place in 1838 but subsequently disappeared.

A similar statue appeared in Leicester Square in 1748. It was brought from Canons, the magnificent, Palladian mansion built near Edgware by that aimiable tycoon, James Brydges, First Duke of Chandos. Pope may have been referring to Canons when he wrote of "trees like statues, statues thick as trees" and the gilded, equestrian figure of George I was a noted feature of the place. However, the second Duke, deep in debt and uninterested in art, sold off the estate and its contents for a song. The statue was given as a birthday present by his friends to Frederick, Prince of Wales, who had been living at Leicester House since his break with his father, King George II.

George I. Born 1660, son of Duke of Hanover. Played courageous part in rescue of Vienna from Turks, 1683. Fought as British ally in wars against France, 1688-94 & 1701-9. Became Elector of Hanover, 1698. Became King of England, 1714. Defeat of first Jacobite rebellion, 1715-6. Played key role in European wars curbing the power of Sweden and Spain, 1715-20. Temporary collapse of national finances in South Sea Company; relied increasingly on first minister, Robert Walpole, 1721. Died 1727.

Statue modelled by C. Burchard and probably cast by Andrew Carpenter. Gilded lead. Leicester Square. Unveiled with ceremony November 19th, 1748, for the birthday of Frederick, Prince of Wales.

The statue was originally erected c.1720, in the North Garden, Canons, Edgware. It came from the Van Nost yard and the casting is usually attributed to John Van Nost; however, recent scholarship has shown that he died in 1711. Cost 250 guineas. It was reguilded in 1812.

According to Horace Walpole, its erection was specially calculated to annoy George II, who in turn had had difficult relations with *his* father George I.

The dramatically glowing form soon became famous – it proved that, if not the streets, then at least something in the capital was made of gold. However, during the nineteenth century the Square's condition deteriorated under a succession of owners. In 1851 James Wyld's Great Globe, a huge inverted representation of the Earth's surface, was set up there and the statue was buried in a pit twelve feet below ground. In 1861 it emerged much damaged and in 1866 received terminal indignities at the hands of vandals. Shortly afterwards the rider disappeared and the horse was sold off as scrap.

The only surviving outdoor statue of George I is not free-standing but on a building, on being the operative word. Conventionally Roman, it crowns the stepped pyramid steeple of St. George's Church, Bloomsbury Way, designed by Nicholas Hawksmoor to resemble the tomb of Mausolus at Halicarnassus, one of the Seven Wonders of the World.

Right. Leicester Square reached its nadir in the 1860's. A builder had cut down all the trees, it was filled with rubbish and the statue of George I, grubby from having been buried for years in a pit, lacked arms and legs. His horse, similarly lacking a leg, was propped up on two sticks. In September, 1866, the statue was given a shining coat of whitewash. A letter then appeared in *The Times*, signed by the statue itself, complaining that one coat would hardly be warm enough for the coming winter. The response came shortly afterwards, to the delight of the crowds who thronged to see the spectacle. Overnight someone had added black spots to the white, tied donkey's ears to the horse and given the King a dunce's cap and broomstick lance.

George II

The first of George II's laurel-crowned statues stands on the Prime Meridian from which the vertical axes of Earth are measured. As one looks up past Wren's breathtaking vistas, one can see Greenwich Observatory crowning the hill and the tall statue of James Wolfe, George's favourite military commander (p283). ("Mad, is he? Then I wish he would bite some of my other generals.") His reign's penultimate year saw England establish a colonial supremacy over the French in two continents and with it the right, during the coming age, to be looked on as the centre of the world.

Nothing so aptly glorious was, of course, originally planned. In fact the erection of George's statue at Greenwich Hospital (the naval equivalent of the home of the Chelsea pensioners) may be seen as a successful fund-raising device. In the 1730's the Hospital was in serious financial difficulties and its Governor, Admiral Sir John Jennings, decided to attract the attention of the most illustrious of possible patrons. If the governing body would provide the marble, he said, he would himself pay for a statue of the King in the Great Court. Fortunately, a block of the very finest marble was to hand. Originally destined to become a statue of Louis XIV, it had been taken from a French vessel as spoils of war by Admiral Sir George Rooke. The Hospital had bought it in 1714 with the intention of fulfilling Wren's plan for statues of William and Mary at the River Gate. Admiral Jennings, however, clearly understood that a living king could do more for the Hospital than a dead one. John Michael Rysbrack's fine, dramatic figure must have caught George's eye as he sailed past Greenwich in May, 1735, on his way to Hanover, and again on his return. He would have appreciated the military touch; the Battle of

George II. Born 1683, grandson of Elector of Hanover. Fought under Marlborough at Battle of Oudenarde, 1708. Accompanied father, now King George I, to England, 1714. Became King, 1727. Overall commander of victorious British, Hanoverian, Hessian, Austrian and Dutch forces at Battle of Dettingen in War of Austrian Succession, the last English king to lead his troops into battle, 1743. Beginning of Seven Years' War with France, 1756. The Year of Victories, 1759: British power established in Canada by Wolfe's victory at Quebec (p283) and in India by Clive's victory at Plessey (p216); French fleets defeated at Lagos Bay and Quiberon Bay. Died 1760.

Statue by John Michael Rysbrack. Marble. Great Court, Greenwich Naval College (until 1869 Greenwich Naval Hospital). Erected March 1st, 1735 and ceremonially unveiled August 1st, during the illumination of the Great Court for the Queen's birthday.

Oudenarde, in which he had fought as a young man, had been the great event of his life. Since his popularity was now at a low ebb, what better way to improve it than by making over the confiscated estates of the Jacobite Earl of Derwentwater to Greenwich Hospital, of whose existence he had just been so pleasantly reminded? Jennings' financial problems were substantially over.

Lord Edward Gleichen, writing in 1928, described the statue's expression as "oddly perky". Since then all traces of animation have disappeared and the face is now an irreparable ruin. This we owe to certain Sandhurst cadets of the early 1950's who raided the Naval College and painted the statue with black stripes; the fluid used to remove the paint broke the stone's protective weathering.

The statue in Golden Square is a more stolid affair. In *Nicholas Nickleby*, Dickens describes how "the notes of pianos and harps float in the evening-time round the head of the mournful statue – the guardian genius of a little wilderness of shrubs." Like the equestrian statue of George I once in Leicester Square (p38), it is said to have come from the gardens of Canons. The story goes that the auctioneer had just opened the bidding on it when an old friend walked in and nodded good day to him. However, the price was so low that he accepted the unintentional purchase and later presented it to Golden Square. The cold light of reason throws doubt on all of this rather too obvious story. The conventions of the statue's dress would seem to indicate a reigning monarch and George did not become King until 1727, several years after the main sculptural work for Canons was done in the van Nost yard. Moreover there is no surviving contemporary evidence of the presence there or sale of a statue of George II.

Statue by an unknown sculptor. Portland Stone. Golden Square. Erected 1753. The picture on the left shows the the statue's dilapidated condition just after the Second World War, when air-raid shelters were dug under the Square. The one on the right shows its 1988 state of restoration, just after Westminster Council had smoothed it over with a wash like that used on Charles II in Soho Square (p25). George had the long nose and protruding eyes of the Hanoverians, so the likeness, if ever there was one, is quite gone. The most unusual feature is the ornamentation of the sword handle, which resembles a lizard.

George III and Queen Charlotte

George III, so we are generally told, was a dull and rather stupid man who was happiest riding around his farms at Windsor. This image is misleading on a number of counts. He was earnest and dutiful, certainly. He was also deeply interested in the arts; he was Handel's patron; his book collection formed the basis of the first National Library; and the foundation of the Royal Academy was largely due to his encouragement. He supervised the composition of the Academy's charter and lent it rooms in the old palace of Somerset House. Later, he agreed to the erection of a completely new building on the site. This was the Academy's home until 1838 and is now the great mansion which houses the nation's wills.

Included in the design of the new building were various sculptural figures, among them the group just inside the entrance way in which the figure of the King took pride of place. Classical costume, so far as the Academy were concerned, was still de rigeur for public statues. Speaking at the 1780 prize-giving, the first President, Sir Joshua Reynolds (p140) severely criticised the modern military uniform worn by the Duke of Cumberland's statue in Cavendish Square (p346). However, the usual royal role of conquering emperor was not really suitable for the patron of an artistic institution. (Nor – with hindsight – was it appropriate for a king who, just as the statue was being made, was presiding over the loss of his country's most important colony). George, then, appears as a benevolent patrician, benefactor and steersman. He holds a ship's tiller; to his left is the ornamental prow of a Roman vessel and to his right the lion of England. Below him is a figure probably representing Father Thames and symbolic of the river's proximity (before the raising of the Embankment, Somerset House ran down to its shore). The cornucopia of course represents his free-flowing generosity towards the Academy.

The group's sculptor, John Bacon, had close links with the Academy; he attended its classes and he won its first ever gold medal for sculpture. He was born in 1840, in Southwark; his father was a poor cloth maker. When he was a child a cart passed over his right hand; however, two large stones lifted the wheel clear and Bacon always saw the event as evidence of the workings of Providence. He learned to model at Nicholas Crisp's porcelain factory and later designed reliefs for Josiah Wedgewood. He became chief designer for Miss Eleanor Coade, the proprietor of Coade's Artificial Stone Manufactory. Coade stone figures were extremely popular during this period and Bacon's Father Thames at Somerset House is not unlike a figure with an urn which he made for the Manufactory.

In 1774 Bacon was commissioned to provide a bust of George III for Christ Church, Oxford, and this involved visiting the Palace for sittings. The King liked Bacon's courteous manners – for example, instead of moistening the modelling clay by spitting on it, as was the custom, he applied water from a silver syringe. "Have you ever been out of England?" the King asked. "No? – I am glad of it – you will be the greater credit for it." George III was the first of the Hanoverian Kings to identify completely with his country and he must have been pleased that here, for once, was a sculptor whose roots were entirely English. The bust was a success and the King ordered three copies.

However, the rather florid figure at Somerset House was less well appreciated, at least by George's Queen. "Why did you make so frightful a figure?" she asked John Bacon, who had to use all his carefully acquired courtly tact in framing his reply. "Art," he said,

George III. Born 1738, London, son of Frederick, Prince of Wales. Death of father, 1751. Became King, 1760. Married Princess Charlotte, 1761. Concluded peace with France, 1762. Played leading role in founding of Royal Academy, 1768. War of American Independence; loss of American colonies, 1775-83. Personal appointment of William Pitt the Younger (p172) as Prime Minister began long period of Tory ascendancy, 1783. Serious illnesses, 1787-9, 1801 & 4. War with revolutionary France, 1793-1801 and 1803-15. Illness became permanent, 1810. Died 1820.

Statue by John Bacon. Bronze. Forecourt of Somerset House. Erected 1788. Cost £2,000.

A hundred years ago, the statue suffered what nowadays would be an inconceivable indignity; the lower part of the pedestal, which was hollow and had an entrance way at the back, was turned into a public urinal. In 1922 Sir Aston Webb, the architect of the Victoria Memorial, wrote in complaint to the Office of Works; it seemed that ladies viewing the statue had to suffer the embarrassment of seeing men emerging from behind it adjusting their dress. The urinal was found to have been there for at least forty years. It was speedily removed and the back wall was filled up with blocks of Portland stone at a cost of £20.

"cannot always effect what is ever within the reach of Nature – the union of beauty and majesty."

The lady who made that sharp remark about George III's statue at Somerset House has also been badly treated by history. The immediate and most essential qualification for the throne of England was simply to be royal but, as young George discovered, finding the right royal bride was not an easy matter. The Princess of Hesse-Darmstadt, so he was reliably informed, was stubborn and bad-tempered, the Princess of Saxe-Gotha was too interested in philosophy and the Princesses of Anhalt-Dessau were the great-granddaughters of a chemist. Only Princess Sophia Charlotte of Mecklenburg-Strelitz was admirable on all counts; she was pleasant and sensible, she could sing and dance well and, though no classic beauty, was lively and attractive. George could not wait to meet her and they were married on her first night in London. So began a long and devoted partnership.

Unfortunately the aura of dullness which built up around George III also attached itself to his Queen. An eminent twentieth century historian attributed the King's breakdown in part to "the sexual strain of his marriage to so unattractive a woman." Such nonsense quite ignores the evidence of her portraits, those by Zoffany and Gainsborough, for example, and the coronation portrait by Allan Ramsay shown opposite. Caroline had a pert beauty: fine, brown hair, an attractive nose, nostrils slightly flared, and a large, generous mouth. Even the National Gallery portrait painted by Sir Thomas Lawrence in 1789 has the same appeal, though tempered by time and worry. Not until she was over sixty did age finally take its toll of her looks. Nor was she dull; she was extremely well read, with a special interest in poetry and in botany, she was musical – in 1764 we find her singing an aria to the 8-year old Mozart's accompaniment – and she actively supported various charities.

The false image of Charlotte helped to fuel later controversy over the identity of the young and pretty figure in Queen's Square. The confusion probably began when it was classified in the Schedule of the 1854 Public Statues Act as being of Queen Anne. Over the years numerous authors and writers to the press argued the matter. Some supported Anne, some her sister Queen Mary, some the able and sophisticated Caroline, wife of George II. The consensus, however, was with Charlotte and in 1962 the Trustees of the gardens placed a plaque on the back of the pedestal identifying the statue as hers. Looking at her portraits, one wonders what the fuss was about; the statue has the same mouth and flared nose and the same look of regal gaiety.

Queen's Square is now the home of the National Hospital for Nervous Diseases, the country's leading neurological hospital. If only George III had been able to receive diagnosis and treatment there instead of at the hands of the Willis brothers, who did little but put him in a strait-jacket and pour cold water over him! George's "madness" is now widely recognised as having been caused by the hereditary metabolic disorder called porphyria. How much suffering could Charlotte have been spared! Yet the siting of her statue is just one more example of the eerie partnership of object and event. For Dr Richard Hunter, the man who did most to establish the physical nature of George III's illness, publishing papers in the *British Medical Journal* and later a full length book on the subject, was Physician in Psychological Medicine at that very hospital in Queen's Square.

Below. The statue's likeness to the young Queen may be seen from this coronation portrait by Allan Ramsay.

William III, *St James's Square*

Statue by John Bacon, finished and cast by his son, John Bacon, Jnr. Bronze. Centre of St James's Square. Erected 1808. Paid for by a bequest of Samuel Travers of Westminster. It originally stood in the middle of a large octagonal lake but by 1845 this had become stagnant and it was later drained.

During World War Two the statue was taken to the safety of Berkhampstead Castle, together with the Cockspur St. George III, Field Marshal Wolseley and The Burghers of Calais.

William of Orange was a brave soldier and an intelligent, effective ruler, but he often found himself isolated from the new subjects whom marriage and the flight of James II had brought him. This was understandable. He had immense responsibilities as the leader of the pan-European resistance to French imperialism, a role which English Parliaments did not always appreciate. He spoke no English and kept no roistering court like that of Charles II. Likewise the majority of his subjects, though they valued the stability which his reign brought them, had few deep feelings of affection for their foreign king.

This, surely, is one of the reasons why London had no outdoor statue of William for over a hundred years. In 1697, after the first peace with France, there had been plans to set up an elaborate bronze monument in St. James's Square "with several devices and mottoes trampling down popery, breaking the chain of bondage and slavery etc.". After William's death the Privy Council resolved on an equestrian statue "in some public place". However, nothing came of either plan. Other schemes failed for lack of funds; in 1718, for example, the sculptor Francis Bird proposed a statue in Cornhill but no one subscribed.

In 1724, Samuel Travers, auditor general to the Prince of Wales and a long-serving royal administrator, left the money for an equestrian statue of William either in Cheapside Conduit or in St. James's Square. The Cheapside scheme was voted down in 1731 by the City's Court of Common Council, despite the support of the Lord Mayor and Aldermen – an early case of the refusal of local planning permission! It was left to the aristocratic residents of St James's Square to pursue a desultory interest in the statue over the decades. Various references to it appear in the Trustees' minutes; however, no decisive action was taken until April 30th, 1794, when an approach was finally made to John Bacon (p42). He was by then the country's leading and most prolific sculptor of memorials. He produced a design and set to work, but died unexpectedly in 1799. It was left to his son John to finish and finally cast the statue in 1807, two years after the Battle of Trafalgar.

William III is therefore the very last of London's royal Roman emperors. Youthful and vigorous, he sits at the hub of St James's Square, his left hand on his horse's reins and his right holding the baton of leadership. The dress is appropriate for a man who spent nearly half his adult life embroiled in war, though one could say that the struggle between the independently minded burghers of the Netherlands and absolutist France more resembled that of the city states of Ancient Greece against the might of Persia than the advance of Imperial Rome. On the other hand, the wide-ranging alliances which William forged may have had a new Pax Romana in Europe as their long-term, unrealised goal.

As a personal portrait the statue is quite misleading. William was a slender, austere figure, with thin lips and a prominent, aquiline nose. He was delicate as a child and later suffered from asthma, made worse by stress and overwork, as well as from anaemia. He was already a very sick man when he fell from his horse in Richmond Park and died a few days later. His horse stumbled on a molehill – hence the perennial Jacobite toast to "the little gentleman in black velvet". The Bacons have given us the molehill; it is there under the horse's rear, left leg. The head of the horse is beginning to skew to the right, so we see the fall forever about to take place.

George III *concluded*

George III was still King when London's great public buildings began to fill with the monuments of those who had fallen in the struggle with Napoleon and the first non-royal statues were beginning to appear in the squares. Despite his illness, his long reign had come to symbolise the nation's continuity and when he died, it was clear that the nation owed him his own outdoor memorial. He was therefore the first of England's monarchs to be commemorated in this way by public subscription, rather than by private gift.

A Memorial Committee was set up under the chairmanship of the Prime Minister, Lord Liverpool. The sculptor was not chosen by public competition, which caused ill-feeling in certain quarters; instead Liverpool went straight to Matthew Cotes Wyatt, a rising member of a highly distinguished dynasty of artists and architects. Sir James, his father, was Surveyor General and Sir Jeffrey, his uncle, was about to transform Windsor Castle for George IV. Matthew had begun his artistic career as a painter and he loved large, dramatic designs. For George III's memorial he planned a massive bronze group: the King in classical dress, riding in a chariot drawn by four horses and accompanied by figures representing Fame and Victory; the extras included a hydra-headed monster, Faction, writhing beneath the chariot's wheels. His drawing of the design is shown on p11.

An advertisement for the memorial was distributed (see also p11) together with a list of subscribers. However, the funds raised were quite inadequate for such an elaborate design. Wyatt therefore prepared a much simpler equestrian figure in contemporary dress, so ending one hundred and fifty years of tradition. The Committee may have been making a virtue of necessity or they may have genuinely felt that a natural approach better suited such a homely monarch. As their spokesman Colonel Trench put it, "We thought that the people of England would rather have George III called to their recollection as they have so often seen him, than clothed in a Roman toga and with a wreath of laurel round his brow and a truncheon in his hand."

Wyatt's work suffered numerous delays but by the beginning of 1836 everything was ready except the hind parts of the horse. An unknown person then sabotaged the final casting by putting charcoal in the tubes down which the molten metal was poured. Then an archetypal spoilsport, a Mr Williams of the bankers Ransom and Company whose premises adjoined the Cockspur Street site, appeared on the scene. Maintaining that the statue's presence would harm his business, he lodged an affidavit against it in the Vice-Chancellor's Court. Two months of "tedious and expensive litigation" were required before the way was cleared for the unveiling of the first ever outdoor, national memorial to an English monarch.

The authorities may have feared trouble in the crowded streets and the police were on the alert; however, there were no serious disturbances. "His Royal Highness (i.e. the Duke of Cumberland) having taken his place," wrote *The Times*, "the curtains were withdrawn and the statue exposed to the eyes of the beholders. This was the signal for waving of hats and loud huzzas." Before them stood plain featured George III, wearing a close-fitting riding wig with an elaborate pigtail down the middle of his back and riding Adonis, the Arab grey with pointed ears and high tail which had been his favourite mount for twenty years. It was not long before the statue was nicknamed the Pigtail and Pump-handle, and Cockspur Street became known as Pigtail Street.

Statue by Matthew Cotes Wyatt. Bronze. Cockspur Street, between the western end of Pall Mall and Trafalgar Square. Unveiled August 4th, 1836, by the Duke of Cumberland, George III's fifth son.

Wyatt made his sculptural reputation with his marble memorial to George IV's daughter, Charlotte, at Windsor; she died in childbirth and he portrayed her spiritual form rising ecstatically from her draped and lifeless body, accompanied by two angels. His other contribution to the streets of London was the great bronze statue of the Duke of Wellington now at Aldershot (pp244-7 & 348).

For his statue of George III, Wyatt was finally paid £4,000, a sum which he always maintained barely covered his expenses. It appears that subscriptions of around £7,000 were originally promised for the memorial, a modest sum comparable to that later raised for the Duke of York (p250). One of the problems in raising money was the matter of social precedence. If George III's children, who had often quarrelled with their father and were chronically in debt, each put up only 100 guineas (about £2,600 in modern terms), then marquises, earls and archbishops might give the same but no more. Those slightly lower in the social scale, such as generals, senior bankers and the Provost of Eton might give £50, and so on down. Moreover, half the subscriptions were only promised, not paid, and so £4,000 was the eventual sum raised. (The tiny colony of Mauritius gave £730, or over one sixth of the total, confirming the observation that the British are at their most patriotic abroad.)

George IV

George IV, "The First Gentleman in Europe", was the most sophisticated of England's kings and we owe much of the present day pageantry and splendour of the monarchy to him. When he died, he was, like his father, given a national memorial. It was designed by Stephen Geary, who later built Highgate Cemetery with its magnificent Egyptian Avenue. However, his Graeco-Roman monument to George was less well regarded. It was, in fact, execrated by highbrow and lowbrow alike and, together with its statue, was taken down and demolished within ten years. All that now remains of it is the name which it gave to its location: King's Cross.

Fortunately, a better memorial remains. In front of the National

George IV. Born 1762, London, eldest son of George III. Established himself in great luxury at Carlton House; held court with Charles James Fox (p174) and other Whigs in opposition to father's Tories, 1783. Began the building of Brighton Pavilion, 1784. Continuing mountainous debts led to marriage to Princess Caroline of Brunswick, 1795. Appointed Regent, 1811; began construction of Regent Street and Regent's Park. Became King, 1820. Held splendid coronation and made popular visits to Ireland and Scotland, 1821-2. Began extensive rebuilding of Windsor Castle, 1824. Began building of Buckingham Palace, 1825. Died 1830.

Left. Statue by Stephen Geary, as shown in this advertisement for George IV's national memorial at King's Cross. On the corners below are St George (left) and St Patrick; St Andrew and St David are on the other side. Erected 1836 and immediately much criticised. Demolished 1845.

Above right. It is not clear what function Geary's pavilion-like structure was intended to have. At least it did not suffer the fate of George III's pedestal at Somerset House (p42). It was used as a *camera obscura* exhibition hall, a police station and finally, as can be seen from this *Illustrated London News* engraving of the demolition, as a beer-shop. Behind, the domed building at the junction of the Pentonville and Caledonian Roads fixes the location.

Below right. A cartoon drawn by "Paul Pry" in 1829, at the height of the controversy over the high cost of Buckingham Palace; it was being paid for out of public funds and incurred a great deal of opposition. John Bull is discussing estimates with John Nash, who is standing in the middle of his designs. The statue now in Trafalgar Square can just be seen at the bottom of the picture in its intended position on the triumphal arch. (The arch was erected but was moved in 1850 to become Marble Arch).

NB. The Figures below represent S.¹ GEORGE of England & S.¹ PATRICK of Ireland on the opposite Corners are S.¹ ANDREW of Scotland & S.¹ DAVID of Wales

ELEVATION OF KINGS CROSS

NOW ERECTING BY PUBLIC SUBSCRIPTION

STEPHEN GEARY ARCHITECT.

JOHN BULL & the ARCH-ITECT WOT BUILD'S THE ARCHES &c &c &c &c

Here is a charge for building Wings — Yes - that ere's all right
Here also a charge for pulling down Wings — Yes - them ere was all wrong
Then there's a charge for building them up again — Yes that ere's all right
But the Bill is more than double the Estimate — Yes that ere's always wrong — we never minds no Estimates

The Architect Glory consists in the designment and Idea of the work : his ambition should be to make the form Triumph over the Matter

Gallery (itself one of George's artistic god-children) the portly, gout-ridden King sheds his fleshy burden and quietly shows us his soul. His route there was circuitous. Throughout his life he had built magnificently and his very last project was the transformation of his mother's modest Buckingham House into a royal palace. John Nash's designs included a triumphal arch with an equestrian statue of the King (just visible in the foreground of the cartoon on the previous page). However, George died while the work on the palace was still in progress. By the time Sir Francis Chantrey had finished the statue, the aged Nash had been driven into retirement by allegations of gross extravagance and all the plans had been changed. It therefore spent several years in store, until in 1843 Queen Victoria approved its "temporary" placement in newly built Trafalgar Square, on one of the two pedestals on the north side. It has remained there ever since, forever begging the question as to who should occupy the corresponding pedestal at the other corner.

Chantrey, who has three outdoor statues in London, was one of Britain's most distinguished sculptors. He was born in 1782, near Sheffield, the son of a farmer and part-time carpenter. He was first apprenticed as a wood carver, but decided to become a painter of portraits. As an artist he was completely self-taught. He came to London and worked hard for years without making any money. Painting led to modelling, and so to sculpture. Around 1809 he married a wealthy widow and set up his own studio; soon afterwards a bust of the aged politician Horne Tooke won him acclaim and brought him many commissions. He became extremely successful, modelling four reigning sovereigns – George III, George IV, William IV and Queen Victoria – from life. His early poverty made him an extremely shrewd businessman and, when he died, he left £150,000 (nearly £4 million in modern terms) in trust to the Royal Academy for the purchase of works of art for the nation.

Chantrey made no attempt to disguise his humble origins; his manners were rough, his language plain and strong. He loved to tease the most exalted of his colleagues. Once at the Royal Academy, on a cold day, he went up to a picture by Turner in which the artist had used a lot of orange and warmed his hands at it, saying, "Turner, this is the only comfortable place in the room." He enjoyed shooting and fishing; he was a good host and after dinner loved to show his guests his collection of fossils, which they examined through his microscope. His bluff manner concealed deeply held views about the moral value of beauty. Simplicity was an essential quality of his work. He disliked unnecessary ornamentation – especially in bronze, which he considered a difficult medium for the dull English climate – and he preferred to show his subjects in contemporary dress. His liking for clear outline is demonstrated here. There are no stirrups and no saddle, and the King wears what look like stocking tights. Nevertheless, the overall impression is one of dignified harmony.

The horse stands with all four legs on the ground, a new thing in equestrian statues. Chantrey gave the matter of stance considerable thought and concluded that, since the eye takes an appreciable length of time to absorb the complete shape of a statue, the most natural solution was to show the animal at rest. It is also said that he presented George IV with cards showing horses in different positions – prancing, trotting, neighing and starting – and that the King chose the one standing still.

Above. An *Art Journal* engraving of the ebullient, prosperous yet sensitive Chantrey.

KING GEORGE IV

FRANCIS CHANTREY
SCULPTOR

William IV

William IV was an informal, jolly monarch who ruled with remarkable good sense. When he died, the City of London erected his statue on their new traffic island at the southern end of King William Street. It belonged to the new, naturalistic period, being, as the *Times* remarked, dignified but natural, representing the King neither as a demigod nor as a boatswain. It was the work of a local artist, Samuel Nixon, who had workshops off Bishopsgate and whose figures of the four seasons at the Goldsmith's Hall were much admired. Its erection, too, was a jolly, local affair, watched by interested crowds. A few days afterwards, a celebratory supper was held at the Adelaide Tavern at the foot of London Bridge. Musical entertainment was provided and the healths of the King, the sculptor and the aldermen of the wards of Bridge and Candlewick were drunk "with every demonstration of good feeling and cheer."

This was the capital's first ever statue carved in granite, which is the hardest of all stones and exceptionally taxing to work (see p113). Prominent detail is especially difficult to achieve since the stone vibrates when struck; William's slender baton must have been a remarkable achievement. One can only hope that Samuel Nixon's skill was properly appreciated, for his immense three-year-long labour permanently affected his health and his fee of £2,200 did not even cover his expenses.

Alas, the gradual transition from horse-drawn to motor transport changed the statue's situation in a way that the revellers at the Adelaide Tavern could not have dreamed of. Matters came to a head in 1933 when a pedestrian subway was planned for the junction. Any tunnel dug beneath the statue would certainly have brought its vast bulk crashing through. It would have to be moved – but where? With the co-operation of five different authorities, an admirable solution was found to an extremely complex problem. At Greenwich, surrounded by centuries of naval tradition, the Sailor King has surely found his perfect resting place.

In the circumstances, it seems appropriate to review William's actual career at sea. He joined the navy as a midshipman at the age of fourteen and he soon demonstrated a cheerful and combative nature and a sailor's eye for a pretty girl. He took part in the relief of Gibraltar and was given his first command at the age of twenty, partly in order to remove him from the attractions of the daughter of the Royal Commissioner of Portsmouth to whom he had proposed marriage. He was posted to the West Indies. Nelson (p252) – and what better recommendation could one have – considered him an energetic and efficient captain. Some of his own officers, however, resented his youth and his obvious enjoyment of ceremony, which goes to show the extreme tact that members of the Royal Family must exercise while on service. William also had a tendency to make up his own sailing orders. When his father first became ill he sailed straight back to England, crossing the Atlantic in a record three weeks. It was then that the Lords of the Admiralty decided that they had had enough of him; though he continued to be promoted, he never again went to sea, much to his sorrow. When, many years later, he was given the largely ceremonial post of Lord High Admiral, he again upset the authorities by trying to take his duties seriously. It all seems a waste of genuine enthusiasm and talent. As King, William continued to champion the navy's interests and his very last public engagement was the delivery of a lecture on naval warfare.

William IV. Born 1765, London, third son of George III. Joined navy at wish of father, 1779. Took part in relief of Gibraltar, 1780. Appointed captain of Pegasus and posted to West Indies, 1785. End of active service, 1790. Appointed Ranger of Bushey Park, near Richmond, 1791; settled down with celebrated actress Dorothy Jordan, who bore him ten children. Crisis over royal succession led to marriage with Princess Adelaide of Saxe-Meiningen, 1818. Became heir to throne after death of Duke of York, 1827. Appointed Lord High Admiral; resigned after trying unsuccessfully to take operational command of Channel fleet, 1827. Became King, 1830. First Reform Bill crisis; supported reform and backed elected Whig government; when the Lords blocked the bill, wrote personally to all the Tory peers, who therefore withdrew their opposition, 1831-2. Died 1837.

Statue by Samuel Nixon. Foggin Tor Devon granite, 15 ft 3 ins, 20 tons. William is dressed in his uniform as Lord High Admiral. Commissioned by the Corporation of the City of London. Cost £2,200.

Left. The statue was originally erected on December 18th and 19th, 1844, on a circular, 25ft pedestal, at the junction of King William Street, Gracechurch Street and Eastcheap, where it towered up like a lighthouse to travellers over London Bridge.

Right. In 1935 the statue was taken down and transported to Greenwich, where it was stored at the National Maritime Museum.

Below. In 1936 it was re-erected, on a new 16ft 6ins pedestal, in a newly laid out garden in King William's Walk, just to the left of the entrance to Greenwich Park.

Richard I

The chivalrous warrior Richard Coeur de Lion has always belonged as much to the realm of myth as to historical reality. His quest for Jerusalem, the symbolic centre of the mediaeval universe, belongs to both; however, his meeting, in disguise, with Robin Hood and the oppressed outlaws of Sherwood Forest, and the troubadour Blondel's musical search for him throughout the castles of Europe, are part of the great corpus of romance and legend which grew up after his death. In this century his statue outside the Houses of Parliament has exercised a similar symbolic appeal. In September 1940 it was damaged by Hitler's bombs; the upper part of the raised sword was bent but remained intact. As Vincent Massey, the High Commissioner for Canada, put it, this showed "the strength of democracy which will bend but not break under attack." At his suggestion the sword was left unrepaired until 1947, when it unfortunately became unsafe and had to be replaced. A photograph of the scene just after the raid appears as the frontispiece of this book.

The statue was erected in 1860 and so looks out in time over the high ground of London's great commemorative age. The "Crystal Palace", that miraculous sixteen acre pavilion of iron and glass built to house the 1851 Great Exhibition Of The Industry Of All Nations, stands at the gateway to that age. Sculpture, because of its links with industrial technology, was one of its prominent features. Works by all the leading British sculptors were on show but the work which attracted most attention was the equestrian statue of Richard Coeur de Lion by Baron Carlo Marochetti, which stood outside the western entrance. Massively dramatic, it perfectly caught the prevailing mood of heroic achievement; manufacture and trade were in some ways the nineteenth century equivalents of feudal allegiance and crusading. When the Great Exhibition was over, it was proposed that the plaster Coeur de Lion should be cast in bronze and erected as its memorial, and £5,000 was subscribed for the purpose. It was later decided that an armed warrior was not a suitable symbol for what had also been a Congress of Peace, but the casting went ahead nevertheless.

The political centre of Richard I's realm was in western France, which explains why he spent only a few months of his ten-year reign in England. It was therefore quite appropriate that his sculptor should have been a French-speaking foreigner. The celebrated Baron was born in Turin and trained in Rome. He was ennobled by the King of Sardinia for his equestrian statue of Emmanuel Philibert of Savoy and he was much in favour at the French Court of Louis Philippe. After the revolution of 1848 he came to England, where he was patronised by the royal family and by the aristocracy, who thought his manner engaging and his work exciting. The more insular distrusted his continental airs and considered him flashy. (Punch, who detested all he did, referred to him as Count Marrowfatty.)

A number of statues of earlier rulers were put up at this time, as England looked back over the sweep of her glorious past. It was now that Thornycroft began his statue of Boadicea (p68). The Westminster Old Boys Memorial Column outside Westminster Abbey (1861) and the Buxton Anti-Slavery Memorial Fountain (1865), now in Victoria Tower Gardens, housed in their niches numerous minor figures of rulers from Caractacus onwards. The most interesting of these Gothic recreations, however, was the Eleanor Cross closely modelled on the original (see p21) and set up in 1865 outside Charing Cross Station by the South Eastern Railway Company.

Richard I. Born 1157, Oxford, third son of Henry II, Count of Anjou and King of England. Made Duke of Acquitaine, 1170. Established military and political control of dukedom, 1175-9. Fought wars against or in alliance with father, brothers Henry and Geoffrey, and Philip, King of France, 1173-89. Became King of England and ruler of Angevin Empire, 1189. Collected extensive funds in England and set out on Third Crusade, 1190. Conquered Cyprus, relieved siege of Acre, defeated Saladin's army at Arsuf and turned back 12 miles short of Jerusalem; established Christian kingdom on coast and pilgrims' rights to visit Jerusalem, 1191-2. Captured and held for ransom by Leopold, Duke of Austria, 1193-4. Recovered control of England and established administration under Hubert Walter, 1194. Regained most of Angevin possessions in war with with Philip of France, 1194-9. Died from arrow-wound at Chalus-Chabrol, 1199.

Statue by Carlo Marochetti (see also frontispiece). Bronze. Old Palace Yard, Houses of Parliament. Erected October, 1860. There was a great deal of controversy about the site and it was Prince Albert, in his capacity as Chairman of the newly formed Royal Fine Arts Commission, who effectively chose the present position. Cost £5,000. Parliament agreed to pay £1,650 for the pedestal and a further £1,000 for the two bas-reliefs; one of these shows the Crusader army attacking Jerusalem, the other Richard on his death bed forgiving the archer who shot him, while a cat sleeps peacefully beneath a chair.

Prince Albert

There has always been something strangely anonymous about Albert of Saxe-Coburg. He was an able, far-sighted and highly industrious man, yet it was only after his death that the nation realised what it had lost and made him one of the most commemorated men in its history. His outstanding achievement was the Great Exhibition of 1851, the world's first truly international trade fair; it was his brainchild and he oversaw every part of its vast and complex organisation. Its business triumphantly concluded, the Exhibition was considered worthy of commemoration (see p56). The Lord Mayor of London proposed a memorial with Prince Albert as the central figure and subscriptions were raised. However, one significant voice of support was lacking – that of Albert himself. As he wrote to Lord Glanville, the Memorial Committee's vice-chairman,

'I can say, with perfect absence of humbug, that I would much rather not be made the prominent feature of such a monument, as it would both disturb my quiet rides in Rotten Row to see my own face staring at me, and if (as is very likely) it became an artistic monstrosity, like most of our monuments, it would upset my equanimity to be permanently ridiculed and laughed at in effigy.'

Albert would have preferred the funds to go on travelling scholarships and the like, but the subscribers wanted something more tangible. A competition was therefore held and Joseph Durham's design for a statue of Britannia with four surrounding figures representing the continents of the world was declared the winner. Later a statue of Queen Victoria was substituted for that of Britannia. The site eventually chosen was the Royal Horticultural Gardens, newly laid out between Kensington Road and Brompton Road.

Then, in December, 1861, at the age of forty two, Prince Albert died. The cause was typhoid, aggravated by years of overwork and exhaustion. The Queen was shattered by the blow and came close to breakdown. In her sorrow, she turned to the physical recreation of her beloved husband's presence. One of her first acts was to inform the Great Exhibition Memorial Committee, through the Prince of Wales, that she wished Albert to have the place of honour on their monument. Durham, himself deeply involved, set to work once more and the new memorial was finished within two years.

Prince Albert. Born 1809, Rosenau, near Coburg, son of Duke of Saxe-Coburg-Gotha. Married Queen Victoria, 1840. Encouraged Victoria to take up position of political neutrality, 1841. Instrumental in passing of regulations against duelling, 1843. Elected Chancellor of Cambridge University, 1847; influential in turning syllabus away from theology and classics towards modern history and science. President of Society for Improving the Conditions of the Working Classes, 1848. Initiated and organised Great Exhibition, 1849-51. Prevented likely war with U.S. by altering government dispatch over seizure of merchant ship the Trent *during American Civil War, 1861. Died 1861.*

Right. Statue by Joseph Durham. Copper electrotype, 10ft. South side of Albert Hall. Originally erected in the Royal Horticultural Gardens and unveiled on June 10th, 1863, by Edward, Prince of Wales. Cost £7,500.

The unveiling took place with great pomp. County and municipal dignitaries, leading academics, volunteer corps officers and diplomatic representatives attended; politicians of opposing parties chatted and joked together. Altogether between twelve and fourteen thousand people were present in the Royal Horticultural Gardens. Between three and four o'clock dark clouds massed and three times the spectators were asperged by downpours of rain as they ran for shelter. At four, the skies cleared and the Prince of Wales, accompanied by his new bride, arrived to the sound of trumpets. The monument was formally unveiled and the likeness to Albert generally admired. (Only the absent Queen was dissatisfied; she thought the neck too thin and the shoulders wrong).

Left. This painting shows an event early in the history of the Great Exhibition Memorial. Once he was satisfied that he would not be displayed upon it, Albert took a great interest in its development. At one stage a water cascade was incorporated into the design and the height of the pedestal was raised. Albert, with typical Germanic thoroughness, had a model set up and, because the model was somewhat under life size, had a viewing pit dug in order to correct the altered perspective. The picture shows the Prince in the pit. Sir Henry Cole and his dog are in the left foreground.

The Horticultural Gardens have long since disappeared under brick and tarmac and the memorial has been moved a few hundred yards northwards. However, its present surroundings only serve to emphasise the Prince's significance. The curve of the Albert Hall with its frieze of classical figures and the circular, mandala-like pavement in front of the memorial lend the scene an almost numinous character. In this man, they say, is the hub of this part of Kensington with its great museums and colleges. Albert in fact planned the development of the area as a centre of instruction and study during his lifetime, not long after the opening of the Great Exhibition, and his principal co-worker in that project, Sir Henry Cole, was one of the men who saw the project through. Albert may have had no love of statues of himself but this one, if it could speak, would be happy to repeat the words on Wren's tomb in St Paul's: *Si monumentum requeris, circumspice.*

The Great Exhibition Memorial was the first of a series of monuments to Albert; Edinburgh, Glasgow, Dublin, Manchester, Wolverhampton,

Salford and the Universities of Oxford and Cambridge were just some of the places to commemorate him. In London the next outdoor statue was erected by the Licensed Victuallers' Association at their home for retired publicans off the Old Kent Road. Albert believed strongly in the mutual interdependence of all classes of society and was the Association's patron. He was also, it seems, no teetotaller.

A few years later came the statue in Holborn Circus, where Albert is on parade as a Field Marshal. This was his military rank. In 1850 the aged Duke of Wellington proposed that he should succeed him as Commander-in-Chief, but he declined the somewhat ill-defined position. He was essentially an internationalist and a man of peace. Both he and the Queen found Palmerston's opportunistic, "gunboat" diplomacy highly distasteful. He made himself almost dangerously unpopular by speaking out against the mood of belligerence which swept the country into the Crimean War, though once the war began he worked extremely hard to improve army administration. It is therefore appropriate that the City has given us a most unmilitary Albert – for Field Marshals return the acknowledgements of their troops by saluting, not by raising their hats!

For Albert's national memorial a work on an unprecedented scale was planned. Eight leading architects were invited to submit drawings and models and George Gilbert Scott's Gothic design was selected by the Queen herself. It was based on the shape of a mediaeval *ciborium*, the altar shrine used to house the sacred host; in this case, however, the sacred object enshrined was to be the figure of Albert himself.

Below. Statue by Thomas Earle. Stone, 8ft. Originally erected at The Licensed Victuallers' Association Asylum, Old Kent Road, and unveiled August 9th, 1864, by Edward, Prince of Wales. Cost 600 guineas. In 1958, the Victuallers' retirement home moved to Denham Garden Village in Berkshire and the statue accompanied it; it is now part of a First World War Memorial.

For the unveiling the Victuallers' Choral Society sang a specially composed hymn in praise of Albert's virtues and ended their programme with the Hallelujah Chorus. The Victuallers had asked for the Prince to be dressed just as he was when he laid the foundation stone of their new wing in 1858 and the everyday, frock coated figure makes an interesting contrast with other royal statues.

Right. Statue by Charles Bacon. Bronze. Holborn Circus. Unveiled January 9th, 1874, by the Prince of Wales. Donated anonymously by a City businessman, Mr Charles Oppenheimer, who paid £2,000 for the central figure.

Yet when the memorial was finally unveiled after more than ten years of work, the precious, central figure was still missing. Two further deaths were responsible for its absence. The Queen's own choice of sculptor had been her favourite, Baron Marochetti (p56); he delayed and in 1867 he unexpectedly died. The commission passed to the conscientious John Foley (p186), already at work on the group for the Memorial representing Asia; by 1870 his full sized model of Albert was ready and approved. A few months later he caught a severe chill – some said he had sat too long on the wet clay of Asia's lap, modelling her breasts. The chill turned to pleurisy and in 1873 only the statue's head had been cast in bronze; the other hundreds of parts, still in plaster form, lay dismembered about the studio. In 1874 Foley himself died and the statue was finally completed eighteen months later by his assistant, Thomas Brock (p132). It was erected and then immediately boarded up for guilding; when the boards were taken away, the figure shone so brightly that its features could hardly be distinguished in the glow. There was no formal unveiling, but on March 9th, 1876, the Queen stopped to view it on her way to Paddington. And the following weekend large numbers of people came to gaze up at Albert, gleaming like a Buddha through the unseasonable snow and rain.

They saw a calm, deeply serious work. The Prince holds not a bible, as many have thought, but the Catalogue of the Great Exhibition. He has, as *The Times* of the day observed, the look of a Chairman; he presides over his juncture of history with a concerned, intelligent eye. The original guilding has gone now, "salvaged" in 1915 to help pay for the war against Kaiser Wilhelm, Albert and Victoria's eldest grandson. Had Albert lived another forty years, could he have exercised a moderating influence on political developments and turned Europe aside from that catastrophic falling out of related nations? The question must always remain unanswered, but one thing is certain – he would have tried his best.

Right. Statue by John Foley. Bronze. The Albert Memorial, Kensington Gardens. The Memorial was unveiled in August, 1872, but the statue was not in place until late in 1875. The overall cost of the Memorial was in excess of £100,000, far more than the sum raised by public subscription. Untypically, Parliament voted £50,000 to make up the difference. Gladstone (p204) spoke against the grant but Disraeli (p194) carried the House in its favour.

Left. A contemporary view of the Memorial. Its familiar, ornate form is based on an ordered transition from Earth to Heaven. At its corners are four groups representing the continents of Europe, Africa, Asia and America. On the frieze around the base are 169 figures comprising the mid-Victorian view of the world's greatest painters, musicians, architects and sculptors. Above them are groups representing Commerce, Engineering, Manufacture and Agriculture, and around the central area, on two levels, are eight figures symbolising the Natural Sciences. There are mosaics representing the various Arts. Then the attention is drawn upwards to spiritual matters; in the niches of the spire stand Faith, Hope, Charity and Humility and at the angles Prudence, Temperance, Justice and Fortitude. Higher still, angels in mourning give way to angels in exultation and at the very top is a globe surmounted by a cross.

Victoria

Left. Statue by Thomas Brock. Marble, 13 ft. The Victoria Memorial, The Mall, outside Buckingham Palace. Unveiled May 16th, 1911, by King George V (photograph, p70). £353,907 was subscribed for the Memorial, of which over £100,000 was paid to Brock for the sculpture.

As with the Albert Memorial, the design is a complex allegory. Around the base of the monument are four bronze lions symbolising Power; embracing them are bronze figures of Peace, Progress, Manufacture and Agriculture. The marble base, with its cascades and triton, mermaid and ship's prow designs, symbolises British Sea-power. Above the cascade basins are pairs of figures representing Painting and Architecture, Shipbuilding and War. The principal figures above (with their attendants) are Truth (winged and holding a mirror, seen here to the left), Justice (also winged and holding a sword, to the right), Motherhood, facing the Palace, and, seen here in the centre, the Queen herself. Over all, magnificently gilded, are Courage, Constancy and the Winged Victory.

Right. Statue by Princess Louise, Duchess of Argyll. Marble. The young Queen wears her coronation robes. Kensington Gardens. Unveiled June 28th, 1893, by Edward, Prince of Wales, in the presence of the Queen. The statue was the contribution of the people of Kensington to the Golden Jubilee celebrations.

We come now to the most familiar royal image of all: the small, round, somewhat severe looking lady who ruled over a good proportion of the inhabitants of the globe and who, during the last period of her reign, became more than ever the magical symbol of the nation's unity. Beginning with the Golden Jubilee of 1887, those last years seemed almost continually occupied with commemorations and out of these came a number of public statues.

One of the most interesting is the figure of the young Victoria in Kensington Gardens. It stands close by the palace where she spent her isolated and somewhat unhappy childhood and where, early one June morning, she received the news that she was Queen of England. Her own daughter, Princess Louise, was the sculptress. The family in general had artistic ability – Albert's musical compositions and Victoria's watercolours were both worthy achievements – but Princess Louise was a serious, dedicated practitioner who worked her statues herself without relying on borrowed labour. Her bronze memorial to the troops of the colonies may be seen on a wall of the South Transept of St Paul's Cathedral. From her youth her artistic tutor and advisor was the Austrian-born Sir Joseph Boehm (p265); sadly, he died of a stroke while she was at work on the Kensington Gardens statue.

The City of London's contribution to the Jubilee commemorative

pageant was the statue close by Blackfriars Bridge. The Lord Mayor, attended by swordbearer and macebearer, was present at the unveiling and the Chairman of the Lands Committee raised loyal rhetoric to its highest pitch. The statue would, he said, "in times to come prove a fitting testimony of the close bond of union existing between the reigning dynasty and our ancient city, begotten by a feeling of unswerving fidelity on our part and of gracious condescension from those in high places who have been called to rule over us."

From that time onwards, nation and Empire erected in the region of one hundred and fifty outdoor statues of Victoria; these included forty in India. Many were the work of Thomas Brock. Besides London, he provided statues or busts for Hove, Worcester, Birmingham, Liverpool, Carlisle, Belfast, Cape Town, Agra, Bangalore and Calcutta. It is clear from the marble statue now outside the National Portrait Gallery Annexe that he was not concerned to flatter her; she was to be loved for what she was. Her death in 1901 brought him the greatest undertaking of his career. As Foley's young assistant he had completed the statue of Albert for Kensington Gardens (p63); now by one of the symmetries of history he was commissioned to provide the statues for Victoria's own national memorial. The Memorial Committee asked him to spend a year travelling through Europe at their expense, studying the great monuments of the past; however, he said that the multiplicity of examples would only confuse him. Indeed, a plan for the long expected memorial based on Britain's unique mastery of the seas was already germinating within him and he had a sketch model ready to show King Edward within a few months.

Below left. Statue by John Broad. Terra-cotta, 8ft. Produced at Doulton's pottery works, Albert Embankment, Lambeth and erected 1900, outside the factory. Removed 1910, for road alterations, and destroyed. Other mass-produced examples went to Newbury and Gravesend.

Below right. Statue by Thomas Brock. Marble, 6ft 6ins. Originally unveiled inside the Constitutional Club on February 5th, 1902, by Lord Salisbury. Removed to Wimbledon that same year on the demolition of the Club by its owner. Purchased by the National Portrait Gallery and re-erected outside its annexe in Carlton House Terrace, 1971.

Far right. Statue by John Bell Birch. Bronze, 9 ft. North side of Blackfriars Bridge. Unveiled July 21st, 1896, by H.R.H. the Duke of Cambridge. The gift of the businessman Sir Seale Haslam. A version of a statue originally erected in Udaipur, India; replicas were also erected in Aberdeen, Scarborough, St Peter Port, Guernsey, and Adelaide.

Boadicea

Meanwhile, with remarkable timing, another statue burst upon the capital which was, in its way, a highly appropriate tribute to the departed Queen. This was the warlike figure of Boadicea. Though Victoria's reign had in fact been comparatively peaceful, no one could deny that the national spirit had once again flourished under the leadership of a woman. Moreover, Boadicea's true name, before it was altered by a series of mediaeval copying errors, was Boudica and *bouda* in the Celtic language meant victory; hence she too was called Victoria.

Boudica is one of those figures who, like Arthur, live "under the hill", in the cave of the national imagination and many people think of her as legendary. She was in fact one of the Iceni people of East Anglia and she led a dramatic revolt against Roman oppression. In A.D.43 Claudius' legions conquered Britain. Boudica's husband Prasutagus, king of the Iceni, offered them no resistance and, on his death, left his land and possessions jointly to the new rulers and to his two daughters. The Romans, however, seized everything, stripped

Right. The bearded, artistic paterfamilias Thomas Thornycroft. This engraving appeared in the *Graphic*, together with his son John's proposal to erect the statue of Boadicea on Parliament Hill.

Statue by Thomas Thornycroft. Bronze. Westminster Bridge. Erected 1902. The plaster model was donated by Sir John Thornycroft to the L.C.C., who paid £1,500 for the pedestal and foundations. The cost of the casting, £2,800, was paid for partly out of public subscription and partly by John Thornycroft.

The inscription on the river side of the pedestal comes from William Cowper's famous *Boadicea, an Ode*, in which, on the eve of the battle, a British Druid prophecies the future greatness of the British Empire:

"Then the progeny that springs
From the forests of our land
Armed with thunder, clad with wings,
Shall a wider world command.

Regions Caesar never knew
Thy posterity shall sway;
Where his eagles never flew
None invincible as they."

The photograph shows the group floodlit for the nineteen hundredth anniversary of the revolt. Boudica is accompanied in her charge by her two daughters; the one in view leans eagerly forward, the one on her right holds up her hand against the approaching carnage.

and beat the protesting Queen and raped the girls. This caused a wholesale revolt. The Roman Governor, Caius Suetonius Paullinus, was absent fighting the Druids in Anglesey. The rebels sacked Colchester, London and St Albans, slaughtering the colonists and their collaborators in a holy war of vengeance. Suetonius returned and a confrontation took place somewhere along Watling Street (probably at Mancetter, just north of Nuneaton). The Romans, through superior skill and tactics, won against the odds and Boudica, rather than be taken captive, took poison. Suetonius' immediate retribution was savage but the revolt showed the Roman central government that Britain could not be successfully ruled by exploitation and oppression. Shortly afterwards Suetonius was recalled and their policies were radically changed.

The statues of Boadicea and her daughters represent a moment of national outrage and defiance in a grand-historical manner; it was, in fact, Prince Albert who recommended the sculptor Thomas Thornycroft to "make the chariot like a throne." Present-day archaeologists would dispute the historical accuracy of the design; British chariots had to manoeuvre fast in muddy conditions and were probably light, wickerwork affairs. Moreover, the famous scythes on the wheels turn out to be quite apocryphal! However, there is no doubt that Thornycroft knew what he was doing in composing an image that would stay in the mind. It was his most ambitious work. He had begun life as the son of a Cheshire farmer but showed no desire to follow the family profession; when his mother apprenticed him to a doctor he used the scalpels to carve marble. He came to London to study with John Francis and married his daughter Mary, who was herself a successful and distinguished sculptress. Wishing to portray the great events of English, rather than Greek or Roman, history, he began work on Boadicea in 1856, around the time of the Great Exhibition. Prince Albert supported him closely and even lent him his horses to use as models. However, with Albert's death all prospects of the group being cast were stalled.

In the 1870's hopes of a commission briefly revived and the whole family rallied round. The daughters acted as models and Thomas's more famous sculptor son, Hamo (p206), set to work on the horses but in the end nothing materialised. Thomas gradually lost interest in sculpture. He was a highly talented mechanical inventor and took more pleasure in helping his other son John in the design and manufacture of steamships. (In this he was only exchanging the land-borne war chariots of the past with those of the sea-borne present, for in 1877 John's company provided the British Navy with its first ever torpedo boats.) When Thomas died in 1885, the statues' plaster parts lay in a shed at Chiswick known to the family as Boadicea's Palace. Then the warrior-queen's own legend came to the rescue. The recently formed London County Council planned to excavate the tumulus on Parliament Hill, which since the 18th century had been spoken of as Boadicea's final resting place. John Thornycroft offered to donate the statue to the Council if they would erect it on the site. They expressed interest and set about raising subscriptions. The vision of Boadicea and her daughters breaking the skyline over Highgate and Kentish Town is a dramatic one. The Society of Antiquaries, however, poured scorn on the story of the tomb and it was on Westminster Bridge that those victims of ancient wrong finally reappeared in the modern world.

Victoria, *concluded*

In July, 1904, the contractors began digging outside Buckingham Palace. Aston Webb's architectural scheme for the Victoria Memorial involved the reconstruction of the entire area, including a new road system. Constitution Hill was straightened and a link driven through to Buckingham Gate (that, fortunately, there is no road north through Green Park from the Australia Gate to Piccadilly is due to a misunderstanding of Edward VII's own wishes in the matter). The Mall itself was widened and Admiralty Arch built to complete the perspective. There were years of chaos to endure but, as *The Pall Mall Gazette* commented, "when these works are completed, the Mall and its magnificent carriage drives will have no reason to fear comparison with the Champs Elysees." This was in fact the only occasion (with the exception of Clive's column outside the India Office) when London did things on the French model, integrating roads, buildings and free-standing sculpture in a single, simultaneously executed plan.

Brock's final statue of the Queen once again refrained from any attempt at softening or flattery. For the whole monument he used 2,000 tons of marble, 800 tons of granite and 70 tons of bronze; despite that, the overall effect is light and soaring, even graceful. He went to Italy to select the very finest Carrara marble and it has kept its quality to this day. By 1911 the Memorial was substantially complete and ready for its unveiling, in beautiful summer weather, by George V. When Brock was presented, the King spontaneously called for a sword and made him a knight; it was the climax of his career. It was the climax, too, of Britain's commemorative age. Cycles peak and, containing the seeds of their own destruction, decline. The guest of honour at the unveiling was Queen Victoria's eldest grandson, Kaiser Wilhelm II of Germany. Three years later the two countries began the most destructive and exhausting war the world had ever seen and afterwards the mood of sublime national self-assurance which had produced so many statues of heroes was changed.

The Victoria Memorial (see also p64) was unveiled by George V with splendid and elaborate ceremony. (Edward VII, as he himself had predicted, had not lived to see the occasion). There were four thousand invited guests and thousands more filled the surrounding parks. The Archbishop of Canterbury, Randall Davidson, performed the dedication and a battery of the Royal Horse Guards assembled in St James's Park fired a salute of canon. The photograph shows the military march-past after the unveiling; Edward, Prince of Wales and Prince Arthur of Connaught are taking the salute.

William III, *Kensington Gardens*

William III. For biography, see p46.

Statue by H. Bauke. Bronze, 9ft 2ins. South side of Kensington Palace, in the centre of a specially laid out Dutch Garden. Erected October 15th, 1907. The gift of Kaiser Wilhelm II of Germany.

The ambivalent relations between England and Germany during the 1900's also form the background to the statue of William III at Kensington Palace. It was presented to the British King and people by Kaiser Wilhelm in 1907. Its duplicate was about to be erected on the terrace of his castle in Berlin in a series depicting the princes of the House of Orange. For not only was Wilhelm Queen Victoria's maternal grandson, but he also included William III among his father's forbears. Later that same year he came to London and was well received on all sides (though he did not find time to visit his statue).

Were the English authorities somewhat embarrassed by the gift, seeing it as part of some kind of propaganda war? According to the *Evening News*, a gang of men placed it in position one wet, misty morning. The Germans had expected a prominent West End site; however, central London already had its own native-born statue of William III, in St James's Square (p47). The site at Kensington Palace was proposed on the official grounds that William, wishing to escape the damps of St James's, had lived there for most of his reign.

Unfortunately, statues cannot prevent wars; the close ties between the English and German royal families only make the First World War more tragic.

Edward VII and Queen Alexandra

Queen Alexandra is one of the shining lights of the English Royal Family. From her arrival in England onwards she was a popular figure, beautiful, natural and charming, with a genuine concern for the sick and poor. To some of these she must have seemed a fairytale character, the princess from Copenhagen to whom Hans Christian Andersen had told his bedtime stories. And though her statue at the London Hospital was put up when she was over sixty, there was little flattery in the portrait; she kept the same slender beauty all her life. The London Hospital, deep in the East End, was her special love and she spent hours visiting the wards. Rheumatic fever had left her permanently lame ("the Alexandra limp" became fashionable and was imitated by society ladies). Once she was passing the bed of an unhappy looking patient who was facing a similar disability. "You have a stiff leg? So have I," she said. "Now watch what I can do with it." She raised her skirt and swung her lame leg over the top of his bedside table. John Merrick, the famous "Elephant Man", was also cared for at the London Hospital. His horrific deformities held no terrors for her and it was largely due to her friendship and support that he was able to lead a tolerable life.

Edward VII. Born 1841, eldest son of Queen Victoria. First visit to Paris began lifelong love of foreign travel, 1855. Married Princess Alexandra of Denmark, 1863. Served on Royal Commission on working class housing, 1885-6. Headed list of prize-winning racehorse owners, 1900. Became King, 1901. Visit to Paris laid basis of Entente Cordiale, 1903. Visit to Russia affirmed friendly relations with Czar, 1908. Died 1910.

Statue by L.F. Roselieb. Bronze, 7ft 6in. Tooting Broadway. Unveiled November 4th, 1911, by the Mayor of Wandsworth. Cost £621.

The message of the bronze panels representing Charity and Peace on the pedestal has clearly been picked up by the contented pigeons who live constantly within the statue's ambit.

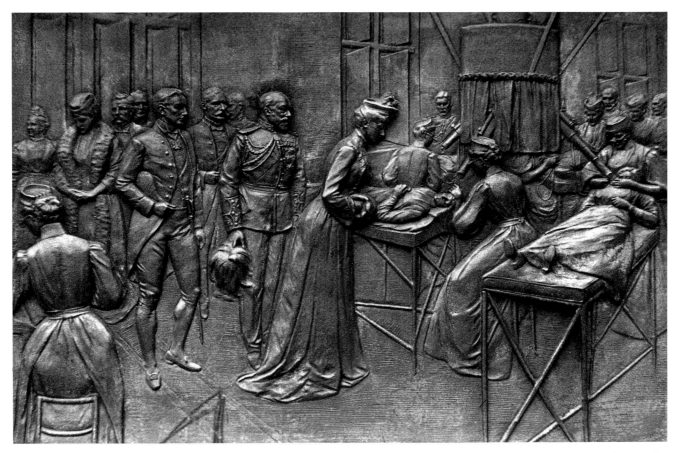

Queen Alexandra. Born 1844, Copenhagen, daughter of Prince Christian of Denmark. Married Edward, Prince of Wales, 1863. Sent out hospital transport and nurses to Boer War and set up convalescent hospital at Sandringham House, 1901. President of newly formed British Red Cross Society, 1905. Founded Alexandra Rose Day to raise money for London Hospitals, 1913. Died 1925.

Statue by George Edward Wade. Bronze. Main Court, London Hospital, Mile End Road. Unveiled July 10th, 1908, by Lord Crewe, Chairman of the Hospital. Cost £1,500, of which Wade waived half.

Above. The plaque shows the operation of the Finsen ultra-violet light cure for lupus (tuberculosis of the skin) which Alexandra introduced into Britain. She bullied the London Hospital into sending a representative to her native Copenhagen to study the cure and they engraved "Nothing but Perseverance" on their first lamp. It proved remarkably successful; they treated one hundred patients a day for twenty five years and the incidence of the disease was reduced for the first time.

Observance and ceremony continued undisturbed throughout the Edwardian era as society enjoyed the calm before the storm. The King himself took a great interest in the statues erected during his reign – as Prince of Wales had he not unveiled so many of them? National commemoration moved towards a second high peak. When Edward died in 1910 the Borough of Wandsworth was so prompt in its memorial appeal that the benignly regal figure by the Clapham sculptor L.F. Roselieb was in place after little more than a year. The committee raised a total of £708-18-4d, the full proprieties of the social order being observed; the Rt. Hon. Lord Wandsworth subscribed one hundred guineas and Mr J. Dobbyn and Mrs A. Smith one shilling. A whist drive held in Tooting raised £13-10s.

The preparations for Edward's national memorial ran far less smoothly and were overtaken by the War. The chief difficulties centred on the site. It seems that even during the great commemorative period there were those who were deeply suspicious of the tide which seemed about to engulf every available space in the capital. Under pressure, the Office of Works adopted an unofficial policy of refusing permission for statues in the parks under their control. The Edward VII Memorial Committee, however, were set on a central, parkland site. Their first suggestion was Green Park, but this was turned down amid protest. Next came a proposal to hive off a comparatively small area of St James's Park half-way along The Mall. This could have provided a pleasant prospect but it was greeted by an even fiercer public storm.

The War then put an end to further deliberations. The site eventually chosen was somewhat second-hand, since Lord Napier of Magdala was

already occupying the centre of Waterloo Place and had to be moved out. The design of the memorial seems to have had more to do with the fact that Britain had just won a war than with any great sensitivity to Edward's life and character. It is true that as a young man he longed to enter the army on a regular, active basis (his parents, however, considered him on the one hand too important and on the other hand too unreliable) and as King he insisted on being consulted on matters of military policy. However, he was, outstandingly, a man of peace, most at home in pleasure-loving Paris (or at Cannes, where his statue was up by April, 1912). If only his memorial could have showed him in neat frock-coat or tweed suit, or wearing the homburg hat which he introduced to England and made famous!

If Edward was, after his death, transmogrified into War, Alexandra was remembered as Love. Her memorial (not free-standing but included for its unforgettable beauty) was the swansong of Sir Alfred Gilbert, better known as the sculptor of Eros (see p96). He was an eccentric, fantastic character. Powerfully imaginative and an original and painstaking craftsman, he was "discovered" at work in Italy by Sir Frederick Leighton, the President of the Royal Academy, and launched

Statue by Bertram Mackennal. Bronze. Waterloo Place. Unveiled July 20th, 1921, by King George V. Cost £10,500 (including £3,000 paid for a statue begun in 1913 and cancelled). The King wears the uniform of a Field Marshal.

Sir Bertram Mackennal was born in Melbourne and studied in London and Paris; he was the first Australian to be elected to the Royal Academy. His most dramatic London work is the group *The Horses of the Sun*, near roof level on the south-east corner of Australia House in the Strand.

The central figures of the Alexandra Memorial by Alfred Gilbert. Bronze. Set into the wall of the gardens of Marlborough House, Marlborough Road. Unveiled June 8th, Alexander Rose Day, 1932. (On the following the unveiling, George V somewhat grudgingly awarded Gilbert a knighthood.) Cost £12,000. The inscription around the base speaks of "Faith, Hope and Love, the Guiding Virtues of Queen Alexandra". It is Love who supports the central figure of the young girl on her journey into life.

onto the London scene. Naive, extravagant, he found it hard to cope with the administrative and financial complexities of the big public commissions which came his way. In 1901 he went bankrupt and left England for Bruges, his relations with the Royal Family strained to breaking point. Alexandra, however, continued to help him out. She sent him money and during the War asked the Kaiser for a guarantee of his safety in occupied Belgium. In 1925, partly through the influence of the sculptress, Princess Louise (p65), it was agreed that he should return to finish, at last, the Duke of Clarence's tomb at Windsor and also provide the memorial for Queen Alexandra. At his own request, he was paid only a workman's living wage. For a studio he was given a large, draughty building at Kensington Palace originally put up as a store and this became his home for the few remaining years of his life.

The Memorial's fin-de-siecle, visionary forms belong more to the 1890's, the period of the symbolists, than to the 1930's. But Gilbert himself encountered these presences directly in his dreams, in some permanent and mysterious substratum of the Anglo-Celtic soul. That they achieved this unexpected public emergence is surely a deep-based tribute to Queen Alexandra's own genius for compassion.

George V

Below. The architect of George V's memorial was Giles Gilbert Scott, the grandson of George Gilbert Scott who performed the same service for Prince Albert. At the beginning of 1939 he submitted his first design which involved the large, ornate gothic canopy shown here. The Memorial Committee approved, as did the King and Queen, but when it was published in the press, there were strong protests. Purists questioned whether gothic ornament should be used in such an isolated, two dimensional way. Others simply thought it awful. In the end the decision went against it, backed by the Royal Fine Arts Commission, who thought the site too cramped. At that time, as one can see from the picture of the unveiling, there were many more buildings on that side of Old Palace Yard. It is true that the canopy might have turned out a huge, anachronistic eyesore, but it might have blended well with Westminster Abbey and Barry's Houses of Parliament. It would certainly have made the monument more of a landmark.

The shy, gruff, conservative naval officer who came to the throne in 1910 successfully shouldered the burdens laid on him and maintained both the honour and the popularity of the monarchy in a more democratic age. His Jubilee Appeal raised over a million pounds – and not a penny was spent on statues. This matched both the mood of the times and also the King's own wishes. Unlike his father, Edward VII, he had no particular love of monuments (see his conversation with Lady Scott, p302); he had had no qualms approving the wartime stripping of the gilt from the figure of Prince Albert. Likewise the bulk of the money raised by his Memorial Appeal was spent on nation-wide recreation grounds; out of the £584,378 4s 11d collected, only £25,037 17s 11d was spent on a statue. How different from the times of Albert and Victoria!

In its plans for his statue, the Memorial Committee turned its attention to a vacant site just beyond Westminster Abbey. They liked to think that George V would be looking towards Parliament whose opening he had so often performed. (But did they realise what an ordeal this had been for him? He was extremely nervous on such occasions and the Speech from the Throne was always printed in large type on thick sheets of paper which would not rustle in his shaking hands). No nervousness, however, is apparent in William Reid Dick's satisfyingly dignified figure. What the King was called upon to do, he did well; now he rests from his labours.

Statue by William Reid Dick. Portland stone. Old Palace Yard, Westminster, beside Westminster Abbey. Unveiled October 2nd, 1947, by King George VI. The King wears Garter Robes over the uniform of a Field Marshal and holds the Sword of State, point downwards.

Sir William Reid Dick was probably Britain's leading public sculptor in the period between the Wars. (For a photograph, see p304). He was born in Glasgow and took up sculpture against the wishes of his Presbyterian father. He went through the First World War as an ordinary soldier; he carved a female figure out of the chalk of the trenches and this became celebrated as an example of resilience and resourcefulness. He both designed and executed the Kitchener Memorial Chapel in St Paul's Cathedral, with its dramatically beautiful figure of Mary holding the dead Christ in her arms. During the 1930's he became the established sculptor of royalty. Unlike the bohemian Alfred Gilbert (pp75 & 97), he was George V's kind of artist, modest and dependable; they shared the same kind of quiet, somewhat dour humour. As well as the London memorial, Reid Dick also carved the effigies of George V and Queen Mary in St George's Chapel, Windsor. He was an excellent craftsman and everything he did has a beautifully finished quality. His 1947 statue of President Roosevelt (p233) shows him adapting that craftsmanship to a more modern, pared artistic style.

George VI

Discreetly angled steps lead up from the Mall to Carlton Gardens; at their head stands the man who never expected to be king. Of the one and three quarter million pounds raised by George VI's Memorial Appeal, by far the largest amount was spent on schemes benefiting both old and young, including the founding of the Duke of Edinburgh Awards. However, his statue, modest though it is, deserves its share of attention. The Garter robes fill out the slight, erect figure. What we notice most is the strength of the features; the sculptor has made good use of his bronze medium in delineating the line of the mouth, showing us one whose essence was the triumph of innate quality over initial disadvantage.

George VI was a second son, much overshadowed in nursery and schoolroom by his clever, extrovert elder brother. He was backward at his lessons and as a naval cadet he came last in his examinations. Recurrent gastric trouble kept him out of most of the First World War, though he discovered a fearlessness under fire during the battle of Jutland, its only major naval encounter. He later joined the R.A.F. and became the first royal air pilot. His health improved, he went on foreign tours and he visited mines and factories. His chronic stammer, however, continued and made an agony of so many public engagements. Nevertheless, he persevered and eventually mastered it. His serious, straightforward approach to life made him friends everywhere.

As King he is perhaps best remembered for the example which he set during the blitz. Buckingham Palace was hit several times but he and the Queen refused to leave. After the nights of destruction they would set out to comfort and encourage those who had suffered in the bombings. On one such visit to the East End an onlooker called out, "Thank God for a good King!" to which he replied, "Thank God for a good people!"

With that tribute we end our account of the commemoration of England's royalty. It would be in poor taste to anticipate the ending of the present reign. However, Queen Elizabeth's Golden Jubilee, which falls due in 2002, provides a far happier prospect and there is the precedent of Queen Victoria for the erection of statues to celebrate the occasion. In the writer's view, the perfect occupant of the long vacant pedestal in Trafalgar Square would be an equestrian statue of the present Queen. Her skill as a rider and her love of horses are well-known. The statue need not be in a military style; rider and animal could be admired for their innate elegance and beauty, rather than for any symbolic associations. Yet being the statue of a ruler, it would complement the calm equestrian figure of George IV (p53) and complete the symmetry of the Square.

The monarchy is a national institution and one would not expect to find foreign royalty prominent on the streets of the capital. However, the young Prince Imperial of France who was killed fighting for Britain in the Zulu War of 1879 was given a statue at Woolwich (see chapter 9, p348). Even more poignant is the memory of the Red Indian princess, Pocahontas (see Captain Smith, p308). She married an English settler, amazed the court of King James I with her culture and intelligence, and died here in childbirth; her recumbent form, known also as "La Belle Sauvage", used to lie in Red Lion Square but the publishers Cassell who commissioned her (they began business over a public house which bore her name) have now taken her indoors at their new offices in Vincent Square, Victoria.

George VI. Born 1895, second son of Duke of York, later George V. Entered navy as cadet, 1909. Fought in Battle of Jutland as sub-lieutenant, 1916. Joined R.A.F. and qualified as pilot, 1917-9. Started annual Duke of York's camps for boys, 1921. Began successful speech therapy for stammer, 1926. Became King after abdication of Edward VIII, 1936. Made first-ever visit of monarch to America, 1939. Remained at Buckingham Palace during Second World War bombing, 1939-45. Created George Cross and Medal for civilian gallantry, 1940. Proposed Ernest Bevin as strong foreign secretary in Labour government, 1945. Died 1952.

Statue by William Macmillan. Bronze. Carlton Gardens. Unveiled October 21st, 1955, by Queen Elizabeth II.

Macmillan was an Aberdonian who had a long and successful career as a sculptor. He was a confident, capable artist, perfectly happy to go on making portraits in the traditional manner while all around him were turning to abstraction. He was sixty eight years old when he completed the statue of George VI. He went on to do three more commemorative statues for London, those of Raleigh, Trenchard and Coram, and his stone figures of Sir John Alcock and Sir Arthur Brown (the first airmen to fly the Atlantic) were erected at Heathrow Airport when he was nearly eighty.

Below. The vacant pedestal in the north-west corner of Trafalgar Square, opposite the equestrian statue of George IV (p53).

CHAPTER 2
PHILANTHROPY AND EDUCATION

After majesty, munificence; after power, wealth and the distribution of wealth. Perhaps the English have always been, at heart, men of property. In London the erection of free-standing statues of philanthropists began more or less simultaneously with those of royalty. It is interesting to compare the slight, ascetically bearded figure of Charles I with portly, jovial Captain Maples, commemorated in 1683 outside Trinity House's almshouses in Deptford. Maples was a sea captain who spent most of his long life in India and when he died he left diamonds, Tonquin musk and other goods worth £1,300 to Trinity House for the care of retired sailors. His executors suggested that a statue would encourage other benefactors. Jasper Latham's figure (of stone, now painted white) is seen here in the entrance hall of Trinity House, where it was placed in 1953. (It has a companion but far less interesting statue, that of Captain Sandes, whose gifts were also commemorated at Deptford, in 1746.)

The first statues of philanthropists belong to a period of prosperity and charitable giving in which City merchants and City institutions played a leading role. The man whose gifts surpassed all others was the bookseller and member of the Stationers' Company, Thomas Guy. Later, as the advancing Industrial Revolution created ever more social dislocation and misery, it was clear that new and wider initiatives were needed. This chapter has its own Royal Duke, Edward Augustus, proto-socialist and fourth son of George III, who was a member of no less than fifty three charitable organisations. From the Victorian Age of Improvement there is an American millionaire-banker and an English stationer, both of whom built houses for the working poor, an East End shipbuilder, and a sugar merchant who initiated the Polytechnic movement. Also included is Eros, the famous memorial to the social reformer, Lord Shaftesbury. Shaftesbury was always spoken of as the greatest philanthropist of his times, not in a financial sense but according to the root meaning of the word, a "lover of mankind".

It is most natural, perhaps, to give to the next generation. That is why philanthropy and education have a natural link and why children, sculpted or real, figure prominently in the following pages. Mrs Margaret MacDonald, wife of the first Labour Prime Minister Ramsay MacDonald, was honoured for her qualities as a friend and mother. Yet at least half the men commemorated here were themselves childless; as Francis Bacon wrote, "So the care of posterity is most in them, that have no posterity."

CAPTAIN RICHARD MAPLES
DIED 1680
A BENEFACTOR TO THE CORPORATION

Sir Robert Clayton

Sir Robert Clayton. Born 1629, Bulwick, Northamptonshire, son of small farmer. Apprenticed to uncle, a wealthy London scrivener (or broker) who later left him his fortune. Elected Alderman of City of London, 1670. Donated £10,000 for building of girls' wing at Christ's Hospital and £1,000 for a new mathematical school, principally designed for the study of navigation, 1675. Lord Mayor, 1679-80. M.P. for City of London, 1678-81; moved Bill to exclude James, Duke of York, from throne and presented petition to Charles II protesting at Parliament's dissolution. Lost seat as Alderman after rewriting of City Charter by Charles II, 1681. Resumed seats as Alderman and M.P. after accession of William III, 1689. President of St Thomas's Hospital, 1691-2. Led St Thomas's rebuilding appeal with donation of £600, 1693. Loaned £30,000 to William III to pay wages of army, 1697. Died 1707, leaving £2,300 to St Thomas's.

Statue by Grinling Gibbons. Marble. Clayton wears his Lord Mayor's robes. St Thomas's Hospital, Lambeth, north wing terrace. First erected 1702, in the centre of Clayton Quadrangle, St Thomas's Hospital, Southwark. Moved to Lambeth 1868-70 and erected in present position 1976. Cost £200.

John Evelyn called the broker and money-lender Sir Robert Clayton "the Prince of Citizens." He was certainly one of the wealthiest men of his age. His banquets were served in a cedar panelled dining room adorned with frescoes of the battles of the gods and the giants. When as Lord Mayor he entertained Charles II, no doubt wearing the rich mayoral robes in which his statue is dressed, his wife appeared "all over scarlet and ermine and half over diamonds." Nowadays governments borrow billions from international banks to balance their budgets; when William III needed the money to pay his troops, he went to Clayton.

Clayton appears in Dryden's pro-Stuart satire *Absolom and Achitophel* as "extorting Ishban," "as good a saint as usurer e'er made." What really lay behind his philanthropy? It was in part the product of a naturally overflowing nature but there was also a sadder side to it. His only son died in infancy. A childless man cannot spend all his money on his wife's jewels and what more natural than to turn his attention to the upbringing and education of orphans? Likewise his great donation to Christ's Hospital was made shortly after a serious attack of typhoid had shown him his own mortal vulnerablility.

There was also a political side to Clayton's connection with St Thomas's, for the Hospital was then a stronghold of Whig opinion and always elected a Whig Alderman as President. Clayton's political views were suited to a poor farmer's boy become independent City magnate. The inscription on his statue describes him as "a brave defender of the liberty and religion of his country". Reading between the lines, this means parliamentarian, anti-Catholic and a determined opponent of the Stuart dynasty in its last years. It was said that Charles II was so incensed by the behaviour of the Whig group in the City during the time of the Exclusion Bill and the Popish Plot that he tried to have Clayton hanged, and that he was only saved by the intervention of his friend, Judge Jeffries. The tale is unlikely to be true, though one of his aldermen, Cornish, did later suffer that fate at the hands of James II.

The governors of St Thomas's commissioned Clayton's statue from Grinling Gibbons and he, so far as is known, carved it himself. Though he was at his best in wood rather than in marble (see page 29), the governors were satisfied. This was just as well, for only three years previously Christ's Hospital had refused to accept a statue of Sir John Moore because the likeness was so bad, and Gibbons had had to re-carve it. The whole Hospital had just been rebuilt and Clayton's donation had covered the entire cost of reconstructing the third, easternmost quadrangle. There, in its centre, his statue was placed. After his death the inscription was re-cut to include mention of his final bequest and the whole monument was "beautified". To judge from the remnants of colour still on the coat of arms, the pedestal must have received a painting. The statue itself was discoloured in a more recent fire.

The statue now stands with Edward VI (p36) and Florence Nightingale (p164) in the line of figures outside the new main entrance. The modern block provides an awkward background and aesthetically it would be far better off in the centre of one of the lawns facing the river. Fewer people would see it there but one wonders whether busy nurses on their way in to work have much time to stop and reflect on the somewhat ponderous, bewigged figure whose money built a third of their Hospital so many years ago.

Thomas Guy

The founder of Guy's Hospital was not, as one might think, a medical man but a bookseller. He owed his wealth to two circumstances: one was the scarcity and poor quality of printed bibles and the other was the navy's bankruptcy, which resulted in the raising of national capital through the infamous South Sea Company. The production of bibles was a monopoly long held by the King's Printers and by Oxford University Press. Guy began by illegally importing them from Holland and later came to an arrangement with Oxford; for fourteen years he printed good, cheap bibles which everyone could afford. They made him a fortune but he had in fact already begun to give it away. The town of Tamworth was the first to profit from his generosity but he abandoned it when its citizens failed to re-elect him as their M.P.; he was reportedly so angry that he threatened to pull down the Town Hall which he had just built them.

Guy had long taken a philanthropic interest in St Thomas's Hospital in Southwark. As a result of the inflation of his South Sea stock, he found himself, in the very last years of his long life, possessed of a huge fortune. He therefore set out to make full and thorough provision for St Thomas's convalescent patients. In practice the result was a completely new general hospital, built on adjacent land. In his will Guy left over £200,000 for its completion and endowment; the modern equivalent would be around £5 million. (One can get a further idea of relative values from the fact that he also left £1,000 for the relief of those imprisoned for debts of less than £5, so bringing about the release of over 600 people.) Out of their bequest the Trustees of the new hospital gave their founder a sumptuous funeral and set aside £2,000 (£50,000) for his portraits and statues.

After Guy's death stories were told which made him into that fairytale character, the "miser with a heart of gold." He ate his dinner off his shop's counter using an old newspaper as a table-cloth. He kept one maidservant, Phyllis Howard by name. A friend persuaded him to propose marriage to her but when she allowed some workmen to pave the area in front of his shop six inches beyond the appointed limit, at his expense, he broke off the engagement. He dressed shabbily; once he was standing thoughtfully on Westminster Bridge when a passer-by, thinking that he was about to throw himself into the river in destitution and despair, gave him a sovereign. He pursued his benefactor and explained who he was; later, discovering that the man had gone bankrupt, he set him up again in business. Such stories, whether true or not, may have reflected some aspect of his character. He lived simply and never married; we know that he was invited to become a Sheriff of the City of London but refused the honour, preferring to pay the statutory £420 fine than have the greater trouble and expense of the office.

In the hospital chapel there is a marble memorial to Guy carved by John Bacon (p42) and put up in 1779 for the chapel's completion. It shows a richly dressed, elegant gentleman stooping to raise a sick man from the ground. Some consider it Bacon's masterpiece but Scheemakers (p36), who was of course working much nearer to Guy's time, has surely got closer to the underlying reality of the man. His figure is lean, ectomorphic, wigless. There is a glow about the face, a charitable intensity, yet within the glow the eyes calculate, the mouth is narrow. As a portrait of combined acquisitiveness and generosity it is a remarkable achievement, the more so for having stood for over two hundred and fifty years in the open air.

James Hulbert

When James Hulbert, citizen of London and Prime Warden of the Fishmongers' Company, made his will, he could not possibly have known how much his estate would shortly be worth. He even left a proviso allowing the members of his Court to scale down his plans for an almshouse if they found it necessary. But just as the South Sea Bubble would shortly shower its benefits on the patients of Mr Guy's hospital (p84), so it now vastly increased the value of Hulbert's bequest. His executors found themselves left with no less than £9,467-2-5d, or about £240,000 by modern reckoning. Of this they spent £1,928-4-5d on the building of almshouses, and this sum was enough to include luxuries like "effigies of the Donor".

The remainder was invested and the interest went to provide the forty poor persons who lived in the almshouses' three courts with a truly safe haven. They were paid three shillings weekly and given a Christmas bonus. They were also kept warm and dry; each year they received a gown and a cauldron of coals. They were visited annually by the Wardens and religious services were said for them in their chapel. They had benefited both from Hulbert's generosity and from the instability of the financial markets; for those poor persons, the Wheel of Fortune had swung well.

Robert Aske

The last of this chapter's four liveried gentlemen was a close contemporary of Sir Robert Clayton (p83). In fact the same political wind which swept Clayton from his office as an Alderman brought the High Tory Aske the Mastership of the Haberdashers' Company. Little is known of his life but he must have been a good businessman to have left the modern equivalent of £750,000.

His bequest brought new and unexpected responsibilities to the Haberdashers' Company. With it they bought a twenty acre site at Hoxton, Shoreditch, and they engaged Dr Hooke, the famous scientist and colleague of Wren, as their architect. He spent, some said, more than he should have done in designing a grand, wide-fronted, classical building to rival the other great hospitals of the period. A statue of Aske stood in a niche over the main doorway. By 1824, however, this building was in such a bad state that it had to be demolished. A new almshouse designed by David Riddel Roper was put up two years later, together with a quite different, free-standing statue of Aske in Coade stone. Later in the century its function became purely educational and in 1875 an entirely new boy's school was built at New Cross; it was there, on the commanding heights known then as Plowed Garlic Hill, that the statue was re-erected.

Robert Aske. Born 1619, London, son of draper. Apprenticed to haberdasher and merchant of East India Company, 1634, Became freeman of Haberdashers' Company, 1643; carried on trade in raw silk and dealt in property. Became member of Court of Assistants of Haberdashers' Company and Alderman of City of London, 1666. Appointed Master of Haberdashers' Company on wishes of James II, 1685. Died 1689, leaving £20,000 to Company to buy land and build an almshouse for twenty poor, single freemen of the Company and pay them £20 per year. The residue of the estate (another £10,000 or more) was to be used to educate twenty boys, who in practice lived in the same building as the pensioners.

Statue by William Croggan. Coade stone. In front of Haberdashers' Aske's School, Pepys Road, New Cross. Aske wears his City livery and to his left are the arms of his Company with its motto, Serve and Obey. In his left hand he holds a scroll bearing a plan of the original almshouse. First erected c.1826, outside the newly rebuilt almshouse at Hoxton. The statue was moved to its position at the present Aske's boys school in 1903.

The use of that astonishingly durable material, Coade stone, began around 1769 and ended around 1837. The Coade artificial stone manufactory was run by the redoubtable Miss Eleanor Coade, the stone having been invented by her father or husband. It was moulded and then fired, though the exact nature of the process was always a secret. The best known London Coade stone figure is the great lion which stands on the south eastern corner of Westminster Bridge. William Croggan took over as the director of the manufactory around 1813. He provided a number of statues for Buckingham Palace, and also reliefs of King Alfred Expelling the Danes and King Alfred Delivering the Laws for its West Front.

The Duke of Kent

The life of George III's fourth son was full of paradoxes. He was a stickler for army discipline and enforced it with all the appalling brutality which the regulations of the day laid down, ordering frequent floggings, and executions for mutiny. He only thought that he was doing his duty. He considered himself a reformer and he was indeed the first commander to establish regimental schools for the illiterate among his troops and for their children. In private life he was hospitable and courteous. He lived luxuriously and, like all his brothers, ran up huge debts. His army career terminated, he spent some miserable years trying to clear his finances, appealing unsuccessfully to Parliament and making over most of his income to trustees.

The Duke was an energetic, zealous man, brawny and tall, a typical mesomorph by constitution. Did condemnation and misfortune teach him to appreciate the sufferings of others? For the last decade of his life he poured his energies into charitable activities of all kinds. He supported over fifty different societies, among them the Bible Society, the Anti-Slavery Society and the British School of Industry, as well as, for example, the Society for the Propagation of the Gospel in the Highlands and Islands of Scotland and the Lying-in Charity for Delivering Poor Women at their Own Habitations. He gave donations (though the money was more his creditors than his own). More importantly he presided – in 1816 no less than seventy-two times. He regularly chaired the annual dinner of the Literary Fund for Distressed Authors and he had an intriguing scheme for establishing a national institution, similar to the Chelsea Hospital for retired soldiers, which would care for aged and worn-out writers.

The Duke also admired the man often called the founder of Socialism, Robert Owen, whose working community at the Lanark Cotton Mills was for a time a centre of harmony and enlightenment. He would eagerly show his visitors Owen's model of society, consisting of a series of cubes with his own tiny class perched isolated at the top. In 1819, shortly after the birth of his daughter, he chaired a meeting to consider implementing Owen's plans for improving the lot of the poor. The prospect of Britain's first socialist crusade led by the father of Queen Victoria is a striking one, but it was not to be. In January, 1820, after a severe cold caught visiting Salisbury Cathedral, the Duke died of pneumonia.

A few months later, a group of noblemen and gentlemen met at the Freemasons' Hall to consider the erection of his statue somewhere in the capital. As sculptor they chose the Irishman Samuel Gahagan, who had just completed an impressive monument to fierce old General Picton, killed at Waterloo, for St Paul's. They placed the statue of Edward Augustus at the top of Portland Place, facing south, where, given good weather, the sun of virtuous self-satisfaction passes daily across its face.

Towards the end of his life Owen, hitherto an ardent atheist, turned to spiritualism. The Duke of Kent, so he believed, (together with those other champions of democracy Thomas Jefferson and Benjamin Franklin) spoke to him through his mediums. There were, said the Duke, no titles in the spirit world. Statues, too, would be superfluous in that equal and eternal flux, though he has not returned to Portland Place to tell us so, speaking Talos-like through that brazen mouth. Now few remember him except as the father of his famous daughter, but his statue stands as a memorial to the principle that nobility, to be appreciated, must oblige.

Prince Edward Augustus, Duke of Kent. Born 1767, London, fourth son of George III. Sent for military training in Hanover, 1785-7. Posted to Gibraltar as colonel of Royal Fusiliers, 1790. Transferred to Canada; took part in capture of Windward and Leeward Islands, 1791-8. C-in-C, North American forces, 1799-1800; resigned through ill-health. Governor of Gibraltar, 1802-3; imposed strict discipline and banned troops from wine-shops, which caused a mutiny. Recalled on charge of excessive discipline, 1803. Began work for charities, 1812. Granted Freedom of City of London for charitable activities, 1816. Crisis over royal succession, 1817; parted from Julie de Saint Laurent, his mistress for twenty six years, and married Princess Victoria of Saxe-Coburg. Birth of daughter, the future Queen Victoria, 1819. Died 1820.

Statue by Sebastian Gahagan. Bronze. The Duke wears Garter robes and supports his weight on a classical column, with books. Park Crescent Gardens, at the top of Portland Place. Erected 1825. Paid for, according to the inscription, by "the supporters of the numerous charities which he so zealously and successfully patronised."

Richard Green

"I have no time to hesitate," was Richard Green's favourite utterance and, looking at the vigour that can still sometimes be seen in the face of his statue, one can imagine him making it. He embodied the energy of Britain's nineteenth century mercantile expansion. The ships he built carried his name to every part of the world. He supplied "East Indianmen" sailing ships to the East India Company and steam frigates to the English, Russian, Spanish, Portuguese and Brazilian navies. When the East India Company lost its exclusive charter, he set up his own fleet and traded with India himself; at the time of his death he owned thirty vessels. He sent his ships to Australia with the 1852 Gold Rush and he imported tea from China (let us hope that he did not export Indian opium in return).

Green also directed his energies and the fruits of his labours towards improving the general comfort, education and status of merchant

Richard Green. Born 1803, Poplar, son of shipbuilder. Became head of family business with brother Henry. Established Thames Marine Officers' Training Ship, founded Poplar Sailors' Home, supported Dreadnought Hospital Ship and Merchant Seamen's Orphan Asylum. Supported local schools and hospitals. Traded with Australia, India and China. Died 1863.

Statue by E.W. Wyon. Bronze. Outside Poplar Public Baths, East India Dock Road. Unveiled May 11th, 1866. Green is seated in his chair while his favourite Newfoundland dog, Hector, rests his head against his master's knee. The Baths were rebuilt in 1931-2 but the statue still stands in its original position.

seamen. The Sailors' Home which he endowed in Poplar was open to any man of good character and provided courses on seamanship and navigation. He subscribed to all the leading marine schools and hostels and he helped to strengthen the link between the Navy and the merchant services. He was also a supporter of local causes on land; he was, for example, the chief contributor of funds to Poplar's schools, in which over 2,000 children were educated and clothed. Not surprisingly, on the day of his funeral all the ships in the docks and on the river flew their flags at half-mast and thousands of people lined the streets. The collection of funds for his statue began almost at once and contributions were also received from India, Australia and China.

Some older residents of the area still remember the shipbuilding firm which continued up to the Second World War on the Isle of Dogs under the name of Green, Siley and Weir. Now, however, all that is gone; the great tide of marine prosperity has ebbed completely. Green would no doubt have shuddered at the statistics displayed in our photograph. His statue grows ever "Greener" with the passage of time. This is partly inevitable and depends on the constitution of the atmosphere in that part of the city (it is noticeable that the statues in the very centre discolour black or dark brown while those on the peripheries often have a greener tinge). However, its generally dull and grubby state at the time of writing would be improved by the application of some of its subject's own vigour.

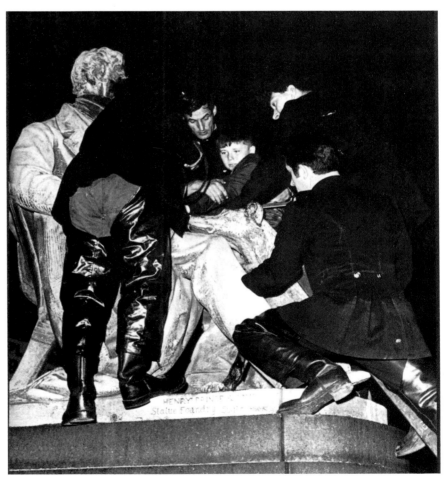

Right. 10-year-old Patrick Heneghan being rescued by firemen after having trapped his leg in the statue. He had climbed up to rescue his swimming trunks thrown there by a friend. To free him, the fireman had to cut off one of the dog Hector's ears. The event occurred in 1967 but the ear is still missing.

George Peabody

George Peabody's statue, tucked away in a leafy corner behind the Royal Exchange, is one of the least of his memorials. A portion of the Arctic was named Peabody Land after he had financed one of the many searches for Sir John Franklin (p298). His home town of Danvers, Massachusetts, was renamed Peabody, for he was an even greater philanthropist in America than in England, chiefly in the field of education (something which he himself had lacked). And in London the numerous Peabody buildings, tall blocks of sturdy, practical flats, are still administered by the Trust which he founded.

London was Peabody's principal home for nearly thirty years and in his quiet way he made a considerable contribution to Anglo-American relations. He liked London air and London life and called himself "somewhat of a Cockney." He lived simply, in rented rooms; he was hospitable and a good conversationalist, he was fond of singing, especially Scottish songs, and he liked a game of backgammon after dinner. His greatest pleasure, clearly, was in well-judged giving. It is pleasant to be able to contemplate the figure of an American millionaire about whom nothing bad can be said.

His decision to devote funds to the housing of London's poor was taken on the advice of Lord Shaftesbury (p96). Both had seen at first hand the appalling conditions created by London's industrial growth and the take-over of so much land by the railways: unbearably over-crowded lodgings, unheated, with no sanitation, breeding grounds for cholera and typhoid. Shaftesbury's so-called Labourers' Friend Society had already built good, clean workers' apartments. The Trust established by Peabody carried on this work on a much larger scale; within twenty years there were eighteen groups of Peabody buildings, housing 20,455 people at an average rent of 5s. per week per flat. Later came similar schemes financed by Sir Sydney Waterlow (p101) and all three men were commemorated with statues.

George Peabody. Born 1795, Danvers, Massachusetts, son of poor parents. Apprenticed to local grocer, 1806-10. Went into dry goods business in Georgetown and Baltimore, 1814; was very successful and opened branches nation-wide. Made first visit to England, selling cotton in Lancashire, 1827. Settled permanently in London as merchant and banker, 1837. Loaned £3,000 to improve sub-standard American display at Great Exhibition, 1851. Arranged first Independence Day Dinner in England, inviting Duke of Wellington and 1,000 other people, 1851. Set up fund of £150,000 to build houses for London's working poor, 1862. First Peabody building opened in Spitalfields, 1864. Refused baronetcy, asking only for personal letter of commendation from Queen Victoria, 1866. Gave £700,000 for education of freed slaves in southern states of America, 1867. Gave further £350,000 for London housing, 1869. Died 1869; his body lay in state for a month in Westminster Abbey and was then ceremonially conveyed to America by battleship.

Statue by William Wetmore Story. Bronze. North corner of Pope's Head Lane, behind Royal Exchange. Cost £3,000. A replica was erected in Baltimore, U.S.A., in 1888.

Story was an American sculptor who worked in Rome and received many of his commissions from England. Peabody went to Rome himself for sittings.

Left. The unveiling of the statue on June 23rd, 1869, by Edward, Prince of Wales.

Sir Rowland Hill

Everybody knows that Rowland Hill invented the Penny Post. Was he then some worthy junior minister or civil servant, charged by his superiors with carrying out the task? No – the scheme which within a few decades had spread to almost every country of the world was essentially the creation of one solitary man and was carried through (with the help of public pressure) in the teeth of government and postal service opposition. No great technical wizardry was involved, just common sense: the introduction of a cheap, standard charge, prepaid and carried on "a bit of paper just large enough to bear a stamp and covered at the back with a glutinous wash."

Hill's genius was many sided. He began in the family business, which was education. By the age of twelve he was both teacher and pupil and by seventeen he had paid off his impractical father's debts. Their school became the Summerfields of the Age of Reform, patronised by the leading radicals of Europe. It was governed largely by its pupils, it had no corporal punishment and it encouraged individual scientific and artistic pursuits. Despite its success, Hill became restless. He went into educational publishing and printed cheap, useful and reliable books. He also invented the first practical rotating newspaper press, which was suppressed by the Treasury on a legal technicality. In all this he was looking for a way in which he could really benefit his fellow men. When in 1835 the government appointed a commission to consider postal reform, he realised that he had finally found his ideal goal.

Hill therefore belongs among the educators and philanthropists, taking the latter word in its root sense of a lover of mankind. Prior to his time, it cost a working man a third of a day's wages to send a letter. If an itinerant Irish labourer – and there were many of them – wanted to write home, he would have to work for a day and a half. During the first two years of the Penny Post, the number of letters sent rose from 72,000 to 208,000 p.a., and by the time of Hill's retirement in 1864 the number was 642,000. The profits naturally rose too, despite the lower charges. The service was extended to rural areas, postal clerks no longer had to work on Sundays and M.P.'s and peers (and their friends) no longer had their letters, pianos and maidservants sent free of charge.

Hill was given three outdoor statues. One of these (by Thomas Brock and considered by Hill's sister to be the best likeness) was erected in Kidderminster, his birthplace, and another (by Peter Hollins) in Birmingham, whence he retired; both of these were put up during his lifetime. After his death, there was no shortage of funds for a London commemoration, for he was, deservedly, one of the most popular men of his day. The memorial appeal raised £16,000, most of which went to benefit sick and elderly postal workers. A public competition was held to choose the sculptor of the statue, the chairman of the judges being the President of the Royal Academy, Sir Frederick Leighton, who was then doing a great deal to usher in a new age of imaginative vigour in English sculpture (see p14). The winner was a young and rising artist, Edward Onslow Ford, who produced a subtly moulded figure, dignified yet human. It is a pity that London does not have more of his work outdoors. There are two versions of his ornate, Levantine statue of General Gordon on a camel but one is at Chatham and the other at Woking. And his equally sumptuous statue of Lord Strathnairn, which used to stand in Knightsbridge, was removed in 1931 (see p349) and is now in Hampshire.

Sir Rowland Hill. Born 1795, Kidderminster, son of schoolmaster. Became teacher as well as pupil in father's school, 1807. Built and ran new school house with brother, 1819-28. Co-founded Society for the Diffusion of Useful Knowledge, 1825. Published pamphlet "Post Office Reform, its Importance and Practicability", which received massive public support, 1837. Penny Post system accepted by Parliament, 1839; Hill appointed to introduce it, with limited powers. Dismissed by Tories, under Peel, 1842. Director of Brighton Railway, 1842-5. Voted £13,000 by public subscription, 1846. Returned to Post Office as second in command, 1846-53. Placed in full charge as Secretary to Post Office, 1854-64. Retired through ill-health, 1864. Published report recommending gradual nationalisation of railways, 1867. Died 1879.

Statue by Edward Onslow Ford. Bronze. King Edward Street, outside the General Post Office. Originally erected outside the Royal Exchange and unveiled June 7th, 1882, by Edward, Prince of Wales. Shortly afterwards children were observed to be sticking stamps on it. Moved to its present position, 1923. Cost £1,800.

Lord Shaftesbury

The figure of Eros in Piccadilly Circus must be one of the best known statues in the world. Less well known is the fact that it commemorates Anthony Ashley Cooper, seventh earl of Shaftesbury. To his century Shaftesbury was *the* philanthropist – not in a financial sense, for he was never a rich man – but as *philos-anthropos*, a lover of mankind. He was passionate and determined, deeply religious and highly strung. His field was parliamentary reform, administration and, above all, publicity; he told one half of the nation how the other half lived and got something done about it.

One can trace Shaftesbury's appreciation of suffering back to his own unhappy childhood. His father was distantly tyrannical and his mother cared only for fashionable society; at his first school (though private and expensive) he met with bullying and starvation. The only person who showed him affection was the family housekeeper, Maria Millis, who taught him to pray. She bequeathed him her gold watch, which he wore to the end of his life. Once it was stolen and what happened illustrates how much he was loved and respected by all classes of society. He advertised the loss; the local community of thieves found out the boy responsible and delivered him, and the watch, tied up in a sack on his doorstep. He found the boy a place in one of his Ragged Schools.

In politics he was no revolutionary; he was not even a democrat and opposed the Second and Third Reform Bills. His motivation was Christian; how could souls flourish or survive at all in the conditions they were forced to endure: the insane chained to beds of straw, beaten and put on view to a curious public; children kept in unhealthy and dangerous factories for up to sixteen hours a day, by adulthood worn out and enslaved to a round of work, sleep and drink; the poor housed thirty to a room in lice-ridden lodging houses, with crime and prostitution the accepted norms? Shaftesbury set out to change all that and to a great extent succeeded. Charles Dickens, for example, called the Lodging Houses Act of 1851 which Shaftesbury pioneered "the best law that was ever passed by an English parliament."

After his death a meeting was held at the Mansion House and a Memorial Committee set up. Joseph Boehm was asked to provide two works. He completed the bust for Westminster Abbey but passed the commission for an outdoor statue to his assistant, the boyish, enthusiastic Alfred Gilbert. To Gilbert, Art was all; he flatly refused to do a "coat-and-trousers job" – a literal representation of the Earl – and instead set out to symbolise his compassionate qualities by means of a figure based on Eros, God of Love. The choice may now seem strange, but his intentions were generally understood at the time. In Greek mythology Eros stood for dispassionate as well as passionate love; in Hesoid and the Orphic mysteries he was the first of all the gods, emerging from the egg of Chaos together with Earth and Underworld and resolving their disharmonies. Gilbert himself explained his figure as "the blindfolded Love sending forth indiscriminately, yet with purpose, his missile of kindness – never ceasing, to breath or reflect critically, but ever soaring onwards, regardless of its own perils and dangers."

However, if Gilbert thought that Lord Shaftesbury never paused for critical self-reflection, he was quite wrong; his diaries are full of it. He might rather have been speaking of his own involvement with the project and Icarus, not Eros, is the figure that comes to mind (coincidentally, he was using the more subtle "lost-wax" method of

Anthony Ashley Cooper, 7th Earl of Shaftesbury. Born 1801, London, son of 6th Earl. Became M.P., 1826. Married Lady Emily Cooper, daughter of future wife of Lord Palmerston (p182), 1830. Chairman of committee of enquiry into treatment of insane, 1829-45. Put through Lunacy Bills, establishing properly run asylums and inspectorate, 1845. Chairman of Lunacy Commission, 1845-85. Became leader of parliamentary movement for reform of factory laws, 1833. Put through Bill prohibiting children under 13 and women from working in mines, 1842. Bill limiting hours of work to ten a day finally passed, 1847. Began work for General Board of Health, organising and improving town sanitation and standards of accommodation, 1842. Put through Lodging Houses Act, 1851. Took up cause of slum children; Chairman of Ragged Schools Union, 1846-1885. Inherited title and entered House of Lords, 1851. Died 1885.

Overleaf. Memorial by Alfred Gilbert. Picadilly Circus. Unveiled June 29th, 1893, by the Duke of Westminster. The figure of the god, its whole weight poised on one slender foot, is of aluminium – the first time that the lightest of all metals had ever been used in a large, public sculpture – and weighs 13-14 cwt.

In 1925 the memorial was removed to the Victoria Embankment Gardens while the Underground line was constructed beneath Picadilly Circus; it was returned in 1931 after much public protest. It spent World War Two at Cooper's Hill, Egham, and was afterwards reinstated in the presence of thousands. In 1985-6 the figure of Eros was taken down and thoroughly restored by the eighty year old Mr George Mancini, who had worked for Gilbert as a young man.

Left overleaf. The scene on January 31st, 1972, when the whole fountain froze solid.

Right overleaf. At Christmas the statue is given an extra bouquet of lights.

casting (see p338) which he had personally helped to re-introduce into England). The original design was for an immensely grand fountain with the central figure seeming to hover on a continually rising liquid dome. But Gilbert had forgotten how expensive it would be to supply such a volume of water and Westminster Council refused to bear the cost. The financial difficulties soon became personal. His original estimate for his work was £3,000, on the understanding that the government would supply the bulk of the metal for the fountain from its store of surplus canon. After four years, however, this promise was withdrawn. The Memorial Committee had no more funds and Gilbert had no firm contract. He had either to put up £4,000 of his own (a huge sum in modern terms) or abandon the project. He went on, but began a downward financial spiral which led eventually to bankruptcy and exile (see p75).

When the memorial was finally completed the nobler spirits of the age were full of admiration but there was much cavilling; the *Manchester Evening Mail* referred to "a curious kind of creature, half mercury and half eagle, who seems bent on self-destruction by precipitating himself straight into the Criterion Restaurant." Others condemned the statue's nudity on moral grounds. But *Amor vincit omnia.* Within a few decades Eros was being called "the hub of the British Empire" and London without it is still unthinkable. If the traffic now no longer flows around it, that only gives a better opportunity for visitors from all parts of the world to gather on its steps. And if they enjoy its beauty, they should also remember the life and spirit of the man in whose honour it was erected.

Below left. The youthful Alfred Gilbert photographed in his studio around 1891, when he was still working on the Shaftesbury Memorial.

Below right. Lord Shaftesbury and donkey. Shaftesbury developed a special relationship with London's costermongers; he protected their interests in disputes and he persuaded them to rest their animals on Sundays, a kindness which greatly improved their performance on the other six days of the week. In 1875 a thousand costermongers assembled and presented him with his own donkey, pictured here. Thanking them he said, "When I have passed away from this life I desire to have no more said of me than that I have done my duty, as the poor donkey has done his, with patience and unmurmuring resignation."

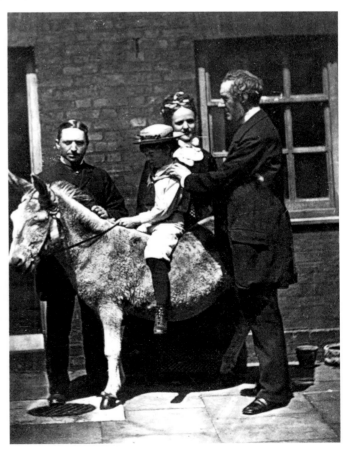

Sir Sydney Waterlow

Sir Sydney Waterlow. Born 1822, Finsbury, son of a stationer. Apprenticed to his uncle, a printer, 1836-43; at age of 18 he was placed in charge of the printing of confidential Cabinet papers. Entered and later took over father's printing and stationery firm, 1844-98; it began with 20 employees and ended with 4,000. Built first workers' flats in Mark Street, Finsbury, 1862. Founded Improved Industrial Dwellings Company, 1863; it built 6,000 flats housing 30,000 people. Four times Liberal M.P., 1868-85. Lord Mayor of London, 1872. Chairman of Westminster Schools, 1873-93. Treasurer of St Bartholemew's Hospital, 1874-92. Gave Highgate home and grounds to L.C.C. as Waterlow Park, 1889. Died 1906.

Statue by Frank Taubman. Bronze. Waterlow Park, Highgate. Unveiled July 28th, 1900, by Princess Louise, Duchess of Argyll (p65). Another version of the statue was unveiled June 27th, 1901, outside Westminster City School, Palace Street, Victoria.

Shortly before his death Waterlow, bent and white haired, took a walk in his park. His second wife, whom he had met in San Francisco on one of his many world travels, described the scene. "To my surprise I saw directly in front of me a great number of people. A gentleman came forward and told me that, having heard that Sydney was in the park, the people had collected there in hope of seeing him as he passed by. So we went on and as we neared the statue the path cleared before us. And then quite suddenly there went up a great shout of welcome to Sydney – there were hundreds of people and they all seemed so glad to greet him." Afterwards they followed him to the lower gate and cheered again as he left in his carriage, never to return.

From Highgate Sir Sydney Waterlow must have the finest view of any statue in London (Nelson and the Duke of York excepted). His tall, commanding presence looks out, past the site of its twin figure in Victoria, to Crystal Palace and the North Downs beyond. Unlike his fellow builder of houses, George Peabody (p92), Waterlow is well equipped for life in the open air, with gloves and overcoat. He also carries a broad-brimmed hat and – unique among London statues – a rolled umbrella.

Sir Sydney was both an original and highly practical man. At one time his printing and stationery business found itself with premises both at the Carpenters' Hall in the City and in Victoria, so he strung a special telegraph line between the two which crossed streets and rooftops and even spanned the River Thames. Part of his prosperity came from printing timetables and tickets for the rapidly expanding railway companies. He well understood one of the major problems of this expansion, the homelessness caused by the wholesale clearance of large areas of land. He therefore set about providing healthy and reasonably priced accommodation for those displaced. He designed his Improved Industrial Dwellings himself. Having heard of a cheap and extremely durable Italian building material made of volcanic lava, he invented an English equivalent using cement and coke cinders. The rooms were well ventilated and safe from fire; in 1896 it was calculated that the death rate among his tenants was a quarter of the average in poorer areas. His projects even ran at a profit. "Philanthropy and 5%" was the charge levelled at him. However, his view was that the independently minded working class (of which he had once been an at least honorary member) would prefer sound business arrangements to charity.

In connection with his position as City Alderman, Sir Sydney became chairman of the governors of Westminster City School, Victoria, outside which a replica of his statue was erected. He carried out a rebuilding programme and increased its roll from 30 to 850. The boys did so well in their examinations that the Examining Board accused their headmaster, Mr Goffin, of giving out the answers beforehand. An independently supervised exam showed that this was not the case, but the Board took Goffin before a Parliamentary Committee and then to court. Sir Sydney raised his salary so that he could pay his legal costs. The case dragged on for five years before it was finally dropped and made Sir Sydney extremely angry. Corporations and governments, he characteristically remarked, had neither a soul to be saved nor a body to be kicked and could therefore behave as disgracefully as they liked.

He also made changes as Treasurer of St Bartholemew's Hospital. He introduced separate wards for contagious diseases and installed a fully trained matron, despite objections from one of the senior doctors that she was too young and pretty. Later he built a new library, lecture theatres and a nurses' hostel. Open spaces were, he felt, as important as well ventilated housing. In 1872 he presented his house in Highgate to Bart's as a convalescent home and when its wards were moved to the country, he gave the house and 29 acres of grounds to the London County Council for use as a public park. It was in the park that the money for his statue was raised. Collecting boxes were left out and emptied at the end of each day. It is said that they contained no silver, only pennies, halfpennies and farthings, so that the poor for whom Sir Sydney had done so much truly paid for his memorial.

John Colet

John Colet, the founder of St Paul's School, was one of England's leading men of the Renaissance. Had he lived out the full span of his life, he might now be as famous as his pupil and close friend, Thomas More (p323). The young Henry VIII listened patiently to Colet's eloquent condemnation of his continental wars and called him "my doctor". Would the doctor also have challenged Henry's Reformation and died, like More, under the executioner's axe? Or would he have welcomed the break with Rome as the sweeping away of indulgence and outdated superstition?

In theology, Colet was a liberal. The systemizations of mediaeval scholasticism seemed to him stultifying and unreal. In his much attended lectures on the Epistles of St Paul he tried to recreate the original time and intention of their writing. He regarded the Genesis creation story as poetry told to satisfy an audience of simple Hebrew tribespeople. However, he had rather less sympathy for the relics of St Thomas Becket (p324), displayed at Canterbury to satisfy the simple tribespeople of England. According to his friend Erasmus, he grew ever more exasperated with the succession of bits of tooth, hair-shirt and bleeding limb. When finally, as a distinguished visitor, the Prior presented him with a soiled rag which was supposed to have been one of the saint's handkerchiefs, he pushed it away with a disgusted snort.

In his private life Colet was disciplined and austere. His efforts to revive preaching and lecturing at St Paul's and his failure to give good dinners made him unpopular with the run of the Cathedral clergy; he probably tried to reform the existing Cathedral grammar

John Colet. Born 1466/7, London, son of rich merchant and twice Lord Mayor. Studied at Oxford, 1483-93. Toured France and Italy, studying at universities, 1493-6. Returned to Oxford and began series of lectures on Epistles of St Paul, 1496. First meeting with lifelong friend, the Dutch scholar Erasmus, 1497. Ordained priest, 1498. Appointed Dean of St Paul's Cathedral, 1503/4. Inherited large fortune from father, 1505; fearing that it would bring out a latent self-indulgence, he decided to devote it to education. Began building new school for 153 boys, dedicated to Christ the Child, at east end of St Paul's Churchyard, 1508. School established by royal warrant, 1510. Preached sermon to Convocation summoned to suppress Lollard heresy, 1512; ignored Lollards and attacked corruption and worldliness of Church. Was himself accused of heresy by Bishop of London. Preached to Henry VIII on evils of waging war, 1513. Serious decline in health began, 1515. Died 1519.

Statue by Hamo Thornycroft. Bronze. End of front drive, St Paul's School, Hammersmith. Given by Mr Edward Howley Palmer, Governor of the Bank of England, and first erected outside the school's buildings in West Kensington. Unveiled December 10th, 1902, by Mr Greville Palmer, the donor's son. Moved to present position 1968.

Colet wrote a Latin grammar for his new school and the prologue touchingly reveals his intentions. It ends as follows: "Wherefore I pray you, all little babes, all little children, learn gladly this little treatise, and commend it diligently unto your memories, trusting of this beginning that ye shall proceed and grow to perfect literature, and come at the end to be great clerks. And lift up your little white hands for me, which prayeth for you to God, to whom be all honour and imperial majesty and glory. Amen." The same spirit is found in the memorial. The scholar is seated between two kneeling pupils and all three have their books open in front of them. Around and above them a circular Gothic canopy gathers itself up into a crown, and at its top is a shrine with figures of the Virgin and of the Child to whom Colet dedicated his school.

Far left. The statue and its canopy were cast by one of the leading foundries of the age, J.W. Singer of Frome (see p356). In the centre of the picture, wearing a bowler hat and a stern expression, is John Goulter, the firm's "walking foreman", whose task was to supervise operations throughout the works. On the near right is a detached head of Queen Victoria.

school, but without success. He decreed that his new school should be administered by married members of the Mercers' Company, since he believed that they would be less corrupt than the clerics. Twice the size of Eton or Winchester, it was an educational milestone. Erasmus wrote a textbook on rhetoric for it which became the standard work of the century. At the heart of the curriculum was the study of the pure, clear Latin of the Classical Age, the works of Cicero, Virgil and Church Fathers like Jerome and Augustine. And, though he himself had little knowledge of it, Colet also introduced the study of Greek.

Colet loved children, finding their innocence a welcome relief from the coarseness and opacity of adults; his memorial, erected nearly four hundred years after his death, beautifully embodies this spirit of study and devotion.

Quintin Hogg

Quintin Hogg transformed further education in London, yet he was not by profession a teacher or administrator. Like Lord Shaftesbury (p96), he was essentially an apostle of Christian goodness. At Eton he started a bible class for his fellow pupils; as one of them said, "We would not have stood it from anyone else." Hogg was always an intensely charismatic character and he also had the advantage of being the school football star. Later he organised the first ever matches between England and Scotland and played half-back for Scotland. He was always keen on the place of sport in education, as the football held by one of the boys in his memorial bears out.

After school he went straight into business, first into tea – which he hated – and then into his brother-in-law's sugar company, where he worked for the rest of his life. After work his hours were spent quite differently. His mission of education began underneath the Arches as, by candle-light, he tried to teach two young crossing-sweepers to read. A policeman came by and the boys fled. In order to find out how the poor really lived, Hogg disguised himself as a boot-black and took odd jobs around Charing Cross. He held prayer meetings for the porters and flower girls of Covent Garden. Twice the criminal fraternity nearly had him killed. Helped by former school-friends, he started a school for the penniless children of the streets and developed it into a residential community. His intensely focused kindness inspired great loyalty, just as his look of disapproval caused agonies of remorse.

The 1870 Education Act, put through Parliament by W.E.Forster (p202), removed the need for the so-called Ragged Schools. However, there was still a great lack of technical education for those who had just left school. As Hogg saw his own protégés grow up, he realised the need to alter the direction of his work. Eventually he took over the ailing Regent Street Polytechnic building and made it into a full-scale educational establishment. For those between the ages of sixteen and twenty-two there were classes in carpentry, plumbing, watch making, tailoring, stone carving and many other trades, as well as a debating society, a magazine, a savings bank, low cost holidays and innumerable sports teams. Charges were modest, initially no more than a few pence a week, with a reduction for boys attending the classes in general education. Some financial support came from the newly founded City and Guilds of London Institute but Hogg put in more than £100,000 of his own money. In return he had the opportunity of befriending, encouraging and advising "his boys." It was his greatest personal satisfaction; the polite society of his peers bored him terribly and straightforward administration was not to his taste.

Despite his poor health, Hogg was always active and curious about every practical aspect of life. For his company he invented new ways of harvesting sugar and as an Alderman of the City of London he became interested in drainage and personally inspected miles of sewers. He was broad minded in religion, happy to build Hindu temples and mosques for his workers in the West Indies. With some pain, he grew out of a literal belief in the Bible; he came to see Heaven and Hell as – primarily – states of mind and wrote a short book about the relationship between science and scripture. Religion was essentially about love and nothing unless practical.

After his death a 50,000 shilling fund was set up so that as many people as possible could contribute to his statue. The artist chosen was George Frampton, now best known as the sculptor of Peter Pan (p136). He was a leading member of the Arts and Crafts Movement

Quintin Hogg. Born 1845, London, son of prominent politician, later Chairman of East India Company. Entered brother-in-law's firm of sugar merchants and rose to become senior partner, 1865-98. Ran schools for poor children near Charing Cross, 1864-78. Parallel school for girls started by his sister Annie, 1868. Caught yellow fever in West Indies, 1869; overdose of medicine containing mercury permanently affected health. Transferred school to Long Acre and developed technical education for older boys, 1878. Took over buildings of Royal Polytechnic Institute in Regent Street, 1882; built up membership of nearly 7,000 in first year. Visited by Commissioner of City Charities, who recommended founding of other polytechnics on his model, 1884. Girls' Institute founded by Annie Hogg, 1888. As member of London County Council, introduced motion which led to founding of further polytechnics, 1890. Died 1902.

Statue by George Frampton. Bronze. Portland Place, opposite former buildings of the Girls' Polytechnic. Unveiled November 24th, 1906, by the Duke of Argyll. Cost £2,500.

Throughout her life Hogg's sister Annie matched her brother's achievements with parallel institutions for girls. There is no statue to her, though on one side of the pedestal is the somewhat low-key inscription "1845-1915. Alice. A. Hogg, whose unfailing love and devotion contributed so greatly to the success of the Polytechnic."

and much influenced by the French Symbolists. His earlier works are mysterious, private and brooding, but success brought him more into the public sphere. His memorial to Hogg links the private and the public with perfect success. The group is intimate without being sentimental and the likeness – the broad brow, deep-set eyes and well trimmed beard – is natural and true.

The unveiling was a solemn, almost religious occasion. The streets were packed and quiet and a trombone quartet played "O God, our help in ages past." By that time there were thirteen polytechnics in London, founded by the L.C.C. and the City Companies directly on Hogg's model. His example had helped to bridge the gap between Victorian deprivation and the modern age in which universal further education seems something taken for granted.

Margaret MacDonald

Mrs Margaret MacDonald must have been a rather special person When she died at the early age of forty one, her husband Ramsay MacDonald, later to be Britain's first Labour Prime Minister, wrote a memoir which has been called the most moving tribute to a wife in the English language. Of their first meetings as fellow socialists he said, "She came very often after a morning's work (as a charity visitor) at Hoxton. She was so very different from the rest of us. She was like a girl who had just left school and was finding the world a delightful, wide place, full of interest and whom the world was finding to be an attractively strange mixture of childlike innocence and mature commonsense...Loving humanity, working humanity, poverty-stricken humanity, was her nearest kindred. With it she was never demonstrative, over it she never gushed. She just liked to be with it, to minister unto it; and there was a great strength about her presence which was more consoling than expressed sympathy."

After their marriage, the MacDonalds settled in Lincoln's Inn Fields. Through Margaret's genius for friendship, a constant stream of visitors, from every country and from every level of life, passed through their flat to be advised, fed, comforted and entertained. These were the days when the growth of Socialism seemed to presage the unity of all mankind. Outsiders saw her running a political salon but she was not political in the usual sense of the word; she disliked organisations and their disputes and power and position held no attractions for her.

Margaret MacDonald was a fellow of the Royal Statistical Society and her innumerable reports on subjects like female unemployment, the conditions of home-workers, the fines imposed on shopgirls and the lives of barmaids were meticulously researched and compiled. She always wanted to get down to the bedrock of fact; the only people she really distrusted were glib sentimentalists and impatient idealists. She thus combined emotional and intellectual power in a remarkable way. She was a deeply committed feminist but guarded her own mystery and would not allow that women should become like men in order to be equal. She broke with Mrs Pankhurst (p220) and her suffragettes over their insistence on the vote above all things and their use of confrontation. "I only saw their hatpins," she said of one of their meetings; "women with hatpins are like men with fists."

She had six children (three less than the number in the memorial) and was an unfussy parent. Ramsay Macdonald again: "Her relationship to her children was that of a big, intimate friend. They played round her and on her knee as she worked. I can see her now in those morning days sitting at the big black table, a little bundle lying at her side, from which arms and legs waved and a gurgle of joy came, she looking over her arm every now and again and joining in the baby ripplings." She brought her children up to be independent and look after themselves and each other. But her emotional ties to them ran very deep and it may be that she never really recovered from the death of her youngest son, which took place a year before her own. As she herself lay dying, she asked one of her oldest friends to do all she could for her children. "See that they have some romance in their lives," she said. "Don't let them marry except for love."

The decision to set up a memorial near her old home was taken at a private meeting of her friends, who saw in her the embodiment of motherhood. This is why their donations also went to set up a baby clinic in Notting Hill and a new ward at the Leicester Children's Hospital, and why they chose Richard Goulden's design for the

Margaret MacDonald. Born 1870, London, daughter of Dr John Gladstone, professor of chemistry and worker for religious and social causes. Studied at King's College, London, 1887-91. Nominated by father as manager of a group of schools in Whitechapel, 1892. Worked for Charity Organisation Society as visitor of poor in Hoxton, 1893-6. Joined Independent Labour Party, 1896. Married Ramsay MacDonald and settled in flat at 3, Lincoln's Inn Fields, 1896. Joined Women's Industrial Council and served on its Statistical, Investigative and Education Committees, 1894-1907; helped establish Trade Schools for women. Chairman of National Union of Women Workers, 1898-1911. Founded Women's Labour League, 1906. Death of youngest son, David, from diptheria, 1910. Died 1911.

Below. Richard Goulden in the uniform which he wore at the unveiling of the statue.

memorial. His ring of children demonstrates the transformation brought about by love and care; those on the right are unhappily seeking comfort, while those on the left are going out into life full of joy.

Goulden was a idealistic and painstaking artist who often used the figures of children to represent a hope in the continuity of life and a faith in the next generation. This is particularly so in the many memorials which he carried out after the First World War. He considered the war a just struggle and enlisted in the Royal Engineers as soon as it began; he thus attended the unveiling of the Margaret MacDonald memorial in uniform. He was invalided out of the front line in 1916 but continued to serve as an instructor and in air-raid rescue work. One of his memorials stands outside St Michael's Church in Cornhill; the tall, winged figure of St Michael leads an ascending line of four children to safety, while repelling two writhing beasts representing strife with his flaming sword. He carried out similar war memorials for Kingston, Reigate and Crompton, and a more lighthearted ring of four, chubby children for the Malvern Pump Room fountain, entitled *The Source*.

Statue by Richard Goulden. Bronze, above a bench of grey, Scottish granite and ship's teak. North side of Lincoln's Inn Fields. Unveiled December 19th, 1914, by Margaret MacDonald's youngest daughter, Sheila, after a speech by Sir Laurence Gomme, Clerk of the London County Council. The statue was dedicated by Professor Gilbert Murray.

Beneath the memorial today are Leo and Alexei Nabarro with Mallet.

Lord Nuffield

Billy Morris, bicycle maker to the undergraduates of Oxford, had no formal engineering training but relied instead on an instinctive feel for machinery. By far and away the most important thing in his life was work; when the 40-hour week came in, he called it "semi-retirement". He saw the coming importance of the motor car and the need for mass production. But when his success in designing and assembling a practical car for the private motorist made him a multimillionaire, he was almost nonplussed. As he put it himself, "If you have so much money that you can buy anything you want, you find you don't want anything. Nothing gives you any satisfaction unless you have to struggle a bit." And so, even as he acquired it, he set about giving his vast fortune away. By the end of his life he had disposed of the equivalent in modern terms of up to half a billion pounds.

Though married, Nuffield had no children and the lack of an heir touched him deeply. He was also strongly averse to the prospect of death duties. These were, so to speak, the reactive aspects of his philanthropy. But he was also an optimist who believed that, just as he had mastered the manufacture of the motor car, so the progress of human knowledge could master the future. He also never lost the common touch; besides his great donations, he made innumerable small, unrecorded gifts to the sick, the old and those in difficulties. His one personal extravagance was the purchase of a golf club near his country home and if he met a tramp on the road, he would tell him to call at the club kitchen for a cup of tea and a sandwich. He was ruthless enough with those whom he considered able to help themselves but he also knew that there were those who could not.

Outside business his greatest interest was in health. He always said that he would have liked to have been a surgeon and he was himself a great taker of pills and potions. (Through pressure of work, he suffered from sleeplessness and from stomach trouble; he always claimed to have a stomach ulcer though no X-ray was able to find it.) Out of this concern came special health clinics for his employees and a great number of donations to medical causes. His medical philanthropy began with gifts to St Thomas's but during the 1930's he "adopted" Guy's as his favourite London hospital. He became its Treasurer and President. He endowed a new private wing and a nurses' home and, during the Second World War, provided £250,000 out of his Special Areas Fund for the repair of bomb damage. Thus the terrors and explosions of the blitz form the background to his statue, for it was in 1944 that the governors of Guy's approved its erection and set about raising subscriptions.

Maurice Lambert's bronze figure is somewhat similar to Macmillan's George VI (p78) in that he has used his medium to show the strength of character – energetic, autocratic – especially in the mouth and prominent brows. According to Lambert, Nuffield greatly enjoyed the sittings. He would come in the mornings and again in the afternoons; he would then offer to come in the evenings as well. Lambert had to explain that an artist, unlike a production line, needs pauses for creative recuperation. This enthusiasm had little to do with personal vanity, for Nuffield had always flatly refused to have a statue of himself put up nearer home at the Oxford Orthopaedic Hospital. It was rather a craftsman's interest in a new technique of manufacture. Not surprisingly, he was particularly fascinated by the various stages of the casting of the metal.

William Morris, Viscount Nuffield. Born 1877, Worcester, son of poor farmer. Moved to Oxford, 1880. Started own bicycle firm with capital of £4, 1893; later took up assembly of motor-cycles and car repair. Designed and built first Morris Oxford motor car, 1912. Annual sales reached 70,000 cars, 1926; turned down offer of £11 million from General Motors of U.S.A. Began philanthropic activities with fund of £10,000 to help parents to visit children in Borstals, 1926. Gave £100,000 to St Thomas's Hospital, 1927-8. Tried unsuccessfully to assist expansion of national aircraft production in anticipation of Second World War, 1935. Gave £2 million to found Oxford University Medical School, 1936. Endowed Nuffield College, Oxford, 1937. Established Nuffield Foundation for the advancement of health, social welfare and education, 1943. First Chairman of British Motor Corporation, 1952. Died 1963.

Statue by Maurice Lambert. Bronze. Western quadrangle, Guy's House, Guy's Hospital. Erected 1949.

Over the customary neat, straightforward suit (of being rich he said, "Well, you can only wear one suit at a time") Nuffield wears the robes of the honorary doctorate given him by the University of Oxford. He had a long-standing love-hate relationship with every aspect of his home town, ever since 1913 when he started up a new motor bus service in the teeth of City Council opposition. He wanted to give the University a college of engineering but was told that the sciences were the preserve of Cambridge. The postgraduate college of social studies which took his name sometimes seemed to him a poor substitute. ("A bloody Kremlin," he would call it in certain moods). More satisfying was the Oxford University Medical School, which he built up to rank with those of London. This, together with the support given by the Nuffield Foundation to Florey during his work on penicillin, was perhaps his greatest contribution in the field of health.

Lord Baden-Powell

Like Rowland Hill (p94), Baden Powell is an awkward man to categorise. His achievement in founding the world's largest ever youth organisation places him among the immortals of education. He was, however, famous twice over. During an interesting and unconventional army career, he found himself the military commander of Mafeking during its 217-day siege by the Boers. His skilful use of the press focused world attention on the small town and the news of its relief produced bonfires and firework displays throughout Britain. It even gave the English language a new word: to maffick, or "celebrate with boisterous rejoicing and hilarious behaviour." So Baden Powell was first of all a hero of Empire, cast very much in its mould and having, it must be said, the limitations of view common to the period; his poor opinion of colonised races meant that at Mafeking the whites remained well-fed while the natives starved. He was also not a very good military strategist. Having escaped from Mafeking, he allowed himself to be besieged again a year later at Rustenburg, much to the annoyance of Field Marshal Roberts (p274). Neither Roberts or Kitchener (p278) considered him a likely general.

As a trainer and inspirer of youth, however, Baden Powell found his perfect metier. Known and applauded wherever he went, he was in an ideal position to carry out the work which made him enduringly famous. His aim was physical and moral reform. Returning to England he saw, in his own words, begging, vandalism and drunkenness on the streets and pale, hunched boys and young men smoking endlessly. The Scout Law of loyalty, honesty and helpfulness would change all that. To it he harnessed the basic, tribal group-instinct and love of uniform, coupled with the challenge and excitement of life in the open air, drawing for the latter on his own extensive experience as tracker and spy. The combination was immensely successful. With skilful magazine publicity provided by C. Arthur Pearson, who later founded the *Daily Express*, the movement gained over 100,000 members in two years. From then on it has been a story of continuous growth until, at the time of writing, the Scout and Guide movement has 25 million members in over 150 countries. Baden Powell's original aim may been the purification of Britain's future manpower but the movement's astonishing internationalism must have carried him far beyond his earlier perspectives.

In 1919 a training centre for scoutmasters was set up at Gilwell, near Epping Forest. To camp and work there at weekends came the young Donald Potter, who lived a short distance away. He was a scout and was then working in a tool factory. Since childhood he had been absorbed by drawing, modelling and carving but had as yet found no training or encouragement. In 1926 he joined the permanent staff at Gilwell and found his artistic abilities put to full use in building log cabins and carving totem poles and ornamental gateways. Baden Powell personally encouraged and advised him. B-P was himself a skilful artist; he exhibited his sculptures at the Royal Academy and his books and letters are full of spontaneous, amusing sketches. Potter found him full of creative imagination, humorous and unobtrusively kind.

So the bond was forged that led eventually to the carving of the statue outside the Scout Headquarters in Queen's Gate. At Gilwell, after years of depressing factory work, Potter came alive and the Scout philosophy has been a permanent influence on him; he describes it as "resourcefulness, imagination, observation, camping and woodcraft,

Robert Baden Powell, 1st Baron Baden-Powell of Gilwell. Born 1857, London, son of clergyman-professor of mathematics. Commissioned into army and served in India, 1876-84; noted for skill in map-making during Afghan War. Posted to Natal, 1884-5; carried out secret reconnaissance of frontier disguised as artist. A.D.C to Sir Henry Smyth, Officer Commanding, South Africa, 1877-90. Led defeat of uprising in Matabeleland, 1896; promoted colonel. Appointed to guard northern frontier of Transvaal in Boer War, 1899; trapped in Mafeking, survived 217-day siege and became national hero. Besieged again in Rustenburg, 1900. Commander of South African Constabulary, 1901-3. Returned to England as Inspector General of Cavalry, 1903-7. Published letter in Eton Chronicle proposing training programme for boys, 1905. Held first experimental Scout camp on Brownsea Island, Dorset, 1907. Published Scouting for Boys, 1908. First Scout Rally of 11,000 held at Crystal Palace, 1909. Girl Guides founded, 1909. Married Olave Soames, who later became World Chief Guide, 1912. Wolf Cubs for younger boys founded, 1914. Acclaimed World Chief Scout at first World Jamboree held at Olympia, 1920. Retired to Kenya, 1938. Died 1941.

and a deep feeling for the wonder and mystery of nature." Later he left to develop his sculpture and worked for six years in Eric Gill's studio at Pigotts in Buckinghamshire; one can see something of Gill's linear, economic style in the Baden-Powell statue. Since 1940 he has taught at Bryanston School, an individualist among the staff but exceptionally capable of meeting the pupils on their own level. At the same time he has fulfilled a number of commissions for sculptures, including several large scale religious works.

The nine foot high figure of Baden Powell is of silver-grey, flecked Cornish granite – not since Samuel Nixon's William IV (p54) had London had a statue in that hardest of all stones. The photographs overleaf show the progress of the statue once the first model had been made and approved. The stone came from the De Lank quarry at St Breward, near Bodmin. A suitable 10 ton block was chosen and then cut down to a more manageable 8 tons. With the assistance of Hedley Methvin, Cornwall's leading granite mason, Potter worked on this block at the quarry for three months to produce an outline form. This was then transferred to his studio at Blandford Forum, where he worked on it over the next year. There were certain technical problems in portraying the Grand Old Man of Scouting. The wide brim of the familiar hat was impossible to carve in granite, so the hat is held and the cavalry cloak which Baden Powell sometimes wore is added to unify and complete the design. The statue's expression is benign and the youthfulness and humour which the sculptor knew so well shine through.

Baden Powell standing next to his sculptor, Donald Potter, during an International Scout Jamboree held at Arrow Park, Birkenhead, in 1929. Potter carved the totem poles out of branches lopped from thousand-year-old elm trees near Baden Powell's Hampshire home and they were presented to the representatives of the five British dominions.

Statue by Donald Potter. Granite, 9 ft on 2 ft plinth, 3 tons. Scout Headquarters, Queen's Gate. Unveiled July 12th, 1961, by the Duke of Gloucester, as President of the Boy Scouts Association.

Above left. The original block of granite lies embedded in its quarry, behind the one about to be split.
Below left. The sculptor (right) and Hedley Methvin survey the emerging form.

Above right. The 10 ton block has been reduced to more manageable 8 ton proportions.
Below right. The completed statue is raised from its bed of straw and put in place.

Captain Coram

Passing between his home in Rotherhithe and his business in the City, the merchant and retired sea-captain Thomas Coram would often see babies lying by the side of the road, some crying, some reduced to exhausted silence, some dying, some already dead. They were the innocent victims of the morality of his day, by which no unmarried woman could admit to motherhood and remain respectable and no institution was prepared to look after babies who bore the stain of illegitimacy. Only the aristocracy, with high hypocrisy, were exempt; a well born bastard had no difficulty in finding a good place in society.

The goodhearted Coram became the champion of these abandoned children and spent seventeen long years canvassing support for a hostel which would bring them up and teach them useful occupations. To get the necessary Royal Charter, a petition signed by a number of prominent people was required. He approached noblemen and bishops without success; as he wrote to a friend with characteristic choler, he could no more persuade them to take up his cause than "to putt downe their Breeches and present their Backsides to the King and Queen in a full Drawing room, such was the unchristian shyness of all about the Court." The breakthrough came when he gained the support of a group of younger ladies of the aristocracy who were, presumably, more sympathetic to the plight of other women and less hidebound by convention. Given their lead, the menfolk followed suit and the petition was accepted. Coram was now seventy years old but still walked around London, sometimes ten or twelve miles a day, enlisting scores of distinguished men to become the governors of his new institution.

The Foundling Hospital became more than just a home for outcasts. Its philanthropic spirit attracted leading men of the arts and it came to play a unique part in the cultural life of the nation. Handel conducted the first successful performance of *The Messiah* there and performances continued annually for twenty seven years. The painter William Hogarth (on whose famous portrait of his friend the present statue of Coram is based) and the sculptor Michael Rysbrack were among the first governors. The meetings of artists and the numerous exhibitions held at the Hospital led on directly to the founding of the Royal Academy. One honest, determined sea-captain became the catalyst for more than he could have imagined.

Coram ended his days as that paradoxical figure, a philanthropist dependent on the charity of others. He soon lost his official position at the Hospital through speaking out too openly on a matter of scandal. His wife died and he ceased to manage his affairs properly. (They had no children). However, he still acted as godfather at Hospital christenings and could be seen wandering sadly through the columned, classical arcades distributing gingerbread to the children. When he died, he was buried in the chapel crypt but was given only a tablet in the cloisters as a memorial. It was not until 1851, a hundred years after his death, that he finally received his well deserved statue; it was carved by William Calder Marshall and stood on the outer gateway facing Guilford Street. The gateway is still there, one of the few parts of the splendid original buildings to survive. The statue was moved with the Hospital to Berkhampstead in 1926. Its site became Coram Fields, a unique kind of playground to which adults are not admitted unless accompanied by children. Coram's second, more recent statue stands in the street just behind the playground and no doubt feels thoroughly at home there.

Captain Thomas Coram. Born 1668, Lyme Regis, son of ship's captain. Managed shipyards in Boston and Taunton, U.S.A., for group of City merchants, 1694-1704; met with opposition from local inhabitants. Returned to London. Tried unsuccessfully to win support for colony for ex-soldiers in Maine, 1713-20. First took up cause of hostel for abandoned children, 1722; aimed to establish non-profit making, joint stock company, but recent collapse of South Sea Bubble created unfavourable climate. Petition for Foundling Hospital's Royal Charter signed by Duchess of Somerset and other ladies of the nobility, 1729-30. Appointed Trustee for colony of Georgia, 1732-8; tried unsuccessfully to change rule on inheritance of land by daughters. Foundling Hospital petition accepted by George II, 1737; Coram asked to provide names of governors. Royal Charter granted, 1739. Plan of operation drawn up and first premises opened in Covent Garden, 1739-41. Death of wife, 1741. Spoke out on charges of misbehaviour against head nurse and two governors, 1741; excluded from committees on building of new Hospital in Lambs Conduit Fields. Tried unsuccessfully to establish second Foundling Hospital in Westminster, 1742/5-50. Granted pension of £161 per annum, subscribed to by Prince of Wales and City merchants, 1749. Died 1751.

Statue by William Macmillan. Bronze. Brunswick Square. Unveiled 1963, by Princess Margaret, as President of the Coram Foundation which works for the fostering of children.

CHAPTER 3
THE ARTS

Do the English find the creative imagination hard to handle, at least in public? Unlike the Latin Americans, they do not appoint their best poets to ambassadorships; instead they ignore them and frequently drive them into exile. Unlike the French and the Italians, they do not make pre-eminent national heroes of their great painters, writers and philosophers; instead, they have tended to treat the inspired creator as someone faintly embarrassing, less than fully heroic and unhelpful to the State. These Anglo-Saxon attitudes may account for London's comparatively modest tally of statues relating to the Arts. London's first outdoor commemoration in that field was of an Italian; the statues of the architect Andrea Palladio and of his English follower and counterpart, Inigo Jones, take us back to the 1720's and the realm of private patronage. Shortly after, in 1744, came the statue of a German, Handel, sculpted by a Frenchman, Roubiliac; this is no longer out of doors and its story is told in Chapter 9. From there we jump straight to the golden decade of the Arts, 1874-84, which saw five statues erected; of these, Shakespeare's is the only one of a true-born Englishman and he owes his commemoration in Leicester Square to the otherwise highly dubious activities of an Irishman named Gottheimer.

Moreover, a closer examination of the list reveals an overwhelming debt to the country's Celtic periphery. Byron, Carlyle and Burns were Scotsmen – and the Scots, as exemplified by the statue of Burns in the Victoria Embankment Gardens (shown opposite), clearly find inspiration no embarrassment. John Everett Millais was a Jerseyman, Henry Irving was Cornish and Joshua Reynolds came from Devon. Take away J.S.Mill, whose father was a Glasgow journalist, and the list grows short indeed.

By the end of the nineteenth century, nevertheless, the Arts had acquired more of a national status. No one worked harder for this than Sir Henry Irving, who is commemorated outside the National Portrait Gallery. It is to him, too, that we owe the Paddington figure of the great tragedian, Sarah Siddons, which has kept its beauty despite the ravages of time and of the M40. There remain that archetypal Londoner, Dr Johnson, commemorated close to the maze of little streets in which he used to live, and that universal clown, Charlie Chaplin, who was South London born and bred. Chaplin was a double exile, first from England and then from the U.S.A., but he made the little tramp of the cockney music-halls into one of the best known theatrical characters in the world.

Andrea Palladio and Inigo Jones

Andrea Palladio. Born 1508, Padua. Worked as mason for humanist Tressino, who gave him his classical pseudonym. Began architectural career, 1540, building villas, palaces and churches in the High Renaissance style. Published I Quatro Libri dell' Architectura. *Died 1580.*

Inigo Jones. Born 1573, London, son of clothworker. Visited Italy and developed admiration for works of Palladio, c.1600 & 1613-5. Designed scenery and costumes for numerous court masques, 1605-40. Surveyor to the Crown, 1615-40. Built Queen's House, Greenwich, 1616-35. Built Banqueting House, Whitehall, 1619-21. Built St Paul's Church, Covent Garden, 1631-8. Died 1652.

Statues by John Michael Rysbrack. Marble. Chiswick House. Erected c.1728, at the time of the building of the house for Lord Burlington by William Kent.

Chiswick House is a perfect example of the architecture of the mid-eighteenth century, which saw a return to the harmonious lines and strict mathematical proportions of the High Renaissance. As their master and mentor, the builders of stately homes looked back to the great Italian Andrea Palladio, together with Charles I's architect, Inigo Jones, who brought the Palladian style to England. The high priest of the revival was Richard Boyle, third Earl of Burlington, who built Chiswick House not as a place to live in, but as a temple of good taste where he could entertain and divert his friends. Since the exquisite house and grounds are now open to the public, this is a category in which everyone may now include themselves.

At each end of the main front Lord Burlington placed statues of the principal deities of his cult. They were early works by the industrious Dutchman, John Michael Rysbrack, who settled in England in 1720 at the age of 26. They have the same fluency of pose as his later statue of George II at Greenwich (p25). He based his melancholy study of the Italian on a probably inaccurate engraving in Burlington's collection. The more weathered Inigo Jones closely resembles the famous, deep-souled drawing by Van Dyck. The pair are a marvellous evocation of past glories. Unfortunately, since our photographs were taken they have been disastrously over-cleaned and their expressive contours have been quite flattened out.

William Shakespeare

More than any other writer in the world, perhaps, Shakespeare had the power to embody the entire range of the human condition. A study of contemporary records reveals little of note; he was a married man, an owner of property in Stratford, a successful actor-playwright with a strong financial stake in his company. But his dramatic scope seems quite universal, as if his own mind were no more than the round O of the stage on which his characters worked out their destinies.

Faced with such paradoxical diversity, it seems best to focus attention on the site of his London commemoration. In 1866 Leicester Square saw the final humiliation of the statue of George I (p38). It was then in the hands of speculators, barren and treeless, accumulating ever more piles of rubbish. In 1873 an aquarium company offered the owners £50,000 for the central area but the angry residents gained a court injunction against any commercial development. No doubt the stalemate would have continued indefinitely but for the arrival of "Baron" Albert Grant. Grant (who claimed his title from the King of Italy) was a newspaper tycoon and M.P. for Kidderminster. He had been born in Dublin, his real name was Gottheimer and he specialised in dubious business and insurance schemes. He was certainly one of life's rogues. However, his involvement with Leicester Square was entirely admirable. With the consent of all parties he bought the site and within a year turned it into a beautiful public garden. Shortly afterwards he went bankrupt, leaving many clergymen, widows and orphans the poorer; he himself retired quietly to Bognor, where he died in 1899.

The man responsible for the overall design of the monument was the architect, James Knowles. He explained it somewhat long-windedly as follows: "The Poet stands isolated and colossal, cut off from the rest of the world by the quasi-Castalian spring which rises at his feet, but brought close to all men by his works, symbolised by the grass and flowers which spring up round the margin of the fountain, and which its water bedews and nourishes. The dolphins playing close to him imply his Arion-like attraction for the "sane and simple" animal part of us, and those memorable words to which his finger points – "There is no darkness but ignorance" – his deep, sympathetic insight into our brighter nature and its needs." No public competition was held for the central figure; one can imagine the in-fighting and hence the delays that would have been generated over the production of an entirely new statue of England's National Bard. Instead a copy of Scheemakers' memorial in Westminster Abbey (see p37) was commissioned from a reliable Italian craftsman.

One might well feel that more could be done by way of free-standing statues of England's national poet. Sometime in the middle of the nineteenth century there was a proposal for a colossal statue on the cliffs of Dover, visible for miles out to sea, but understandably nothing came of it. In 1875 Shakespeare found a place on the Poetry Memorial in Park Lane (p351) but this was demolished in 1950. In the 1900's there were plans for a grand National Memorial at the top of Portland Place, displacing the Duke of Kent (p88), but, typically, these did not survive the First World War. The little statue erected in London's Stratford was hardly an adequate substitute. However, the present-day rebuilding of the Globe Theatre in Southwark and the opening up of the Embankment on that side of the river surely provide an opportunity for some new and striking representation of Shakespeare and the mystery of his works.

William Shakespeare. Born 1546, Stratford, son of glovemaker. Married Anne Hathaway, 1582. Went to London and joined theatrical company, possibly Queen Elisabeth's, c.1587. Career as dramatist in progress with Henry VI, *1592. Joined Lord Chamberlain's company under Richard Burbage, 1594. Wrote early histories and lyric comedies, from* Richard III *to* Merchant of Venice, *1593-6. Death of son, Hamnet, 1596. Wrote middle comedies and histories, from* Henry IV *to* Twelfth Night, *1596-1601. Bought New Place, second largest house in Stratford, 1597. Shareholder in building of Globe Theatre on Bankside, 1598. Company taken under active patronage of James I, performing a number of plays at Court each winter season, 1601. Wrote tragedies, from* Troilus and Cressida *to* Anthony and Cleopatra, *1602-7. Birth of granddaughter, 1608. Wrote late romances, from* Pericles *to* The Tempest, *1608-11. Globe Theatre burnt down, 1613. Retired, 1613. Died 1616.*

Statue by Giovanni Fontana. Marble. Leicester Square. Unveiled July 2nd, 1874, by Mr Richardson, as representative of the Metropolitan Board. The gift of "Baron" Albert Grant.

Below. Statue from an original mould by the Coade Company. Outside Stratford Reference Library, Water Lane. Erected in its present position 1923. The gift of Councillor J.C. Carroll. The statue was originally cast in 1840 and stood inside Lord Harrington's house in Kensington Palace Gardens.

THIS ENCLOSURE
WAS PURCHASED, LAID OUT
AND DECORATED AS A GARDEN
BY ALBERT GRANT, ESQRE M.P.
AND
CONVEYED BY HIM ON THE 2ND JULY 1874
TO THE
METROPOLITAN BOARD OF WORKS
TO BE PRESERVED FOR EVER
FOR THE FREE USE AND ENJOYMENT
OF THE PUBLIC

John Stuart Mill

Progress through reason, representative government, individual freedom of expression and the greatest happiness of the greatest possible number: these are ideas which have dominated the political agenda for the last two and a half centuries. The writings of J.S.Mill have played a central part in the debate. They have been translated into numerous languages and have been banned by a great number of the world's dictators.

Mill himself had a most unusual upbringing. From early childhood his father prepared him to be the prophet of freedom and he responded to the challenge with remarkable facility. His powers of argument were formidable, his devotion to his task intense – especially since, for the greater part of his life, he wrote in his spare time.

Thomas Woolner, shown below, was a lively, ebullient character and one of the more vigorous Victorian portrait artists. He was the sculptor member of the short-lived Pre-Raphaelite Brotherhood (see Millais, p132). Despairing of recognition, he spent two years in Australia as a gold digger but later returned to build up a successful conventional practice. His statue of Mill is almost too good a human likeness. Gladstone called the philosopher "the saint of reason" but he was also to some extent its martyr. The statue wears a thoughtful, almost pained expression and the compression of the lips show the emotions tightly reined in. According to a contemporary, it closely resembles Mill during his short period as an M.P., when Disraeli unsympathetically referred to him as "the finishing governess". He scolded, however, in a good cause; he was, for example, the first to propose votes for women in the House and his motion was only defeated by 196 votes to 73.

J.S.Mill. Born 1806, London, son of James Mill, self-made Scottish radical journalist and colleague of Utilitarian philosopher Jeremy Bentham. Began study of Greek under father's tuition, aged 3, 1809. Wrote own history of the government of Rome, aged 11, 1817. Began serious political writing and campaigning in support of radical parliamentary reform, aged 16, 1822. To earn living, worked full-time for East India Company, rising to high administrative position, 1824-58; (by contrast he regarded India as an essentially static society, incapable of full self-determination, and would have been surprised by the spread of his own ideas there). After a period of intense melancholy, developed greater interest in poetry and close friendship with Thomas Carlyle (p126), 1827-8. Began lifelong relationship, initially platonic, with free-thinker Harriet Taylor, 1830; they married in 1857. Wrote immensely successful A System of Logic, *advocating reason as against "magical" or superstitious modes of thought, 1840-2. Wrote* Principles of Political Economy *with Harriet Taylor; it became the textbook for the development of socialism in England, 1846-8. Published best-known work,* On Liberty, *1859. M.P., 1865-8. Died 1873; his last words were, "You know that I have done my work."*

Statue by Thomas Woolner. Bronze. Victoria Embankment Gardens. Erected January 26th, 1878.

Left. Thomas Woolner in his studio, standing next to his bust of Tennyson.

Lord Byron

In 1816 Byron left England, never to return. The reasons for his self-exile were many: Celtic wanderlust and a deep love of the Mediterranean, debts, political pressure (the authorities were genuinely terrified that, with his Stuart blood, he would assume the revolutionary mantle of Napoleon), rumours of incestuous fatherhood and of marital sodomy (at that time still a capital crime) and a loathing of English cant and of English weather.

Given all this, it is not surprising that the history of Byron's commemoration in England was not a smooth one. Dean Ireland refused him burial in Westminster Abbey. His admirers raised subscriptions for a memorial during the 1830's; however, the Abbey again rejected him and Thorwaldson's statue ended up in the library of Trinity College, Cambridge. It was not until 1968 that a plaque was finally unveiled in that Mecca of writers, Poet's Corner.

In 1875, however, Prime Minister Disraeli lent the weight of his support to an outdoor statue in London. In his youth Disraeli had been poetically Byronic himself and Byron appears as the hero of one of his novels. The competition for the memorial was won by Richard Belt. His statue looks well in a good light; however, it was criticised by Byron's friend Trelawney as being a poor likeness of the noble-browed hero, in his day the most beautiful and the most famous man in the world. It does not, for example, show Byron's cleft chin or his darker

George Gordon, Lord Byron. Born 1788, London, son of Guards' Captain and Scottish heiress. Inherited title from great-uncle, 1798. Studied at Cambridge, 1805-8. Toured Mediterranean, 1809-11; swam Hellespont, 1810. Spoke in House of Lords against sentence of death for machine-breaking and in defence of Major Cartwright (p176), 1812-3. Published Childe Harold's Pilgrimage *and became overnight celebrity, 1812. Affair with half-sister Augusta, 1813-4. Married serious, intellectual Annabella Millbanke, 1815; they parted in 1816. Lived in Switzerland and Italy; became close friend of Shelley circle, 1816-22. Began publication of* Don Juan, *1819. Joined Greece's struggle for independence from Turkish Empire; made C-in-C of Greek forces at Missolonghi, 1823-4. Died of fever, 1824.*

The scene during the Belt v. Lawes libel trial. A model of the statue of Byron is half-way down on the right.

Statue designed by Charles Belt. Bronze. South end of Park Lane, formerly Hamilton Gardens, behind the house where Byron lived during his marriage. Unveiled 24th May, 1880, by the writer Lord Houghton. Cost £3,500. The pink granite for the pedestal was presented by the Greek government. The dog is the Newfoundland Bo'sun, the favourite pet of Byron's youth. (He always loved animals; in his Ravenna palazzo he kept 10 horses, 8 large dogs, 3 monkeys, 5 cats, an eagle, a crow and a falcon.)

physical attributes, his club foot and non-existent ear lobes (the latter sometimes regarded as the sign of a murderer).

It is in fact questionable just how much Belt was responsible for the finished statue (see also Queen Anne, p32). The Dutchman Pierre Verhyden, who worked in Belt's studio, claimed to have done all the work beyond the original design. When this and similar allegations were published by the aristocrat-sculptor and proprietor of *Vanity Fair* Charles Lawes, Belt sued for libel. The celebrated case ran over two years and at times it seemed that the sculptured occupants of the courtroom outnumbered the living. Belt finally won, owing to the difficulty of defining the exact nature of artistic assistance, but his reputation was not improved. He was later jailed for selling fake jewellery.

Thomas Carlyle

Carlyle left his native Scotland at the age of thirty nine and came to London. He settled in Cheyne Row, Chelsea, where he remained for the rest of his life. His house, now number 24, is preserved as a museum and his statue stands close by. Across the river was open countryside where he would often go riding. In old age he became a loved and respected *genius loci*. A stranger remarked to a Chelsea bus conductor, "That old fellow 'as a queer 'at." "Queer 'at?" came the reply, "Aye, 'e may 'ave a queer 'at, but what would you give for the 'ed-piece what's inside it!"

As an explicator of the phenomenon of hero worship, Carlyle must have a special place in a book devoted to statues. His rehabilitation of Cromwell, for example, led directly through to the great dictator's commemoration outside Parliament at the end of the century (p208). The charisma of heroes, said Carlyle, is something ultimately mysterious, springing from the depths of their being. But without their ability to draw and inspire, society has no cohesion and the history of the world is the biography of great men. Thus he gave utterance to what many of the thinking people of the mid-nineteenth century wanted to hear. Linking the gods and prophets of the far past with the writers and political leaders of recent history, he gave them a sense of destiny at work through the individualism of the modern age. He is sometimes accused of simply maintaining that "might is right" but he also urged social responsibility on those in power.

To create the effect he wanted, Carlyle evolved a new kind of narrative style, accumulating, dramatising, questioning; Swinburne called him "the stormy sophist with the mouth of thunder". Like his friend J.S. Mill (p122), he was intensely inner-directed. Years of reading and research were followed by the "paroxysm of clairvoyance" needed to integrate them into a whole. The nervous tension under which he worked produced frequent dyspepsia. Noise of any kind drove him to delirium; when in 1844 some neighbours acquired hens, it was his wife, Jane, who saved the situation with a tactful letter. She was in many ways as able as he was but she subordinated her genius to his. They had no children. After she died he was overcome with remorse at his shortcomings towards her and wrote a reminiscence which revealed the private failings of the public hero. Published in the year of his death, it caused a storm of disillusionment.

Carlyle had a generally low opinion of artists, whom he used to call fools and rascals. Joseph Boehm (see p265) was an exception. Carlyle employed him in historical research and later agreed to sit for a statue. "I'll give you twenty two minutes to see what you can do with me," he exclaimed at their first sitting. Boehm in fact completed two principal statues, both of which were reproduced a number of times; this is the second, more successful one, in which the old Scotsman sits in his dressing gown with a pile of books under his chair. It was said to be an uncannily good likeness.

With all his scholarship and irascibility, the Sage of Chelsea was essentially a mystic of nature and nature's processes, for which the Norse Tree of Life, Iggdrasil, was his favourite metaphor. "Not a leaf rotting on the highway but is indissoluble portion of solar and stellar systems; no thought, word or act of man but has sprung with all out of all men, and works sooner or later, recognisable or unrecognisable, on all men! It is all a Tree; circulation of sap and influences, mutual communication of every minutest leaf with the lowest talon of a root, with every other greatest and minutest portion of the whole."

Thomas Carlyle. Born 1795, Ecclefechan, Dumfriesshire, son of master mason. Enrolled at Edinburgh University, 1809. Married Jane Baillie Welsh, 1826. Translated Goethe and Schiller and gained reputation as literary pioneer, 1820-30. Moved to London, 1834. Published immediately successful History of the French Revolution, *1837. Gave celebrated series of public lectures, 1839-40; the last was later published as* On Heroes and Hero Worship. *Co-founded London Library, 1840. Published* Life of Cromwell, *1845. Published* Life of Frederick the Great, *1858-65. Death of wife, 1865. Elected Rector of Edinburgh University, 1865. Died 1881.*

Statue by Joseph Boehm. Bronze, life-size, on red granite pedestal. Chelsea Embankment. Unveiled October 26th, 1882, by the scientist and friend of Carlyle, Professor Tyndall. The poet Robert Browning proposed a vote of thanks to Boehm.

A replica was erected in Ecclefechan in 1929.

Robert Burns

On the night of January 25th, as the fumes of whisky rise like incense, Scotsmen all over the world celebrate Burns' birthday and recite his poems, even though they may think little of literature during the rest of the year. For he is not only Scotland's bard, he is also her pre-eminent national hero. No other poet in the world, perhaps, is so comprehensively honoured.

Burns is the most natural of poets. His plough drives a "wee, sleekit, timorous beastie" from its nest and shows him how chancy are the schemes of mice and men. He was a ploughman from his boyhood. The family farm was difficult to work and the rent extortionate; hardship and his father's early death gave him his strongly egalitarian character: "The rank is but the guinea's stamp, The man's the gowd for a' that." He was, however, well educated at home and he had a keen ear for local song and story. His principal poetic inspiration was love. He had several affairs and finally proposed marriage to Jean Armour, who was already carrying his child. Her family rejected an alliance with a poor, irreverent and roistering farmer and threatened a lawsuit. Burns was on the point of emigrating to Jamaica but first he decided first to show the world what he could do by publishing his poems.

The effect was instantaneous. Scottish culture was then in the doldrums and Burns swept all before him. The Edinburgh literati acclaimed him, housemaids and farm labourers saved their wages to buy his writings, and duchesses and coachmen clambered round to get a sight of him as he travelled round the country. His later poetic energies were given to reviving traditional song; to him we owe *Auld Lang Syne, My Love's Like a Red, Red Rose* and many others. He never became even adequately well off from his writings; he eventually worked as an exciseman, his chief task being – ironically – to prevent the brewing of illicit liquor. He died at the early age of thirty nine of rheumatic heart disease which had its origins in the overwork and malnutrition of his early years.

After his death, Burns became a national institution and monuments to him were erected throughout Scotland. He became, retrospectively, all things to all men. As another great Scottish poet, Edwin Muir, put it, "He is a Protean figure; ...to the respectable, Burns is a decent man: to the Rabelaisian, bawdy: to the sentimentalist, sentimental: to the Socialist, a revolutionary: to the Nationalist, a patriot: to the religious, pious: to the self-made man, self-made: to the drinker, a drinker. He has the semi-miraculous power of making any Scotsman, whether generous or canny, sentimental or prosaic, religious or profane, more wholeheartedly himself than he could have been without assistance; and in that way perhaps more human."

Which Burns do we find in Victoria Embankment Gardens? The statue was the gift of John Gordon Crawford, a retired Glasgow merchant living in London. He was "known in most of those circles which are identified with philanthropy, progress and patriotism", so we may take it that he identified with Burns the self-reliant Scot and spokesman of the disadvantaged. The statue itself is somewhat different. A restless energy animates the folds of the cloak but the eyes' lack of pupils makes the expression withdrawn. We see the poet in the quiet aftermath of composition; he holds a pen while on the ground below lie the just completed sheets of the *Ode to Mary in Heaven*, written to a dead sweetheart. This, then, is Burns the inspired, sorrowing lover, so deeply satisfying to the sentimental romantic.

Robert Burns. Born 1759, Alloway, Ayrshire, son of gardener and tenant farmer. Wrote first poem to Nellie Kirkpatrick, farmer's daughter, 1773. Death of father; took over management of farm with brothers, 1784. Wrote first satires, 1785. Published Poems Chiefly in a Scottish Dialect, *1786. Invited to Edinburgh; new edition of poems published, 1787. Toured Border Country and Highlands, 1788. Worked for Johnson's* Scots Musical Museum *and Thompson's* Select Collection *, compiling, restoring and rewriting great corpus of traditional Scots song, 1788-96. Began work as excise officer, 1789. Published* Tam o' Shanter; *settled in Dumfries, 1791. Tour of Galloway, 1793. Died 1796.*

See also frontispiece to chapter, p117. Statue by John Steell. Bronze, 9ft on 6ft pedestal. Victoria Embankment Gardens. Unveiled July 26th, 1884, by the Earl of Rosebery. The gift of John Gordon Crawford. This photograph was taken in 1921, during a misty January, as Crawford's worthy successors were laying their anniversary wreaths. Sir John Steell was Scotland's foremost sculptor. Sir Francis Chantrey encouraged him to come to London but he preferred to remain pre-eminent in the "Athens of the North". In 1846 he sculpted the marble figure of Sir Walter Scott for the Scott Memorial in Princes Street, Edinburgh, and he also introduced the casting of bronze figures to Scotland. He was 80 years old when his London Burns was unveiled, so it is perhaps understandable that it is a smaller replica of the statue erected some years previously in Central Park, New York. Steell moulded the head from a cast of the poet's skull in the Museum of the Edinburgh Phenological Society.

Sarah Siddons

"Her voice is naturally plaintive, and a tender melancholy in her level speaking denotes a being devoted to tragedy, yet this seemingly settled quality of voice becomes at will sonorous or piercing, overwhelms with rage or, in its wild shriek, absolutely harrows up the soul. Her sorrow, too, is never childish; her lamentation has a dignity which belongs, I think, to no other woman."

So wrote a contemporary journalist of Sarah Siddons, whose effect on her audiences was generally devastating. She lived in a time of restrictive social codes and restricting underclothes, when women regularly fainted in the theatre; it was said that when Siddons played, the orange girls sold only hartshorn and lavender pills. The most eerie occurrence of this kind took place when Catherine Gordon, the future mother of Lord Byron (p124), was, long before her own betrothal, attending *The Fatal Marriage*. She went into convulsions just as Sarah was declaiming, "Ah! Biron, Biron!"

As an actress, Siddons had the capacity to empty herself out and identify completely with the part she was playing. Occasionally this ability passed into hallucination. Her most famous role was as Lady Macbeth; when she first played it in London, she was still rubbing her hands and saying, "Here's the smell of blood," as she handed her cloak to her dresser. Not until the alarmed woman had assured her that it was only pink dye did she return to normal. In general, however, she had her powers of identification under full control. She had an able and original mind and thought out her interpretations with great care. Dr Johnson met her and was deeply impressed with her good sense. "Neither praise nor money," he said, "the two powerful corrupters of mankind, seem to have depraved her."

Sarah's own life had its difficulties. Her first season in London was a failure. Both her elder daughters died young, Sally at twenty nine and Maria of consumption at nineteen. Richard Sheridan, who managed the Drury Lane Theatre, was a notoriously bad paymaster and she had to go on exhausting summer tours far longer than she need have done. When she did finally retire, it was to Paddington, to Westbourne Green Farm, situated by what is now the junction of the Harrow Road and Cirencester Road, very near the site of her statue. She was closely connected with the world of art and during her retirement she passed some of the time making portrait busts. She herself had been painted by many artists. Gainsborough produced the clearest likeness – those eyes which could be seen to glare or sparkle from an immense distance and her other, strong features – "Dammit, madam," he remarked during one of their sittings, "there is no end to your nose."

When Sarah died she was buried in the churchyard of St Mary's, just next to Paddington Green where, sixty six years later, her statue was erected by members of the theatrical profession. Its design is loosely based on Sir Joshua Reynolds' sublime portrait of her as the Tragic Muse, hence the mask and dagger beside the chair. Despite the damage which it has suffered over the years (there *is* no end to the nose) it still casts a powerful spell, even though the front part of the Green has been ludicrously chopped away by the M40 motorway extension and Sarah sits no more than thirty yards from the roaring traffic. The remaining finger of her left hand is held against her ear as if to shut out the noise, though her beautiful, penetrating gaze seems not to notice it. If her soul, from the stage on which it is now playing, still maintains a tenuous link with her earthly memorial, then perhaps she hears it as applause.

Sarah Siddons. Born 1755, Brecon, as Sarah Kemble, daughter of proprietor of travelling theatre company. Acted from early age. Engaged by Garrick at Drury Lane, but failed to impress, 1775-6. Acted with great success at Bath, 1777-82. Returned to Drury lane and triumphed in first role as Isabella in The Fatal Marriage, *1782. Performed at Drury Lane and toured in the summer, 1782-1802. Performed at Covent Garden, where her brother John Kemble was actor-manager, 1802-12. Retired from stage with final performance as Lady Macbeth, 1812; the audience insisted the curtain be rung down after the sleep-walking scene. Lived at Westbourne Green Farm, 1806-17. Died 1831.*

Statue by Leon-Joseph Chavalliaud, for Farmer and Brindlay Ltd. Marble. Paddington Green. Unveiled June 14th, 1897, by Sir Henry Irving (p138), who also set up the fund for the statue. The unveiling was a grand occasion for the Stage; George Grossmith, Ellen Terry and Marie Tempest were present and Irving commented on the greater esteem in which the profession was now held.

Sarah Siddons' own descendants also subscribed generously. Col. Siddons Young sent a sum to be buried beneath the statue in a silver casket but the committee declined the idea.

Below. Detail: Lady Macbeth's dagger and the Mask of Tragedy rest against the right side of the chair.

Sir John Millais

Millais' statue outside the Tate Gallery is clearly the portrait of a successful man. It was not always so. After an exceptionally precocious youth, he formed an alliance with two other painters, William Holman Hunt and Dante Gabriel Rossetti, and established the Pre-Raphaelite Brotherhood. The sculptor Thomas Woolner (p122) was another member. These young men wanted desperately to escape from the sombre-tinted, sentimental imitations of Renaissance forms prevalent at the time and show nature in vivid and exact detail. They used scenes and faces taken from real life and glowingly bright colours (achieved by painting on a wet, white canvas) and they also drew on tales of mediaeval romance. It was all far too extreme for most contemporary taste. Millais' *Christ in the House of His Parents* (now in the Tate) showed the carpenter's shop with woodshavings and all, and raised a storm of pious protest.

The support of the author John Ruskin gained the Brotherhood some acceptance but then Millais fell in love with Ruskin's wife, Ellie. Two years later they were married, after an annulment and much public scandal. Out of favour again, Millais decided to abandon the enchanted world of *Ophelia, The Blind Girl* and *Autumn Leaves* and proceeded to make himself into the public man we see outside the Tate. Ellie, intelligent and perceptive, was the ideal support for what he called his "wretchedly nervous temperament". He concealed his heightened sensitivity to form and colour behind a bluff heartiness of manner; in his frock coat and winged collar he looked more like a successful businessman than an artist. His portraits of children, for which his growing family provided the models, proved the most popular. As a colour supplement to *The Graphic, Cherry Ripe* sold 600,000 copies in a few days and reached to the furthest corners of the Empire.

Millais' genius survived in his later portraits of the great and famous. Having moulded his own character, he became fascinated by its manifestations, particularly in public men. In judging likenesses of Carlyle, Irving, Disraeli, Gladstone and Cardinal Newman – all of whom have outdoor statues in London – one compares them first of all with Millais' penetrating studies. (Of course, as Art's first baronet, he could be jocular even with the great. When the aged Newman (p316) came to sit for him in 1887, he pointed to the raised chair and said, "Oh, Your Eminence, on that eminence, if you please," and, when the Cardinal hesitated, shocked his entourage of priests by adding, "Come, jump up, you dear old boy.")

The statue of Millais is the work of that artistic stalwart, Sir Thomas Brock. He fitted so perfectly into his age that today he receives comparatively little attention. He was born in Worcester and learned design at the Royal Worcester Porcelain Factory. At the age of 19 he came to London and apprenticed himself to John Foley (p186). He took over Foley's studio when he died, his first task being to assemble and cast the unfinished statue of Albert for the Albert Memorial (p63). He helped his friend Sir Kenneth Leighton, more experienced as a painter, to complete his *Athlete Wrestling with a Python*, the work which is generally held to have ushered in a new period of freedom in British sculpture. Brock profited by that freedom but he also knew how to respond to the needs of the Establishment. The figures for the Victoria Memorial (pp64 & 70) were his crowning achievement and won him his knighthood. He died in 1922 and was buried at Mayfield, Sussex, where he had his country home.

Sir John Everett Millais. Born 1829, Southampton, son of prominent Jersey artist and militia officer. Showed extreme youthful talent and was taken by parents to study art in London, 1838. Youngest ever pupil to enter Royal Academy Schools, 1840. Founded Pre-Raphaelite Brotherhood, 1848. First Exhibition of Brotherhood at Royal Academy met mixed but generally hostile response. Break-up of Brotherhood, c.1852. Married Ellie Ruskin, 1855. Founded Artist's Orphan Fund, later Artist's Benevolent Fund, 1871. Made baronet, 1885. Helped in founding Tate Gallery and recommended present site, 1892. Elected President of the Royal Academy, 1896. Died 1896.

Statue by Thomas Brock. Bronze, 10ft on 12ft pedestal. Outside Tate Gallery. Unveiled November, 1904, without ceremony, by the sculptor. Edward, Prince of Wales, was Chairman of the Memorial Committee and continued in that office after he became King.

Besides the statue of Millais, Brock's outdoor London works include those of Irving (p138), Bartle Frere (p200), Robert Raikes (p300) and Captain Cook (p296 & 301), as well as two of Queen Victoria (p64 & 66), a tally equalled only by Sir Joseph Boehm (p265).

Dr Johnson

Some of Dr Johnson's best-known sayings concern the city he loved so much: "No, sir, when a man is tired of London, he is tired of life, for there is in London all that life can afford." A large, bear-like man, Johnson lived always in the maze of little lanes and courts around Fleet Street, in Gough Square, Inner Temple Lane, Johnson Court and Bolt Court, just to the east of the place where his statue now stands. There he ate, drank and talked with the other leading spirits of his day, Edmund Burke, Joshua Reynolds, Oliver Goldsmith and the faithful Boswell, sipping his tea or lemonade (for most of his life he was terrified of becoming addicted to alcohol) in the Ivy Leaf, the Mitre or the Turk's Head.

Johnson was a phenomenon of his age. He rendered the pursuit of learning unforgettable and serious discourse a delight. Physically he was extremely short-sighted, half-deaf and bore the childhood scars of scrofula (he had been "touched" by Queen Anne for the disease and always wore her golden touchpiece around his neck). He dressed in stained old clothes, his wig burned bare in front from reading too near the candle flame. He rolled about, through some metabolic affliction, performing strange and unexpected gyrations. But when he began to speak those who did not know him were astonished. His flow of conversation was measured and effortless, his wit pungent, his vocabulary rich and orotund. Being constitutionally idle he enjoyed conversation more than writing, yet he produced the first ever thorough, etymological English dictionary and the most perceptive commentaries on Shakespeare since the Bard's own time.

Johnson attended St Clement Danes's church with some regularity and the erection of his statue there in 1910 was largely due to the enthusiasm of its rector, the Rev. Septimus Pennington, whose family had a long ecclesiastical connection with the church. His forebear, Montague Pennington, was a curate there in Johnson's day and had the uneasy experience of preaching his first sermon with the critical Doctor sitting in the front row. Johnson's original connection with the church probably came through Pennington's aunt, the liberated Elisabeth Carter, who published a celebrated translation of the maxims of Epicetus and used to accompany Johnson on his visits to inns, an unheard-of thing for a single woman. Johnson was a devout and conservative Christian who feared Hell, much as he feared the madness which he felt lurking in his soul. Boswell records his Good Friday visits to the church during the last years of his life. "I shall never forget the tremulous earnestness with which he pronounced the aweful petition in the Litany: In the hour of death and at the day of judgement, good Lord deliver us."

The statue itself does not reach these psychological depths, just as it does not give us Johnson's commanding physical height; we have instead the ever-sociable gourmand and witty frequenter of inns and coffee houses. It could not be be in greater contrast to John Bacon's marble figure in St Paul's Cathedral, half a mile or so further east. There Johnson towers up grim and serious, one shoulder bare, in a classical toga. He was the first man ever to be given a statue in that building; Sir Joshua Reynolds (p140) organised the commemoration and was almost certainly responsible for the classical nature of the design (see p42). Johnson had a fascinating physiognomy and Reynolds himself produced several penetrating studies of his great friend, so there is still room for a masterly sculptural study of one of England's most paradoxical men of letters.

Dr Samuel Johnson. Born 1709, Litchfield, son of bookseller and parchment maker. Went into father's business, 1726. Studied at Oxford but gave up studies because of poverty, 1728-9. Married 45-year-old widow, Tetty Porter. Started unsuccessful school, 1735. Went to London, 1737; worked as journalist, contributing to The Gentleman's Magazine *and writing and publishing* The Rambler. *Compiled* A Dictionary of the English Language, *1746-54. Wrote and published* Rasselas, or the Prince of Abyssinia, *1759. Granted a pension of £300 p.a. by George III, 1762. Published new and more accurate edition of Shakespeare's plays, 1765. Visited Highlands of Scotland with Boswell and published account of journey, 1773 & 5. Published* Lives of the English Poets *at behest of George III, 1781. Died 1784.*

Statue by Percy Fitzgerald. Bronze, 6ft. Behind St Clement Dane's Church, The Strand. Donated by the sculptor and unveiled by him, August 4th, 1910.

Below. On the pedestal there is a plaque of the young James Boswell, Johnson's great friend and biographer.

Amusingly for a lexicographer, Johnson's degree of Doctor of Law is abbreviated wrongly (it should be Ll.D.).

Peter Pan

Peter Pan. "Born" c.1898, during J.M.Barrie's storytellings in Kensington Gardens. All the children in that part of London were once birds in the Gardens. Seven-day-old Peter, however, decided to fly back to the island in the Serpentine from which he had been sent. Once there, he lost the power to fly away again. Eventually he persuaded the thrushes to make him a great mud-lined boat. With his nightgown as a sail, he was blown towards the shore, landing at the spot where the statue now stands. He made friends with the fairies who inhabit the Gardens after locking-up time and became the musician at their revels.

Statue by George Frampton. Bronze. Kensington Gardens. Erected secretly behind screens on April 29th & 30th, 1912, so that it appeared as if by magic on the morning of May 1st.

Below. Barrie's map of the Gardens, with Peter's landing-place at the top right. Over all looms the spirit of growing up, the schoolmaster Pilkington.

There are several good reasons for including Peter Pan with London's more strictly historical immortals. To begin with, he *is* immortality itself, an embodiment of the *puer aeternus*, the Eternal Child. His is also the only free-standing figure of – allowing the contradiction – a real fictional character. And he has more than once been voted London's most popular statue, so that a book without him would be bare indeed.

Peter actually grew up in Kensington Gardens, through the meetings of his creator, J.M.Barrie, with the Llewellyn-Davies boys, George, Jack, Peter, Michael and Nicholas, grandsons of the playwright George du Maurier. Childless himself, Barrie found them the perfect audience for his stories. Peter first appeared in print in the story *The Little White Bird* as a seven-day-old child who decides to revert to his pre-human, birdlike state. It was later, in the famous play first performed in 1904, that he assumed his identity as the joyful captain of the boys of Never-Never Land. This play rapidly became so popular that the First Commissioner of Works asked Barrie's permission to use scenes from it on panels in a new shelter in Kensington Gardens. Barrie went one better and himself commissioned a statue, sending George Frampton pictures of Michael Llewellyn-Davies dressed as Peter. However, Barrie never really liked the final result, which he felt lacked the devilment of the conqueror of Captain Hook. Tragically, Peter's chief inspirer never *did* grow up; Michael died with a friend in a swimming accident during his first year at Oxford.

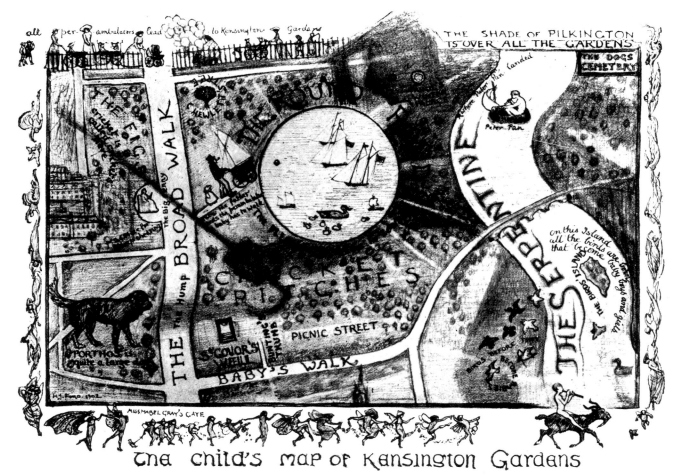

The child's map of Kensington Gardens

Sir Henry Irving

Like Garrick, like Keene and like Sarah Siddons, Henry Irving sprang to fame overnight. As a young actor he had known failure. He played generally in the provinces, and in Dublin he was once booed continuously for three weeks. Then in 1871 he persuaded the proprietor of the unsuccessful Lyceum Theatre to stage an adaptation of the French melodrama *The Bells*. Irving took the part of Matthias, the respectable burgomaster who is hounded to destruction by remorse for a murder committed earlier in his life. It was a triumph and Irving later took over the Lyceum himself as actor-manager. He was always at his best in tragic roles. He brought a new dimension to guilt and villainy – he was, for example, the first actor to bring out the pathos in the part of Shylock. He did not stride or rant; indeed, he seemed to glide rather than walk, sing rather than speak and his face was endlessly expressive. His effects were unpredictable, yet he knew exactly what he was doing as, within the warm glow of his theatre and its expertly handled machinery, he exposed and purged his audiences' guiltiest, gloomiest fears.

Irving was the first of Britain's Knights of the Theatre. He was first offered a knighthood in 1883 but refused it; he was an unhappily married man and perhaps he was afraid that the honour would add to the scandal should his new affair with Ellen Terry became public knowledge. In 1895, however, he accepted, stating that he did so on behalf of the whole acting profession. His gentlemanly manner and intellectual air had brought a new distinction to the stage; indeed this persona was itself one of his greatest theatrical creations. He had little formal education; he was a West countryman and the broad vowels of that part of the world would sometimes break through at moments of high tension. What sustained him was a considerable native intelligence and a deep and abiding passion for acting. He successfully projected himself to all classes of people; he was courteous to the humblest and the banquets which he gave after the show at the Lyceum were attended by the greatest in the land. Prime Minister Gladstone (p204) was a personal friend; when he grew deaf Irving provided him with a special chair in the wings.

Shortly after the award of his knighthood, Irving embarked on another status-enhancing project: the organising of London's first outdoor, theatrical commemoration, the statue of Sarah Siddons on Paddington Green (p130). In fact its unveiling coincided with the high peak of his fortunes. In the following year all the elaborate Lyceum sets were destroyed by fire and Irving himself fell seriously ill with pleurisy. Financial troubles followed thick and fast. He had hoped to retire quietly to Tintagel but it always remained impossible. The last words he spoke on stage were as Thomas Becket: "Into Thy hands, O Lord – into thy hands"; he died that same evening.

Irving's statue, like that of Millais at the Tate (p133), was undertaken by Thomas Brock during the decade in which he was working on the Victoria Memorial. Understandably, he did not quite make the Committee's deadline and the unveiling had to be postponed until the autumn. He successfully combines expressiveness with the dignity required for the portrayal of an established figure, taking the actor's fine air of detachment and clothing it in the gown of a Doctor of Literature of Cambridge University. Irving's son Henry spoke at the unveiling; deeply affected, he explained how the statue showed above all his father's courage, his self-possession in the face of both success and failure.

Sir Henry Irving. Born 1838, Keinton Mandeville, Somerset, as John Brodribb; brought up in Cornwall. Apprenticed to Cheapside lawyer, 1851, Attended City elocution classes, 1852. Made acting debut in Sunderland, 1856. Attained overnight celebrity with The Bells, *1871. Played Hamlet with immense success; acknowledged as country's leading actor, 1874. Took over lease of Lyceum Theatre, off Aldwych; engaged Ellen Terry as leading lady, so beginning a long theatrical partnership, 1878. Went on series of eight winter tours of U.S.A., travelling in all weathers, 1883-1904. Successfully staged Goethe's* Faust, *in which he played Mephistopheles, 1886-7. First staged Tennyson's* Beckett, *1893. Revived Shakespeare's* Richard III, *1896. Destruction of all sets by fire; ill with pleurisy, 1898. Lyceum Theatre closed after financial losses, 1902. Moved to Drury Lane, 1903. Died 1905.*

Statue by Thomas Brock. Bronze. Irving Street, on the north side of the National Portrait Gallery. Unveiled December 5th, 1910, by the comic actor Sir John Hare, who was also the President and Treasurer of the Memorial Committee. Subscriptions came entirely from the theatrical world.

Brock resisted suggestions from the First Commissioner of Works that he should show Irving dressed as one of his stage characters. Apart from anything else, it had been done before, by Edward Onslow Ford, whose marble statue of Irving as Hamlet is now in the Guildhall Museum.

The pavement around the statue is now used for the practice of another branch of the arts, especially for the benefit of London's summer visitors.

Sir Joshua Reynolds

Sir Joshua Reynolds has several related claims to greatness. He was the leading portrait painter of his age and for nearly forty years captured the richness, grace and elegance of eighteenth century society. He worked extremely hard, sometimes receiving sitters all day at his house in Leicester Square, and after work he liked the pleasure of varied company. He had the ability to see the best in all men; lords, bishops, doctors, lawyers, writers, actors and musicians all joined his informal suppers, where the only subject barred from conversation was politics. Dr Johnson (p134) was his closest friend; Johnson admired him as a man of equable, independent mind, while Reynolds' own powers of analysis were greatly strengthened by his association with the older, weightier thinker.

Reynold's genius both for painting and for friendship made him a key social figure. Just as Johnson advanced the profession of letters, so Reynolds increased the status of art. When the new Royal Academy was formed, he was the obvious choice as its first President and George III (p42) – though he never favoured him – was obliged to agree to his appointment. (The reasons for the antipathy are not at all clear. Perhaps George found his manner too egalitarian; Reynolds was once tactless enough to tell the King who had knighted him that his election as the mayor of his home town, Plympton, was the greatest honour he had ever received!) He devoted a great deal of his time and energy to the Academy, arranging exhibitions and supervising appointments. At the annual prizegivings he delivered his views on inspiration, beauty and taste, later published as his *Discourses*. They are a fascinating enquiry by a practising artist into the nature of art. For Reynolds inspiration did not descend pre-given in a sudden flash of lightning (hence Blake's quarrel with him) but was won by careful study and observation. Beauty was the golden mean, the generalised and perfected whole, something which he put triumphantly into painting for his age.

The statue at the Royal Academy was, appropriately enough, the final fruit of Alfred Drury's own quest for beauty and truth in form. Drury was a great admirer of Reynolds and saw the statue (with all its delays) as the summing up of his creative life. He first developed an interest in carving as a chorister at New College, Oxford. (Music was always important to him and the rhythmic qualities of the statue of Reynolds are obvious.) Working in Paris in the 1880's as assistant to the great Jules Dalou, he developed the lyric skills of the best exponents of the New Sculpture. In 1905 he completed four great allegorical groups for the outside of the new War Office in Whitehall. These evocative figures attracted universal attention, especially the woman holding the skull representing the Horror of War, soon to do her full work in the Western world. He also carried out a number of representations of eminent Edwardians, including a statue of the Duke of Devonshire for Eastbourne in which the handling of the drapery is, as with the statue of Reynolds, particularly fine.

Here Drury portrays the master at work. In fact Reynolds was extremely energetic while painting. As Lady Burlington reported, "His plan was to walk away several feet, then take a long look at me and the picture as we stood side by side, then rush up to the portrait and dash at it in a kind of fury. I sometimes thought he would make a mistake and paint on me instead of on the picture." Drury has of course sublimated the outer frenzy to reveal the inner judgement and poise, the beauty of one of England's greatest exponents of beauty.

Sir Joshua Reynolds. Born 1723, Plympton, Devon, son of quiet, gentle clergyman schoolmaster. Apprenticed to portrait painter Thomas Hudson in London, 1740-3. Visited Rome and Italy, 1750-2. Began pre-eminent position as painter of portraits; in 1758 he received no less than 150 sitters. Bought large house on west side of Leicester Fields (later Leicester Square), 1760. Founded the Club (later the Literary Club) with Dr Johnson, 1764. Elected President of the Royal Academy, 1768. End of painting career, due to blindness, 1789. Died 1792; his funeral procession stretched unbroken from Somerset House to St Paul's Cathedral.

Statue by Alfred Drury. Bronze, 9ft 6ins. Forecourt of Royal Academy, Picadilly. Unveiled December 10th, 1931. Cost £2,500, paid for out of the Academy's Lord Leighton Trust Fund for commissioning decorative works in public places.

Drury first received the commission in 1917, when his model was preferred to that of Derwent Wood. After the War he was much occupied with memorials, including the London Troops Memorial in front of the Royal Exchange. In 1926 his first clay figure of Reynolds suffered a disaster; the studio assistant detailed to keep it moist every night failed to do so and it disintegrated irrevocably. He had to begin all over again but as a result introduced the new and more dynamic pose which is one of the joys of the present work.

Charlie Chaplin

All the world knows Charlie Chaplin; fewer people know that he was a Londoner and that his art had its roots in the London music-hall. Both his parents were stage performers. His father was a successful singer and composer but his addiction to drink caused the early break-up of the family. His mother, to whom he was devoted, was also a singer but when he was only four years old she lost her voice and had to turn to dressmaking. They lived in extreme poverty in lodgings off the Kennington Road. His mother spent periods in the workhouse and in asylums, when Charlie and his elder brother Sydney were separated and sent to sombre orphanage schools or lodged with their father's drunken mistress. Charlie tried to earn money at a number of jobs – errand boy, printer's assistant, woodcutter, toy maker – but his great longing was for the stage. He spent a year with a dancing troupe called The Eight Lancashire Lads, which gave him the chance to observe artists like Marie Lloyd and Dan Leno at first hand. During his teens he had a long-standing part as a page boy in *Sherlock Holmes*; its West End run earned him a pass to attend the funeral of Sir Henry Irving (p138) in Westminster Abbey, a very proud day for him. His first music-hall appearance was with Fred Karno's company, when he won applause for some ad lib trips and falls and comic business with trousers and cane.

While on tour with Karno in America, Chaplin was spotted and engaged by Mack Sennett, who made silent film comedies in Hollywood. For ten days he hung around his set doing little or nothing. Then, suddenly, came the emergence of the character commemorated in Leicester Square. Chaplin described it as follows:

"Sennett was standing looking into a hotel lobby set, biting on a cigar. "We need some gags here," he said, then turned to me. "Put on a comedy make-up. Anything will do." I had no idea what to put on. However, on the way to the wardrobe I thought I would dress in baggy pants, big shoes, a cane and a Derby hat. I wanted everything a contradiction: the pants baggy, the coat tight, the hat small and the shoes large. I was undecided whether to look old or young, but remembering Sennett had expected me to be a much older man, I added a small moustache which, I reasoned, would add age without hiding my expression."

"I had no idea of the character. But the moment I was dressed, the clothes and the make-up made me feel the person he was. I began to know him and by the time I walked on the stage he was fully born. I assumed the character and strutted about, swinging my cane I began to explain the character: You know this fellow is many-sided, a tramp, a gentleman, a poet, a dreamer, a lonely fellow, always hopeful of romance and adventure. He would have you believe he is a scientist, a musician, a duke, a polo-player. However, he is not above picking up cigarette-butts or robbing a baby of its candy. And, of course, if the occasion warrants it, he will kick a lady in the rear – but only in extreme anger!"

From that point on Chaplin's career ignited and his million dollar a year contract with First National in 1917 made him the highest paid employee in the history of the world. He made a brief return to London in 1922 as an international star. Artists and politicians sought him out; H.G.Wells introduced him to J.M.Barrie, who talked to him about a proposed Hollywood production of *Peter Pan*. Yet on his first evening he slipped incognito from his hotel and revisited the scenes of his childhood in Kennington and Brixton. They seemed to

Sir Charles Chaplin. Born 1889, East Lane, Walworth, South London, son of stage artists. Played page-boy in Sherlock Holmes, *1903-6. Engaged by Fred Karno's Music Hall, 1908-13. Joined Keystone Film Company, 1913. Made 47 short films in Hollywood and Chicago, 1914-5. Signed lavish contracts with Mutual Film Company and First National Exhibition Circuit, 1916-8. Founded own company, United Artists, with Douglas Fairbanks and Mary Pickford, 1919. Came to London for premier of* City Lights, *1931; revisited Hanwell Orphanage School and met Gandhi and Churchill. Made* Modern Times, *satire of machine age, 1933-5. Made* The Great Dictator, *satire of Hitler, 1938-40. Married Oona O'Neill, with whom he finally found permanent romantic happiness, 1943. Attracted hostility of Un-American Activities Committee; accused of Communism, 1946-52. Attended London premier of* Limelight; *surrendered U.S. re-entry permit and moved to Switzerland, 1952-3. Received knighthood, 1975. Died 1977.*

Left. Statue by John Doubleday. Bronze, 6ft. Leicester Square. Unveiled April 16th, 1981, by Sir Ralph Richardson. Cost £8,500.

At the time of writing (the centenary year of 1989) the statue has been moved from Leicester Square for the building of a new electricity sub-station. So as not to disappoint his public, Chaplin will stand for eighteen months on the roof of the Vanguard Engineering building, overlooking the A40 at Alperton.

Right. By a burlesque misunderstanding which Chaplin himself would have relished, this statue by Tommy Steele was in 1980 delivered by mistake to Leicester Square instead of to the foyer of the Prince of Wales Theatre. It was impounded overnight by the police and the singer-sculptor had to rescue it the following morning from Bow Street Station.

him dreamlike, yet drained his emotions; poverty still had the power to trap him in its hopelessness. In all his later films he continued to play the pathetic outcast, the little man whose persistence triumphs over adversity in the end.

Chaplin's London statue owes its existence to the enthusiasm of Councillor Illtyd Harrington, deputy leader of the Greater London Council, who immediately after his death proposed a commemoration either at the Elephant and Castle or in the Old Kent Road. Disputes about the site followed and an appeal failed to reach the target. In 1980 the city of Calcutta beat London to the mark with a Chaplin statue. Then the Bristol and West Building Society, as patrons of the chosen sculptor John Doubleday, came forward with funds for the site in Leicester Square. Westminster Council gave permission, despite a petition signed by forty-seven objectors protesting that Chaplin had been a Communist. At the insistence of the Royal Fine Arts Commission the size of the pedestal was much reduced, so giving the statue a needed informality and avoiding a visual clash with the more traditional figure of Shakespeare. So did the little tramp thread his way back to his roots in London's theatreland.

CHAPTER 4
SCIENCE AND MEDICINE

The arts and the sciences have run roughly parallel courses in the field of commemoration. The statue of the doctor and botanist Sir Hans Sloane was erected in the Chelsea Physic Garden around 1737, only ten or so years after the honouring of the architects Palladio and Inigo Jones at Chiswick House (p104). The Garden was then the property of the Apothecaries Society and is now open to the public at certain times. London's next "scientific" statue maintained this close contact with the soil; when Francis Russell, Duke of Bedford, was commemorated in 1809 in Russell Square, the theme was his sterling experimental work in agriculture.

Freud (commemorated in Swiss Cottage, close to his last home) once compared the acquisition of scientific knowledge to the procedures of sculpture. "Science," he wrote, "works... like a sculptor at his clay model, who tirelessly alters his rough sketch, adds to it and takes away from it, till he has arrived at what he feels is a satisfactory degree of resemblance to the object he sees or imagines." This is an excellent description of Dr Edward Jenner's long and painstaking observations on the relations between cowpox and smallpox in the health of Gloucestershire milkmaids. The Jenner statue, erected in 1858, was London's first public memorial to a truly international, as opposed to a national, benefactor.

Speaking at the unveiling of the statue of the water-bearer Sir Hugh Myddleton, Gladstone maintained that those who transformed human life through technology were now as highly honoured as any of the heroes of the past. In London it did not quite work out like that. Within three years of its unveiling the statue of Jenner was moved out of Trafalgar Square to the obscurer pastures of Kensington Gardens. And those of Robert Stephenson and Isambard Kingdom Brunel, the principal architects of the world's first railway system, also failed to achieve their promised places in Parliament Square, as science, like the arts, took a back seat to politics.

The spotlight turned to war and the horrors of war, with the incomparable Florence Nightingale and the martyr-heroine Nurse Edith Cavell. Yet the statue of Sir Francis Bacon at Gray's Inn also honoured the man whose writings prepared the ground for the scientific revolution. Sigmund Freud, mentioned above, broadened that revolution to include hitherto unexplored regions of the mind. And Brunel has recently achieved the unusual distinction of a second statue, shown opposite, at his former Great Western Railway terminus of Paddington.

Sir Hans Sloane

In 1712 the physician Sir Hans Sloane bought Chelsea Manor as his country home. With it came the freehold of the herb garden established forty years earlier by the Apothecaries' Society. At this time herbs provided the great majority of medicines so the garden was a veritable scientific laboratory. It held the largest collection of herbal plants in the country, some of them brought from distant parts of the world. As a young man fresh from Ireland, Sloane had studied there himself. In 1722, a highly respected national figure, he presented the Apothecaries with the perpetual freehold, making only one condition: that every year for forty years specimens of plants should be presented to the Royal Society, of which he was soon to become President in succession to Sir Isaac Newton. Later the Apothecaries expressed their gratitude by commissioning a marble statue of their benefactor and erecting it in the garden.

Property therefore played a part in this earliest medical and scientific commemoration. However, there were other good reasons for remembering Sir Hans. Consulted by numerous members of the royal family, chief physician to the army and to Christ's Hospital, he was very much an establishment figure. He was also an archetypically good doctor, cheerful, practical and hard-working. He brought his own aura of health into the sick-room; after a serious illness in his teens, he adopted a lifelong regime of moderation which kept him fit until the age of 92. He rose early and would spend until 10 o'clock treating poor patients without charge. His treatments were generally traditional, though he also popularised the use of the newly discovered Peruvian bark cinchona, the source of quinine, wisely investing much of his early savings in it. He also tested and pioneered the technique of preventing smallpox by giving children a mild form of the disease. This method, learned from Turkey, remained in use until the time of Jenner (p152). It was risky, but anything was better than the current, all-prevalent scourge. Sloane successfully inoculated one of his own grandchildren and two of the royal princes.

Sloane was a distinguished botanist as well as a doctor. On his expedition to Jamaica he classified over 800 plants, most of them unknown in Europe. He also observed the behaviour of humming-birds and earthquakes and speculated on the nature of phosphorescence at sea. His open, enquiring mind made him part of the expansive search for knowledge so characteristic of Western civilisation since the Renaissance. He worked indefatigably for the Royal Society and built up a large network of contacts, being a member of the scientific societies of Paris, Berlin, Madrid, Gottingen and St Petersberg. In his later years he devoted all his time to his great collection. Visitors to Chelsea Manor could inspect over 100,000 items, jewels, minerals, fossils, plants, insects, ancient coins and medals, and scientific books and manuscripts. When he died the collection was, by his bequest, purchased for the nation and it became the basis of the British Museum.

In the photograph Sir Hans looks out across a sea of herbs: ladies' bedstraw, taken for kidney problems, lavender, useful as a sedative, and in the foreground the South American yucca, which sends up its gloriously flowering spike every seven years; in homeopathy it is used in cases of biliousness and despondency. For the last hundred and fifty years herbs have been out of favour as medicines but their popularity is now reviving and their efficacy is being reassessed, a move of which Sloane, with his practical good sense, would no doubt approve.

Francis Russell, Duke of Bedford

The Russell family is an illustrious one. Henry VIII granted them their title and lands and since then they have changed the face of England in more ways than one. The fourth Earl of Bedford laid out Covent Garden and, with the first Duke, drained the fenlands of East Anglia. Both the fourth and fifth Dukes were in the forefront of the agricultural reforms of the later part of the eighteenth century, and the fifth Duke oversaw the building of a great part of Bloomsbury on the former site of the family home, Bedford House.

It is in Bloomsbury that the fifth Duke's statue stands. Indeed two members of the family are commemorated in that area, the other being Bertrand Russell, the philosopher, peace campaigner and scourge of the establishment, who has a bust in Red Lion Square. As a young man Francis Russell quite lacked his distinguished descendant's natural brainpower. At the age of twenty four, despite Westminster School and Cambridge, he confessed that he had hardly ever opened a book. However, his companion the cultured Lady Maynard took him in hand and he was also inspired by the political example of his uncle, the radical Whig leader, Charles James Fox (p174). As a young nobleman of immense wealth, he could have led a life of idleness and dissipation; it is to his credit that he did not. He steeled himself to address the House of Lords and acquitted himself well. His speeches were always sound and well informed, though his natural diffidence made him appear rather offhand. One has the impression of great physical energies held in check by a sincere desire to do good and be worthy of the family tradition.

The Whig party suffered an almost complete eclipse during the

Francis Russell, fifth Duke of Bedford. Born 1765, son of Marquis of Tavistock. Became Duke in succession to grandfather, 1771. Entered House of Lords, 1778, becoming in due course Whig leader. Member of first ever Board of Agriculture, 1793. Signed protest at suspension of Habeas Corpus; motion for peace with France heavily defeated, 1794. Withdrew from politics, frustrated by complete Tory domination. Started annual sheep shearing exhibitions at Woburn, 1797. Died 1802.

Statue by Richard Westmacott. Bronze, 9ft on 16 ft pedestal. South side of Russell Square. Unveiled August 3rd, 1809. The Duke's right hand is resting on a plough and his left hand holds a sheaf of corn.

Below. A nineteenth century engraving shows the statue presiding over a summertime scene in Russell Square.

struggle with Napoleon and long dominance of William Pitt (p172). The Duke eventually abandoned politics and devoted himself entirely to running his estates in Bedforshire and East Anglia. There he employed the latest methods of science, conducting controlled trials of different techniques of sowing grain, species of grass, and breeds of cattle and sheep (the diehards complained that all these "new, Whig sheep" were ruining the stock). On one occasion he sat a party of farmers down to dine on South Down and New Leicester mutton, unidentified and identically cooked; the latter was judged the tastier against all expectations. At his annual sheep shearing exhibitions, he offered prizes for improved agricultural machinery and to farmers who introduced the new and better breeds. There were also ploughing matches, stalls, exhibitions and banquets. These occasions made Woburn the centre of the farming universe. As the great agricultural reformer Arthur Young wrote, they were "the most respectable agricultural meetings ever seen in England, that is, in the whole world, attended by nobility, gentry, farmers and graziers from various parts of the three kingdoms, from many countries of Europe and from America."

The Duke died young, of a strangulated hernia after a game of tennis. How much more might he have achieved! When Fox rose to address the House of Commons on his behalf he was so moved by memories of their steadfast friendship that he could hardly speak. The sense of tragic loss was felt by all his friends and no doubt played a considerable part in bringing about his commemoration.

His monument in Russell Square was the work of Sir Richard Westmacott, the sculptor most patronised by the aristocratic Whig circles to which the Duke belonged. At the age of fifteen Westmacott's father had sent him to Rome, where he studied under the great Canova, won a number of prizes and was known as "the youngest student." He was an ambitious man, determined to transplant the grandeurs of Rome to the damper, less exuberant soils of home. The Bedford memorial, which *The Times* called "the most magnificent work of art which was ever cast in England", was an early success. His statue of Fox (p174), erected a short distance away from Russell's, was an excellent likeness, his Canning in Parliament Square (p179) perhaps less so, and his Duke of York (p250) too elevated to assess. His Achilles in Hyde Park (p241), commemorating Wellington, was initially a near disaster. The Earl of Egremont, who encountered him at work at Petworth House, thought him a fussy little man and nicknamed him "Westmacotteles" for his displays of classical erudition. However, the artist who created the exquisite figures which circle the fifth Duke's pedestal can be forgiven a great deal of personal pomposity.

Russell too had his detractors. He was once foolish enough to attack George III's grant of a pension to the right-wing Whig, Edmund Burke. Burke employed all his oratory in a celebrated attack on Russell's own inherited wealth, calling him "the Leviathan among the creatures of the crown". "His ribs, his fins, his whalebone, his blubber," he wrote, "the very spiracles through which he spurts a torrent of brine against his origins and covers me all over with spray — everything of him and about him is from the throne." It was quite unfair; well built he may have been, but he was no monster of privilege. He made himself a truly public-spirited aristocrat, no rock-stranded sea-beast but rather, as Westmacott has shown him, the ruler of flocks and herds, the Master of the Turning Year.

Right. On the sides of the pedestal are the heads of cattle, and plaques showing scenes of labour in harvest and farmyard. A sheep grazes upon its upper slopes. These life-sized figures of boys represent the four seasons: Winter, Spring, Summer and Autumn.

Dr Edward Jenner

Above all men, Jenner deserves his statue for virtually eliminating the disease which in the England of his day caused one in ten of all deaths and left countless others scarred for life. Yet the story behind his commemoration is one of the most involved of all. It began in 1849 when the hard-working, if somewhat prosaic sculptor William Calder Marshall found himself left off the list of competitors for the statue of William Bentinck (p182). Why not, he thought, choose some universally worthy man and raise subscriptions for a statue which he himself would sculpt? He decided on Dr Jenner, who had died some twenty six years before, and set about studying his life.

At first the fund-raising committee of medical men whom Calder Marshall recruited did not realise the extent to which the sculptor himself was to profit by the venture. When they did, the majority resigned. Funds came in at a trickle. Then the eighty year old Chevalier Jean de Carro made contact from the city of Carlsbad; he had known Jenner in his youth and had been responsible for introducing his vaccine into the Middle East and India. He set about raising funds abroad and canvassed the crowned heads of Europe. The King of Prussia gave twenty friedrich d'ors and Napoleon III five hundred francs. Even so, nine years' labour succeeded in raising only £750, just enough, as it happened, to pay Calder Marshall's expenses of production. The Fates, it seemed, had taken his altruism at face value and rewarded him with minute exactitude.

Prince Albert himself agreed to unveil the statue in Trafalgar Square. His support undoubtedly tipped the scales with the Office of Works, who had been most unwilling to allow the site on which Calder Marshall had always set his heart. That royalty should sponsor a public statue of a commoner, principally subscribed to from abroad, was unprecedented, but Albert was both an idealist and an internationalist. He was also swayed by the practical information that five thousand people a year still died from smallpox and that a demonstration of vaccination would be held in connection with the unveiling. Three years later Albert himself died. Without his protection the powers-that-be, in the person of William Cowper, Palmerston's First Commissioner, struck and removed the Jenner memorial. Trafalgar Square now belonged to Nelson (p252), to Napier (p256) and to Havelock (p258), who more clearly displayed the national interest.

For a while it was uncertain where the statue would be put and *Punch* produced the following ironic jingle:

> England, ingratitude still blots
>   The escutcheon of the brave and free;
> I saved you many million spots,
>   And now you grudge one spot to me.

Its final removal to an obscure site in Kensington Gardens was a poor reflection on the spirit of officialdom but Jenner himself would not have minded much. Once again, the fate of the likeness mirrors the nature of the man. Despite becoming one of the most celebrated men in Europe – during the Napoleonic Wars, Jenner's signature on a passport was a sure guarantee of safe passage – he remained at heart a country doctor. He was feted in London and on occasions went there to fight for his deserts, but he never stayed for long. The man who won his fellowship of the Royal Society with a paper on the behaviour of cuckoos, and whose great discovery was based on long and painstaking observations of the health of milkmaids, is surely happier among the grass and trees.

Dr Edward Jenner. Born 1749, Berkeley, Gloucestershire, son of clergyman. Apprenticed to surgeon in nearby Sodbury, 1763; first heard a dairymaid remark that those who had had cowpox never caught smallpox. Studied in London as resident pupil of the great Dr John Hunter, with whom he maintained a lifelong scientific correspondence, 1770-3; catalogued botanical specimens collected by Captain Cook (p296). Began practice in Berkeley, 1773. Elected Fellow of the Royal Society, 1778. First definite observation that inoculation with smallpox (see Sloane, p147) would not take on those who had had cowpox; began collecting data on different infections, 1778. Inoculated 8-year-old James Phipps with with lymph from cow; vesicles of dairymaid Sarah Nelmes, Phipps with lymph from cowpox 1796. Conducted further trials and published conclusions in London, 1798. Vaccination of army ordered by Duke of York (p250), 1800. Mediterranean Fleet vaccinated, 1801. Voted £10,000 by Parliament, 1802. Jennerian Institute, subsequently National Vaccine Establishment, founded in London, 1803. Returned permanently to practice in Berkeley, 1804; gave numerous free vaccinations. Statue of Jenner erected in Guatemala City, 1821. Died 1823.

Statue by William Calder Marshall. Bronze. Originally erected April 30th, 1858, in Trafalgar Square (it appears that Prince Albert was not in the end able to unveil it). Removed to Water Gardens, Kensington Gardens, February, 1862. Cost £750.

Dr Bentley Todd

Dr Robert Bentley Todd. Born 1809, Dublin, son of well-known surgeon. Qualified as doctor and came to London, 1831; lectured in anatomy. Began publication of Cyclopaedia of Anatomy and Physiology, *1835. Appointed to new Chair of Physiology and Morbid Anatomy at King's College, London, 1836. Elected Fellow of Royal Society, 1838. Played leading part in founding King's College Hospital, 1838-40; Physician to Hospital, 1840-60. Published* Physiological Anatomy, *which became standard textbook of the day, 1845. With Bishop of London, organised formation of nurses training sisterhood at St John's House, 1847-8. Resigned from professorship and expanded private practice, 1853-60. Completed publication of* Cyclopaedia, *1859. Died 1860.*

Statue by Matthew Noble. Marble. King's College Hospital, Denmark Hill. First erected 1863, inside the Hospital's Great Hall, in the Strand. Moved with the Hospital 1913.

   Of course Noble (p191) did not select his stone for life in the open air but the statue is terribly worn. A comparison with his McGrigor, opposite, erected only two years later shows how much more enduring bronze is as an outdoor medium.

During the 1830's great advances were made in the technology of the microscope and a new world of anatomical enquiry was opened up. As a young man, Dr Todd was determined to make the best possible use of the new precision. He came to London, as he said, without a sixpence in his pocket determined to become *the* anatomical physician and by diligence, patience and a clear, logical mind he succeeded in that aim. He was an excellent teacher, his lectures being straightforward, well illustrated and delivered without notes. He also took an interest in the general welfare of his pupils. He was one of the reformers of nursing and was active several years before Florence Nightingale (p165), to whom the credit is generally given; six nurses from his St John's House went with her to the Crimea. As a physician he introduced several new techniques. In treating inflammation and delirium he changed the current practice of "cooling" the organism by bleeding and emetics. Instead he tried to stimulate recovery by giving alcohol, generally brandy, at regular intervals. In some (though understandably not all) cases this was successful.

Sir James McGrigor

Before the discovery of bacteria and of antiseptics the British army's most dangerous foe was Disease, with his General Staff of Gangrene, Dysentery, Typhoid and Yellow Fever. Dr McGrigor was a modest, compassionate army doctor who did everything he could to alleviate their terrors. His finest hour came during the Peninsular War. As Wellington's Chief of Medical Staff, he brought treatment into the front line of combat for the first time, so avoiding the usual long, agonising journeys in bumpy carts suffered by the wounded. He speeded up supplies, he organised individual regimental hospitals and he cut re-infection by separating those suffering from different illnesses. Between 1812 and 1814, out of a total of 62,000 troops, 9,000 died of injuries and 25,000 of disease. It was horrific; nevertheless, it was an improvement. Wellington (p242) reckoned that McGrigor had given him an extra 4-5,000 men and helped him to win the war. In private he called him "Mac" and in his public testimonial "one of the most industrious, able and successful public servants I have ever met".

SIR JAMES
M^c GRIGOR BAR^t M.D.
K.C.B. K.C. K.C.T.S.
F.R.S.
DIRECTOR GENERAL
OF THE ARMY
MEDICAL DEPARTMENT
1816 ___ 1851

BORN 1771 DIED 1858

Sir James McGrigor, Bart. Born 1771, Cromdale, Invernesshire, son of Aberdeen merchant. Studied medicine at Aberdeen and Edinburgh, 1788-91. Joined 88th, Connaught Rangers as army doctor. Served in Flanders, West Indies, India and Ceylon, 1793-1801; employed successful preventive, hygienic measures against plague in Egypt. Inspector-general of Hospitals, responsible for national regions, 1805-11. Dispatched to Holland to deal with fever epidemic on Walcheren expedition; survived shipwreck and purchased private supplies of drugs over heads of superiors, 1809-10. Chief of Wellington's medical staff during Peninsular War, served in all major battles and sieges; improved health situation through numerous innovations, 1811-4. Made Director General of Army Medical Department just before Waterloo and continued during long period of peace, 1815-51; raised standards of training and instituted keeping of medical records. Founded National History Museum. Made K.C.B., 1850. Died 1854.

Statue by Matthew Noble. Bronze. Outside Royal Army Medical Corps Barracks, Atterbury Street, facing Tate Gallery. Originally erected 1865, in the grounds of Chelsea Hospital, and moved to its present position 1909.

McGrigor resigned after 35 years as Director General just before the Crimean War and he died as the furore over the appalling loss of life there was breaking. Chelsea was the heartland of army conservatism and one wonders whether some of the medical men who subscribed to his statue did so as part of the general retrenchment against the assaults of the reformers led by Florence Nightingale (p165).

Sir Hugh Myddleton

It may seem highly odd that a worn marble statue of a tall gentleman wearing an Elisabethan ruff should represent the establishment of the age of modern technology, but Gladstone (p204) said it did and he should know. As he pointed out at the unveiling, this was London's first public statue of an engineer. It marked a new chapter; those who transformed the material means of life for the benefit of their fellow men would now be as highly regarded as the prophets and philosophers of the past. "It will be our own fault," he added with typical Victorian optimism, "if the addition of that new chapter be not a great blessing," and he proceeded to drink the health of the assembly in the water brought to the fountain from Myddleton's New River Head a short distance away.

In Myddleton's day Londoners purchased their water from carriers with buckets or carts, or crowded around the lead conduits at the ends of the streets. From 1581 a tidal water-wheel on London Bridge had brought up the polluted water of the Thames for supply to individual houses, but the range of its pumps was limited. The New River was designed to bring fresh, clean water from springs in Hertfordshire, employing nature's own force of gravity as its motive power. It ran for no less than 39 miles at almost exactly 100 feet above sea level, ending at a reservoir sited on the nearest high ground overlooking the City. From there the water was conveyed to the houses of individual subscribers in pipes bored out of elm wood.

Myddleton was (*pace* Gladstone) more of an administrator and financier than an engineer, but only a man with his authority and connections could have brought the difficult and complex scheme to completion. The experts were happy to work under him: Edmund Colthurst, to whom the original credit for the scheme must be given, the Cambridge mathematician Edward Wright and his successor as surveyor, the appropriately named Edward Pond. Resistance to new technology meant that Myddleton never made much money out of the New River Company. Happily his silver mines in Wales were more profitable. However, by the nineteenth century the original shares in the Company had become extremely valuable and im-poverished Welsh descendants of Sir Hugh would arrive in London in the vain hope of claiming some unexpired fortune.

Sir Morton Peto, who paid for the memorial, was Myddleton's nineteenth century counterpart. Entrepreneur and Liberal M.P., he built railways in almost every continent in the world and a number of London clubs and theatres. He and the sculptor-architect John Thomas had a long and productive association. This was their last work together, as Thomas died shortly before the unveiling. A quietly spoken, patient man and a natural artist, he was also responsible for the decoration of Sir Charles Barry's Houses of Parliament. As the *Illustrated London News* put it, "Hundreds of kings, queens, angels, saints, griffins, heraldic devices and rich ornamental decorations came from his hands." His skills were also manifested in the Islington fountain's attendant figures, their hair entwined with bulrushes.

Alas, at the time of writing no passing Chancellor of the Exchequer could toast the nation's taxpayers in its waters, something one hopes will soon be remedied. The New River now ends at Stoke Newington, close by the stunning Gothic castle which is its Victorian pumping station. Just to the south of the statue stands the modern headquarters of the Thames Water Authority and the New River Head survives there as an ornamental pond.

Sir Hugh Myddleton. Born 1560, Galch Hill, Denbighshire, son of governor of Denbigh Castle. Served apprenticeship to Goldsmiths Company, London, 1576-85. M.P. for Denbighshire, 1603-28. Prime Warden of Goldsmiths' Company, 1610 & 1624. Invited by City to take over control of New River venture, 1609. Financial difficulties led to King James I taking half-share in project, 1610-11. Construction completed and resevoir opened at Clerkenwell, to the accompaniment of drums, trumpets and canons, 1613. Number of customers exceeded 1,000, 1618. Took over silver mines near Aberystwyth, 1617. Drained Brading Harbour, Isle of Wight, 1620-1. Died 1631.

Statue by John Thomas. Sicilian marble, 8ft 6ins, on 17ft grey Devonshire granite pedestal and fountain of Portland stone. Islington Green. Unveiled July 26th, 1862, by W.E.Gladstone, then Chancellor of the Exchequer. Cost £900; the statue was paid for by Sir Morton Peto and the fountain by local subscription.

The chain and pendant around Myddleton's neck is generally taken to be a badge of office; in fact it was a reward given to him in 1623 by the City Aldermen after water from the New River sluices had put out a dangerous warehouse fire. His water put out many such fires and may well have postponed the Great Fire of London until such time as Sir Christopher Wren was available to redeem its ravages.

The same year, 1862, saw technology celebrated nationwide; statues were erected to George Stephenson (see p158) at Newcastle, to Samuel Crompton, the eighteenth century inventor of the "Mule" spinning machine, at Bolton, and to the Boston M.P., Herbert Ingram, who like Myddleton had been the prime mover in a scheme to bring water to his town.

Robert Stephenson

The building of Britain's railways was perhaps the greatest undertaking of the Industrial Revolution; it was certainly the most romantic. Two names stand out, those of Stephenson and Brunel. Rail transport had its origins in the needs of the mining industry, especially in the North where George Stephenson worked as an engineman. A tough, determined mechanical genius, he taught himself to read at eighteen and went on to solve the immense problems involved in making rail travel a practical possibility not only for goods but also for passengers. His son Robert, more tolerant and flexible in character but even more gifted, was his closest collaborator. Robert's early and happiest years were spent working on the design of the new engines, the *Lancashire Witch*, the *Rocket*, which won the competition for the new Liverpool to Manchester Railway (see Huskisson, p180) and the *Planet*, which fixed the optimum form of the railway locomotive once and for all.

The climax of Stephenson's authority came during his thirties with the building of the London to Birmingham Railway. He personally planned and surveyed the route and negotiated with the often hostile landowners (Sir Astley Cooper accused him of being about to destroy the nobility). He was served by thirty contractors and a force of twenty thousand men, who laboured and drank with astonishing vigour. He brought the line out from Euston through the blue clay of Primrose Hill by means of a special inverted arch lined with eight million bricks. Tunnelling under Kilsby Hill he encountered a huge quicksand and nineteen months of continuous pumping were required to clear it. Nothing on such a scale had ever been attempted before. Samuel Smiles compared the undertaking to the building of the Great Pyramid of Egypt.

Bridge building dominated his later years, work of even greater uncertainty and nervous strain. In 1847 his new bridge over the River Dee collapsed, killing five people. For the crossing of the Menai Straits he decided on a revolutionary design which would carry the lines in two fifteen hundred foot, solid tubes. "Often at night," he wrote to a friend, "I would lie tossing about seeking sleep in vain. The tubes filled my head. In the grey of the morning when I looked across the Square it seemed an immense distance to the houses on the opposite side. It was nearly the same length as the span of my bridge!" In the end all went well and the structure remained in use until badly damaged by fire in 1970. Four huge, couchant lions carved by John Thomas (p156) still guard the approaches to the bridge.

By 1850 Stephenson's health was broken; he always smoked cigars heavily and during the building of the London to Birmingham Railway may have resorted to the stimulus of drugs. Nevertheless he continued working. Ocean cruises and the society of his friends were his only recreations. His charm made him universally popular and he was twice elected as the leading representative of his profession. The name of Stephenson was known world-wide, as Britain took the lead in developing railways on every continent.

A marble statue of George Stephenson by E.H. Baily (p252) used to stand in the Great Hall at Euston until the appalling decision to demolish the old station was taken in 1968; it is now in the Railway Museum at York. The history of Robert Stephenson's London statue is closely tied up with that of Brunel (overleaf, p160). It too was moved in 1968, from Euston Square, and now stands behind a bare pool of stagnant water in a setting which recalls the grime rather than the grandeur of the Railway Age.

Robert Stephenson. Born 1803, Willington Quay, near Newcastle, son of George Stephenson, engineer. Apprenticed to manager of Killingworth Colliery, 1819. Assisted father in surveying Stockton to Darlington Railway, the first public line in the world, 1821. Took over management of father's locomotive factory in Newcastle, 1823. Managed gold and silver mines in Columbia, 1824-7. Returned to Newcastle; designed and built engines for passenger railways, 1827-33. Sole overall charge of building of London to Birmingham Railway, 1833-8. Built High Level Bridge over Tyne at Newcastle and Royal Border Bridge over Tweed at Berwick, 1846-9. Built Conwy River Bridge and Britannia Bridge over Menai Straits, 1847-50. M.P. for Whitby, 1847-59. Consultant to building of Norwegian railway, 1850-4. Built Victoria Bridge over St Lawrence at Montreal, then the longest bridge in the world, 1854-9. President of Institution of Civil Engineers, 1856 & 7. Died 1859.

Statue by Carlo Marochetti. Bronze, 9ft. Forecourt, Euston Station. Originally erected in Euston Square in 1871 and moved to its present position 1968. Cost £2,500.

Isambard Kingdom Brunel

Marc Isambard and Isambard Kingdom Brunel, like George and Robert Stephenson (p158), were a partnership of father and son. Marc was an inventor of genius whose greatest work was done in shipbuilding and Isambard inherited his prodigious mathematical and engineering skills. He showed his abilities young. At the age of ten he took a bet with friends that some buildings being erected opposite their school would collapse; they were down within a week. At the age of twenty he took over the direction of his father's massive project to bore a tunnel under the Thames from Wapping to Rotherhithe, the first of its kind in the world.

Brunel's principal achievement was the building of the Great Western Railway. If the Stephensons' genius was of the North of England, simple, monumental and grand, then Brunel's was Gallic, ingenious and daring. He was a poet among engineers. To him we owe the rolling, wrought iron ovals of Saltash Bridge and the poised, economical span of the Clifton Suspension Bridge, the soaring glasswork at Paddington and Bristol Temple Meads stations and the elegant decorative entrance to Box tunnel, near Bath, which is the longest in the country and so aligned that the sun shines through it on his birthday, April 9th. Unlike Robert Stephenson, Brunel did not engage contractors to carry out the work of construction but supervised every detail personally. He even designed his own railway engines but these were a failure. He had more success with his epoch-making steam-ships, though the *Great Eastern*, through no fault of his own, exploded on its first voyage.

Worn out by their Herculean labours, Brunel and Stephenson died in the same year, 1859, and of the same disease, nephritis. The same committee, chaired by Lord Shelburne, undertook the commemoration of both men and commissioned a pair of bronze statues from Baron Marochetti (p56). The list of subscribers to the Brunel memorial was enormous; the tycoon Sir Morton Peto (see p156) contributed the maximum of £10 and Mr R. Rowse and his five men of the Cornwall railway 2s 3d. At that time the heart of the engineering profession was located in Great George Street, which runs along the north side of Parliament Square. The Institute of Civil Engineers had its offices there and so did the company, Pritt & Co., where the memorial committee's first meeting was held. Brunel himself lived there, a short walk away from the House of Commons before whose committees he had argued out so many of his plans. This, then, was the site proposed for the statues. No less than three successive First Commissioners of Works, William Cowper, Lord John Manners and Alfred Austen, approved their erection, first where Smuts and Palmerston now stand and then just to the north of Canning (see map chapter 11). In December 1868, however, after many delays, Austen suddenly withdrew permission, saying that the pair were out of scale with the statue of Canning and that the Square was to be reserved for statesmen.

One motive for the change of heart was undoubtedly Parliament's vote earlier in the year for the destruction of Baron Marochetti's statue of Peel (p185). Seven years before, after the death of Prince Albert, Dr Jenner (p152) had been removed from Trafalgar Square and now another opportunity to honour science in the heart of the city had been lost. The two engineers were boxed up and consigned to the crypt of the Whitehall Chapel. Later they parted company. Stephenson was disinterred in 1871 but Brunel had to wait until 1877 before the Victoria Embankment Gardens were ready to receive him.

Isambard Kingdom Brunel. Born 1806, Portsea, son of French-born engineer, Marc Isambard Brunel. Began work in father's office, 1822. Took over from father as director of Thames Tunnel project, 1826-8; badly injured after second collapse in tunnel roof. Design for Clifton Suspension Bridge adopted, 1831; due to lack of city funds he worked on it intermittently between 1836 and 1854 and it was finally finished after his death. Improved Bristol Docks, 1823. Chief Engineer for Great Western Railway Company; built line from Paddington to Bristol, 1833-41. Built successful transatlantic steamship, the Great Western, *1835-8; it made 67 crossings to New York in 8 years. Completed extension of railway to Exeter, 1844, and Gloucester, 1845. Built Saltash Bridge, 1848-59. Built largest ship in the world, the* Great Eastern, *1854-9; due to the closing of the stopcocks on some water heaters, it exploded on its first voyage. Died 1859, shortly after receiving the news of the disaster.*

Statue by Carlo Marochetti. Bronze, 8ft 5ins. Victoria Embankment Gardens, corner of Temple Place. Unveiled July 1877. Cost £2,500.

Colour frontispiece to chapter, page 145. Brunel now has the unusual distinction of two London statues, the other being a modern work by John Doubleday; its postion at Paddington, the former Great Western terminus, earns it a honorary outdoor status. The two could not be a greater contrast. Marochetti's Victorian Brunel is magnificently dignified, the perfect image of the great engineer judging a curve or assessing a stress factor. Doubleday's figure has no such dignity; it is more like a friendly station mascot to whom we may nod as we pass down into the Underground, of which Brunel's Wapping to Rotherhithe tunnel now forms a part.

Left. Neither of the statues, however, captures the human being, the ebullient, cigar-smoking workaholic in the stove-pipe hat familiar from this famous photograph.

Sir Francis Bacon

Until he was forty-five, Francis Bacon lived in rooms at Gray's Inn and after his calamitous fall from office he returned there once again. The pedestal of his statue records the many positions which he held, from student up to Treasurer. His is therefore the only outdoor commemoration of a lawyer in London. He took up the law after his father had unexpectedly left him unprovided for in his will (some see this as evidence that he was illegitimate and, like the Earl of Essex, the son of Queen Elisabeth and the Earl of Leicester). The law was his livelihood and his gateway to political life. Through it he rose to the highest offices in the land; as Lord Keeper and as Lord Chancellor he was James I's principal adviser and the equivalent of today's Prime Minister. Unfortunately "the wisest fool in Christendom" was a difficult man to advise. Bacon could not restrain James' follies and James likewise did nothing to prevent Bacon's downfall – indeed, he may even have engineered it in order to divert hostility from his own beloved favourite, the young Duke of Buckingham. The charges on which he was tried were obviously staged; he was accused of having taken bribes even though he had actually given judgement against the people who had sent him gifts.

However little Bacon may have achieved politically, as a philosopher of science he ranks with the greatest. He was a pioneer, setting the scene for the great change that was about to come over human thought in Europe. His example encouraged the founding of the Royal Society and he inspired the French Encyclopaedists. From his early teens, when he was a student at Cambridge, he wanted to reform the sum of human knowledge. Oppressed by the sterile repetition of what Aristotle had said two thousand years before, he stressed the importance of personal deduction based on direct, factual observation and organised according to consistent, rational principles. He saw no limit to the improvement of human life through the exercise of reason. He himself arrived at a dynamic theory of heat – "Heat itself, in its essence and quiddity, is Motion and nothing else" – stressed the importance of atomic theory, and maintained that the movements of the stars and those of objects on Earth were governed by the same laws. He wrote a history of the wind and carried out numerous experiments with windmills. It has been said that he predicted the principles of anaesthetics, plastics and other synthetic materials, genetic engineering, weather forecasting and weather control, the pressure cooker and the septic tank.

Bacon was also a lover of gardens and he regarded the laying out of a good garden as a higher and more evolved art than architecture. "God Almighty first planted a garden," he wrote, "and, indeed, it is the purest of all human pleasure." At Gray's Inn the great open area which, at the time of writing, runs up to Theobalds Road and which is known as The Walks was his personal creation. He acquired the land through a series of legal coups and laid out the lawns and paths. He planted "cherries, pincks, violetts and primroses and standards of roses" and in the centre he raised a circular mound on which stood an ornamental summer-house. He may even have established the catalpa tree which still grows opposite no.5 Raymond Buildings. But statues, he said, though great princes indulge in them, add nothing to the pleasure of a garden, and he erected none in The Walks. Nevertheless in 1912 Gray's Inn ignored this advice and placed a statue of their most famous student beneath the windows of their library, among the flower-beds of South Square.

Francis Bacon, 1st Baron Verulam and Viscount of St Albans. Born 1561, London, son of Sir Nicholas Bacon, Lord Keeper to Queen Elisabeth. Studied at Cambridge, 1573-5. Entered Gray's Inn Began friendship with Earl of Essex, 1591. Published first edition of Essays, *1597. Took part in trial and execution of Essex on behalf of Crown, 1600. Published* The Advancement of Learning, *1605. Solicitor General, 1607-13. Attorney General, 1613-7. Lord Keeper, 1617-8. Lord Chancellor, 1618-20. Published* Novum Organum, *1620. Accused of bribery and deprived of all offices, 1620. Died 1626.*

Statue by F.W. Pomeroy. Bronze. Gray's Inn, South Square. Unveiled June 27th, 1912, by Rt. Hon. Arthur Balfour.

Behind the statue is the library. The present, somewhat functional building was opened in 1958, its predecessor having been destroyed during the Second World War; its square lines may remind us of the purely logical side of Bacon's philosophical outlook.

Florence Nightingale

From an early age Florence Nightingale believed that she had a divine mission to perform. She was a member of the upper classes at a time when the opportunities for gentlewomen were severely restricted. But having discovered that her call was to the despised and degrading profession of hospital nursing, she clung to it with single-minded tenacity. The heroic role which she played in the Crimea and the influence which she gained transformed the status of nursing and had an incalculable effect on medical services throughout the world.

She was known as the Lady of the Lamp, gliding gentle and compassionate through the cholera-stricken wards. Her reality, however, was stranger and more complex. She did indeed comfort the dying and the troops loved her. But she was also a ruthless administrator with a highly efficient, statistical mind, and she maintained her own, personal influence by any means she could. On her return to England, exhausted by all the suffering and by the fury of her efforts, she began to suffer from breathlessness and fainting fits. On the advice of her doctor, she retired to her room and barely left it until her death fifty years later, at the age of ninety. This protective cocoon of isolation only made her spell more potent. She took up the cause of India, and no less than five Viceroys called to receive her advice before taking office. She was, as it were, the hidden Queen of England.

Not surprisingly, she was the first woman commoner to be given a statue in London. It was erected while the First World War was still in progress, so a proposal to rename Lower Regent Street Crimea Street was abandoned for fear of offending the Russians, then Britain's allies. Yet even now, when the street is deserted, one can feel the spirit of that earlier conflict, as the tall, cavernous buildings turn themselves into the defiles of the road from coast to encampment, choked with mud, dead horses and unused supplies. It was not entirely a disaster; out of it came a new care and compassion for the life of the ordinary soldier and in that Florence Nightingale played her God-appointed part.

Florence Nightingale. Born 1820, Florence, Italy, daughter of dilettante political idealist. Received call to God's service, 1837. Entered Kaiserwerth Hospital, Berlin, to train as nurse, 1851. Appointed to run sanitarium for gentlewomen in Harley Street, 1853. Sent by Sidney Herbert (p186), then Secretary at War, with party of 38 nurses, to Crimea, 1854. Re-organised appalling conditions in Scutari military hospital; greatly reduced death rate and introduced recreation and savings schemes for ordinary soldiers, 1854-6. Enlisted support of Queen Victoria and played key role in setting up of Royal Commission of Enquiry into Crimean and army health, chaired by Sidney Herbert, 1856-7. Founded Training School for Nurses at St Thomas's Hospital, 1860. Played key role on Royal Commission on health of Indian Army; wrote to every hospital in India and contributed to 2,000 page report, 1859-63. Contributed to improved design of maternity hospitals, 1872. Awarded Order of Merit, 1907. Died 1910.

Statue by A.G. Walker. Bronze, 9ft on 11ft pedestal. Waterloo place. Unveiled February 24th, 1915, without ceremony. Cost £2,500. The new statue, the statue of Sidney Herbert (p186), and the Guards' Crimea Memorial of 1860 (which was moved back 40ft) were all brought together in one unified design.

Walker's original plaster figure used to stand outside the nurses' dining room at St Thomas's Hospital, where it attracted some probably uncomplimentary nickname. In 1955 the Hospital decided to commission a new bronze version. The 6ft statue was completed by Frederick Mancini and erected in 1958. In 1970 it disappeared, presumed stolen (for profit or for jest?). A further version was cast in a composite material and erected in 1975. It now stands on the North Wing Terrace.

Edith Cavell

Nurse Cavell was a wartime heroine. In 1915 she was shot by the Germans, on the charge that she had helped British and French soldiers to escape and return to the battlefront. She had indeed aided perhaps as many as six hundred men to reach the Belgian frontier, hiding them in her Brussels clinic or in safe houses and arranging their rendezvous with other members of her resistance group. She considered her verdict just and, so far as she could, she accepted it. But when the news of her execution became known to the world, it caused a wave of revulsion against German inhumanity. She had been a non-combatant medical worker, she had not been engaged in spying and – above all – she was a woman. Three of those convicted with her (two of them also women) were reprieved at the personal appeals of the Pope and of the King of Spain, and the Kaiser ordered that any further such cases should be referred personally to him.

In England her death became a focus for an increased commitment to the war; army recruitment (at that time still voluntary) doubled in the two months following it. It was the proprietors of the *Daily Telegraph* who originated and promoted the scheme for her statue and subscriptions were collected from its readers. The members of the Memorial Committee included the Bishop of London, the Mayor of Westminster and the Chairman of the London County Council, and the sculptor, George Frampton, carried out his work at cost.

Edith Cavell was an unexceptional girl with a quiet sense of humour. The reports on her by the ever critical Matron of the London Hospital were not particularly flattering. She owed her position in Belgium to the reputation of English nursing and to her knowledge of languages. Those who knew her there found her efficient, trim and possessed of a rarely-used, marvellous smile. In sheltering the soldiers she had at first, no doubt, acted spontaneously, partly out of a sense of national loyalty and partly from a nurse's natural desire to help those in trouble. After her arrest she spent a period of ten weeks in solitary confinement, thinking over her life and what faced her. She had with her a copy of Thomas Kempis' *The Imitation of Christ* and she underlined certain passages: "Occasions of adversity best discover how great virtue and strength each one hath", "Thou must come through fire and water before thou come to the place of refreshing" and "It were more just that thou shouldest accuse thyself and excuse thy brother". The night before she died she was visited by the Rev Stirling Gahan, the only English priest still remaining in Brussels. She explained that she had often seen death and did not fear it; before it, lesser motives fell away. "Standing as I do in the view of God and Eternity," she said, "I realise that patriotism is not enough. I must have no hatred or bitterness in my heart for anyone."

These words, recorded by Gahan, are inscribed on the pedestal of her statue. They were not part of the original design, which was made while the war was at its height. In 1923, however, the National Council of Women of Great Britain and Ireland, a well known pressure group for humanitarian causes, urged that they be placed there as a contribution to international understanding. In 1924 F.W. Jowett, the First Commissioner of Works in the new Labour government, agreed. There were protests from various sources. Some said that it was not clear that the words on the pedestal were Edith Cavell's and Sir Lionel Earle, the Permanent Under-Secretary at the Office of Works, instructed that inverted commas should be added. However, this nationalistic piece of pedantry was never carried out.

Edith Cavell. Born 1865, Swardeston, Norfolk, daughter of clergyman. Worked as governess in Brussels, 1886-90. Entered London Hospital (see Queen Alexandra, p73) as nurse probationer, 1890, rising to staff nurse, 1895. Invited to Brussels to set up nurses' training school, 1906; became Matron of Berkendael Medical Institute, 1907. Invasion of Belgium, 1914; took charge of Institute and did Red Cross work, caring for German and Allied wounded. After retreat from Mons, helped British and French soldiers to escape country, 1915; arrested, court-martialled, and executed at dawn, October 12th, 1915. Body brought to England and buried in precincts of Norwich Cathedral, 1919.

Statue by George Frampton. Marble, 8ft. St Martin's Place. Unveiled March 17th, 1920, by Queen Alexandra.

Above the statue (not shown here) the granite column extends to a height of 25ft and becomes a cross surmounted by a sorrowing woman protecting a child in the folds of her cloak. This symbolises humanity protecting the smaller nations of the world, among them, of course, Belgium. The overall design was modernistic and somewhat top-heavy and was much criticised at the time of its erection.

Sigmund Freud

Dr Sigmund Freud. Born 1856, Freberg, Moravia, son of Jewish wool merchant. Moved with family to Vienna, 1860. Medical student at Vienna University, 1873-81. Worked at Vienna General Hospital and Kaisowitz Children's Institute as neurologist with special interest in hysteria and hypnosis, 1882-93; built up private practice, making special use of technique of free association. Researched into anxiety and obsession; introduced term "psychoanalysis" and developed theories of infantile sexuality and Oedipus complex, 1893-8. Published The Interpretation of Dreams, *1900. Founding of International Association of Psychoanalysts, 1908; first meeting held at Salzburg. Lectured in U.S.A., 1908. Published* Totem and Taboo, *giving anthropological background to theories, 1913-4. First signs of cancer of the mouth, caused by heavy smoking, 1923. Books publicly burned by Hitler regime in Berlin, 1936. Elected Corresponding Member of Royal Society, 1936. Left Vienna and settled in London, 1938. Died 1939.*

Freud spent the last fifteen months of his life in Hampstead as a fugitive from the Nazis. Though seriously ill with cancer, he saw patients and completed his book *Moses and Monotheism.* He was then a world figure. Permission to leave Austria came through the personal intervention of President Roosevelt (p232) and his financial resources were transfered to England through the King of Greece. While living at 20 Maresfield Gardens, he was visited by the Secretaries of the Royal Society and he signed his name in its Charter Book alongside those of Newton and Darwin.

Freud was very happy in England. He had always had a longing for the country, ever since his half-brothers had emigrated to Manchester and he had visited them there at the age of nineteen. If only, he said, he had been an ordinary, straightforward, beer-drinking Englishman, looking out at the clear world, instead of living in Vienna, plumbing its dark, ingrown depths – but such a paradise of the alter-ego was, of course, not to be.

Though many of Freud's ideas and concepts have now become a part of everyday conversation, they were deeply shocking to most of his contemporaries. At the same time he became a cult figure to the artistic avant-garde, who saw him as an explorer of the same anarchistic, paradoxical territory as themselves. During the 1920's many artists begged to be allowed to portray him but he was always secretive about himself, preferring to work through the impersonal mask of science. Nevertheless, on his seventy fifth birthday he agreed for the one and only time to be sculpted and the task was given to the young Oscar Nemon (p290). The two got on well and Nemon completed a statue in plaster. At first only the head was cast in bronze (it may be seen at 20 Maresfield Gardens, now the Freud Museum). The full-sized figure remained uncast for nearly forty years until a successful, world-wide appeal for funds was launched among members of the

Above left. The appeal for the casting of the statue was organised by the great child psychiatrist, Dr Donald Winnicott. It was also his idea that the statue should be unveiled, not by some public figure, but by Freud's own great-grandchildren, Dominic, Emma (now a well-known broadcaster) and Matthew. They are the children of Sir Clement Freud, gourmet and former Liberal M.P., whose father was Sigmund Freud's youngest son Ernst.

Freud in fact conducted his investigation into the traumas of childhood from the security of an extremely happy and stable family life. His youngest daughter, Anna, followed him into psycho-analysis and became one of his closest co-workers.

psychiatric profession.

The completed statue was put up next to the Swiss Cottage Library complex, a short distance from Freud's last home. It stands somewhat isolated on a lawn on the south side, facing Adelaide Road, rather than in the busy, open pedestrian thoroughfare to the north. One reason for this was undoubtedly the fear of vandalism and the pedestal is still sometimes disfigured by graffiti. One wonders how Freud viewed the phenomenon of commemorative statues, those erect, unmoving representatives of society's super-ego, ever vulnerable to the retributions of the id.

Statue by Oscar Nemon. Bronze. Swiss Cottage. Unveiled October 2nd, 1970, by Dominic, Emma and Matthew Freud. Cost £10,000.

CHAPTER 5
POLITICS

It was William Pitt's retirement after the first, long war with Napoleon which initiated the first raising of public funds for a statue of an English statesman. This golden age of heroism happened also to be a golden age of political satire and the cartoonist's comment shown opposite – entitled *John Bull and his favourite Statue of Bronze* – illustrates how the colossal expense of the war had undone all Pitt's earlier good work on the economy. It also illustrates the abiding and necessary ambivalence felt by an emerging democracy towards its political rulers.

These funds eventually bore fruit in an outdoor statue of the Father of the Tory Party erected in Hanover Square in 1831. In the meantime the Whigs had commemorated two of their heroes, the Fifth Duke of Bedford and Charles James Fox, though the Duke, as we saw in the previous chapter (p148), was remembered more as a successful agriculturalist than as an unsuccessful politician. These celebrations were somewhat private in character and took place on Whig-owned land in Bloomsbury. From 1831 onwards, however, the outdoor, public commemoration of statesmen was fully established and for the next one hundred years their images – twenty four in all – filled the streets. This was no State enterprise; the statues were, without exception, paid for by public subscription. (Lord Rosebery's attempt to commemorate Oliver Cromwell at government expense ended in ignominy.) All shades of opinion were represented: radicals like Richard Cobden, John Cartwright and Sir Wilfrid Lawson stood together with traditionalists like Lord George Bentinck and Lord Curzon. It was Curzon's statue, together with that of the only woman represented, Mrs Pankhurst, which completed the century.

From 1932 up to mid-1989 the commemorative picture has been quite different. There have been statues of only three English politicians: Winston Churchill, Fenner Brockway and, most recently, Clement Attlee (who appears on his own in chapter 8). The British have certainly become less inclined to put their leaders up on pedestals, real or metaphorical. At the same time their links with the world at large have become more important. Since the First World War (in effect the real watershed) there have been no less than seven statues of foreign statesmen, four of them presented from abroad: United States Presidents Lincoln, Washington, F.D. Roosevelt and Eisenhower (chapter 10, p362), Smuts of South Africa and the Commonwealth, Gandhi of India and Bolivar of the greater part of South America.

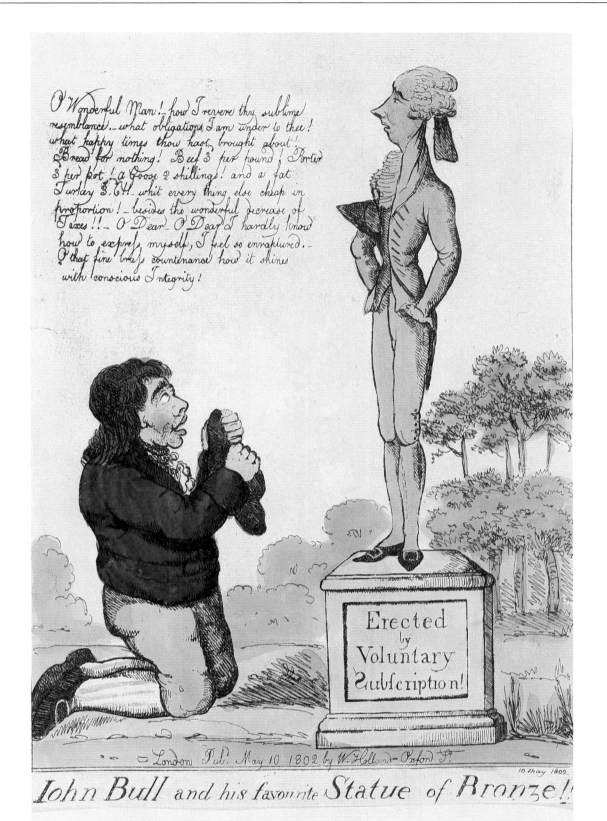

O Wonderful Man! how I revere thy sublime resemblance.— what obligations I am under to thee! what happy times thou hast brought about! Bread for nothing! Beef 3d per pound! Porter 3d per pot! a Goose 2 shillings! and a fat Turkey 3.6d.! whit every thing else cheap in proportion!— besides the wonderful decrease of Taxes!!— O Dear O Dear I hardly know how to express myself, I feel so enraptured.— O that fine brass countenance how it shines with conscious Integrity!

Erected by Voluntary Subscription!

London Pub. May 10 1802 by W. Holland - Oxford St.

10 May 1802

John Bull and his favourite Statue of Bronze!

WILLIAM PITT
BORN
MDCCLIX
DIED
MDCCCVI

William Pitt

William Pitt the Younger. Born 1759, Hayes, Kent, son of William Pitt, Earl of Chatham, Prime Minister. Studied at Cambridge, 1774-7. Entered House of Commons, 1780. Chancellor of Exchequer, 1781. Appointed Prime Minister and First Lord of the Treasury, 1783. Reduced duties and taxes, stimulated trade and raised government revenue, 1784-9. War with France. Successfully raised huge loans and introduced income tax. Fearing revolution, suspended Habeas Corpus, introduced press censorship and control of public meetings, 1793-1801. Passed Bill uniting British and Irish parliaments. Proposal to grant greater rights to Irish Catholics blocked by George III; resigned, 1801. Returned as Prime Minister after renewal of war with France, 1804-6. Died 1806; his last words were, "Oh, my country! How I leave my country!"

Statue by Francis Chantrey. Bronze, 12 ft on 15 ft granite pedestal. South side of Hanover Square. Unveiled August 22nd, 1831, in the presence of the Marquis of Camden and other subscribers. Cost £7,000.

Our political roll call begins with William Pitt the Younger, who holds one clear, all time record – how extraordinary, *not* to be Prime Minister of one's country for only six years of ones adult life! During his first years in office he purged the country's tax system of irrationality and excess and ushered in a new period of prosperity. When later the war with Napoleon involved the raising of huge loans, Pitt's personal standing with the men of money was such that the lines of credit were maintained. It was, one may note, their subscriptions which paid for his statue in Hanover Square.

Pitt was a precociously intelligent, aloof figure. He was close to his family and one or two drinking companions but to the general public his private life was a closed book. He was unmarried and had no mistresses. His only vice was the heavy consumption of port (begun in his teens as a cure for supposed hereditary gout) which contributed to his later ill-health; it was the solace of a genuinely lonely man, isolated from his fellows by the range of his abilities.

In 1801 he retired from office, ill and exhausted. In the following year, as we saw in the introduction to this chapter, a committee was formed with the purpose of erecting his statue. Its pioneering chairman was John Julius Angerstein, a Russian-born broker who had come to England at the age of 15 and was a noted connoisseur of art; his collection of paintings later formed the basis of the National Gallery. He was also a leading underwriter and the first meetings of subscribers were held at Lloyd's. Controversy soon broke out. Some felt that it would be improper to erect the statue while Pitt was still alive. Others pointed out that, as he was still a young man, they might never see their gifts bear fruit. Motions were passed and rescinded. Pitt himself intimated that he would prefer his admirers to wait until he had reached, in the words of the *Morning Chronicle*, "those happy realms where resignations are unknown." However, the majority were undeterred and by the end of 1803, £5,410-6s. had been collected and invested at 3%. However, Pitt's unexpected return to power the next year made the putting up of his statue an impossibly partisan act and the project came to a halt.

After Pitt's early death, statues were erected in Glasgow and Cambridge and monuments placed in Westminster Abbey and the Guildhall. It seems certain beyond all reasonable doubt that Angerstein's fund paid for the the bronze, seated figure by Richard Westmacott which was erected in 1815 inside the National Debt Office (an institution which Pitt himself founded) at 19 Old Jewry. This statue was made homeless during the Second World War and narrowly escaped being melted down by the Ministry of Works; it now reposes gravely beneath the library windows of Pitt's alma mater, Pembroke College, Cambridge. Meanwhile – through long accumulated interest, perhaps – a healthy surplus of £7,000 remained in the fund. For decades after his death the Tories were still "the party of Mr Pitt" and in 1825 the trustees approached Sir Francis Chantrey (p52) for a second figure.

This statue began its career most dramatically. By the time it was ready, the country was in an uproar over the slow progress of the First Reform Bill. To the new generation of reformers Pitt was the old arch-enemy and symbol of the Establishment. On the morning of its erection, while the workmen were having their breakfast, a group of protesters threw a rope around it and tried to pull it down. Chantrey was told what was going on but he smiled and said, "The cramps are leaded and they may pull till Doomsday!"

Charles James Fox

Charles James Fox. Born 1749, second son of the politician Henry Fox, later the first Lord Holland. Educated Eton and Oxford. Became M.P., 1768. Junior Lord of Treasury. Attacked Clive's actions in India; dismissed by King, 1772. Gambling debts of £140,000 paid off by father, 1773-4. Became leader of Whig party in House of Commons; opposed war with America, 1773-8. Foreign Secretary; tried unsuccessfully to reform finances of East India Company and lost majority in Commons, 1782-3. Introduced Libel Bill which extended trial by jury, 1792. Foreign Secretary, 1806. Died 1806.

Statue by Richard Westmacott. Bronze, 9ft on 8ft pedestal. North side of Bloomsbury Square. Erected June 19th, 1816. The Square was at the time the property of Fox's political colleague, the sixth Duke of Bedford.

Below. A contemporary cartoon showing the Empress Catherine the Great of Russia taking possession of the bust of Fox which she had ordered to be sent to her (see paragraph 3).

Fox and Pitt (p172) are, like Gladstone (p204) and Disraeli (p194), archetypically opposite figures; Pitt tall, aloof, perforce authoritarian, Fox plump, convivial, the champion of individual liberties. As a young man Fox certainly had style, gambling all night yet arriving at the House of Commons fresh and ready for debate in the morning. His debts were astronomical, his affairs with women notorious, yet his charisma and oratorical skills soon established him as the country's leading radical. He opposed the war with America and he expressed sympathy with the French Revolution in its early days. King George III profoundly mistrusted him, while the Prince of Wales, later George IV (p50), was his bosom friend.

What Fox stood for – the rights of Parliament and the subject against the King, civil liberties, the abolition of slavery – was far more important than what he actually achieved. His views, together with a certain instability and political maladroitness, kept him for most of his life on the sidelines of power. During the long period of Tory dominance his wing of the Whig party lost all influence and even stopped attending Parliament. Despite, or rather because of, these difficulties, Fox himself became an ever greater cult figure to his followers. His aristocratic friends, among them the Duke of Devonshire and Francis Russell, Duke of Bedford (p148) drew close around him; when Russell built a Whig "shrine" at Woburn House, a "Temple of Liberty", it was Fox's bust which occupied pride of place.

At that time busts (unlike statues) were widely used as icons during the lifetimes of their subjects. Catherine the Great, Empress of Russia, also felt the glamour of such neo-classical celebrations. She was a free-thinker in theory, though an autocrat in practice. In 1891, after Fox's parliamentary eloquence had headed off the possibility of war between England and Russia, she ordered his bust to be sent to her at St Petersburg, where she placed it between those of Demosthenes and Cicero. Since she was a passionate woman, humourists suggested that her partiality for Fox was physical rather than political.

After Pitt's death, Fox enjoyed a late political summer. As Foreign Secretary in "The Ministry of All the Talents", he conducted peace negotiations with Napoleon – and demonstrated a very British fair-mindedness by telling the French of a plot against their Emperor's life. But it was too late; after less than a year in office, he died of dropsy. His aristocratic friends at once formed a committee for his commemoration and over the next three years obtained promises of £12,450. This was enough both for a marble monument in Westminster Abbey and also a bronze, outdoor statue, the two commissions being given to the same sculptor, Sir Richard Westmacott (p150).

Some regard the former as his masterpiece, especially the figure of the negro which exemplifies Fox's support of the campaign for the abolition of slavery. The outdoor statue, though not exactly a masterpiece, is good fun. Fox's widow thought it an excellent likeness. It stands – or sits, rather, for it would be impossible for such a portly politician to stand with any dignity – in Bloomsbury Square, which was at that time owned by the Bedford family. It looks north towards Westmacott's statue of the fifth Duke of Bedford in Russell Square (p149). As a champion of freedom, Fox the Consul holds a somewhat anachronistic Magna Carta, its seal carefully copied from the original in the British Museum. And finally, as if to complete the picture of his life, a fig tree – whether intentionally planted or not – has grown up around the convivial, pleasure loving hero.

Major John Cartwright

JOHN CARTWRIGHT,
BORN 28ᵗʰ SEPᵗ 1740 DIED 23ᵗʰ SEPᵗ 1824.
The Firm, Consistent & Persevering Advocate
OF
UNIVERSAL SUFFRAGE,
Equal Representation, Vote by Ballot
AND
ANNUAL PARLIAMENTS.

Major John Cartwright. Born 1740, Marnham, Nottinghamshire, son of gentleman farmer. Joined navy, 1758. Published writings in favour of American independence and resigned from service, 1774. Began campaign for universal suffrage, 1780. Dismissed from rank of major in Nottinghamshire Militia after attending public meeting celebrating fall of Bastille, 1789. Helped inventor-brother Edward with financial side of world's first power-driven loom, 1799-1802. Arrested during tour of North of England, but released; supported by Lord Byron (p124) in House of Lords, 1812-13. Presented petition for reform bearing half a million signatures to Parliament, 1817. Arrested for sedition in Birmingham and fined, 1819-20. Died 1824.

Statue by George Clarke. Bronze. Cartwright Gardens. Unveiled July 20th, 1831. That same evening a dinner for 500-600 guests was held at the White Conduit House, Pentonville; they included the M.P.'s Burdett, Hume and Hunt. The first toast was drunk to "the people, the only source legitimate power." The second toast, however, was drunk to the King, so one should not overestimate the revolutionary character of the occasion.

The statue was first erected close by no. 19, where Cartwright lived for the last seven years of his life. The location was then called Burton Crescent; this was changed to Cartwright Gardens in 1908 after a series of murders had made the original name notorious.

John Cartwright was one of that breed of English eccentric whose ideas, held with unyielding conviction and transparent honesty, are so straightforwardly sane as to seem impossibly mad. He had one major preoccupation: the need to reform parliament. His programme was simple: annual assemblies, constituencies of equal size, secret ballots and universal male suffrage. But Cartwright lived in the age of patronage and the rotten borough, when the right to vote was still held by only eight per cent of the adult population.

For forty four years, until his death at the age of eighty four, Cartwright wrote, talked, toured the country, addressed meetings and got up petitions in support of his ideas. He became the father figure of the radicals of his day, men like Sir Francis Burdett, Joseph Hume and Henry Hunt, though few had his complete dedication and some found his approach naive. He risked hostility, violence and arrest, though his obvious integrity and his status as a gentleman protected him. In 1819, the year of the Peterloo massacre, he was arrested in Birmingham for sedition. This was a serious charge and three of his companions were imprisoned. Cartwright, however, defended by the able elder brother of Rowland Hill (p94), was let off with a £100 fine.

Some reformers place their vision of an ideal society in the future, some in the past. Cartwright was of the second type; he believed that true representative government had been realised in the "folkmeets" of Anglo-Saxon England. If he had lived today he would have followed ley lines and campaigned for organic farming. In reality, he was a prophet far ahead of his time. It is fascinating to note that he was also a prophet in the field of commemorative architecture. In 1802 he published the design of his *Heironauticon*, an immensely elaborate temple celebrating British naval achievement. Ever since the Battle of the Nile there had been talk of such a monument; the sculptor Flaxman had, for example, proposed a colossal statue of Britannia on Greenwich Hill. Cartwright's plan involved a central shrine containing innumerable statues of naval heroes, surrounded by halls and gymnasiums for ceremonial displays and dances. At the heart of the design was a figure of King Alfred as the Genius of Albion surmounted by a naval trident, in all 600 ft high. It was all somewhat like a gigantic "theme-park", except that Cartwright was quite serious about its propaganda purposes; he feared, as well as admired, revolutionary France and wanted to be sure that Britain had the might to resist her. It was, of course, far too expensive to build. Nevertheless its scale and allegorical complexity were not unlike those of the Albert Memorial sixty years later (p62). Moreover, the symbolism of the Victoria Memorial (p65) would be largely based on British sea-power.

Cartwright's own statue, rather more modest in scale, was erected by the small band of his political supporters. Its sculptor, George Clarke, was a pupil of Chantrey who had set up in Birmingham, the scene of Cartwright's trial, and later moved to London. He went bankrupt in 1832, so it is a pity that he did not do better out of this particular commission; £2,000 was well below par for a outdoor bronze statue at this time. One of Cartwright's obituaries described his face as "bearing the marks of deep thought" and this is clearly the image Clarke was trying to convey. The statue has been described as looking like Houdon's Voltaire, without the smile. It has also been called "a small shoemaker seated on a tomb, making reflection on the vanity of human wishes".

George Canning

Canning was a nervous, fiery politician largely defeated by his own ambitions; a brilliant, if theatrical orator, after Fox the greatest of his age; a clever handler of public opinion and of the press; and an able and quick-minded administrator. During his second period as Foreign Secretary he claimed to have "called the New World into existence to redress the balance of the Old" by recognising the independence from Spain of the new South American republics. However, it is more likely that the real motive behind his political strategy was to counter the growing influence of the United States.

Canning died having been Prime Minister for only four months. In London subscriptions of £9,500 were quickly raised for his statue. It seems that the Memorial Committee wanted Sir Francis Chantrey (p52) as their sculptor; however, they were too embarrassed to admit that he had refused their request to submit plans. Chantrey intensely disliked having his work judged by those who knew little of art and for that reason always refused to enter public competitions. However, he managed to get the commission for another Canning statue on his own terms. As he wrote to a friend, "I have refused the London monument and accepted the one for Liverpool; many honourable men have daubed their fingers with the London job; mine, thank God, are clean, for I have not touched it."

Sir Richard Westmacott (p150) was their second choice and was presumably more obliging. He was also more fearful. The deceased politician had been no friend of parliamentary reform and so, remembering the crowd that had tried to pull down Chantrey's statue of Pitt in Hanover Square (p173), Westmacott delayed the erection of his Canning for as long as possible. Controversy over the First Reform Bill raged throughout 1831 and the first part of 1832. He waited until five weeks after the Bill had successfully passed its second reading in the Commons and then went ahead. Four days later, however, the Lords threw out the Bill and passions rose again. But his statue was greeted with ridicule rather than with violence, at least in certain quarters. As the *Observer* commented,

"The statue of Canning, erected in Palace Yard, continues to excite the surprise and regret of all who look upon it. Nothing so vile in taste, or so defective in execution, has outraged public opinion for some years, and we apprehend that it must eventually be consigned to the furnace. The only pretence for placing it in such a position was, that the figure should be made to look towards the House of Commons; but the artist has, with most perverse ingenuity, turned his back to the house, and at the same time attempted to realise our conceptions of the light and fragile figure of the orator by giving him the paunch of a Falstaff and the muscles of a Hercules. The colour – a pea-green – has a very curious effect. The wags of the neightbourhood have already established their pleasantry in nmaing the erection the Green Man and Still."

Westmacott had obviously given the bronze an artificial patina (long since gone). The figure stood inside a railed enclosure surrounded by trees and shrubs, and was so pale in colour that its outline was almost lost among the leaves – a Green Man indeed! Nevertheless, despite the *Observer's* comments, *and* despite the burning down of the old Houses of Parliament around it two years later, the statue has survived and seems rather a dignified work, worthy of admiration. It stands now on the opposite side of Parliament Square next to that of Abraham Lincoln (p228), another champion of the New World.

George Canning. Born 1770, London, son of impoverished barrister. Father died, 1771; mother became actress. Brought up in cheap theatrical lodgings, then sent by uncle to Eton and Oxford. Offered leadership of English Jacobins but turned Tory after French Revolution, 1791. Became M.P., 1794; follower and friend of Pitt. Foreign Secretary, 1807-9; master-minded seizure and neutralisation of Danish and Portuguese fleets, so preventing Napoleon from gaining control of them. Wanted to supply more troops for Peninsular War and quarrelled with Lord Castlereagh, Secretary for War; fought duel (both were slightly wounded) and resigned. Offered Foreign Secretaryship but refused to serve in same administration as Castlereagh; hoped for Premiership, 1812. Foreign Secretary after suicide of Castlereagh, 1822-7; claimed to have countered French influence over Spain by recognising independence of Mexico, Colombia, Argentina and Brazil. Prime Minister, 1827. Died 1827.

Statue by Richard Westmacott. Bronze, 11ft 8ins, on 14ft 6ins pedestal. Erected May 2nd, 1832, at the west end of New Palace Yard, near the entrance to the House of Commons. It was moved to its present position in the north-west corner of Parliament Square (formerly known as the Canning enclosure) in 1867, because of fears that it would fall through into the Underground tunnel about to be dug beneath it. Cost £7,000.

Left. Canning's burly, be-toga'd statue pushes idealisation to its limits. Compare its build with this rather more probable likeness, the portrait by Sir Thomas Lawrence now in the National Gallery.

William Huskisson

Today Huskisson is an obscure figure, best known for having been the world's first ever victim of a public railway accident. At the time, however, his death was felt as a genuine national tragedy. He had been the country's foremost financial genius, the inheritor of the mantle of Pitt. Like Pitt, he had worked to cut back the mass of taxes and duties which had once again proliferated during the Napoleonic Wars, so freeing the progress of the Industrial Revolution. Huskisson was M.P. for the thriving port and commercial centre of Liverpool and his constituents, especially, thought well of him.

The manner of his death makes him a sacrifice to the very industrialisation he worked to promote. However, the more immediate cause of his downfall was the Duke of Wellington (p242ff), whose quasi-hypnotic hold over the populace of England he intensely disliked. They clashed over the Corn Laws, an issue that was to play an increasingly crucial role in the politics of this period. During the War large duties had been imposed on grain imported from abroad, so keeping the price of bread artificially high and increasing the hardships of the poor. Huskisson wanted to curb these duties, while Wellington (though he was later to change his views) represented the interests of the English landowning and corn producing class. In 1828 Wellington became Prime Minister. A few months later Huskisson offered his resignation on an electoral issue; he had not expected Wellington to accept it, but he misjudged him.

Two years later both men were attending the ceremonial opening of the Liverpool to Manchester railway. Two convoys of trains set out from Huskisson's constituency on parallel tracks. A halt was made on a narrow embankment while the engines went to take on water. Against the orders of the railway company, Huskisson got out to pay his respects to his old political foe. As he was standing beneath the Duke's carriage, Stephenson's Rocket (see p158) came back up the parallel line at great speed. Huskisson could not get off the embankment and, in trying to clamber up to safety, he stumbled and fell into the path of the train. He died a few hours later.

After the tragedy, a Liverpool Memorial Committee was formed and a statue commissioned for the city's cemetery. The sculptor was John Gibson, a Welshman brought up in Liverpool, who had made a considerable reputation for himself in Rome. An idealistic, unworldly man, he was a passionate believer in the dignity of classical forms and he set about sculpting Huskisson in a toga with arm and shoulder bare. Reports of this nudity alarmed the Committee and Mrs Huskisson went out to Rome to investigate. However, when the widow saw this new image of her husband, she fell in love with him all over again. She found a new interest in life in becoming Gibson's champion, organising his visits to England and taking him to tea with Queen Victoria.

Huskisson was a stooping, ungainly man, shy, accident prone, quietly humorous and a poor public speaker. Of this statue (Gibson's second and even more idealised portrait) Sir Robert Peel remarked, "It is very like Huskisson, but you have given a grandeur of look to the figure which did not belong to him." To this Gibson replied, "I fancy that a hundred and fifty years hence people will not complain of that." Unfortunately he was wrong. Osbert Sitwell dubbed the statue "boredom rising from the bath" and nowadays, despite an undoubted nobility, we would probably rather have had the man himself in all his awkwardness.

William Huskisson. Born 1770, Birch Morton Court, Warwickshire, son of landowner. Became M.P., 1796. Secretary to the Treasury; did important backroom work on reform of currency, 1807-8. Became M.P. for Liverpool, 1823. President of the Board of Trade, 1822-7; re-organised taxation system, reducing duties on raw materials such as cotton, wool and glass; prepared Bill to reduce import duties on corn. Colonial Secretary and Leader of House, 1827-8. Resignation unexpectedly accepted by Duke of Wellington, 1828. Despite poor health, attended opening of Liverpool to Manchester railway, 1830; killed by train.

Statue by John Gibson. Marble, 8ft. Pimlico Gardens. It was originally commissioned by Mrs Huskisson for Liverpool Customs House but the site was found to be too dark and cramped and so she donated it to Lloyd's of London. Lloyd's had had no particular love of Huskisson's policies but they accepted it for the sake of the sculptor. It was unveiled on February 7th, 1848, and stood in the upstairs hallway of their offices at the Royal Exchange. In 1915 Lloyd's gave it to the London County Council, who erected it in its present position.

Lord George Bentinck

William George Bentinck. Born 1802, fourth son of Duke of Portland. Entered army, 1819. Private secretary to his uncle, George Canning (p178), 1822-5. Became M.P., 1826. Won key High Court action which established legality of betting, 1843. Took up active politics in support of Corn Laws; became leader of Protectionist party, 1845. Failed to prevent repeal of Corn Laws, but acted to bring down government of Sir Robert Peel (p184) over law and order in Ireland, 1846. Proposed programme of Irish railway building; opposed abolition of preferential duties on colonial sugar, 1847. Died 1848.

Statue by Thomas Campbell. Bronze, 12ft on pedestal of polished red granite. Cavendish Square. Erected November 4th, 1851, and paid for by his political supporters who were, necessarily, far richer than those of his arch opponent, Richard Cobden (facing page). The Duke of Cumberland (p346) was then occupying the centre of the Square, so Lord George was placed at the southern end, facing down Hollies Street.

William George Frederick Cavendish Bentinck, for so his statue is inscribed, was the epitome of the English gentleman at play. For all but the last three years of his life, he was a part-time soldier and politician and a full-time sportsman; he used to appear in Parliament with his hunting dress on underneath his overcoat. "I don't know much," he said, "but I can judge of men and horses." He owned over forty racehorses and in 1840 his mare Crucifix won the Oaks, the One Thousand and the Two Thousand Guineas. He was a leading member of the Jockey Club and did a great deal to improve the efficiency and honest conduct of racing.

Why then is he commemorated in London and not at Newmarket? The restrictions on imported corn (see p180) – the so-called Corn Laws – were *the* key issue in the politics of the period. Bentinck, unlike Huskisson, favoured the barriers which kept prices high and protected home producers. When in 1845 Prime Minister Peel (p184) changed his mind over their removal, Bentinck felt it his duty to fight what he saw as the betrayal of his country and his class. He laboriously studied the details of the issue and, backed by Benjamin Disraeli (p194), became the leader of the Protectionist party in the House of Commons. He also sold his racehorses. It was, however, all in vain; the Corn Laws were repealed. In 1848 his former colt Surplice won the Derby. "All my life I have been trying for this," said Lord George bitterly, "and for what have I sacrificed it?" He had, nevertheless, become a national figure and when he died later that year the ships in all the ports flew their flags at half-mast.

Richard Cobden

Cobden was the moving spirit behind the anti-Corn Law campaign which shortened Bentinck's life with overwork (facing page) and split the government of Peel (p184). Cobden was an upright, generous-spirited man, respected even by his opponents, who stirred the nation's conscience over the hunger of the poor. He was also an extremely efficient campaigner. Making good use of the newly established Penny Post (p94) and of the railways (pp158-60), his Corn Law League sent out pamphlets to every elector in the land. One could even say that it was Britain's first properly organised political party, the Whigs and the Tories being more like loose coalitions of gentlemen. Cobden went on working for free trade all his life. The Anglo-French commercial treaty, which was his own idea and which he negotiated in Paris throughout the freezing winter of 1859-60, played a key role in keeping the two countries at peace. He was an internationalist, admired even more abroad than at home as an apostle of liberty.

He was also, it seems, especially admired in Camden Town, where the erection of his statue was organised by a small, private group of supporters – there is no other connection between him and the borough. Fund raising events included a last minute concert held in the Agricultural Hall, Islington, attended by 15,000 people at 6d. a head. To help the sculptors, Cobden's widow Catherine came up from the country to their premises on the Euston Road in order to demonstrate her husband's favourite stance while speaking. However, the moderate quality of the figure – necessarily, the cheapest post eighteenth century statue in London – has left it little more than an interesting relic.

Richard Cobden. Born 1804, son of poor Sussex farmer. Worked in uncle's London goods warehouse, 1819-25. Set up own textile business in Manchester and became successful calico manufacturer; educated himself by reading and foreign travel, and supported public causes, e.g. workers' education and Penny Post, 1828-38. Became M.P. for Stockport, 1841. Founded Corn Law League and led successful campaign for repeal of duties, 1838-46. Received as hero in Italy, Russia and Spain, 1847. Lost his money through unwise speculation in the Illinois Railway Company (how would he have managed the nation's finances? asked Palmerston) and his seat in Parliament through opposing wars with Russia and China, 1856-8. Regained seat but refused office, 1859. Negotiated Cobden-Chevalier trade treaty with France, 1859-60. Died 1865.

Statue by W.J. and T.Wills. Marble, 8ft, on 15 ft pedestal of Portland stone. South end of Camden High Street. Unveiled June 27th, 1868, by H.Lewis and T.Chambers, M.P.'s for Marylebone. Cost £320. The sheaves on the sides of the pedestal are an allusion to the Corn Laws. A later inscription records that the Emperor Napoleon III was the "principal contributor," though there seems to be no contemporary evidence for this. The statue stood originally on a 200ft wide site made free by the removal of the old toll gate but is now hemmed in on all sides by traffic barriers and street lighting.

Sir Robert Peel

Sir Robert Peel. Born 1788, son of M.P. and Lancashire cotton magnate. Won double first at Oxford, 1808. Became M.P., 1809. Chief Secretary for Ireland, 1812-18; founded Irish police. Home Secretary, 1822-7; passed numerous acts reforming the Criminal Law. With Wellington, changed sides over the granting of greater legal rights to Catholics in order to avoid chaos and violence in Ireland, 1828. Home Secretary, 1829-30; founded Metropolitan Police by integrating various scattered London watches into one uniformed body. Rebuilt Tory Party after its defeat over First Reform Bill, 1833-40. Briefly Prime Minister at behest of William IV, 1834-5. Prime Minister of full Conservative administration, 1841-6; re-introduced income tax and reduced indirect taxation, so greatly stimulating national prosperity; reformed banking system. Continued to support import duties on corn (see p180) but, faced with sufferings of Irish potato famine, changed policy; carried through repeal of Corn Laws, 1846, but split party and ended premiership. Died 1850, after riding accident.

Right. Statue by William Behnes. Bronze, 11ft. Originally erected May, 1855 at the west end of Cheapside, on the present site of St Paul's Underground station. Cost £7,000. Owing to the build-up of traffic, removed 1939 to the Bank of England but never erected, as planned, in a recess in the outer wall. Re-erected 1951 in Postman's Park, Aldersgate Street. Transferred 1971 to Hendon Police Training School, where it was unveiled by Her Majesty the Queen on May 31st, 1974. The estate of which the Training School is a part is private, so the statue is now out of the public domain.

The untimely death of the charismatic Sir Robert Peel was a great shock to the nation; there had seemed no doubt that he would one day return to power. His heroism in sacrificing his career for a principle – that of cheaper bread in a time of famine – was widely admired and there was even a memorial fund to which thousands of working men contributed their pence.

Peel was the first significant British Prime Minister to come from the middle classes. His political base was in the North, and Leeds, Liverpool, Manchester, Salford, Bury, Bolton, Huddersfield and Preston all undertook statues, so making him the most commemorated politician in English history. What the solid burgher members of the various memorial committees wanted was the man himself, hence the many tall, commanding, frock-coated figures.

The sculptor William Behnes succeeded in winning the custom of Leeds, Bradford and the City of London. Since Peel had done so much for banking and, indeed, for the general prosperity of the country, the City committee wanted their statue erected near the Royal Exchange (despite the comment that its proximity to the equestrian statue of Wellington (p245) would make it look like the policeman walking in front of the City Marshal). However, they fell foul of the relevant administrative body, the City Commissioners of Sewers, who insisted on the site at the St. Paul's end of Cheapside.

With Peel as with Wellington, London divided east and west. The story of the Westminster commemoration was long and complex (see right); its final result was the statue in Parliament Square.

Right. Statue by Matthew Noble. Bronze, 8ft 6ins on 9ft pedestal. Parliament Square. Erected January 1877.

The appearance of the statue 27 years after Peel's death requires some explanation. The London Peel Testimonial Committee, under the chairmanship of the Prime Minister, Lord Aberdeen, had originally approached Baron Marochetti (p56). He produced a statue even larger than that in the City, 12ft tall with a proposed pedestal of 17ft. It was planned to erect it in New Palace Yard next to the considerably less elevated statue of Canning (p178) but Sir William Molesworth, the First Commissioner of Works, refused permission; he judged the juxtaposition invidious and "in consequence of their antagonistic political feelings, in bad taste." In fact the two men had been on perfectly good terms but it seems that some of Lord George Bentinck's slurs had stuck. At the height of his Protectionist campaign (p167) he had accused Peel of hounding Canning to his death; the normally restrained Peel had been so incensed that he had had to be prevented from challenging Bentinck to a duel.

Later a more suitable position in the Yard was found but the statue was still considered too large. Marochetti, at his own expense, produced another only 8ft tall. After two quiet, unnoticed years this was moved to an awkwardly sloping site just inside the new ornamental railings. Here it attracted the hostility of Lord Elcho, who in 1868 moved a special motion against it in Parliament. It was, he said, rough and ungainly and looked like a policeman (the inevitable jibe!) directing the members' cabs. By 182 votes to 71 the House voted for its removal! It was melted down and the metal was handed over to Matthew Noble (p191); with it he made the last public statue of his long career. It took its place alongside his Lord Derby (p190) and proved entirely acceptable, though by the year of its erection the style of dress already looked somewhat old-fashioned.

Sidney Herbert

Sidney Herbert is best known for having arranged for Florence Nightingale (p165) and her nurses to go out and minister to the thousands of British soldiers who lay ill and dying in the Crimea. He was her personal friend and political spokesman, a gentle, industrious man who did a great deal to improve army education, health and sanitation. He was often spoken of as a future Prime Minister and might well have attained that office had he not died of kidney disease at the early age of 51. (For this Miss Nightingale, who drove him unmercifully, must be held partly responsible.) He was thus commemorated more in anticipation of achievement – and for a certain indefinable inner grace which was recognised by everyone who knew him.

His rather beautiful statue was the product of like minds. It was the work of the conscientious John Foley, who died while sculpting the central figure of Albert for the Albert Memorial (pp62-3). The natures of the artist and his subject seem to have been remarkably similar. S.C. Hall, the editor of the *Art Journal*, described Foley as "pensive almost to melancholy…He was not robust, either in body or in mind; all his sentiments and sensations were graceful: so in truth were his manners. His leisure was consumed by thought." The result was an outdoor statue of exceptional expressiveness, especially for its times.

Sidney Herbert, 1st baron Herbert of Lea. Born 1810, second son of the Earl of Pembroke; his mother was a Russian countess. Became M.P., 1832. Secretary to the Admiralty, 1841-5; reformed Greenwich Naval School. Secretary at War, 1845-6 and 1852-5; was partly responsible for conduct of Crimean War and organised sending out of nurses under Florence Nightingale. Appointed to Committee for investigating Crimean disasters, 1855-9; continued to work for army reform and drafted reports on sanitation and medical care. Secretary for War; built up Volunteer Force, 1859-61. Died 1861.

Statue by John Foley. Bronze. Waterloo Place. Unveiled June 1st, 1867, by W.E.Gladstone, in front of old War Office in Pall Mall. Moved to new War Office in Whitehall in 1906 and in 1915 to present position in front of the Crimea Memorial, balancing the newly erected statue of Florence Nightingale (pp164-5). The plaque on the front of the pedestal shows Florence Nightingale instructing her nurses.

Left. An *Art Journal* portrait of the sculptor John Foley as a young man.

Lord Holland

With Lord Holland we move from the controversies over the Corn Laws back to the aristocratic Left, whom we last saw gathered around Fox's statue in Bloomsbury Square (p174). Indeed a full-sized, bronzed plaster cast of that statue stood for many years by the entrance to the breakfast room at Holland House, much to the alarm of unprepared visitors. Holland was Fox's nephew and his political disciple in all things. He was pro-French, his many travels abroad having made him an internationalist, and he actively supported the abolition of slavery.

In his time Holland House was a magnet for the progressive and the unconventional – Lord Byron came there and complained of the cold – yet William IV was also among the guests. Husband and wife complemented each other well: he agreeable and urbane, full of anecdote and reminiscence, she strikingly beautiful, energetic and dominating. Some found her influence excessive. In 1827-8, when some members of the Whig party were brought into office, Lord Holland wished very much to be Foreign Secretary but, as Lord John Russell regretfully explained, no one in the Cabinet would work with a man whose wife opened all his letters. So during the 1830's he more or less ran an alternative British foreign policy from Holland House; while Palmerston (p192) worked from expediency, he supported liberal regimes on principle.

G.F. Watts lived for a number of years in the rambling farm house in the grounds of Holland House, having been befriended while in Rome by Henry Edward, the 4th Baron Holland. He is better known as one of the finest of Victorian painters but he was always interested in sculpture. Modelling in wet clay gave him rheumatism and he eventually learned the technique of using "gesso grosso", tow mixed with size and plaster, which dries quickly and can easily be worked when dry. His statue of Lord Holland was an early piece modelled in clay, so it no doubt cost him some pains.

Henry Richard Fox, 3rd Baron Holland. Born 1773, Winterslow House, Wiltshire, son of 2nd Baron. Brought up by his maternal grandmother and by his uncle, Charles James Fox. Travelled abroad and formed relationship with Elisabeth Vassall, then Lady Gregory Webster, who bore him a son, 1791-7; they subsequently married. Took seat in House of Lords, 1798; followed policies of his uncle and became Whig leader in the Lords. Lord Privy Seal in Ministry of All The Talents, 1806-7. Chancellor of the Duchy of Lancaster, 1830-4 & 1835-40. Died 1840.

Statue by G.F. Watts, assisted in the casting by Joseph Boehm. Bronze. North side of Holland Park. Erected c. November 1871 in Watts' garden at Little Holland House and later moved to the southern end of the Park. Moved to its present position 1926. Cost £2,600, paid out of surplus funds from Holland's memorial in Westminster Abbey.

Towards the end of his life Lord Holland suffered much from gout, hence the stick held by the statue.

Left. G.F. Watts at work on the gesso grosso horse and rider which was his greatest work of sculpture. The photograph was taken around 1895 in the garden of New Little Holland House, now 6 Melbury Road. The statue was finally cast in bronze and erected in Cape Town in 1903 as a memorial to Cecil Rhodes. Watts disliked the cast and set to work again, so contracting the chill from which he died. The second version was cast and erected in Kensington Gardens with the title of Physical Energy (see map, chapter 11).

LORD
HOLLAND

1799 — DERBY — 1869

Lord Derby

Edward George Geoffrey Smith Stanley, 14th Earl of Derby. Born 1799, Knowsley, near Liverpool, son of 13th Earl. Became Whig M.P., 1820. Secretary for Ireland; opposed independence and brought in Irish Education Act, 1830-3. As Colonial Secretary, settled arrangements for abolition of slavery in colonies; resigned over State appropriation of Irish church revenues and formed third party known as the Dilly, 1833-4. Joined Tories under Peel, 1837. Colonial Secretary, 1841-4; made peace with China. Went to House of Lords, 1844. Split with Peel over Corn Laws (see pp180-4) and became Tory Protectionist leader in Lords, 1845-6. Steward of Jockey Club, 1848. Elected Chancellor of Oxford University, 1852. Prime Minister of minority ministry, 1852. Prime Minister; introduced unsuccessful parliamentary reform bill, 1858-9. Published translation of Illiad, 1864. Became Chairman of Central Committee for the relief of Midlands workers unemployed through cotton shortage during American Civil War, 1865. Prime Minister; passed Second Reform Bill, giving vote to all male borough ratepayers, 1866-8. Died 1869.

Statue by Matthew Noble. Bronze, 8ft 2ins on 9ft pink granite pedestal. Parliament Square. Unveiled July 11th, 1874, by Prime Minister Benjamin Disraeli (p194).

Below. An informal photograph of the sculptor, Matthew Noble.

Edward Stanley, Earl of Derby, was one of the mainstays of English politics for nearly forty years. He was three times Prime Minister; on two other occasions the Queen asked him to form a government, but he refused. His first administration was so inexperienced that it became known as the "who-who" ministry, since, as the names of the new office holders were read out in the Lords, the aged and near-deaf Duke of Wellington had called out, "Who? Who?" Derby's brief periods of power, nevertheless, did more to extend the parliamentary franchise than decades of Whig rule. With his abilities, background and basic lack of ambition, he was the ideal man to lead the Right and yet yield to the pressures for change when the clear will of the country demanded it. He was a politician out of a sense of obligation; he would have been more than happy looking after the vast family estates near Liverpool and pursuing his classical studies. He was England's Colonial Secretary, yet imperialism had no appeal for him; he preferred to direct his warlike instincts at the rabbits on those estates, naming them after his political opponents as he banged away at them.

Derby was renowned as an orator, his fine, cutting style earning him the title of "the Prince Rupert of Debate." He always cared deeply about Ireland. In the 1830's he introduced state education for Catholic and Protestant alike, more than thirty years before the same thing was done in England, and his final speech in the Lords opposed, unsuccessfully, the disestablishment of the Irish Anglican church. Old, infirm, stricken with gout, his voice rang out for the last time and then he quit the red-lined chamber looking, as a contemporary poet observed, like some strong, pathetic, wounded prophet passing from the littleness of men.

Noble was a word easily applied to Lord Derby, and Noble (as someone pointed out at the unveiling) was also the name of the sculptor of his statue in Parliament Square. The Yorkshireman Matthew Noble was one of the most prolific statue makers of the Victorian Age. The photograph opposite shows a man slight of build, sharply and sensitively featured. His constitution was never strong. His friends were always surprised that he was able to produce the amount of work he did: 42 full-length statues, some of them in immensely complex settings, 50 busts and 27 church monuments are listed in Gunnis' *Dictionary of British Sculptors*. (Of course, once he became established he was able to employ a number of assistants in his studio.) His renderings of the deities of his Age, Albert and Victoria, were generalised and insipid; in fact the Queen disliked his work and expressed the intention of getting her 17 year old daughter Louise (p65) to alter his statue of her for Bombay. He was at his best with less formal, more vigorous subjects. His statue of the Arctic explorer Sir John Franklin in Waterloo Place (p299) is particularly good, as is the decorative work around the pedestal of Sir James Outram's (p262).

The plaques around Lord Derby's pedestal (which are in fact not by Matthew Noble but by Horace Montford) are also interesting. The plaque on the east side of the pedestal, seen here, shows Derby addressing the Commons in 1833 on the subject of slavery, so this is the debating chamber of the old building which was destroyed by fire shortly afterwards. The others show him accepting the Chancellorship of Oxford University (his Latin speech was the envy of all present), chairing the Manchester Famine Relief Committee in 1865, and chairing the Cabinet Council in 1867, when they must have been discussing the Second Reform Bill.

Lord Palmerston

Wishing to be complementary, a French diplomat once said to Palmerston, "If I had not been a Frenchman, I would wish to be an Englishman." "If I had not been an Englishman," the statesman replied, "I would wish to be an Englishman." Palmerston represented a certain side of the national character, self-confident, supremacist. The intellectuals distrusted him, the idealists thought his foreign policy little short of criminal, but the people loved his vitality and the way he made the country respected. Behind the arrogant exterior, however, lay a considerable understanding of the darker, aggressive side of human nature. Palmerston saw man, however governed, as a fighting, quarrelling animal and he was expert at manipulating those instincts in the interests of his country. He knew exactly how to pursue hostilities to the brink without ever stepping over the edge into all-out war. In fact England remained at peace throughout his long period as Foreign Secretary. The Crimean War occurred when, and perhaps because, he was no longer in charge of foreign affairs. When he became Prime Minister he finished off the war and negotiated a very successful treaty.

Yet his career and abilities developed remarkably slowly. There were, according to his biographer Jasper Ridley, three Lord Palmerstons. The first was the charming and somewhat ineffectual man-about-town who was happy to remain Secretary at War for nineteen years and was widely known as "Lord Cupid". Only after the death of Canning (p178) did there emerge "Lord Pumicestone", who kept distinguished ambassadors waiting for hours and dispatched gunboats to the corners of the globe. Finally he mellowed and became "Good Old Pam", Prime Minister and the wise and jovial father-figure of the nation. The transformations were physical too, from soft to hard to a well weathered roundness, and presented the sculptors of his memorial statues with a problem: which of these different Palmerstons would they portray?

Robert Jackson, who carved the national memorial in Westminster Abbey, chose the Grand Old Man and made a passable job of him. Thomas Woolner (p122) seems to have settled for a kind of compromise between all three. He was one of the better Victorian portrait sculptors and his statue of J.S. Mill in the Embankment Gardens (p123) is almost too good a likeness. However, Palmerston gave him a lot of trouble. He got the job without a competition, through William Cowper, the First Commissioner of Works, and was certainly excited about the prospect of having a statue in Parliament Square. "Any sculptor," he wrote to Mrs Tennyson, "would have crawled 100 miles on his hands and knees to have got this commission." He had two attempts at it. A model of the first figure was put up on trial in 1869 but was rejected as too small and, it seems, too withdrawn and dull in expression. The second, by contrast, was jaunty and athletic but was also not well received. It was true, said the *Art Journal*, that Palmerston had often described himself as the "judicious bottle-holder" to the squabbling nations of the world (the bottle-holder was the man who stood by at a prize-fight holding the combatants' coats – just as the statue seems to do – and who revived them with stimulants when they were knocked down). However, in this case the athleticism had been overdone. And if one wants to see a representation of Palmerston at the height of his powers, then the portrait by John Partridge in the National Gallery collection, rapier-slim, hawk-eyed and hawk-nosed, presents a more satisfying image.

Henry Temple, 3rd Viscount Palmerston. Born 1784, at Broadlands, Hampshire, son of politician and socialite 2nd Viscount. Became M.P., 1806. Offered Chancellorship of the Exchequer by Canning but refused it, 1809. Secretary at War, mainly concerned with army finance, 1809-28. Foreign Secretary, 1830-4, 1835-41 & 1846-51; ensured independence of Belgium, successfully intervened in British interest in Portugal, Spain, Turkey and Egypt, and worked for abolition of slavery and slave trade. Blockaded Greek ports over arrest of British subject (the Don Pacifico affair); Civis Romanus Sum speech on freedom of British citizens abroad brought pinnacle of popularity, 1850. Antagonised Queen Victoria by not informing her of his actions, and was dismissed, 1851. Home Secretary, 1853-5; introduced Lord Shaftesbury's Factory Acts (p96). Prime Minister, 1855-8 & 1859-65; pursued Crimean War to conclusion, improved relations with Queen Victoria and opposed parliamentary reform. Died 1865.

Statue by Thomas Woolner. Bronze, 8ft 3ins on 8ft granite pedestal. Parliament Square. Unveiled without ceremony February 2nd, 1876.

Benjamin Disraeli

Benjamin Disraeli (later Lord Beaconsfield). Born 1804, London, son of Jewish free-thinker. Articled to solicitor but preferred journalism and novel writing. Joined Tory party, 1834; wrote Vindication of the British Constitution. *Became M.P., 1837, but failed to win office under Peel. Published novels* Conningsby *and* Sybil, *satirising current Tories, 1844-5. Joined forces with Bentinck (p182) over Corn Laws, 1845-7. Became Tory leader in the Commons, 1852. Chancellor of the Exchequer, 1852, 1858 & 1866-8. Prime Minister, 1867-8 & 1874-80. Introduced Second Reform Bill, 1867. Purchased major shareholding in Suez Canal, 1875. Created Lord Beaconsfield and moved to House of Lords, 1876. Gained "Peace with Honour" at Congress of Berlin, 1878. Died 1881.*

Statue by Mario Rossi (or Razzi). Bronze. Parliament Square. Unveiled April 19th, 1883, by Sir Stafford Northcote (see following page). Disraeli wears peer's robes over diplomatic dress. Cost 3,000 guineas.

Right. A *Punch* cartoon satirising Disraeli early in his political career, when he was M.P. for Shrewsbury. The hats are symbolic of a Jewish old-clothes pedlar.

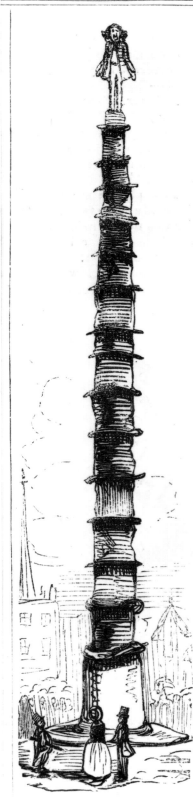

Disraeli was the unlikeliest man to rule England. He even looked like a foreigner, this Jewish writer's son with his long, dark curls and sallow complexion. His overriding ambition, from boyhood on, was political power. In 1832 he stood for Parliament as a radical but got only nine votes. Realising that this was a path without a future, he applied his powerful imagination to divining the true nature of England's political soul. It lay, he decided, with "a real Throne, a generous aristocracy," and a party that would represent all classes impartially. This was his vision of the Conservative Party, which he now joined.

At first, despite his obvious abilities, he was not trusted; his manner was too outlandish and affected, his background suspect. (Hence the *Punch* cartoon of the "Shrewsbury column" opposite.) The Corn Law crisis, however, gave him his perfect opening and he exploited it ruthlessly. Lord Derby (p190) came to like and trust him. He gained the affection of Queen Victoria (p65) with his amusingly written reports of parliamentary business and his sincerely expressed sympathy after Prince Albert's death. He called her (though not to her face) his Faerie Queen and she sent him violets and primroses every spring from Osborne House. Thus did he put his philosophy of monarchy into effect, for it was he more than anyone who gave the Queen back her confidence and brought her once again into public life.

Finally, he became Prime Minister; he had, as he put it, "climbed to the top of the greasy pole." Under his watchful eye a number of excellent measures were passed regulating working conditions, housing and public health. His most conspicuous triumph was his handling of the conflict between Russia and Turkey, sparked off by atrocities committed by Turkish troops against Bulgarian peasants. England was passionately divided. Some wanted to put a military stop to Russian territorial ambitions but Disraeli bided his time. He believed, rightly, that merely by threatening war he could win peace and get a lasting settlement. This he achieved at the Congress of Berlin. Bismarck, who presided, was full of admiration for Disraeli's practical wisdom. "Der Alte Jude," he exclaimed, "das ist der Mann." The mocking playboy had become the sanest head in Europe.

His statue in Parliament Square was unveiled exactly two years after his death. G.J. Shaw Lefevre, a First Commissioner of Works with a real concern for the statues under his care, called it the best of the Square's politicians; it had exactly Disraeli's "inscrutable and slightly cynical expression, well known to all those who sat opposite to him in the House." It was true that Sir Wilfrid Lawson (p210) was the only M.P. who ever made him laugh during a debate. This impassivity was a mask which he had learned to wear but his quiet, almost condescending manner of speaking only made what he had to say more deeply impressive.

From the time of its unveiling the statue assumed the status of a shrine. To Disraeli's funeral at the country church near his home Queen Victoria had sent a wreath of the primroses which were the symbol of their friendship, with the inscription, "His Favourite Flower." As April 19th, the first anniversary of his death, approached, it was reported in the press that London's florists were running short of primroses. In fact the observation was a deliberate "plant," placed there by Sir George Birdwood, a former Indian civil servant. However, the association took root and on the day itself people of *all* political persuasions were found to be wearing primroses in their buttonholes. Another year and the custom was firmly established. For the unveiling

of the statue, thousands upon thousands of primroses were sent from all parts of the British Isles. A bunch had been gathered that dewy morning by Princess May of Teck and her sisters. Flower girls bore trays of buttonholes and a great wreath of primroses and violets spelling out "Peace with Honour," given by a leading Hong Kong businessman, lay at the departed statesman's feet.

Did the newspapermen gathered behind the pedestal see the mythic dimension of it all, unmistakable at this distance of time? A member of the outcast race triumphs over disadvantage and wins the affection of the widowed Queen, keeping throughout his long life his sprightly intelligence and quizzical humour. He makes peace and dies in Spring, to become the Spring hero, honoured with flowers like Adonis, or like Pan, rather, whom Disraeli, with his half-slumbering, Mediterranean looks and short tuft of beard under the chin, so much resembled. Gladstone, not understanding, said that the gilded lily should have been his flower, but in Parliament Square the top hats waved to see their hero ringed with the colours of the earthly resurrection.

Left. The unveiling of Disraeli's statue as recorded by the *Illustrated London News*.

Right. The scene on Primrose Day towards the end of the century. The Tory Party soon adopted the day and the emblem for its own purposes, founding the highly popular, grass-roots organisation called The Primrose League and holding annual rallies at the Albert Hall on April 19th. However, Spring celebrations continued around the statue on essentially non-party lines at least until the First World War.

Lord Lawrence

Three Viceroys of India are commemorated in the streets of London and they could not be more different from each other in character and approach: Lord Curzon (p218), who thought the Raj would last for ever, Lord Mountbatten (p294), who brought it to an end, and the blunt soldierly John Lawrence, who arrived in India at the age of 18 and rose through the ranks of the Civil Service. Hard-working, hard-riding, Lawrence was at his happiest in the field, learning to appreciate local customs and settling disputes with authority. Throughout his career, his sympathies were with the peasant farmers rather than their landlords. As controller of the newly annexed province of Jullundur, for example, he took away the power of the Sikh chieftains and reduced land taxes. When further unrest threatened, he acted promptly to prevent its spread. He ordered his district officers to issue a proclamation, which aptly illustrates the personal, down-to-earth and paternalistic style of his administration:

"I expect, and am fully confident, that you are in your villages and have kept clear of any rebellion... Consider that I have in person visited every one of your villages, and I know the position of every one of you: what is your injury, I consider mine: what is gain to you I consider my gain. The rule of the British is in favour of the agriculturist. If your lands are heavily assessed, tell me so, and I will relieve you: ... but if you excite rebellion, as I live, I will severely punish you. I have ruled this district three years by the sole agency of the pen, and if necessary I will rule it by the sword..."

This proclamation, recorded by Robert Cust, one of the district officers, was to play an important part in Lawrence's commemoration. Having issued it, Cust (presumably on Lawrence's instructions) proceeded to tour his area and confront his village headmen; he presented them with a pen and a sword and asked them to choose between them. When Sir Joseph Boehm (p265) was commissioned to provide Lawrence's statue, he based it on this story and showed him holding the alternative instruments of government, one in each hand. However, when the figure was exhibited at the Royal Academy, some of Lawrence's family were embarrassed and disputed the truth of the story. Moreover, a humorist parodied the statue's rather fierce expression with: "Who the deuce has been trying to cut pens with my sword?" Boehm therefore produced a new version and the Waterloo Place figure has what looks like a notebook in its right hand. The original statue was dispatched (free of charge) to Lahore. It is now at Lawrence's old school, Foyle College, Londonderry.

It was the Indian Mutiny which made Lawrence a national hero. It has been described as something more than a soldiers' revolt and something less than a national rebellion, and it had an immense impact on English consciousness. Though a civilian, Lawrence played a key role. He organised immediate and severe measures against the first mutineers in the Punjab and this had the effect of containing the situation. He then raised a force of seven thousand, including some Indian troops, and marched on Delhi, the home of the last descendants of the Moghul Emperors and the focus of rebellion. When the city eventually fell, he did what he could to ensure the justice of the retributions meted out and reduce their severity.

He was not an outstanding Viceroy; he was conservative and, some considered, parsimonious. During his last years in London he lived quietly, writing to the press and working for various medical charities. He had, said Lord Derby, "a certain heroic simplicity."

Sir John (later 1st Baron) Lawrence. Born 1811, Richmond, Yorkshire, son of army officer. Joined Indian Civil Service, 1829. Assistant to Political Resident in Delhi, 1831-5. District officer in surrounding countryside, 1835-46. Commissioner of Jullundur, annexed after First Sikh War, 1846-8. Chief administrator of Punjab, annexed after Second Sikh War, initially with his brother Henry; established "non-regulation" informal, de-centralised system of control, 1848-57. Indian Mutiny; acted swiftly to contain revolt and joined siege of Delhi, 1857-9. Returned to England in poor health; made national hero, 1859. Viceroy of India, 1863-9. Chairman of London Schools Board, 1870-3. Died 1879.

Statue by Joseph Boehm. Bronze, 8ft 6ins. Waterloo Place. Erected March 1882, without ceremony. Lawrence wears informal dress and holds the old-fashioned cavalry sword which he always carried with him during the Mutiny.

Sir Bartle Frere

There seems to have been extraordinarily wide agreement about Bartle Frere's charm, intelligence and breadth of vision. Though he spent his life in the Colonial Service, he saw British rule as essentially transitional and he did all he could to encourage the political development of native peoples. He also worked to establish the infrastructure of the modern state, roads, canals, water supplies and sanitation, in the territories which he administered. In 1860 Florence Nightingale (p164) informed him that Bombay had a lower death rate than London, which in turn, thanks to the work of Lord Shaftesbury's General Board of Health (p96), was the most disease-free city in Europe.

Had Frere been appointed India's Viceroy after Lord Lawrence (p198), he might have accomplished much. Instead, he was sent to South Africa with the over-idealistic aim of achieving a confederation of its peoples similar to the one just established in Canada. He found the Boers incensed at the recent annexation of Transvaal and the Zulus, under their king Cetywayo, in arms; the ancient custom whereby no Zulu might marry until he or she had killed an enemy had just been revived. Frere judged, correctly as it turned out, that the prompt use of force was the only way to defuse the situation. However, the news of an early defeat in which one thousand British soldiers had been killed turned the home Government against him and the post-war political settlement was left to the hasty and unsubtle General Wolseley (p272). Had Frere's subsequent success been acknowledged and had he been able to build up an administrative network similar to the one so long established in India, the later history of South Africa might have been very different.

Sir Bartle Frere. Born Abergevenny, son of engineer, 1815. Entered Bombay Civil Service, 1834. District officer 1835-42; reduced land taxes and gave security of tenure to peasant farmers. Political Resident of native state of Sattara, 1847-50; supported Rajah's right to appoint deathbed heir but was overruled by Governor General. Chief Commissioner for Sind, 1850-9; popular rule ensured peace during Mutiny. Lord Canning's "right-hand man" on Governor General's Council, 1859-62; supported his plan to give more political representation to Indians. Governor of Bombay Presidency, 1862-7; founded schools and universities. Returned to England as member of India Council, 1867-77. Successfully negotiated treaty with Sultan of Zanzibar to close principal East African slave market (see Livingstone, p304), 1872-3. Guided Edward, Prince of Wales, on successful tours of Egypt and India, 1875. Governor of Cape Colony and High Commissioner for Native Affairs, 1877-80; recalled after defeat of British force by Zulus at Isandhewana. Died 1884, some said of a broken heart at his recall.

Statue by Thomas Brock. Bronze, 11ft. Victoria Embankment Gardens. Cost £3,000. Frere wears Civil Service uniform with the robe and collar of the Star of India and the insignia of the Order of the Bath.

Unveiled June 5th, 1888, by Edward, Prince of Wales, who was Frere's most distinguished champion.

Left. The allegorical figure on the front of the pedestal represented "victory achieved, peace sought and the readiness to maintain honour with the sword." This was how Frere's supporters viewed his policies in South Africa.

W.E. Forster

W.E. Forster. Born 1810, Bradpole, Dorset, son of Quaker missionaries. Went into weaving business in Darlington, 1836-41. Set up successful partnership in Bradford, 1842. Distributed Quaker famine relief in Ireland, 1846 & 7. Liberal M.P. for Bradford, 1861-86. Appointed Vice-President of the Privy Council with special responsibility for Education, 1868. Brought in Endowed Schools Act, which reformed grammar school system, 1869. Brought in Elementary Education Act, which for the first time provided compulsory state education for all children, 1870. Proposed as leader of Liberal Party after resignation of Gladstone but refused to stand, 1874. Chief Secretary for Ireland, 1880-2; obliged to impose martial law and suffered attempts on life; resigned after release of Parnell. Died 1886.

Statue by Henry Pinker. Bronze, 9ft. Victoria Embankment Gardens. Unveiled August 1st, 1890, by Viscount Cranbrook, President of the Privy Council. The *Times* commended the homely cut of the clothes as extremely lifelike. At that time the London School Board, of which Sir John Lawrence (p198) was the first Chairman, had its offices immediately behind the statue.

The man who brought in state education for all seemed an archetypally blunt Yorkshireman, though he also got his directness of speech from his Quaker parents. He was a serious, precocious child, discussing politics even before he had begun to play with other children. On his father's insistence, he went into commerce and became a prosperous mill owner; the understanding of the labouring class which this experience brought him stood him in good stead in his later political career. He eventually settled in Wharfedale and built a mill close to his own house. He was always a strong believer in the right of every person to an education and there he set up a special school for the part-time workers at his mill.

In Parliament he joined the radical wing of the Liberal party led by Richard Cobden (p183). He was the workers' champion, though in an essentially moderate way. When the Chartists came to Bradford in 1848 agitating, sometimes violently, for social change, he sympathised with their aims but not their methods. He had the physical courage to say so and once harangued a meeting of seven thousand for several hours from the top of a cart on the advantages of peaceful change.

Forster's chance for immortality came when Gladstone (p204) appointed him a Privy Councillor. The question of a national system of education was in the air but Gladstone was too preoccupied with Ireland to give it his own attention. He therefore allowed Forster a free hand to bring in a nationwide scheme as he saw fit. He had to reconcile a number of conflicting claims. He proposed local School Boards to cater for the individual needs of different areas and a national Inspectorate to ensure overall standards. Every child between five and thirteen was guaranteed a place and the cost was shared equally between the State, the local ratepayers and those parents who could afford it. Existing Church schools were allowed to continue but, in response to strong demands from Non-conformist groups, it was agreed that religious teaching had to be interdenominational if the school was receiving money from outside. Other pressure groups, like the Birmingham Education League, wanted a completely secular system but Forster disagreed; it would be absurd, he said, if the Bible were the only book not allowed to be taught in English schools.

His Bill passed in a very short time and within his lifetime the number of children attending school in the United Kingdom rose from just over a million to three and a half million. The remainder of his political life was not so happy; he bore the sorrows of Ireland and was censured by his constituents for condemning his Party's failure to rescue General Gordon (p268). However, so far as education was concerned, it was a case of the right man at the right time. He had the good sense and the experience required and he was convinced (as some were not) of the importance of what he was doing. One can imagine him making the peroration to his speech introducing the Education Bill, standing, as his statue does, with one arm behind his back and speaking out in his direct and homely way.

"Let each of us think of our homes, of the villages in which we live, of the towns in which it is our lot to be busy: and do we not know child after child – boys or girls – growing up to probable crime, to still more probable misery, because badly taught or utterly untaught? Dare we, then, take on ourselves the responsibility of allowing this influence and this weakness to continue one year longer than we can help?"

William Gladstone

Gladstone often wondered whether he should have been a clergyman rather than a politician. The causes which he took up were many and varied – Home Rule and the relations between state and religion in Ireland, human rights in Italy, Bulgaria and China, and the rescue of London's prostitutes, to name but a few. Indeed it was the very unpredictability of his campaigns which his opponents found so alarming. Partly because he changed his opinions so often during his long career, a picture has grown up of him as a sanctimonious hypocrite; however, nothing could be further from the truth. He was a man of intense energy and conviction who became, when all is said and done, the prophetic conscience of his age.

Gladstone has two outdoor statues in London. The first was erected in Bow and marked his fiftieth year as a Member of Parliament. It was the gift of Mr Theodore Bryant, a prominent Liberal and one of the Bryants of Bryant and May the matchmakers, whose factory until recently stood in the neighbourhood. This links the statue to two interesting events. Gladstone was an extremely skilful Chancellor of the Exchequer, raising or lowering income tax by a penny and taxing and untaxing tea or spirits to general approval. But in 1871, when Gladstone had become Prime Minister, his new Chancellor, Robert Lowe, proposed a tax of a halfpenny a hundred on matches. This was an appreciable sum and, fearing loss of trade, Bryant and May organised a protest march of hundreds of their employees to Westminster. Soon afterwards the proposed tax was dropped and in celebration a Gothic-style drinking fountain bearing a figure representing Justice was erected by public subscription outside Bow Railway Station. (It was destroyed in 1953 by Council vandalism.) In 1880 Gladstone took on the Exchequer once again. Did the Bryants and the Mays confer and decide that a gentle, statuary reminder of their existence would help to keep matches tax-free?

By the time of his death, Gladstone was indisputably the Grand Old Man of English politics and he was widely commemorated. The commission for the London memorial went to Hamo Thornycroft.

W.E.Gladstone. Born 1809, Liverpool, son of wealthy merchant. Became Tory M.P., 1832. Wrote book advocating Church of England State theocracy. 1838. Denounced First Opium War in China, 1840. Vice-President and later President of Board of Trade, 1841-5; helped Peel (p184) with financial reforms. Condemned persecution of political prisoners in Naples, 1850. Chancellor of Exchequer, 1852-5; extended death duties. Joined Liberals and became Chancellor of Exchequer under Palmerston (p192), 1859-65; won House of Commons' right to control taxes against objections of House of Lords. 1859-65. Prime Minister; defeated over Irish Universities Bill, 1868-74. Resigned from politics but returned over atrocities committed by Turkish soldiers against Bulgarian peasants; "whistle-stop" campaign for seat of Midlothian began new tradition of populist oratory, 1875-9. Prime Minister and Chancellor of the Exchequer, 1880-6; brought in Third Reform Bill which raised electorate from three to five million; attempted to bring in Home Rule for Ireland and split party. Prime Minister, 1892-4; Second Irish Home Rule Bill rejected by House of Lords. Died 1898.

Left. Gladstone's statue at Bow "in mourning" a few days after his death.

Right. Statue by Albert Bruce-Joy. Bronze, 10ft, on polished red granite pedestal. Bow Road, just outside Bow Churchyard. Unveiled August 19th, 1882, by Rt.Hon. Lord Carlingford. The gift of Theodore Bryant.

The donor's family connection with Bryant and May the matchmakers has linked the statue to another well-known historical event: the Matchgirls' Strike. Conditions in their factory were in fact far from pleasant. The girls who worked there were badly paid and fined for trivial offences; they were made to eat their meals at their benches and habitually suffered from a paralysis brought about by phosphorus poisoning known as "fossy-jaw", for which no compensation was given. In 1888 they went on strike. Annie Besant, the social reformer and future leader of the Theosophical Society, took up their cause. She considered bringing the statue into her campaign but, though the girls clearly resented its presence, she could find no evidence that they had been made to contribute to it. Not so the author of *A Match To Fire The Thames*, Anne Stifford. It had, she wrote, been been paid for by shillings compulsorily taken from their wages and at the unveiling some of them had cut their arms and let their blood trickle down onto the marble pedestal. Whatever the true role of the statue, the matchgirls were successful; they formed a union, the first women ever to do so, and won better pay and conditions. There is at the time of writing a proposal to erect a statue in their memory on the former site of the Bryant and May factory.

He was a sympathetic admirer of Gladstone, believing like him that mankind was aspiring towards some distant perfection. But he also caught, with his usual penetrating insight, that unpredictable intensity which some found so inspiring and some so terrifying. Partly on the advice of G. Shaw Lefevre, who was by then Chairman of the London County Council Improvements Committee, he put most of the dynamic movement of the monument into the surounding allegorical figures. The statesman himself stands stiffly, armoured in his Exchequer robes like a watchful iguana, his head deliberately turned a little to the left to face the direction of the sun.

The poet and critic Edmund Gosse, writing to Thornycroft shortly after the statue's unveiling, put its mood exactly. "It is so dignified, so solid and the head so magnificent; the jaws have just gone "snap" in a paroxysm of self-will. It is curious that you have got that look of frenzy in the eye that all his best portraits have – it is alertness and nerve and determination carried *just* over the verge of normal. It always seems to me that if Gladstone had ever had the leisure to take up madness as a profession, he might have been a first class lunatic. But – to be serious – he was kept mentally whole by ceaseless occupation and excitement."

Statue by Hamo Thornycroft. Bronze, 11ft, on a 22ft pedestal of Portland stone on which are set figures representing Brotherhood, Aspiration, Education and Courage. East end of the Strand, outside St Clement Dane's Church. Unveiled November 4th, 1905, by John Morley M.P., Gladstone's cabinet colleague and biographer. Gladstone wears the robes of the Chancellor of the Exchequer. Cost £8,000 for the whole memorial.

That the Strand does not bow south, as the Aldwych does to the north, but runs straight to give an uninterrupted view of the memorial, we owe to a campaign started by Thornycroft in *The Times*.

Left. Hamo Thornycroft in his studio at work on the figure of Courage for the Gladstone Memorial.

Oliver Cromwell

Cromwell looms large in history as England's only military dictator. He has always been the subject of passion and the story behind his London commemoration bears this out. For a century and a half after the collapse of his Commonwealth, history's verdict on him was universally hostile: a brave, bad man at best, at worst a tyrant bound for hell. The tide turned with the Romantic Age. It was essentially Thomas Carlyle (p126) who brought about his rehabilitation. His immensely popular *On Heroes and Hero Worship* shows Cromwell as a giant; he is England's strongest soul, melancholic, half-inarticulate, inspired, between the structurelessness of Puritan Belief and the feebleness of Stuart Make-Believe the only possible bringer of Order.

This vision strongly appealed to the boyish, cultured Lord Rosebery, whom Queen Victoria chose as Prime Minister after Gladstone's resignation in 1894. This being the Imperial Age, Rosebery also admired Cromwell for having built up Britain's navy and, as a liberal, for having been the first of her rulers to accept and encourage the Jews. He revived earlier plans for a statue of Cromwell at the Houses of Parliament and included a downpayment of £500 in the 1895 July estimates.

But the Irish (as Rosebery should have known since he was proposing to give them Home Rule) never forget. The members for Roscommon, Clare and Waterford rose in passionate denunciation of the perpetrator of the massacre of Drogheda. In their constituencies the worst thing that one could say to a man was still, "The curse of Cromwell be upon you." The estimates were only passed by the slenderest of margins and a few days later the plan for a subsidised commemoration was withdrawn. A few days after *that*, Rosebery's government fell, it would be an exaggeration to say over the statue – in fact the cause was a suddenly discovered shortage of army ammunition. Nevertheless, it had certainly contributed to the general sense of disarray.

Fortunately for art, Rosebery did not give up. Shortly afterwards an "anonymous donor", his identity known to everyone, came forward with the necessary funds. The Conservative government decided to "honour the commitments of its predecessor" and agreed to the site in front of Westminster Hall. At the last moment a tiny group of peers called a debate on Prorogation Day and voted the statue down; however, this procedural sleight of hand was ignored. And in the event Hamo Thornycroft's portrait was so compelling that it was extremely well received and has remained popular ever since.

The statue is strangely placed; its pedestal rises up from a grassy lawn well below the level of the road ("like Mephistopheles from the pit," as Lord Hardwicke said in the 1899 debate) and nowadays is enclosed in a giant steel fence whose chief function is to keep out the Irish Republican Army. The site has other powerful associations. After the Restoration Cromwell's body was disinterred and hung, and for twenty years the head was displayed on a pole outside Westminster Hall. It is all a tale of heads. Thornycroft had a lot of trouble with the statue's and at one point had to resort to decapitation: a head for a head, he observed, thinking of the Martyr King. And in fact the sculptured head of Charles I (above) gazes out at his executioner from a niche beside the door of Saint Margaret's Church. Within the broad sweep of history, this seems more like a reconciliation than a perpetuation of conflict: the God-appointed King and the God-appointed Commoner look across at one another; the fire and the rose are one.

Oliver Cromwell. Born 1599, Huntingdon, son of landowner. Became M.P. for Huntingdon, 1628. Experienced conversion after long period of religious depression, 1638. Civil War, 1642-9; became Commander of Horse in New Model Army. Co-signed Charles I's warrant of execution, 1649. Put down army Levellers, 1649. Lord Lieutenant of Ireland, 1649-50; crushed rebellion with great severity and slaughter of civilians. Became C-in-C of army, 1650. Ended Rump Parliament, 1652. Refused kingship but accepted title of Protector; supervised appointment of clergy and issued edicts forbidding duelling, cock-fighting, horse-racing and swearing; made peace with Holland and treaties with Sweden, Denmark and Portugal, 1652-4. Finally dissolved Parliament; divided country into 12 divisions, each under a Major General, 1655. Made war with Spain over colonisation of West Indies, 1656-8. Died 1658.

Right. Statue by Hamo Thornycroft. Bronze. Outside Houses of Parliament. Unveiled November 14th, 1899, without ceremony. Cost £3,000, the gift of Lord Rosebery in the person of "an anonymous donor".

Above. From Parliament, Cromwell's statue looks across at this lead bust of Charles I on St Margaret's Church, Westminster. Like the bust on the Banqueting House, it was found in a builders yard by Mr Hedley Hope-Nicholson, the secretary of the Society of King Charles the Martyr (see p23), and was erected in 1950.

Sir Wilfrid Lawson

Sir Wilfrid Lawson was a Temperance man. He was also a "Little Englander", a phrase which he was proud of having invented. However, if one were to think of him as inevitably dour and moralistic, one would be quite wrong. For nearly fifty years he was Court Jester to the House of Commons, keeping everyone amused with his friendly witticisms and the satirical poems which he scribbled down on order papers. He was known as the only man to have made Disraeli (p194) laugh during debate. Yet his humour had a dry, serious heart. Two things he considered did most evil in the world, war and drink. Of them he said, "We raise thirty millions by killing our people with alcohol; and expend the same on gunpowder to kill people abroad. These sums balance very nicely; that is the beauty of the system."

For years he battled for the Local Option or Local Veto system, by which each area of the country would vote on whether to allow the sale of alcohol; if more than two-thirds opposed it, it would be banned. This scheme actually became part of the Liberal manifesto in 1891 but nothing was done to make it law. Lawson won minor victories, for example over a Bill forbidding the paying of wages in cider, but the brewer's lobby and the habits of the nation were too strong. It did not seem to embitter him and he was always on the best of terms with his opponents. The brewers Whitbread and Bass were both Members of Parliament. On one occasion Lawson and Whitbread were crossing Great George Street arm-in-arm when they were nearly run down by a bus. Each pulled the other to safety. "Had we been killed," Lawson remarked, "there would have been joy in both our camps!"

At home Lawson was a J.P. and deeply interested in agriculture. He was a typical country squire; he really did "ken" the legendary huntsman John Peel and bought his hounds from him when he retired from hunting. In the Commons anything pretentious or inconsistent became the quarry for his wit. Of the complications of the Public Worship Regulation Bill, designed to check excessive high church ritualism he said, "Why cannot (the clergy) be brought before the magistrates when they are charged with illegal practices and, if found guilty, be fined five shillings and costs?" He ridiculed the military objections of Lord Napier (p266) to a Channel Tunnel, which was in prospect as long ago as 1883. "We are told that the French army coming through the hole might surprise us," he said. "I know nothing whatever of tactics, but I still have the strongest conviction that to have a hostile French army in a hole would be the very best place for it: and if all the English forces – horse, foot and artillery – could not prevent it getting out, those forces must be incompetent, impotent and idiotic."

The erection of Lawson's statue was organised by the members of the Temperance Society of which he was president for many years, the United Kingdom Alliance. It was unveiled by no less a person than Prime Minister Asquith. However, this was 1909 and, before he could proceed, two protesting suffragettes (see Mrs Pankhurst, p220) had to be ejected from the Embankment Gardens. Lawson, who was in fact an early supporter of women's rights, would have had something ironically witty to say about the occasion – and again when, in 1917, the statue of the man of peace was damaged during an air raid and once again when, in 1979, the small surrounding figures representing Temperance, Charity, Fortitude and Peace were stolen from the pedestal.

Sir Wilfrid Lawson. Born 1829, Brayton, Cumberland, son of Radical landowner. M.P. for Carlisle and for Cockermouth, 1859-65, 1868-85 & 1886-99; opposed sale of alcohol, opium trade and all foreign military intervention. Introduced annual parliamentary resolutions on "Local Veto" over the sale of alcohol, 1864 & 1869-83; the resolution passed in 1881-83 but did not become law. President of United Kingdom Alliance, 1879-1906; campaigned for Temperance in towns all over Britain. Won motion against practice of making Derby Day a parliamentary holiday, 1892. Strongly opposed Boer War and lost parliamentary seat, 1899. Re-elected M.P. for Camborne, 1903. Offered membership of Privy Council but refused, 1906. Died 1906.

Statue by David McGill. Bronze, 9ft. Victoria Embankment Gardens. Unveiled July 20th, 1909, by Herbert Asquith.

The statue was considered a good likeness of the politician while speaking. The editor of Lawson's memoirs wrote, "The easy, almost negligent position and the disposition of the hands are absolutely lifelike."

The Duke of Devonshire

One day, perhaps, when mankind is calmer and wiser, positions of authority will only be given to those with absolutely no desire for them. Then men like Lord Hartington (as he was better known in politics) will come into their own. Once a speaker in the House of Lords was expounding his own greatest political achievement; Hartington turned to his neighbour and said, "The proudest moment of my life was when my pig won first prize at Skipton Fair." He would have much preferred a country life, hunting, shooting and running his many estates. But all the Cavendishes served their country. His great-great-grandfather was Prime Minister. His scholarly father was Chancellor of Cambridge University and founded the Cavendish laboratories. So politics became his painful duty, patiently borne. In the middle of his maiden speech, he yawned. (He became known as the man who yawned at his own speeches but then, as he said, some of them were damn'd dull). Disraeli (p194) was deeply impressed and prophesied, correctly, that a man who could show such languor on so important an occasion would rise to the very top.

It was Lord Palmerston (p192) who saw what he had to offer the political life of England and who, in the face of considerable protest, gave him office. As Secretary for War he fielded hostile and detailed cross-questioning with detached calm. He became known as incorruptible, independent and reliable. His speeches, delivered in a monotonous sing-song, set out clearly and without deception the steps which had led him to a particular position; his arguments, as an American visitor remarked, were rather like a man driving in piles. On Gladstone's resignation (p204), he became Leader of the Liberal Party. The two men were as opposite as possible, though each respected the other. However, it was Gladstone's rhetoric which won the subsequent election and, though the Queen sent for Hartington and asked him to form a government, he knew that he could not compete with "the people's William." So he became Secretary of State for India, resolving the crisis in Afghanistan with estimable sang-froid. Following the famous victory won by General Roberts (p274), he withdrew British troops from Kandahar and established a friendly, independent regime under Amir Abdurahman. No doubt his own stubborn nature realised that the Afghanis would never accept domination of any kind, neither from Britain on the one side nor from Russia on the other. Later he broke with Gladstone over Home Rule for Ireland. He was twice more offered the Premiership and twice refused it. In the end he became a massive and indispensable presence in English politics, supporting in coalition one of the most stable governments for decades. As Chairman of the Cabinet Defence Committee, he presided over the expansion of the British Empire to its maximum of power and extent.

So his statue, which stands half-way down and at right angles to London's main administrative thoroughfare, is aptly sited. It was subscribed to by admirers from all sides of politics and also from the City, where he was respected as a "solid man." King Edward VII, who was a close friend, took a personal interest in the memorial and asked Herbert Hampton to bring his model to Buckingham Palace for royal inspection. As a young man, Hartington was good looking in a sombre sort of way. Then the hereditary, somnolent droop of the mouth and around the eyes asserted itself and he began to look, pleasantly enough, a little like his prize Skipton pig. Rendered suitably heroic and impressive, a measure of this can be seen in Hampton's statue.

Spencer Compton Cavendish, Marquis of Hartington and 8th Duke of Devonshire. Born 1833, Holker Hall, Lancashire, eldest son of Earl of Burlington. Became M.P., 1857. Under-Secretary and Secretary for War, 1863-6. Postmaster General, 1868-70. Chief Secretary for Ireland, 1870. Leader of Liberal Party, 1875-80; offered Premiership by Queen. Secretary of State for India; resolved Afghan crisis, 1880-2. Secretary of State for War; threatened to resign over Gladstone's hesitancy in rescuing General Gordon (p268), 1882. Became leader of group opposing Gladstone's Irish Home Rule Bill known as Liberal Unionists, 1886. Offered Premiership, 1886 & 7. Supported Conservative government of Lord Salisbury, 1886-95. Joined coalition government, 1895-1903; became President of Council with responsibility for education and President of Cabinet Defence Committee. Resigned over introduction of preferential trade tariffs for colonies, 1904. Died 1908.

Statue by Herbert Hampton. Bronze, 11ft on 13ft pedestal of Darley Dale stone. Junction of Whitehall and Horseguards Avenue, near former War Office. Unveiled February 14th, 1911, by Lord Landsdowne. The Duke wears Garter robes.

SPENCER COMPTON
EIGHTH DUKE
OF
DEVONSHIRE
K·C·
BORN 1833·DIED 1908

Colonel Bevington

Known to everyone in Bermondsey as "the Colonel", Samuel Bevington occupies a special place on the streets of London as her only purely local hero. He ran the family leather business in St Thomas's Street, which specialised in fine leathers. He employed five hundred men and he was known as a lively and generous employer. Instantly recognisable by his magnificent beard, it is not surprising that he was spoken of as the most popular man in the Borough.

In politics Bevington was first a Liberal, then a Hartington Unionist (p212) and, after Gladstone's resignation (p204), a Liberal once more. He was at the local end of many of the age's movements for social betterment. He helped the Ragged Schools and, after the passing of W.E.Forster's 1870 Education Act (p202), he became the Chairman of Bermondsey's School Managers. He later served on the Council of Borough Polytechnic, which was one of the very first to follow Quintin Hogg's example at Regent Street (p104). He helped to found an Institute School of Tanning and he supported the Free Library. He played a leading role in the Leather and Hide Trade's Provident and Benevolent Institute. His colonelship was in the Volunteers, that association of part-time militias launched by Sidney Herbert (p186). He believed that military training was good both for self-discipline and for health and he conducted an annual camp at Aldershot. He was a friend of all the Bermondsey churches, though he himself was an enthusiastic follower of the Swiss philosopher and mystic, Emmanuel Swedenborg. That he therefore believed in the literal reality of angels and in the existence of a complex hierarchy of heavens and purgatories adds a final touch of mystery to the public man.

In 1900, after the London Government Act had brought Bermondsey Borough Council into existence, Bevington was elected as Bermondsey's first Mayor. During his first year of office he inaugurated a new electrical works and a new incinerator. During his second year he was responsible for the local arrangements for the Coronation of Edward VII. His colleagues clearly thought he should have been given a knighthood. When this was not forthcoming, they hung instead a resplendent portrait of him in the Town Hall and, after his death, put up a similarly splendid statue. Both works expressed Bermondsey's new civic pride and its sense of itself as a locality of artists and craftspeople.

Samuel Bourne Bevington. Born 1832, Bickley, Kent, son of Bermondsey businessman. Entered father's leather business, 1851; became Chairman, 1892. Joined 1st Surrey Rifles as Volunteer, 1859; Colonel of 3rd Volunteer Battalion of the Queen's Royal West Surrey Regiment, 1885-99. Chairman of Bermondsey's School Managers, 1871. Master of the Leathersellers' Company. President of the Swedenborgian Society, 1890. First Mayor of Bermondsey, 1900-2. Died 1907.

Statue by Sydney Marsh. Bronze. Tooley Street. Unveiled March 18th, 1911, by Alderman Haybod and Colonel Dixon. Burlington wears his mayoral robes. Cost c.£650. Marsh had seven brothers and two sisters, all of whom were artists; they cast their own statues *en famille*.

Left. A press photograph of "the platform" at the unveiling, valiantly taken in rain and amid a great mass of people. The assembled worthies are, from right to left: the be-wigged Town Clerk, the bearded Alderman Haybod (like Bevington a successful manufacturer and the moving spirit behind both his commemorations), the Mayor in his chain of office, Mrs Haybod, trying hard to get a view, and next to her the somewhat blurred figure of Father Murnane, the local Catholic priest, who is telling the crowd how much Bevington appreciated his own Irish blood; English public life, he is saying, would be a dull affair without the contribution of the Irish. To his left is the youthful, creative-looking sculptor, Sydney Marsh, who looks ill at ease in a top hat.

Sir Robert Clive

Robert, 1st Baron Clive. Born 1725, near Market Drayton, Shropshire, son of impoverished country gentleman. Entered East India Company as junior clerk, 1743. Volunteered for military campaign on behalf of English candidate for throne of Carnatic against French-backed forces, 1750-1; led capture and defence of Arcot and won numerous other battles. Returned to England, married and stood for Parliament, 1752-5. Sent to Madras as prospective Governor. Commanded troops sent to relieve Calcutta after murder of English civilians in "black hole"; defeated armies of Nawab of Bengal at Plessey, 1756-7. Became effective ruler of Bengal, 1758-60. Returned to England, much enriched; became M.P. and purchased country estates; awarded Irish baronetcy, 1760-4. Sent to Calcutta as Governor; reformed administration and established East India Company as receiver of revenues for states of Bengal, Orissa and Bihar, 1764-7. Cross-examined by Parliamentary Committee of Enquiry; censured but finally succeeded in clearing name, 1772-3. Committed suicide, 1774.

Statue by John Tweed (p276). Bronze. King Charles St. First erected 1912 in garden of Gwydyr House, Whitehall; moved to present site 1916, on completion of new India Office. Cost £5,000.

On three sides of the pedestal are plaques showing Clive in action at the siege of Arcot, receiving the revenues of Bengal, Orissa and Bihar, and brooding in a mango grove on the eve of the Battle of Plessey.

The British Empire reached its apogee in the early years of the twentieth century and Robert Clive was revered as one of its greatest heroes. Looking back, it all seemed clear. As Macaulay had written so sonorously in his famous essay: "From Clive's first visit to India dates the renown of English arms in the East... From Clive's second visit to India dates the political ascendancy of the English in that country... From Clive's third visit to India dates the purity of the administration of our eastern Empire." The erection of Clive's statue was masterminded by that Empire's most dedicated champion, Lord Curzon (p218), and was destined to stand beside the great new India Office buildings in King Charles Street, between Whitehall and St James's Park.

Clive's own life was dramatic and controversial. He went out to the marshy, coastal outpost of Madras as a young adventurer determined to make good. He volunteered for arms, (though, like Sir John Lawrence (p198), he was always officially a civil officer rather than a soldier) and had the luck of the gods in battle. Both in South India and in Bengal he was involved in intrigue with rival claimants to a native throne, the standard method of advance in the early days of British colonial expansion. In each case he won great victories and in Bengal, mainly through personal charisma, he became the *de facto* ruler of the State.

On his return to England, he was both admired and resented. The elder Pitt called him "our Heaven-born general" but his relationships with the East India Company were stormy. Nevertheless, he was sent back to Calcutta to deal with the administrative chaos which had arisen in his absence. He negotiated a complex arrangement with the Moghul Emperor which greatly increased British influence and he also tried to regulate the vast sums of money which employees of the East India Company were receiving on their own account. However, his own wealth and past intrigues were coming under increasing scrutiny. His enemies massed and eventually brought him before a House of Commons Committee of Enquiry, threatening to destroy both his reputation and his income. He defended himself with great dignity and was finally exonerated. Within two years he had committed suicide, cutting his throat with a penknife. Some blamed the enquiry, but for years he had suffered from periods of elation followed by deep depression, made worse by severe gastric trouble and chronic malaria.

Clive's statue stands on one of the taller pedestals in London, though it is not quite high or isolated enough to qualify for the lightning conductor sported by the nearby Duke of York's column. Is this rash, since a careful reading of Clive's triumphs reveals the extraordinary role played in them by the electricity of the elements? He marched his army to Arcot through a torrential thunderstorm and the defenders, awe-struck at the feat, fled without fighting. At Plessey another thunderstorm drenched his enemies' gunpowder; he kept his hidden under tarpaulins and so, to their complete surprise, was able to turn their key attack. Moreover, the overlordship of Bengal was achieved by paying off the young and pleasure-loving ruler, Najm-ud-duala, ("more-dancing-girls," he exclaimed happily); his elder brother, the proud, warlike Miram, had shortly before been killed by lightning. It seems that the Indians were right to regard Clive with an almost superstitious awe, for their god Indra, wielder of the thunderbolt, was clearly on his side. Nevertheless, gods can be fickle and one hopes that Clive's statue will continue to enjoy Indra's favour.

Lord Curzon

George Nathaniel Curzon, Marquis of Kedleston. Born 1859, Kedleston, Derbyshire, son of clergyman Baron Scarsdale. Suffered under obsessively strict nanny and sado-sentimental prep-school master. Became M.P., 1886. Travelled in Japan, China, India, Russia, Afghanistan and Persia, and wrote definitive works on travels, 1887-94. Under Secretary for India, 1891-5. Married Mary Victoria Leiter, daughter of Chicago millionaire, 1895. Under Secretary for Foreign Affairs, 1895-8. Viceroy of India, 1898-1905; established separate North-west province, founded agricultural credit banks, expanded railway system. Rescued Taj Mahal from dilapidation. Organised Delhi Durbar, 1903. Resigned, 1905. Death of first wife deeply affected spirit, 1906. Appointed Chancellor of Oxford University, 1907. Filled political vacuum by restoring ancient buildings, among them Tattershall and Bodiham Castles. President of Privy Council and member of War Cabinet, 1916-8. Foreign Secretary, 1919-24; personally laid basis for peace between Greece and Turkey at Conference of Lausanne, 1922. Narrowly failed to be appointed Prime Minister, 1923. Died 1925.

Statue by Bertram Mackennal. Bronze. Carlton Terrace. Unveiled March, 28th, 1931, by Stanley Baldwin. "Erected by his friends in recognition of a great public life."

Curzon was India's most resplendent Viceroy. Among his most spectacular achievements was the staging of the Delhi Durbar of 1903, which celebrated the coronation of Edward VII. In the State procession walked elephants draped in cloth of gold, carrying Rajahs and Maharajas, Nawabs and Sultans, Khans and Mehtars. Before them rode Lord and Lady Curzon, borne in a howdah of solid silver on the most splended beast of all. It was the ceremonial climax of British rule in India.

Curzon was popular with the Indian people, both for his sense of display and for his enlightened reforms. His fellow administrators, however, found him a difficult man to work for, psychologically incapable of delegating responsibility. The politicians at home also found him alarming, as he pursued his own policies of safeguarding Afghanistan, Tibet and the Persian Gulf. Under Curzon, it was said, India's relations to Britain were those of a foreign and not always friendly power. He clashed, finally and fatally, with Lord Kitchener (p278), whom he had specially asked for as his military Commander-in-Chief. Their dispute was a largely technical one of respective powers and Kitchener proved the stronger and more devious man. Curzon threatened to resign once too often and his resignation was accepted. Kitchener's statue stands not far away from Curzon's, on Horseguards Parade, but their gazes fail to meet.

Curzon just failed in his last and greatest ambition, to become Prime Minister, when in 1923 the King unexpectedly chose Stanley Baldwin. On ability he should have been appointed, but his aloofness had made him too many enemies – a fellow M.P. once described his method of speaking to the Commons as "a divinity addressing blackbeetles" – and his temperament was suspect; as at Eton, he would still sometimes burst into tears when thwarted.

Curzon's statue stands opposite his London home at no. 1, Carlton Terrace, where he gave his fashionable dinner parties, where he would sit up until four in the morning reading Foreign Office telegrams, and where he had such difficulty in getting servants to stay. As India's youngest ever Viceroy – he was only 39 when appointed – he was impressively good-looking, his rich, dark hair brushed back across his high forehead. In later years his features became more strained and angular. Bertram Mackennal, who also sculpted Edward VII in Waterloo Place just a short distance away (p74), has mingled age and youth in a somewhat idealised portrait. The stance is stiffly upright. At nineteen Curzon developed curvature of the spine due to an earlier fall from a horse; it gave him constant pain and he had to wear a leather harness. The specialists pronounced nothing organically wrong; if only he would rest, his back would get better but this he would not, or could not, do.

In other ways the likeness is more questionable. Curzon's children objected to the statue (though his second wife approved) and Harold Nicolson thought it bore little resemblance to its subject. The face has a disconcertingly oriental look, as if a high caste brahmin had taken rebirth in England in order to become his former country's ruler. Curzon, of course, could never have seen it like that. He loved the mysterious East but the modern West, with its technical knowledge and administrative efficiency, was far superior. "The secret of the mastery of the world," he wrote, "is, if only they knew it, in the hands of the British people." What exactly that secret was, and is, eluded him; nevertheless he dedicated his life to its pursuit.

Mrs Pankhurst

With the unveiling of her statue close by the Houses of Parliament, the much imprisoned Mrs Pankhurst was formally accepted as a national heroine. Twenty years earlier she and ten thousand of her supporters had marched on Westminster to be met with police violence and arrest. Not long afterwards her own campaign of violence had begun: damaging works of art, blowing up unoccupied railway carriages and breaking the windows of government offices. (She herself, as it happened, was a bad shot with a stone – she twice aimed at the windows of 10 Downing Street and missed). Yet now a recent Prime Minister, who had himself opposed votes for women, was unveiling her statue. There was, as Baldwin said, something peculiarly English about such a resolution of former discord.

To many her sense of outrage and frustration had seemed entirely justified. A majority both in the Cabinet and in the Commons was in favour of votes for women and change was blocked only by a small group led by the Liberal Prime Minister, Asquith. He saw all women as credulous, irrational creatures and there is no doubt that the suffragettes' confrontational tactics – we have just seen them attempting to disrupt his unveiling of the statue of Sir Wilfrid Lawson (p210) – simply increased his resistance. But Mrs Pankhurst was one of those people who can only find fulfilment in complete dedication to a cause. She tested that dedication to its limits when in 1911 the so called "Cat-and-Mouse" Act was brought in. Suffragettes who went on hunger strike in prison were released on point of death; when they had recovered sufficiently, they were re-arrested to serve the remainder of their sentence. This treatment seriously and permanently damaged Mrs Pankhurst's health. Was her sacrifice heroic or misguided? We shall never know, for the War changed everything. The Government needed total support, especially from those who could mobilise large numbers behind a cause. It was clear that, as soon as the War was over, the women who were now working so hard to win it would be rewarded with the vote.

After her death, Mrs Pankhurst's friends and supporters, led by Mrs E.K.Marshall, put the same kind of determined campaigning into getting her a public statue. They initially asked for a site on the lawn at the end of Downing Street (close to the spot from which she had launched her wayward stones) but this was rejected out of hand by the officials at the Office of Works, who were highly antagonistic to the whole project. The turning point came when the ladies persuaded Prime Minister Baldwin to agree to unveil the statue and published his notice of acceptance in the press. A slightly less prominent site in Victoria Tower Gardens, currently under construction, was assured. The B.B.C. broadcast the unveiling ceremony. Music for the occasion was provided by the Metropolitan Police Band! It seems the ultimate irony but according to Dame Ethel Smythe, who conducted them in one of her own compositions, they had especially asked for the honour. The ordinary, solid policeman knew that the suffragettes were no criminals (they were, quite apart from anything else, mostly upper-middle class ladies) and retained a deep respect for them.

Mrs Pankhurst was a consummate public speaker. She loved to go to the West End theatre and study the techniques of her favourite actors. Her quiet voice had an immense range, now pitying, now scornful, now tender, now scathing. She used few gestures but the outstretched, imploring arm of the statue was her most characteristic one; a close associate called it "maternity pleading for the race."

Emmeline Pankhurst. Born 1858, Manchester, the daughter of a wealthy, radical factory owner. Attended first women's suffrage meeting aged 14, 1872. Married Richard Pankhurst, barrister devoted to socialist causes, 1879; ran political salon and did social work for the poor. Abandoned Independent Labour Party and founded own Women's Social and Political Union, 1903. Organised street protests and demonstrations; interrupted speeches by Home Secretary, 1905. Votes for women passed by Parliament but not made law by Asquith's government; first imprisonment and hunger strike, 1907. Violence at opening of parliament, "Black Friday", 1910; suffragette campaign of active violence began after Asquith introduced voting reforms for men only, 1911. Refused to drink or sleep in prison; re-arrested twelve times, 1913. Sentences remitted, 1914; encouraged women in war work. Led march of 50,000 women war-workers to Lloyd George's Ministry of Munitions, 1916. Visited Russia and tried to persuade Kerensky to continue war, 1917. Lectured on venereal disease for Canadian Government, 1920-5. Conservative parliamentary candidate for Whitechapel, 1926. Died 1928, the year the vote was given to all women over twenty one.

Statue by A.G.Walker. He was chosen since he had also sculpted the first non-royal statue of a woman in London, that of Florence Nightingale (p164). Bronze. Victoria Tower Gardens. Unveiled March 6th, 1930, by Stanley Baldwin. Cost £2,500. Inside the pedestal is a metal box containing Mrs Pankhurst's letters and obituary in *The Times*, suffragette brooches and other mementoes.

Sir Winston Churchill

Churchill *was* Britain at war. Had he died in 1938, he would have been remembered as an interesting, able, somewhat maverick political figure and no more. As it turned out, his independence of will and love of action, his knowledge of warfare and history, and his brilliant oratory made him the ideal representative of his country's fighting spirit. Of the day in 1940 when he became Prime Minister he wrote, "As I went to bed at about 3 a.m., I was conscious of a profound sense of relief. At last I had the authority to give directions over the whole scene. I felt as if I were walking with destiny, and that all my past life had been a preparation for this hour and this trial."

It was in this role as war-leader that the Churchill Memorial Committee wished to commemorate him when they commissioned his statue. The limited competition was won by the Welsh sculptor, Ivor Roberts-Jones, who produced one of the best known, if not *the* best known statue in London, its silhouette instantly recognisable from every side of Parliament Square. Roberts-Jones aimed to show his subject's indomitable qualities by building up the figure in simple, continuous, bastion-like sections. Churchill's military greatcoat, the one he wore on his journeys to the front line in Normandy in 1944, was the basis of his design. This gives the figure its abstract massiveness while keeping a link with the real world. One of the chief images present in the sculptor's mind as he worked was Rodin's famous statue of Balzac, in which the looming yet self-contained bulk of the body is similarly important. He believed that Rodin was influenced in the making of that statue by a small Egyptian hawk of Horus which he had in his possession (and which is now in the Rodin Museum in Paris). These Egyptian hawks (the one shown below is in the British Museum) seem to gather up their spiritual, fighting energy by resting back on their tails. The figure of Churchill likewise leans slightly backwards, as if receiving and absorbing the full brunt of the Nazi onslaught before moving onwards once again.

Sir Winston Spencer Churchill. Born 1874, Blenheim Palace, Woodstock, son of politician Sir Randolph Churchill. Commissioned in army, 1895. Served in India, 1896-8. Fought in Battle of Omdurman under Kitchener (p278) and published account of campaign, 1898. War Correspondent during Boer War; captured by Boers but escaped and re-joined army, 1899-1900. Became Conservative M.P., 1900, but attacked re-armament policies of his own party. Joined Liberals, 1904. Under-Secretary of State for the Colonies, 1905-8. President of the Board of Trade, 1908-10; set up Labour Exchanges. Home Secretary, 1910-11. First Lord of the Admiralty, 1911-5; mobilised fleet some weeks before outbreak of war, resigned after failure of expedition to Dardanelles. Rejoined army as Lt.Col.; commanded regiment in France, 1915-6. Minister of Munitions, 1917-8. Secretary of State for War, 1919-21; planned unfulfilled attack on Bolshevik Russia. Colonial Secretary, 1921-2; set up Transjordan and Iraq. Lost seat in Parliament, 1922. Elected as "Constitutional and Anti-Socialist" candidate for Epping, 1924; rejoined Conservatives. Chancellor of the Exchequer, 1924-9. Out of office, 1930-8; opposed self-government for India; warned against growth of Nazi power and advocated re-armament and conscription. Criticised Chamberlain's Munich agreement with Hitler, 1938. Appointed First Lord of the Admiralty on declaration of war, 1939. Prime Minister and Minister of Defence, 1940-5. Defeated in election by Labour party under Clement Attlee (p328ff), 1945. Prime Minister, 1951-5; resigned through ill-health. Died 1965.

Left. Two of the sources of inspiration to the sculptor Ivor Roberts-Jones as he worked on his statue of Churchill: Rodin's statue of Balzac, here photographed by moonlight in its plaster form, and the Egyptian hawk, symbol of the god Horus.

CHURCHILL

Roberts-Jones' full conception included the distribution of various semi-abstract, rectangular, bronze shapes in the grass about the base. These, lit up on special occasions, would represent burning beams and so would show Churchill walking through the ruins of London during the blitz, encouraging and inspiring. However, this design would have been extremely expensive and would also have meant placing the statue on its own in the centre of the square. This the committee did not want to do, since Churchill had in fact selected the north-east corner for himself during his lifetime.

The looming form became so celebrated that the sculptor was asked to provide statues of Churchill for two other, far-distant parts of the world. One was erected in New Orleans in 1978; it has him raising his arm to give a V-sign, just as he did when he visited that city after the War. The other, shown below, is in Oslo. Norway was occupied by the Nazis; however, the peace-loving Scandinavians wanted the statue to express Churchill's more thoughtful qualities as a statesman. The head is therefore larger in relation to the body and the expression more contemplative.

Left and previous page. Statue by Ivor Roberts-Jones. Bronze, 12 ft, on 8ft pedestal. Parliament Square. Unveiled November 1st, 1973, by Lady Spencer-Churchill. Cost £32,104.

Right. Another variation on an international theme. Statue by Ivor Roberts-Jones. Bronze, 9ft. Oslo. Unveiled May 1975.

Lord Fenner Brockway

As a young journalist and member of the Independent Labour Party, Fenner Brockway went to hear George Bernard Shaw lecture on the evolution of the Superman. Afterwards he asked him, "What are we to do with our lives?" "Find out what the life force is making for," replied Shaw, "and make for it too." "These words," Brockway wrote, "directed my thinking and feeling all through subsequent life. The life force – the creative element in life which is making for the good. Sometimes in great moments of beauty one can feel it, linking oneself with all that has been and is and will be, and then working within it and with it for the harmony of all life which expresses it. The realisation of oneness with a universal life had come to me in the deep silence of Nature ...Shaw gave it an objective reality."

If the life forces preserves and vitalises those who struggle on its behalf, then Brockway must have done its work well. He was still vigorous when, at the age of ninety six, he attended the unveiling of his statue in Red Lion Square, and he lived on to the age of ninety nine. He was a veteran campaigner for peace, social equality and human rights. During the First World War he was imprisoned as a conscientious objector. For leading a revolt against the rule forbidding prisoners to speak to each other, he was sentenced to nine months solitary confinement. After the War he compiled an influential report which led, among other things, to the abolition of the silence rule.

To Brockway the British Empire was itself a kind of extended prison and he saw the passing of colonialism as one of the great themes of the twentieth century. He was a supporter of Gandhi (p236) and adopted his philosophy of passive resistance. In Parliament during the 1950's and 60's he became known as "the Member for Africa". He was a close friend of Kenya's Jomo Kenyatta, who created him an honorary Kikuyu chief. It led to his being vilified in England as a supporter of Mau Mau, but his personal endorsement of the government amnesty offered to its warriors was important in bringing about peace and subsequent independence. Equally crucial was the part he played in Tunisia as an advisor both to Bourguiba and to the French Premier, Mendés-France. In the 1950's he was nominated for the Nobel Peace Prize but he withdrew in favour of the president of the African National Congress, Chief Luthuli.

At home he was always unhappy with mainstream politics and spent a number of years outside the Labour Party, a decision which he later regretted. Nevertheless, he made skilful use of parliamentary procedure, particularly in the House of Lords where, it was said, he asked more questions than all the other lords put together. Though they differed totally in their views and attitudes, he was in his way as clear-cut a figure as Churchill (p222), the only other English politician to be given an outdoor London statue between 1932 and 1987. He was the voice of idealism, of hope, of peace and sanity in a mad and destructive – or, as he later came to see it, an adolescent and growing – world.

Ian Walters, a committed Socialist, originally undertook a bust of Fenner Brockway out of a personal admiration for his ideals. They had a number of sittings together. From this came a plan for a full-size statue initiated by the organisation Liberation, formerly the Movement for Colonial Freedom, which Brockway had founded in 1954. A national appeal was launched, to which the Greater London Council made a major contribution. The pose is based on a joyful wave which Brockway gave to his supporters while delivering a C.N.D. petition to No 10 Downing Street in 1980.

Archibald Fenner Brockway, Baron Brockway of Eton and Slough. Born 1888, Calcutta, son of Nonconformist missionaries. Went into journalism in London, 1904. Converted to socialism during interview with Kier Hardie, 1906. Became editor of Labour Leader, *the newspaper of Independent Labour Party. Imprisoned for refusing military service and distributing leaflets against conscription, 1916-8. Became Secretary of British Committee of the Indian National Congress, 1920. Became Chairman of League Against Imperialism, 1929. M.P. in second Labour government, 1929-31. Left Labour Party over issues of parliamentary discipline, 1932-45. M.P. for Eton and Slough, 1950-64. Introduced nine Bills against racial discrimination, 1950-9. Introduced Bill applying United Nations Declaration of Human Rights to colonial territories, 1950; visited and obtained reforms in Sudan, Uganda etc. Worked for independence, political rights and peace in Kenya, Nigeria, Tunisia, Morocco, Congo, Cyprus and Malta. Organised the first ever national movement against nuclear weapons, 1954. Created Baron and entered House of Lords, 1964; championed numerous immigration cases and introduced Civil Rights Bills for Ireland. Opposed Vietnam War and visited both sides in peace mission during Nigeria-Biafra War. Promoted conferences on world hunger and new economic order. Died 1988.*

Statue by Ian Walters. Bronze, life-size. Red Lion Square. Unveiled July 25th, 1985, by Michael Foot, M.P.

In the 1987 autumn hurricane the statue was hit by a tree; the arm was broken off at the welds and the plinth cracked. Fortunately, the damage was made good within a year and a new plinth of polished granite erected.

FENNER BR
PRESIDEN
BORN 1 NOVEMBER

ERECTED BY GLC
HONOUR OF HIS
UNTIRING EFFOR

Abraham Lincoln

The presence of an American President in Parliament Square alongside Canning (p178) and Peel (p184) and the various other British statesmen expresses the long-standing political accord between Britain and the land which was once her colony. The two countries were last at war in 1815. (On his deathbed, Prince Albert (p58) altered the Cabinet's belligerent dispatch over the seizure of Southern agents from the British ship the *Trent*, so avoiding an almost certain conflict with Lincoln's Northern States.) In February 1914, therefore, the American Committee for the Celebration of the Hundredth Anniversary of Peace Among English-speaking Peoples wrote to their counterpart in England with the offer of a statue of Lincoln which, they hoped, would be erected in Parliament Square. The figure would be a replica of August Saint-Gaudens' dignified Lincoln Memorial in Chicago. The Office of Works agreed to the proposed site but the outbreak of the First World War brought a halt to proceedings.

A year or two later a new and shocking statue by George Grey Barnard burst on the American scene. Erected in Cincinnati, it was of Lincoln the backwoodsman, huge-handed and huge-booted. Reactions were extreme. "The greatest statue of our age has revealed the greatest soul of our age," said Theodore Roosevelt, while Lincoln's son, who was known as something of a snob, called it "grotesque and defamatory." The millionaire art patron Charles Taft obviously approved of it and in 1917 he offered to pay for the erection of a replica in Parliament Square in place of the Saint Gaudens (for which, in fact, no money had been raised). The English Peace Committee were agreeable. However, the artistic controversy quickly straddled the Atlantic and powerful voices were raised for and against both works. The secretary of the American Executive Committee, John A. Stewart, strongly supported the Barnard statue, which had at least been paid for. In November 1917, in exasperation, he sent a telegram to the Office of Works purportedly signed by the President, the Vice-president (Charles Taft's brother) and half the American cabinet saying that its erection would have "an incalculable influence in creating goodwill and understanding" between the two countries – this being just seven months after America's entry into the First World War. At this point the Office of Works, the American Ambassador and the Foreign Office got their heads together and a statement was issued saying that during hostilities shipping could not be spared to transport such a heavy object. After the War a compromise was clearly reached. The American Government presented the Saint Gaudens statue to Parliament Square and the Barnard was found a suitable home in Manchester, a city which, unlike London, had expressed strong support for the American North during the Civil War.

The two statues vividly reveal different aspects of Lincoln the man and the myth. One is of the boy who was born in a tiny, dirt-lined log cabin and who worked his way up to be President of the United States. Lincoln was six foot four and immensely strong, and one of the part-time jobs which he had taken as a young man in New Salem was cutting logs to make the sleepers for railway lines. This is Lincoln the "rail-splitter", beloved by the common man, uncouth and melancholy in appearance until transformed by his powers of oratory. One wonders what casual passers-by would have made of Barnard's statue in Parliament Square; said to be a full thirteen and three quarter feet high, it would have been gloriously out of place.

The figure which did find its way there is of Lincoln the fatherly

Abraham Lincoln. Born 1809, near Hodgenville, Kentucky, son of failed farmer. Clerk and storekeeper at New Salem, 1831-7. Elected member of Illinois legislature; began study of law, 1834. Moved to Springfield and set up practice as a lawyer, 1837. Became member of Congress; attacks on injustice of peace settlement with Mexico caused extreme unpopularity, 1847-9. Returned to politics with campaign against Senator Douglas's Bill to extend slavery to West, 1852. Stood for Senate against Douglas with series of public debates; narrowly defeated, 1858. Adopted as Republican candidate for the Presidency and elected against divided opposition, 1860. Secession of Southern States; took summary powers and ordered military defence of Fort Sumpter and naval blockade of South, 1860-1. Civil War, 1861-5; entrusted strategy to generals and personally encouraged troops. After victory, refused to impose dispossession or disenfranchisement on South. Issued proclamation freeing slaves, 1862. Assassinated while at theatre, 1865.

Left. Statue, replica of Auguste Saint-Gaudens' Lincoln Memorial at Chicago. Bronze, 12ft. Canning Enclosure, Parliament Square. Unveiled July 28th, 1920, by the Duke of Connaught. Cost £3,612. Presented by the American Government.

Right. Statue, replica of George Grey Barnard's Lincoln in Cincinnati. Bronze, 13ft 9 ins. At one time proposed for Parliament Square but erected in Platt Fields, Manchester, and unveiled September 15th, 1919, by the Lord Mayor. Since 1986 it has stood in Lincoln Square, a pedestrian precinct in the centre of that city.

statesman. He grew his beard shortly after he became President – and some said it spoilt the peculiar power and pathos of his face. This statue bears a close resemblance to photographs taken of him during the last year of his life, his craggy features lined by the sufferings of the Civil War, yet mellowed and dignified by his mission of reconciliation. Lincoln's genius was for unity. He kept his country undivided, first by taking summary powers in the struggle with the South and finally by framing a non-vindictive peace. From his belief in unity came his view that slavery was morally wrong; first he opposed its extension to the new lands of the West and then, only when the time was right, he had it outlawed by the Constitution. The words he spoke at the Gettysburg burial-ground have become the timeless embodiment of the democratic ideal; they are so well known, yet they always will bear repetition.

"Four score and seven years ago our fathers brought forth upon this continent a new nation conceived in Liberty and dedicated to the proposition that all men are created equal... We here highly resolve that these dead shall not have died in vain; that this nation, under God, shall have a new birth of freedom; and that government of the people, by the people, for the people, shall not perish from the earth."

George Washington

The statue of Washington in front of the National Gallery was, like that of Lincoln (p228), a gift from America proposed just before the First World War and made all the more appropriate after it. The donor was the Legislature of Virginia, Washington's home State, and this time there were no competing statues. This is in fact a replica of one of the world's most famous memorials. After the ending of the American War of Independence, Virginia wished to erect a statue of its greatest hero and, since no one in America was capable of producing one in the appropriate style, Thomas Jefferson and Benjamin Franklin, who were in Paris, approached Jean Antoine Houdon, the leading portrait sculptor of his age. As soon as he had received the commission, it is said, Houdon put aside his work for the Empress Catherine the Great and set out for Mount Vernon, Washington's country estate. He and his three assistants arrived late one night after the great man and his wife had gone to bed. He stayed for seventeen days, observing, sketching, making measurements of the various parts of the long-suffering hero's body and taking a plaster cast of his face.

The intention was to produce an exactly lifelike figure. Washington's visible presence – his great height and strength, his dignified bearing– was immensely important for the new nation. In his poised, soldierly air both the French ally and the British foe had been able to recognise the type of the true European gentleman. Because of Washington the Americans were seen as more than a collection of roughneck rebels; they became a people. When completed, the statue was erected in the State Capitol at Richmond, so helping to bring the little country town into the mainstream of Western civilisation. Since that time it has become one of the best known icons of American greatness. Between 1865 and 1971 no less than twenty two bronze castings were made of it and, besides London, there are replicas in San Francisco, Versailles, Lima and Montevideo.

The statue's design says a great deal about how and why Washington was admired. Having held together the disparate American forces during a long drawn out and difficult war, he resigned his commission and returned to the ordinary life of a planter. It was this disinterestedness, repeated in 1797 when he gave up the Presidency, that his contemporaries valued most of all in him. Their first leader was no autocratic tyrant, no Caesar, but a true servant of the Republic. He was most frequently compared to Cincinnatus, the Roman farmer who led the repulsion of the Equi and the Volsci and then returned to his four acres of ground. Houdon's statue, combining the contemporary and the classical, shows Washington in the act of retiring. He still wears his military uniform but holds a walking-stick in his right hand. His sword and riding cloak are hung on a conveniently placed pillar, against the back of which rests the shaft of a plough. Around the pillar, in the style of the Roman *fasces*, are bound staves representing the thirteen states of the new Union, intertwined with Red Indian arrows. In Rome the *fasces* were carried in procession before the civil magistrates. In the United States they were often used as a symbol of federal unity and equality – we can also see them around the chair of Saint-Gaudens' Lincoln (p229).

On the other side of the entrance to the National Gallery is James II's statue, also Roman (p30). It is fascinating to compare the banished, discredited Caesar with the victorious Cincinnatus, the King who declared himself supreme under God with the President who always began his speeches, "My fellow-citizens".

George Washington. Born 1732, Wakefield, Virginia, son of farmer. Appointed surveyor of Culpepper County, 1749. Military leader of Virginian forces in British-led campaign against French, 1753-9. Retired from army, married and settled as planter at family estate of Mount Vernon; became local representative and magistrate, 1759-75. Beginning of independence movement marked by Boston Tea-party, 1773. Attended First inter-State Conference at Philadelphia as a Virginia delegate, 1774. Attended Second Conference in military uniform; elected Commander-in-Chief of American army, 1775. Led War of Independence; victory at Yorktown and alliance with French ensured eventual success, 1775-83. Resigned commission and returned to Mount Vernon, 1783. Elected Virginia delegate and then President of Federal Convention in Philadelphia; signed draft of American Constitution, 1787. Unanimously elected President of United States, 1789. Re-elected President; issued proclamation of neutrality, 1792. Made wide-ranging tours; backed national bank and close federal unity. Resigned from Presidency and returned to Mount Vernon, 1797. Died 1799.

Statue, replica of marble original by Jean Antoine Houdon in the State Capitol, Richmond, Virginia. Bronze, 6ft 2ins (Washington's exact height). Outside the National Gallery, Trafalgar Square. Unveiled June 30th, 1921, by Miss Judith Bower, daughter of the Speaker of the Virginia House of Delegates. Presented by the Commonwealth of Virginia.

GEORGE WASHINGTON

PRESENTED TO THE PEOPLE
GREAT BRITAIN AND IRELAND
BY THE COMMONWEALTH OF
VIRGINIA 1921

Franklin D. Roosevelt

The erection of Franklin Roosevelt's statue, unlike those of the previous two American Presidents (pp228-31), was deliberately kept an all-British affair. Subscriptions were raised as widely as possible. Both Churchill and Attlee broadcast appeals, memorial brochures were sold on railway stations and three special public booths were opened in London. The £40,000 required was raised in six days and 160,000 people contributed, so making the average donation just 5/- (25p). It was a communal expression of gratitude to the man who had been principally responsible for bringing America into the Second World War.

Roosevelt spent all his life fighting for democracy in one form or another, whether against the political dominance of Tamanny Hall, the economic strait-jacket of the Great Depression or the military tyranny of Fascism. He relished the struggle, mixing astute cunning with a great and fundamental decency. He saw beyond the difficulties; as he said at the beginning of his Hundred Days, "the only thing we have to fear is fear itself." Always at ease and relaxed, he combined, as someone wisely said, passion and the golden mean.

There was considerable discussion over the stance of the statue in Grosvenor Square. At the age of forty Roosevelt contracted polio. Horrible though the experience was, it undoubtedly gave greater depth to a man who up to that time had had most things his own way. For years he struggled to walk again but he left the task half-finished when his colleagues demanded his return to politics. He therefore usually moved about in a wheel chair and the sculptor William Reid Dick (pp77 & 304) produced several seated designs. On other occasions, however, Roosevelt stood supported by a stick, most notably during his four inaugurations as President. The controversy was eventually settled by the intervention of his widow, Eleanor Roosevelt, who insisted on a standing figure. Symbolically it seems correct for, by some strange parallel of destiny, it was the man who had fought so hard to overcome his own paralysis who once more set in motion the economic life of his country and who sent out his country's troops to complete the liberation of Europe.

Franklin Delano Roosevelt. Born 1882, son of New York businessman. Called to New York Bar, 1907. Democratic Senator, New York State Senate; leader of group opposed to party bosses, 1910-3. Assistant Secretary of the Navy, 1913-20. Unsuccessful Vice-Presidential candidate, 1920. Contracted polio on sailing holiday, 1921. Governor of New York State; began radio "fireside chats", 1928-32. Elected President, 1932; faced with mass unemployment and banking chaos, introduced "New Deal", reorganising banks, reviving agricultural credit and funding huge new industrial and conservation schemes. Supported Britain with arms and prepared for war, 1938-41. Brought America into Second World War after Japanese attack on Pearl Harbour, 1941. Attended key conferences with Churchill and Stalin, 1943-5. Re-elected for fourth term as President, 1944. Died 1945.

Statue by William Reid Dick. Bronze, 10ft. Grosvenor Square. Unveiled April 12th, 1946, by Eleanor Roosevelt. The gardens were presented by the Duke of Westminster and specially re-designed as a setting for the statue. Cost £40,000.

Left. One of the special contribution booths, in Trafalgar Square; the others were at the Royal Exchange and Selfridges.

Jan Christian Smuts

Smuts became the Prime Minister of South Africa and a Field Marshal in the British army, yet he was as much a man of ideas as a man of action. He spent his childhood under the wide skies of the western Cape Colony, within sight of the majestic Winterhoek mountains. It gave him a deep, almost mystical feeling for nature and this, combined with a brilliant intellect and a strongly religious upbringing, set him on a lifelong philosophical quest. He worked out a theory which he called "holistic evolution". Its universal principle was unity: the formation and self-perfecting of a successive order of "wholes", moving from the inorganic, through the organic and the ethical-mental to the free and balanced human personality. For this he was made a Fellow of the Royal Society, though his theory of progressive, self-organising fields cut right across current reductionist materialism and is only now becoming acceptable as a scientific paradigm.

In the meantime the world of ideas was hardly rewarding enough for someone of Smuts' abilities. Cosmic principle led him to the study of human law, the practice of law led to politics and politics to warfare. In the Boer War he fought as Britain's enemy. During the two World Wars, however, he played a key role in the struggle against Fascism. In 1916 he led the military campaign against German South-West Africa. In 1917-18 he was in London as a member of War Cabinet; it was his report which was largely responsible for bringing the R.A.F. into existence as an independent fighting force (see p286). During the Second World War, he sent the South African army into Kenya, Abyssinia and North Africa. It was for this and for his role as one of the architects of the British Commonwealth that he was commemorated in Parliament Square.

Apart from the South African granite of the pedestal (which was used at the suggestion of the sculptor) the erection of the memorial was an entirely British affair. This was due principally to Britain's worsening relations with the government of the National Party which in 1948 had removed Smuts from power. One would not see the South African flag flying in Parliament Square today as it did at the statue's unveiling. However, Smuts' own views on race were not essentially different from those of the National Party, only less extreme. He knew that his country would have one day to face the problem of its racial divisions but he deferred the solution; for all his later internationalism, his political holism remained essentially a White Man's Dream.

The statue was one of Jacob Epstein's least controversial contributions to the London scene. Epstein was born in 1880 in the Jewish quarter of New York and came to England at the age of 26. His early works were too "primitive" in style for public taste; his *Rima* memorial to the naturalist W.H.Hudson in Kensington Gardens was tarred and feathered several times by protesters. In the 1930's he turned to the more intimate and acceptable art of the portrait bust and in the 1950's the outdoor, public commissions returned, notably the beautiful Madonna and Child on the north side of Cavendish Square. His statue of Smuts gives us the statesman's erect and wiry figure. The most unusual thing about it is the tiptoeing, forward glide. Epstein intended this to convey Smuts' physical and and mental energy, to show him moving into the future as if climbing a mountain (at the age of 70 he could still reach the top of Table Mountain in two hours). However, the stance, especially from the side, seems precarious, the future unsure.

Field Marshal Jan Christian Smuts. Born 1870, Bovenplaats, Cape Colony, son of farmer and member of Cape legislature. Came to England and studied law at Cambridge, 1891-4. Appointed state Attorney of Transvaal; curbed illicit gold trade and police corruption, 1898-9. Supported South African unity and independence; took a leading part in the Boer War as military commander and negotiator, 1900-2. Colonial Secretary and Minister for Native Affairs; conducted struggle with Indian community led by Gandhi (p236) over compulsory registration and marriage rights, 1907-13. Supported England in First World War 1914-16. Member of British War Cabinet, 1917-8. Criticised harshness of peace terms, presented plan for British Commonwealth of Nations under Crown and helped to draft Covenant of League of Nations, 1919. Prime Minister of South Africa, 1919-24; set up special areas for black occupation. Published Holism and Evolution, *1926. Founded United Party and became deputy Prime Minister, 1933. Voted for participation in Second World War; became Prime Minister and Minister of Defence, 1939-45. Played part in founding United Nations and was responsible for placing affirmation of fundamental human rights in Preamble to Charter, 1945. Defeated by National Party over more extreme apartheid policies, 1948. Elected Chancellor of Cambridge University, 1948. Died 1950.*

Statue by Jacob Epstein. Bronze, 9ft. Parliament Square. Unveiled, as shown here, on November 7th, 1956, by W.S.Morrison, Speaker of the House of Commons, deputising for Winston Churchill. Cost £16,500, paid for out of government funds. (The money from the Smuts Memorial Appeal was used to fund a Chair of Commonwealth Studies at Cambridge.)

Mahatma Gandhi

The young Mohandas Gandhi cut his political teeth on General Jan Smuts (p234) when the latter was South Africa's Minister of African affairs, so it is appropriate that their London statues should have been erected next to each other in time. Gandhi's early days in Bombay were undistinguished; he was an indifferent lawyer and so shy that he was quite unable to stand up and plead in court. But confronted with the racial inequalities of South Africa he found his voice. It was there that he worked out his political philosophy. *Satyagraha* is usually called passive or non-violent resistance, but the literal meaning is more dynamic: "soul-force" or "truth-force". Gandhi thought of himself as an experimenter with this new kind of force, more powerful than Galton's electricity or Darwin's evolution. Many times – with the boycotts of foreign cloth, for example, and the marches to gather forbidden salt – he judged that he had awakened it in the people of India. At other times – especially during the horrific scenes of destruction following Partition — he judged that he had failed. Sometimes he felt that he had acted too early and asked too much – a view which was also held by his assassins. Nevertheless he is still regarded as the father of his nation and his example lives on in human rights movements throughout the world.

Gandhi's connections with London are strong. As a young student he thrived in her utopian, vegetarian and theosophical circles. In 1931, when he returned as the Indian delegate to the Round Table Conference, he chose to stay at Kingsley Hall, Bow, where he took great pleasure in meeting and talking to the poor of London's East End, a conspicuous figure in loin-cloth and dhoti. Though he fought the British, he respected them and trusted in their ultimate fair-mindedness. They were, he said no worse than any other people on Earth and, since they always wished to appear just, they could more easily be shamed into doing the right thing.

Mohandas Gandhi. Born 1869, Porbandur, Gujarat, youngest son of city's Prime Minister. Came to London to study law; became leading member of London Vegetarian Society, 1888-91. Practised law in South Africa; took up struggle for Indian minority rights and organised passive resistance to government measures, 1893-1914. Given hero's welcome on return to India; after Amritsar massacre, emerged as leader of Indian National Congress with programme of non-cooperation and development of village industries, 1915-1920. Imprisoned for sedition, 1922-4. Organised Salt March to Dandi to challenge government monopoly, during which 100,000 were arrested, 1930. Attended Round Table Conference in London, 1931; arrested on return and went on fast to death to protect rights of "untouchable" castes. Initiated final campaign of civil disobedience, 1940-4. Indian Independence and Partition; took no part in final negotiations but went on public fasts to minimise violence in Calcutta and Delhi, 1946-8. Assassinated by Hindu extremists, 1948.

Statue by Fredda Brilliant. Bronze. Tavistock Square Gardens. Unveiled May 17th, 1968, by Prime Minister Harold Wilson. Cost £10,000, raised by public subscription, with Camden Council contributing £1,000. The erection of the statue was first proposed in 1948 and in 1953 Pandit Nehru marked the site by planting a copper beach tree close by.

Gandhi prided himself on being the ugliest man in the world, so the statue must be flattering to some degree; it certainly has more hair than he was usually seen to have. The intention was, of course, to convey his inner, spiritual beauty. Fredda Brilliant, who was born in Poland and lived in India for six years, used a factory cleaner from Southall, Ram Lal Singh, as her model.

Left. The statue is being garlanded during celebrations of Gandhi's birthday on October 2nd, 1988. The way in which the plinth is hollowed out underneath adds to the air of lightness and serenity, and also makes it doubly easy for the statue to become a shrine.

MAHATMA GANDHI
1948

Simon Bolivar

Our last commemoration of a foreign politician brings this chapter back where it began, to the tumultuous, hero-worshipping period of the early 1800's. The take-over of Spain by Napoleon Bonaparte's forces sparked off declarations of independence by all Spain's South American colonies. In the ensuing struggle to retain that independence, one man emerged as champion: Simon Bolivar. No less than six countries – Venezuela, Ecuador, Colombia, Peru, Panama and Bolivia – hail him as their liberator and one of them is named after him.

Bolivar came from an old landowning and slaveowning family. He was educated along progressive lines and journeyed to Europe. In Madrid he married; he might have settled down quietly and become no more than a marginal figure, but after a few months his young wife died. It was a tremendous shock – from then on, what did he have to lose? Among the ruins of Rome, he dreamt of South American independence. He joined the first revolutionary government of Venezuela and in the ruthless war that followed emerged as supreme leader. His life took on extraordinary qualities of heroism and endurance. He came back from defeat, leading his forces on seemingly impossible journeys across the Andes and winning battles against all the odds. With his sense of honour and loyalty, his steely rhetoric and his quixotic temperament, he was more Spanish than the Spaniards. Yet he kept a hard-headed realism about the political possibilities in lands which had lived for so long under a control far more rigid than that experienced by Britain's colonies.

In urbane, diplomatic Belgrave Square his statue, arm upraised, seems more likely to be hailing a taxi than haranguing his troops or expounding his political philosophy. When he himself came to London in 1810, it must have seemed like a haven of peace and reasonableness compared to harsh, semi-feudal Venezuela. He always thought of British institutions, with their slow, organic growth towards freedom, as the best in the world. The people of London, on the other hand, found him an exciting, romantic figure. Byron (p124) once thought of fighting for the freedom of Peru rather than of Greece. Many Britons did go out to join him, much as they went more than a century later to fight for Republican Spain. They were so numerous that they formed their own special battalion and they played a key role in a number of battles.

Despite his immense endurance, Bolivar was a slight, narrow-chested figure; the statue's odd proportions are based on reality. So too is the military uniform (complete with a pair of the original Wellington boots). He wore it habitually, not out of vainglory but as a symbol of the task which he had undertaken. Besides, he said, if he went round in a plain coat people would think that he was aping Napoleon, something he had not the slightest wish to do. The rest of the world, however, found it difficult to imagine a dictator with no dreams of personal aggrandisement and so did not give him the political and financial support he had hoped for at the Congress of Panama. He dreamt of uniting the whole continent but even the territories which he had liberated began to quarrel and fragment. He ended a bitter, disillusioned man, predicting most of the political woes that would come to afflict South America. "The three greatest idiots in history," he said, "have been Jesus Christ, Don Quixote...and myself." Would it have mollified him to see, a hundred and fifty years on, representatives from all the lands which he freed gathered around his statue in the country which he so much admired?

Simon Bolivar. Born 1783, Caracas, son of wealthy planter. Joined army, 1798. Came to Europe; married Teresa Rodriguez del Toro, who died shortly afterwards, 1799-1802. Came to London as emissary of revolutionary government of Venezuela, 1810. Played leading part in war with Spain; became military dictator of Venezuela until defeated by pro-Spanish army of llaneros, wild cowherding plainsmen, 1812-14. Recaptured Venezuela and delivered political testimony to Parliament of Angostura, 1817-9. Crossed Andes and freed New Granada (later Colombia) after Battle of Boyaca, 1819. Won final victory in Venezuela with Battle of Carabobo; chosen as first President of Columbia (which then included New Granada and Venezuela), 1821. Conquered Quito (later Ecuador) and incorporated it into Columbia, 1822. Invited to join struggle in Peru; won Battles of Junin and Ayacucho and proclaimed dictator, 1823-4. Bolivia created from Upper Peru; made triumphal entry into La Paz and organised government, 1825. Called Congress of Panama. Returned to Bogota to deal with unrest and rebellion, 1826. Assumed dictatorship of Columbia; adopted more conservative policies and censorship. Survived assassination attempt, 1828. Secession of Venezuela, 1829. Resigned from office. Secession of Ecuador, 1830. Died 1830.

Statue by Hugo Daini. Bronze. Belgrave Square. Unveiled June 12th, 1974, by James Callaghan, as Foreign Secretary, in the presence of former President Carera of Venezuela. Presented by all the Bolivarian countries, on the initiative of Venezuela.

Several other European capitals have statues of Bolivar. Those in Paris, Rome and Madrid are equestrian, a tribute to his exceptional skill as a horseman. However, because of his admiration for the stability of British political institutions, the one in London presents his role as a maker of constitutions. He is portrayed delivering his political message at Angostura. On one side of the pedestal is the quotation: "I am convinced that England alone is capable of protecting the world's precious rights as she is great, glorious and wise."

CHAPTER 6

THE ARMED FORCES

As one might expect, this chapter begins with that great campaigner, Arthur Wellesley, Duke of Wellington. With five outdoor London commemorations, the Iron Duke was more honoured than any other non-royal personage. His story, which merits telling in full, begins in 1822 with the neo-classical Achilles shown opposite, whose initial nudity so shocked public taste. Wellington was in fact not the first soldier to have an outdoor memorial. That honour belongs to the be-pistolled Duke of Cumberland, the victor of Culloden, whose equestrian statue (chapter 9, p346) was put up in Cavendish Square in 1770 and removed in 1868. And the first personal likeness was that of the royal and grand old Duke of York, whose column preceded Nelson's by nine years.

After Waterloo, England enjoyed a remarkably peaceful nineteenth century. The only European war was fought in the Crimea and its outstanding hero was Florence Nightingale (chapter 4, p164). The true field of endeavour was India, where seven of the nineteen soldiers commemorated saw their major service. What strikes one most about the commanders of Victoria's day is their range and diversity of character, from the missionary Havelock to the daring, chivalrous Outram, from the sentimental Duke of Cambridge to the efficient, belligerent Wolseley. The most remarkable figure of all was General Charles Gordon, who never commanded a British army and whose death in the Sudan elevated him to the status of a religious martyr.

By the end of the century the heroic mould seemed set and in the persons of Roberts, Kitchener and Haig carried Britain into and through the First World War. Marshal Foch, commemorated at Victoria, also belongs to that time and was the French general most closely connected with British forces. The military tide of the Second World War was stemmed and turned in the West by Montgomery and Alexander, whose contrasting but complementary natures won such success in North Africa, and in the East by Slim (soon to be commemorated in Whitehall) and by Mountbatten, who later became First Sea Lord as he so much desired.

With only one outdoor, free-standing figure of a full-time admiral – Nelson – the Navy has been the victim of its own success; between Trafalgar (1805) and Jutland (1916) it ruled the world's seas more or less unchallenged. The Air Force, on the other hand, has made steady commemorative progress since its foundation and, with statues of Trenchard, Portal and now Dowding (chapter 10, p354), has surpassed the Navy.

To ARTHUR DUKE OF WELLINGTON
And his Brave companions in arms
This Statue of Achilles
cast in French Brass
Is inscribed by their Countrywomen!!
June 18th 1822

Making Decent

Pub.d by G Humphrey 27 St James's St London — august 5th 1822.

This Print Commemorative of Anglo French BRASS & true British Chastity, is inscribed with veneration to that worthy man M.r Wilberforce who with saintlike regard for the Morals of his Country, has undertaken to make the above fig. Decent from 10 in the M.g till Dusk.

The Duke of Wellington

The erection of statues on a national scale was, as we have seen, inspired by the victories against Napoleon, as England's heroes took light from the fall of that great star. Two men stood out as guardians of the nation's life: Nelson by sea and Wellington by land. In 1817, two years after Waterloo, it was proposed to celebrate their triumphs by building two gigantic towers, one with an observation room, in Greenwich Park. The treasury set aside £310,000 for the purpose but in the end only Nelson soared to the skies; the commemoration of the Duke turned out to be a much weightier matter.

On the battlefield Wellington seemed to be everywhere. At Waterloo, wrote an observer, "the eye could turn in no direction that it did not perceive him, galloping to charge the enemy, or darting across the field to issue orders. Every ball also…seemed fired, and every gun aimed at him. But he suffered nothing to check or engage him". There was, however, nothing superficially gallant or showy about his presence. He was always supremely calm, as his aristocratic detachment and his outstanding mental gifts enabled him to shrink to the core of the task in hand.

At home, too, his distinctive features seemed everywhere. As his victories in Spain and Portugal made him a household name, his face began to appear on wallpapers, tea services, fans, clocks, barometers and razors. Prints and portrait busts of him were in great demand. However, the erection of a public statue presented certain difficulties. The chief was the taboo, already observed over the statue of Pitt (p173), against such likenesses of the living. Nelson died at the height of his victory in true mythic style ("Kismet, Hardy" is the more likely version of his final words) but Wellington lived on for thirty seven years after Waterloo.

The patriotic, upper-class society known as the Ladies of England were the first to take the matter in hand. In Wellington's honour they commissioned a symbolic horse, to be modelled on the fiery, Classical Roman beast on the Monte Cavallo. However, their sculptor, Sir Richard Westmacott, modified the commission. Having lived in Rome, he knew that the symbolism was wrong; the horse in question was *being* tamed – by one of the Dioscuri, Castor or Pollux, just as Wellington had tamed Napoleon. He therefore took the human figure of the Monte Cavallo group as his model. And lacking Wellington's own innate modesty, he set about creating a colossus, calling it "the greatest task which has been achieved in this or any other century for hundreds of years". Following the canons of Greece and Rome, which knew no Serpent and no Fall, he made his figure naked and unashamed. Loosely named "Achilles", it was erected in 1822 at the south-east corner of Hyde Park. The Ladies of England were horrified and immediately insisted that a fig-leaf be applied to the most intimate parts of the statue. Wellington, as was his custom, said nothing, though the figure stood in close proximity to Apsley House, his London home. The humorists had a field-day, especially since the Duke was known as a ladies' man; in private he was full of Irish gaiety and good humour and was always surrounded by a coterie of fashionable and intelligent women.

The unfavourable reception given to Westmacott's Achilles clearly illustrates the English lack of artistic sophistication and their mistrust of grand gestures. The sculptor was deeply hurt; however, he believed that its qualities would one day be recognised, as on the whole they have.

Since it had become clear that Wellington would go on living for ever, the taboo against a living likeness was in the end allowed to lapse. After the glory of Waterloo, it may come as something of a surprise to find that the City of London commemorated him for his help in putting through the Parliamentary Bill required for the rebuilding of London Bridge. This was carried out by John Rennie and his son between 1824 and 1831. It was a major engineering project with considerable implications for commercial development and the City fathers must have been very proud of it. The Duke had a great interest in technology, whether military or civil, and the bridge was his especial concern as an M.P. and Master of the Ordnance.

After Waterloo, Wellington could have retired and lived sumptuously but out of a sense of duty he re-entered politics; he believed that the State needed him, as indeed it did. He embodied the Right and could carry the Ultra-right; he even had the status to treat on equal terms with the monarch. Three times – over greater rights for Catholics in Ireland, over the extension of the parliamentary electorate and over the repeal of the duties on imported corn – he rose above his own and party opinion and acted to preserve the country from political chaos by supporting necessary change. We see this calm, quiet holding to the centre of events in Chantrey's statue. The figure has an almost Wordsworthian simplicity; as with the statue of George IV, on which he was also working at the time of his death, Chantrey aimed for unencumbered clarity of line (p52). Some of Wellington's contemporaries found the lack of military detail disturbing: why, the Duke had no boots, no saddle and no hat! He rode again, *Punch* said, with bedspread and rolling pin! However, one must see the figure whole.

The story of Wellington's commemoration now shifts once more from the simple and sublime to grandeur tinged with pathos and farce. The chief organiser of the statue at the Royal Exchange was a Mr Thomas Bridge Simpson, a member of the City's Court of Common Council and a particular admirer of Matthew Cotes Wyatt, whose "pigtail and pump-handle" statue of George III (p48) had recently been erected. However, by the Lord Mayor's casting vote, the Royal Exchange commission had gone not to Wyatt but to Chantrey. Simpson therefore turned his energies to another Wellington commemoration, this time in the West End, and due mainly to some crafty dealing by the Duke of Rutland, the chairman of the executive committee, Wyatt was engaged. Now he was more like Westmacott than Chantrey in his approach to commemoration. When he could get the funds – and in this case £30,000 was available, mostly donated by the army – he loved the full scale and dramatic. He therefore produced what he believed to be the largest equestrian statue in existence, 30 ft high and weighing over 40 tons. With the Queen's permission, it was agreed to place it on top of Decimus Burton's triumphal arch at Hyde Park Corner, even though Burton himself condemned its proportions as entirely wrong.

After three years' intense work, the figure was ready. Rutland's committee were determined to erect it in style and its journey from Wyatt's studio off the Harrow Road was made into a national spectacle. The statue was winched onto a vast, specially made carriage drawn by twenty-nine brewer's horses. In front marched the band of the 2nd Life Guards; behind, the bands of the Fusilier, Grenadier and Coldstream Guards poured more music into the air. A hundred Fusiliers held emergency ropes attached to the carriage in case gravity should

Statue by Francis Chantrey. He died before the statue was completed and it was finished by his assistants Henry Weekes and Alan Cunningham. Bronze, 14ft on a 14ft red Aberdeen granite pedestal. In front of the Royal Exchange. Erected June 18th, 1844. Cost c. £4,200 plus metal worth £1,520 donated by the government. The photograph shows the statue backed by the new Stock Exchange building.

Sculptor and sculpted make an interesting comparison. Both had active, hearty, social selves and both had the grace of humour. But the inner natures of both men remained to some extent mysterious, concealed partly out of temperament and partly from necessity, for both began obscure and ended famous. Essentially, Chantrey was a deeply sensitive man who loved beauty and art's completeness while Wellington, in his detached way, loved his county's safety, which he had the foresight to preserve. There is, perhaps, more of Chantrey in the Royal Exchange figure; it is soft and rounded and lacks something of the Duke's cutting edge.

Below and also page 348. Statue by Matthew Cotes Wyatt. Bronze, from captured enemy canon; 30ft, 40 tons. Erected September 29th, 1846, on top of the triumphal arch at Hyde Park Corner. During the 1880's the arch was moved forward and erected at a different angle (the one it occupies today) and in 1883 the authorities at last took the opportunity to remove the statue which they had never liked. After a great deal of controversy, the army took it to Aldershot and re-erected it on Round Hill (p348).

Left. The *Illustrated London News* gave considerable coverage to Wyatt's statue. Above is "The Atelier or Model-Room". In the centre the plaster model of the horse (without head or tail) together with the lower part of the Duke's cloak stands on a revolving platform. Compare the real-life horse and rider standing under the belly. More than 100 tons of plaster were used in the modelling.

Below is "Mr Wyatt's Foundry". Eight separate moulds were taken from the model. Here the completed cast of the Duke in his saddle has been hauled up to the first floor ready for cleaning, smoothing and polishing. The building was more or less demolished for the statue's final removal.

get the better of the procession. The sun shone brilliantly and spectators thronged the windows and rooftops along the route. Wellington himself was in the country for the entire proceedings, but royalty from all the nations and principalities who had triumphed at Waterloo were gathered at Apsley House to witness the statue's arrival.

The following day it was hoisted onto the arch. However, a trial period of only three months had been agreed on, after which "competent persons" would decide its fate. The general public seemed happy enough with it. *Punch* declared war on it and showed it falling through the centre of the Earth or interrupting the Astronomer Royal's observation of the Moon. And just as it was getting itself established as a part of the urban scene, the artistic and administrative bigwigs of the day, the Royal Academicians and the Commissioners for Woods and Forests, pronounced against it; it was an eyesore and would have to come down. The Duke had all along maintained his usual disinterestedness but the news that the young Queen herself was coming up from Windsor to order its removal seems to have touched a raw nerve in him. He let it be known that he would consider this an expression of Her Majesty's personal disapproval and would resign as Commander-in-Chief – even, it was learned later, renounce his peerage. His intervention of course locked the situation solid and the statue remained in place for the next forty years as one of London's best-known landmarks, the metal plumes on the great hat soughing in the wind.

After this, the placing of a marble statue next to Tower Green must have seemed a mere routine operation. It honoured the Duke as Constable of the Tower, one of the many ceremonial posts which he held, and is now to be found at Woolwich. It was the work of the sculptor Thomas Milnes, who did the first set of lions for Nelson's

Left. Statue by Thomas Milnes. Marble, 8ft. Erected December 12th, 1848, at the Tower of London, in front of the steps leading to Traitor's Gate, and moved to the Royal Arsenal, Woolwich, in 1863, where it commemorates Wellington's Mastership of the Ordnance. It was re-sited in 1974; in the photograph the 8th Duke of Wellington looks up at his ancestor after a ceremony commemorating the move.

Right. Statues by Joseph Boehm. Bronze. Hyde Park Corner. Unveiled December 21st, 1888, by the Prince of Wales. Cost £8,000, of which £6,000 was voted by Parliament. The Duke rides his favourite charger, Copenhagen. On the corners of the granite pedestal are soldiers from regiments representing the four countries of the United Kingdom. These are (*anti-clockwise from top left*):

The 42nd Royal Highlanders (the Black Watch), who bravely resisted Napoleon's first major attack at Quatre Bras, two days before Waterloo; their strange bonnets and kilts rising suddenly out of the tall corn stopped the French in their tracks.

The 23rd Royal Welsh Fusiliers, who turned defeat into victory at Albuera; they were, said Wellington, just the men to hold a dangerous gap.

The 6th Inniskilling Dragoons, who led the charge of the Union Brigade at Waterloo; they broke the French but overran into danger.

The 1st Foot Guards who, with graceful nonchalance, took on the final charge of Napoleon's crack Imperial Guards at Waterloo and drove them back.

Column (rejected as being unworthy of their subject). If Wellington sat for him, it is to be hoped that Milnes was on time. The Duke was usually courteous during these frequent inroads into his time, but E.H. Baily (p252), who sculpted Nelson for his Column, was once a day late for a session. Wellington raised his arms above his head and cursed all artists and sculptors, crying out that he had sat for 400,000 sittings!

When in the 1880's Hyde Park Corner was re-structured and the great statue of the Duke removed from the triumphal arch, it was decided to replace it with a new and smaller memorial. This stood originally on its own central island in the midst of horse-drawn carriages and leisurely, parasolled pedestrians. Now it is clamped inside the steel ring of motor traffic and also, at the time of writing, obscured by a tree. However, if one can find the right subway, Wellington's final memorial, guarded by soldiers representing the four countries of the United Kingdom, is well worth inspecting; the soldiers, especially, are the accomplished work one would expect from Sir Joseph Boehm.

The Duke of York

This is indeed the grand old Duke of York who had ten thousand
men, who marched them up to the top of the hill and marched them
down again. It is one of the cruelties of history that he is better
known by a nursery rhyme than for his genuine achievements and
for the handsome one hundred and thirty five foot, ten inch column
which stands at the bottom of Waterloo Place. From there he looks
across to Horseguards Parade, the home of the army of which he was
for thirty years the conscientious and enterprising Commander-in-Chief.
However, at that height his figure can only be seen in silhouette and
most people probably do not even know who he is.

According to his biographer and greatest military champion, Lt.
Col. Alfred Burne, this is the Duke of York who might have become
King of France. In 1793, after his victory against the raw troops of
the French Revolution at Valenciennes, the townspeople hailed him
as their King. He wanted to march on Paris, but was obliged to follow
the orders of Pitt's ultra-cautious Minister of War, Henry Dundas,
and go north to Dunkirk. Here the command was split, the called-for
reinforcements failed to arrive and he eventually had to withdraw.
He was in fact a perfectly competent but unlucky general who was
made to take the blame for others' failures. His royal status, far from
protecting him, made him all the more open to ridicule in certain
quarters.

The Duke was also unlucky in his principal mistress, the wily
adventuress Mrs Clarke. She had his ear on the matter of army
promotions and she sold her recommendations for large sums. When
the scandal broke, the Duke was forced to resign as Commander-in-
Chief, though he was reinstated soon afterwards. It is perfectly possible
that he was, as he claimed, totally unaware of the origins of her
wealth. Like all his brothers, he had no conception of the value of
money and was, as a result, chronically in debt all his life. In his
last years his creditors relied on the expectation that he would soon
succeed George IV as King, but his portly brother outlived him. The
subsequent announcement that a huge sum was to be spent on his
memorial column was for the creditors the final straw; they held an
angry meeting and demanded that their names, rather than the Duke's,
should be inscribed upon its base. Their protests were ignored but the
situation caused much hilarity. The Duke, it was said, had at last
been raised out of their reach and the lightning conductor on his
head was a spike for unpaid bills.

One might wonder why, if Frederick Augustus was so pilloried, he
was given such a grand memorial. Post-Napoleonic national pride
was, of course, still vibrant and the Duke's recent, forthright support
of Church and Constitution had won him many political admirers.
But he was also much appreciated as a military Commander-in-Chief.
In 1814 Wellington told the House of Commons that it was only his
reforms which had made the victories in Spain possible. Working at
his desk overlooking Horseguards Parade, the Duke founded the school
for officer cadets which eventually became Sandhurst and cut back
the system of purchasing commissions. He also increased the pay of
private soldiers by 80%, he gave them greatcoats and he vaccinated
them against smallpox. So it is not surprising that, two days after he
died, the officers of the Royal Artillery at Woolwich opened a fund
for his statue and a month later Wellington chaired the large and
distinguished public meeting which formally inaugurated the fund for
a major memorial. To this many regiments in the army contributed

Frederick Augustus, Duke of York. Born 1763, second son of George III. Studied soldiering in Hanover and Prussia, 1780-7. Commanded British army in unsuccessful campaigns against the French in the Netherlands, 1793-4 & 1799-1800. Commander-in-Chief of the Army, 1795-1809 & 1811-27. Examined for corrupt sale of commissions before House of Commons; narrowly exonerated but resigned as C-in-C, 1808. Reinstated, 1811. Spoke passionately in House of Lords in support of Protestant basis of English Constitution, 1825. Died 1827.

Statue by Richard Westmacott. Bronze, 13ft 10ins, on 10ft pedestal and 112ft column. South end of Waterloo Place. Raised April 8th, 1834. Cost of statue £4,000; costs of column, raising, etc., £17,527-6-0d. The Duke is in Roman dress, with a military cloak.

a day's pay and no doubt did so with some good feeling, whatever has been said to the contrary.

Eventually the time came to install the seven ton, bronze statue on Benjamin Wyatt's one hundred and twelve foot, classical column. However, bad luck and mistiming dogged the Duke's occasions in death as in life. Mr Nowell, of Grosvenor Wharf, Pimlico, who had erected the scaffolding, recommended that a further week be allowed for the raising; however, the authorities decided to do everything in one day. So when large numbers of people assembled in Waterloo Place expecting a military occasion, all they could see was a large object wrapped in a canvas sheet creeping imperceptibly up the side of the column. No bands played, the wind was bitterly cold and six hours later, when the statue was finally in place, everyone had gone home.

Is it now time to rehabilitate the man whom Thackeray called "big, burly, loud, jolly, cursing and courageous"? We should remember his good-heartedness and look again at his statue, made more dramatic by the great cloak that seems to billow in the winds at that exalted altitude. His column, more nobly rounded than Nelson's, occupies an axial position in the city's architecture – something which is especially clear when one catches sight of it, distant and impressive, from the top of Lower Regent Street.

Lord Nelson

The fluted column which rises from Trafalgar Square is London's most immediately recognisable landmark, as familiar as red buses or rain. The eye may not be able to pick out the detail of the one-armed hero aloft, "sailing the sky", but heart and memory know that he is there.

Nelson is said to exemplify the genius of England at its active best. Certainly he won his battles in a most unconventional and daring manner. At the Battle of the Nile, for example, he engaged towards nightfall and took his fleet close up to a sandbank to catch the French on their undefended side. Yet he was a strange figure for a national hero, physically slight, frail and almost white-haired. The future William IV (p54) met him early on in the West Indies and found him a quaint figure – "the merest boy of a captain I ever beheld" – but irresistibly pleasant in manner. He kept this youthful charm and enthusiasm all his life and, paradoxically for a man of war, there is something of the eternal child in his appeal.

There is also something elemental about him, perhaps because he commanded by water, the medium with most appeal for the island British. He was the only man Napoleon feared and the Emperor used to keep a bust of him on his desk as if in an attempt to control a natural force of equal magnitude. He was like a light bursting on the scene of conflict, burning up at his triumphant zenith and bathing the English navy in an aura of invincibility which lasted more than a century. If the metaphor of light seems fanciful, it was Nelson's own. At the age of seventeen he had a bad attack of malaria and during the subsequent depression wished himself at the bottom of the sea. Then everything was changed by a "sudden glow of patriotism" which swept over him; from then on, heroic devotion to King and Country became the "radiant orb" which gave his life meaning. He put himself in the hands of Providence, and that same Providence delivered Britain – and Europe – from the French and raised Nelson

Vice Admiral Horatio Nelson, 1st Viscount Nelson of the Nile. Born 1758, son of Norfolk parson. Entered navy as midshipman on uncle's ship, 1770; served chiefly in the West Indies. Promoted captain, 1779. Married Elisabeth Nisbet, 1787. Lived unemployed and frustrated with father in Norfolk, 1787-92. Posted to Mediterranean, 1793. Played decisive part in Battle of Cape St Vincent, 1797; promoted Rear Admiral. Lost arm in foolhardy attack on Spanish treasure ships in Tenerife, 1797. Pursued French fleet around Mediterranean; finally encountered them off Alexandria and won Battle of the Nile, 1798. Fell in love with Emma Hamilton, wife of British ambassador at Naples, 1798. Put down revolt for Queen of Naples against Admiralty's instructions, 1800. Second in command at Battle of Copenhagen; ignored order to withdraw, 1801. Spent two continuous years at sea pursuing and blockading French fleet, 1803-5. Battle of Trafalgar, October 21st, 1805; French fleet destroyed, Nelson killed by sniper's bullet.

Statue by E.H.Bailey. Stone, 16ft on 12ft 6ins pedestal (the overall height of the column, including the statue, is 170 ft 6ins). Installed November 3rd and 4th, 1843. The total cost of the monument was £47,000 (including £20,000 for the lions).

Left. The sculptor E.H.Baily at work on Nelson's statue. If the detail seems somewhat crude, one must remember that the statue was specifically designed to be seen from a distance. The stone came from the Duke of Buccleuch's quarry at Granton, near Edinburgh. Baily wanted a single block but, as this would have weighed at least 20 tons, the shipping company refused to transport it. He therefore had to complete the statue in two parts. Note the two smaller sized models from which he is working.

Right.. The two sections of the statue were brought to the top of the column on November 3rd and 4th, 1843. Each was lifted, inch by inch, by means of an engine placed on the upper platform of the scaffolding; the lower section took six hours to reach the top. This engraving from the *Illustrated London News* shows the scene two weeks later, with the scaffolding still up. The huge framework, a new type of construction, was made of wooden beams slotted into each other by tenons and secured by clamps.

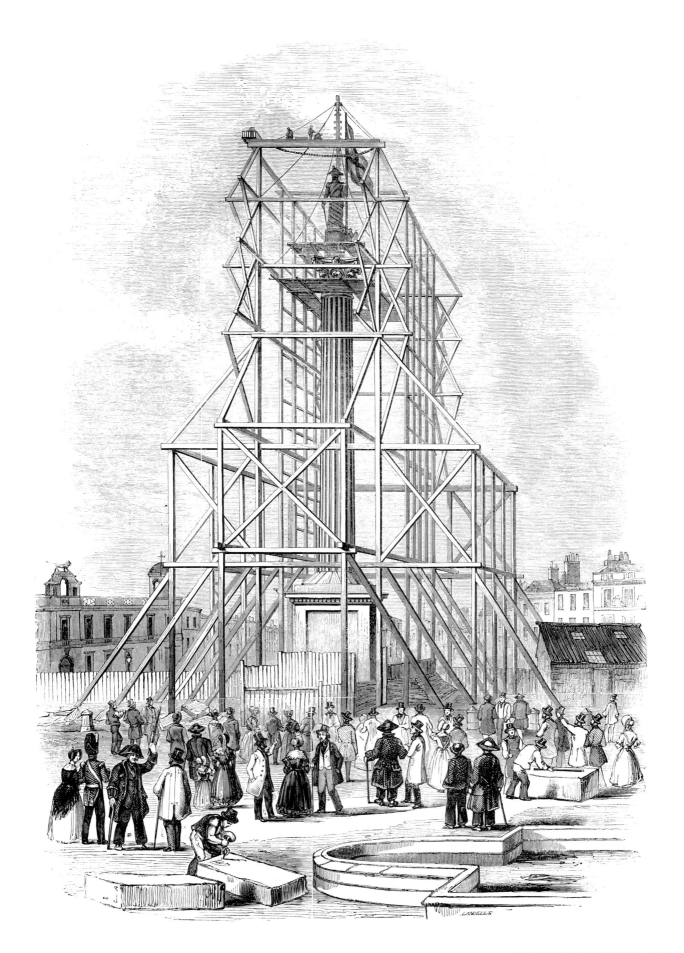

higher than any of his fellow countrymen.

The column in Trafalgar Square was in fact the last of a long series of memorials. London's first commemorations took place indoors, in St Paul's and the Guildhall. Birmingham, Liverpool and the Barbados had statues up within ten years of the hero's death; Glasgow, Dublin and Yarmouth (which was close to his birthplace) raised columns, though Glasgow's was destroyed by lightning in 1810. However, it was not until 1838 that plans for an outdoor London memorial were seriously considered. The building of Trafalgar Square was then more or less complete and it was decided to use its open and inviting centre to celebrate Britain's naval might. A Nelson Memorial Committee was formed and subscriptions invited. Scores of designs were submitted by all the leading figures and two controversial and somewhat inconclusive competitions were held. On both occasions the first prize was awarded to the architect William Railton for his Corinthian column, taken from the temple of Mars the Avenger in Rome. The second prize went initially to the sculptor E.H.Baily for his statue of Nelson in front of an obelisk and in the end it was decided to combine the two winning designs, the Duke of Wellington as usual having the final word on the matter.

The main part of the memorial was completed in 1843. By then the funds subscribed by the general public were running out and the government, in the persons of the Commissioners for Woods and Forests, were obliged to take over the expense. The bas-reliefs on the base of the column, which show Nelson's victories at Cape St. Vincent, the Nile, Copenhagen and Trafalgar, were not in place until 1852. (The firm casting the Trafalgar relief was prosecuted for cheating on the content of the bronze.) The famous lions took a full sixty two years to assume guard. The first sculptor commissioned, John Lough, failed to provide any. Thomas Milnes' lions were so lacking in spirit that they were rejected. Finally, on the strength of his skill as a painter of animals, Sir Edwin Landseer was brought in. His models were excellent; they were cast in bronze by Baron Marochetti and unveiled in January 1867. *Punch* showed Nelson in front of his column shaking hands with the bearded artist and congratulating him with the words, "Thank you, Sir Edwin. I see that England has at last done her duty".

For many years the anniversary of Trafalgar was celebrated at the column. At the turn of the century thousands would watch as steeplejacks scaled its precipitous surface and decorated it with wreaths. In other ways, however, the Square has turned out to be as much a platform for dissent as a symbol of national solidarity. Significant Chartist and Socialist protests were held there and broken up by the police in 1848 and 1886-7. The suffragettes, the hunger marchers of the 1920's, the Campaign for Nuclear Disarmament and numerous other protest groups have all held meetings there. Does Nelson look on approvingly? He was a man of his time, patriotic and conservative in politics; however, his putting of his telescope to his blind eye at Copenhagen is one of the most famous acts of insubordination in history. If Emma Hamilton had taken up votes for women – and, a hundred years on, who knows what she might have done – he would no doubt have incurred the wrath of the Establishment and backed her to the hilt. It was his human unpredictability and his sensitivity to the moment which made him great, as much as his loyalty to his country and his knowledge of warfare, and it is reassuring to find such a man enskied at the heart of the nation's capital.

Above right. In 1987 statue and column were given a major clean-up. Poised high above the capital, Richard Paffett gets to work. How has the all-round view been achieved – is Nelson perhaps looking back at himself in time through the lens of his telescope?

Below right. The statue is now clean and Christopher Chope, M.P., the Minister responsible for the Public Services Agency, has chosen Nelson's sighted left eye (he did not always wear a patch over his blind one) through which to get a view down Whitehall.

Sir Charles Napier

Above. In contrast to the formality of the statue, this eyewitness sketch shows how Napier actually looked as he received the homage of 3,000 Sindi chieftains after his conquest. He wore an old flannel jacket, dirty white trousers without braces and a peaked hunting cap. His staff signed a certificate to say that the sketch was accurate and no caricature.

Major General Sir Charles Napier. Born 1782, eldest son of army colonel (he was the great-great-grandson of Charles II (p24) and his mother, Lady Sarah Lennox, twice refused George III (p42) in marriage). Brought up on family estate in Ireland. Entered for army, 1794. Commanded regiment in Peninsular War; five times wounded, 1808-12. Military Secretary of Greek island of Cephalonia, 1822-30. Handled Chartist unrest in North of England, 1839-40. Conquered Sind, 1841-3. Administered Sind, 1844-6. Marched north for First Sikh War; his forces were not required and he resigned when he was not thanked for his presence, 1847. Appointed Military C-in-C in India on recommendation of Wellington, 1849-50; resigned over issue of Indian soldiers' pay. Died 1853.

Statue by George Ganon Adams. Bronze, 12ft, on 17ft granite pedestal. South-west corner of Trafalgar Square. Unveiled November 26th, 1855, without ceremony, in sleet and slush. Napier is in full military uniform and he holds a scroll symbolising the "giving of government" to Sind. He was much loved by his own soldiers and the inscription reads, "Erected by public subscription from all classes, civil and military, the most numerous subscribers being private soldiers." According to the *Times*, most of the contributions were of £1 or £2.

The statue was much criticised. The *Art Journal* called it dull and soulless and "perhaps the worst piece of sculpture in England". They blamed not so much Adams as the gentlemen of the memorial committee who had hedged him round with demands for a publicly acceptable likeness. In Napier's case this was undoubtedly a difficult task. His appearance was even more extraordinary than his life. He was very short-sighted and his piercing eyes gazed out through thick spectacles. His nose was so fearsomely hooked that his regiments called him Old Fagin and his whiskers and beard fell in wild profusion to his chest. How could such whiskers be translated into bronze? Adams adopts the somewhat artificial stratagem of curling the beard in below the chin, making the face look more like a lion's than a man's.

The life of Sir Charles Napier reads more strangely than fiction. He was the cousin of Charles James Fox (p174) and like him a radical in politics. By temperament, however, he was an autocrat, at his happiest as the uncrowned king of the Greek Ionian island of Cephalonia, where he put down banditry and built roads, hospitals and a lighthouse. Lord Byron, on his deathbed, spoke of him as the man to command the Greek armies of independence.

As a young major in the Peninsular War, Napier was captured and reported killed, and his life was saved only through the kindness of the French officers. The gallant responded to his gallantry; lesser men, or so it seemed to him, envied his accomplishments and he was loved or hated for his outspokenness and fiery temper. The East India Company found him intolerable. Two strands intertwined in his nature: a thirst for military glory and a sympathy for the sufferings of ordinary humanity. Sometimes the strands broke apart; war was his profession, yet he wrote to his mother this eerie description of the Peninsular campaign:

"To me military life is like dancing up a long room with a mirror at the end against which we cut our faces, and so the deception ends. It is thus gaily men follow their trade of blood thinking it glittery, but to me it appears without brightness and reflection, a dirty red."

At other times, however, glory called him and he found the call irresistible. Sind, the dry plain which is now southern Pakistan, has had many conquerors. Napier succeeded the warlike Baluchi princes known as the Amirs who had for sixty years run a comparatively mild and stable Islamic autocracy. However, the English government, its eye on Sind's strategic importance and on the Indus as an artery of trade, judged them uncooperative over certain treaty arrangements and ordered Napier to mount a campaign. He reconciled himself to the task by viewing it as a crusade against an oppressive tyranny on behalf of the ordinary people of Sind. Others, notably Sir James Outram (p262), saw it differently, but Napier wanted his war, calling it a "very advantageous, useful, humane piece of rascality". The English troops were generally outnumbered but their canon was far superior. At Miani and at Hyderabad, Napier led the slaughter of huge numbers of Sindi and Baluchi soldiers, riding unprotected between the lines of fire rallying his men. It is said that after the victory he sent a one-word telegram to England: "Peccavi" (I have Sind), but the story may be apocryphal. Kindness after severity was his policy and his brief administration was generally regarded as benevolent and just. He initiated the building of Karachi harbour and imposed the death penalty for the burning of widows.

Two episodes show his understanding of ordinary people. In 1839 he was sent to the North of England with regiments of troops to deal with Chartist unrest. He personally sympathised with their aims of better conditions for the working classes; he met the leaders in secret and allowed a mass demonstration to go ahead, at the same time insisting that it remain peaceful. The Chartists had no chance of winning their programme at that time and Napier's firm and balanced action prevented bloodshed. As Commander-in-Chief in India he he realised the dangers of reducing the "foreign service" pay and status of the Indian troops after the annexation of the Punjab. He restored their losses on his own authority and resigned when the Governor General Lord Dalhousie overruled him. Had he been listened to, one of the significant causes of the Indian Mutiny would have been avoided.

Sir Henry Havelock

At the age of sixty Henry Havelock was an obscure, somewhat eccentric but respected army staff officer in India. At the age of sixty three, thrust into the limelight by the events of the Indian Mutiny, he was a national and international hero; to some, he was little short of a saint.

His colleagues had always known him as a far from ordinary soldier. To begin with, he held prayer meetings for his men and preached them extemporary sermons; those who attended were called "Havelock's Saints". He was not, however, in any way a bigot; in character he was clear-minded and quietly humorous. His fellow officers were scornful of such familiarity with the lower ranks but those in overall command appreciated the results. Once his regiment was roused by a night alarm and the C.O. was disgusted to find most of the men drunk. "Send for Havelock's Saints," he shouted, "at least they're always sober on duty." Camp life in India was often degradingly monotonous and drunkenness was common. When Havelock became adjutant he started a regimental coffee-house, the first of its kind.

Havelock eventually became Quartermaster General of the Queen's troops in India. At sixty he could look forward to a few quiet years before retirement but the Mutiny changed everything. Returning from Persia, he was appointed to lead the so called "movable column" which set out in the intense heat and drenching monsoon rain to relieve Cawnpore and Lucknow. At Cawnpore his long study of military history bore fruit. Instead of the usual, costly, frontal assault which the Indians had come to expect from English generals, he announced that he was repeating a manoeuvre made by Frederick the Great at the battle of Leuthen. He sent just eighteen crack cavalry soldiers up the road against a force of five thousand and wheeled his regiments round to attack the enemy's left flank, scattering them completely.

The conflict became ever more bitter and atrocities were committed by both sides. Havelock marched on like an Old Testament avenger though, it must be said, he set his face against what he considered to be deliberate or unnecessary cruelty. In front of Lucknow, he was joined by the forces of General Sir James Outram (p262) but it was he who led the final, perilous charge down the street to the Residency where the English were confined. Having won through, they could proceed no further and they settled down to wait for the better equipped relief force led by Sir Colin Campbell (p261). However, they had won an important psychological victory and Havelock was now the war's leading hero. In England he was made a baronet and granted a life pension, but he never knew the extent of his celebrity. Having fought to the limits of his endurance, he died shortly after Campbell's arrival of dysentery and exhaustion.

Today Havelock is all but forgotten and it is difficult to realise that he was as deeply mourned as Nelson after Trafalgar. Sermons on his qualities were preached to overflowing churches and Queen Victoria said that she felt as if she had lost a brother. He was a brave soldier and also a true Christian; the combination made soldiering a more noble profession and set a seal on the Victorian age. His statue was erected by public subscription; significantly, it was the philanthropist and Christian peer Lord Shaftesbury (p96) who approached Lord Palmerston (p192) with a petition for the site in Trafalgar Square. The statue is dressed informally, in fighting kit of frock coat and thigh-length leggings. Havelock was also white haired at the time of his triumph, a detail which the pigeons have conspired to perpetuate.

Major General Sir Henry Havelock. Born 1795, Sunderland, son of shipbuilder. Joined army as junior officer, 1816. Posted to India; experienced religious conversion on board ship, 1823. Fought in First Burmese War, 1824-6; conducted prayer meetings in deserted Great Pagoda, Rangoon. Fought in First Afghan War and published controversial history of campaigns, 1838-42. Fought in Sikh Wars, 1845-6 & 1848-9. Indian Mutiny; led relief of Cawnpore and first relief of Lucknow, 1857. Died 1857.

Statue by William Behnes. Bronze, 12ft on 17ft pedestal. South-east corner of Trafalgar Square. Unveiled April 10th, 1861, without ceremony. On the front of the pedestal is a quotation from one of Havelock's pre-battle orations and on the back a list of the regiments, Indian and English, which served under him during the Mutiny.

This was the first statue ever to be modelled from a photograph. Behnes was an excellent artist who unfortunately bankrupted himself through buying unsuitable premises for his work. Three years after sculpting Havelock, the apostle of temperance, he was found drunk in the street and died in hospital shortly afterwards.

TO
MAJOR GENERAL
SIR HENRY HAVELOCK
K.C.B.
AND HIS BRAVE COMPANIONS
IN ARMS
DURING THE CAMPAIGN IN INDIA
1857

"SOLDIERS! YOUR LABOURS
YOUR PRIVATIONS YOUR SUFFERINGS
AND YOUR VALOUR
WILL NOT BE FORGOTTEN BY
A GRATEFUL COUNTRY"

H. HAVELOCK.

Sir Colin Campbell

*Field Marshal Sir Colin Campbell, 1st
Baron Clyde. Born 1792, Glasgow, son
of carpenter. Fought in Peninsular War,
1808-9 & 1810-13; twice wounded at
siege of San Sebastian. Fought at siege of
Dutch island of Walcheren; contracted
persistent fever, 1809-10. Served in
America, Gibraltar, West Indies and
Ireland, 1814-31. Controlled Chartist
unrest in North of England, 1839-40.
Served in China, 1842-6; garrisoned
Hong Kong and Chusan (the inhabitants
of the island of Chusan presented him with
a letter congratulating him on the good
behaviour of his troops). Fought in Second
Sikh War, 1848-9. Conducted operations
against tribes on Indian North-west
Frontier, 1849-53; resigned after being
criticised for over-caution. Senior
commander in Crimean War, 1854-6; led
Highland Brigade in the storming of
Alma. Commander-in-Chief during
Indian Mutiny, 1857-60. Died 1863.*

Statue by Carlo Marochetti. Bronze, on
cylindrical, red granite pedestal. Waterloo
Place. Erected latter part of 1867.
Campbell wears the informal uniform in
which he fought during the Mutiny: patrol
jacket, corduroy breeches, high boots and
pith hat. In his left hand is the 50-year-old
cavalry sword given him by the Governor
General, Lord Hardinge.

The overall design is different from the
other memorials in Waterloo Place. This is
because the statue was originally intended
for a site on Horseguards Parade, near the
entrance to the old walled garden in front
of the Admiralty. The pedestal was erected
there but the rival service objected that it
was blocking their entrance. The Duke of
Wellington was obliged to intervene in the
controversy and the pedestal was
eventually moved to its present position.

Colin Campbell was a canny, quick tempered Scot who made laborious
progress through the ranks of the army and became a hero late in
life. His Islay forbears lost their land for having taken part in the
'45 Stuart rebellion and Campbell grew up poor at a time when most
army commissions had to be bought and private means were important
to advancement. He also supported his father and sister out of his
pay. It was therefore a matter of satisfaction to him when after nearly
forty frugal years of service he found himself a colonel and free of
debt. He spoke of retirement but his county's needs kept him in
service for a further dramatic decade. This steady progress in the
face of disadvantage and devotion to duty were things which the
Victorian age admired and which contributed to his image as a hero.

Sir Charles Napier (p257) was Campbell's close friend and colleague.
They were together as military commanders in the North of England
during the Chartist disturbances of 1839-40. They shared the same
sympathetic attitude to the workers' cause and the same refusal to be
panicked into action. Campbell also formed the view that the majority
of the workers did not want violent confrontation and were being
intimidated by their own leaders.

Napier dubbed Campbell "war-bred Sir Colin". In his first battle,
at the age of sixteen, his company commander walked him up and
down in front of the enemy's fire, a somewhat shocking initiation
which completely hardened his nerve. As a young officer he was
determined to make his mark and was recklessly brave. At the siege
of San Sebastian he twice tried to scale a narrow breach in the walls
and twice fell back wounded. He and a fellow officer crawled their
way out of hospital, their wounds unhealed, to take part in the next
engagement; he was reprimanded for it, but his courage noted.

The discipline of the regiments which Campbell commanded was
always good and the morale high; he achieved this by a close personal
involvement with his men. His favourites were his fellow countrymen,
the troops of the Highland Brigade whom he commanded in the
Crimea and whose bonnet he wore in place of his general's cocked
hat. He was, an observer noted, one of the few men who remained
consistently cheerful during that miserable conflict.

As a senior officer Campbell could be irascible but had none of
the recklessness of his youth. During the Mutiny he became known
as "Old Kharbardur" – "Old Take Care". He spent the first months
of his command waiting in Calcutta arranging food and horses before
moving to relieve Lucknow. There he won through to the Residency
and rescued its defenders, but immediately withdrew. Five months
later he returned, leading the largest British force seen in the field
since Waterloo. He entered the city but refused the request by Sir
James Outram (p262) to encircle it completely if it would lose a single
life. As a result, several thousand of the rebels escaped and the war
dragged on another summer. However, Campbell's caution was on the
whole justified in a situation where the British were, to begin with,
so vastly outnumbered. His strategy did in the end hold India.

That rule is symbolised by the laurel-crowned figure of Britannia
at the foot of the Field Marshal's statue, and by the lion couched
beside her. Campbell was of medium height, in appearance thick-set
and broad shouldered, with a high, deeply lined forehead and crisp,
curly, grey hair. According to an old soldier who had dressed his
wounds after the Battle of Chillianwallah which concluded the Sikh
Wars, Marochetti's statue was "the man himself".

Sir James Outram

Outram was a different kind of hero from the fiery Napier, the saintly Havelock or the tough, dour Campbell. He spent the first twenty years of his military life as a frontier man; subsequently he mixed soldiering and politics in every part of the Sub-continent and was known for his understanding of native peoples. "A fox is a fool and a lion is a coward compared with James Outram" was the saying in Bombay, where he first served. Two hundred miles to the north west lay the province of Khandesh in whose jungle-covered hills lived the pre-Aryan Bhil people, given to hunting, blood sacrifice and banditry. Outram captured their stronghold and won their trust by living and hunting with them. Like a Kipling hero, he shot man-eating tigers and held their loyalty by his daring, swimming in a tank with a young alligator and rolling down a mountainside gripped in a tiger's claws. He formed their warriors into a regiment of the British army and established peace in the surrounding territory; after ten years he had a well disciplined troop of a thousand men. Posted to Afghanistan, he was again at the very edge of the action, storming the ancient fortress of Ghazni and subduing the chieftains of Ghilzai. After the taking of Kelat, the capital of Baluchistan, he was ordered to carry the news to Karachi by a route never before travelled by a European. He made his way disguised as a Muslim holy man, concealing his ignorance of Persian by muttering charms and spells.

Wishing to broaden his activities, Outram settled into an administrative career. He was appointed political resident – an ambassador and advisor with wide ranging powers – to the Amirs of Sind, whose trust he won by his open dealing. On his deathbed the eldest of the Amirs, Nur Mohammed, entrusted his brother and his youngest son to Outram's care, saying, "from the days of Adam no one has known so great truth and friendship as I have found in you". Outram took the charge to heart and did everything he could to prevent and delay Napier's campaign of conquest (p257), though he eventually fought in it. He received £3,000 as his share of the prize money but gave it all to various Indian charities. To the end of his life he spoke of the annexation of Sind as unnecessary and unjust.

He was, however, less sympathetic towards some of the other princely rulers of India. At Baroda he discovered that court business was heavily laced with bribery; after a long struggle involving a personal appeal to the East India Company directors in London, he eventually succeeded in removing the officials involved. He also found the voluptuary and decadent ruling house of Oudh more than he could stomach and he reluctantly master-minded the British take-over.

It was his part in the Indian Mutiny which made him a household name. He took command at Lucknow after its first relief by Havelock (p258) and defended the town's fortress from repeated attacks prior to the final relief by Campbell (p261). He remained in India long enough to ensure justice and continuity in Oudh and then returned to spend the last three years of his life quietly in England.

Unusually, the subscriptions for his statue were raised during that time. He was given, in fact, two statues, one in Calcutta – a dramatic equestrian masterpiece by John Foley – and one in London, the very first to be erected in the gardens along the new Victoria Embankment (see p12). Outram was regarded with immense romantic deference. Napier, despite their differences, called him "the Bayard of India, a knight sans peur et sans reproche" and the epithet clung.

Lieutenant General Sir James Outram, Bart. Born 1803, Butterley Hall, Derbyshire, son of engineer. Brought up in Aberdeen. Entered Indian army, 1819. Served in wild, jungle territory in Bombay region, 1819-35. Military commander and political resident in Mahi Kanti, Gujurat, 1835-8. Fought in First Afghan War, 1839. Political resident in Sind, 1839-42; opposed British annexation. Political resident in Baroda; waged campaign against bribery, 1847-52 & 1854. Political resident in Oudh, 1854-6; organised peaceful annexation and was subsequently appointed Chief Commissioner. Military commander in Persia, 1856-7. Indian Mutiny, 1857-8; took command at Lucknow after its first relief. Military Member of Governor General's Council, 1858-60. Ill health forced return to England, 1860, Died 1863.

Statue by Matthew Noble. Bronze, 12ft, on 18ft Aberdeen granite pedestal. Victoria Embankment Gardens. Unveiled 17th August, 1871, by Lord Halifax. Outram stands calmly surveying the battlefield, a telescope in his left hand, his right hand on his sword. Behind him lies a broken field gun.

Below. On the corners of the pedestal are piled the trophies of his wide flung victories: bayonets, helmets, shields, grenades, rifles with chased butts, ornamented daggers, axes and quiverfuls of arrows.

Sir John Fox Burgoyne

John Fox Burgoyne spent the first years of his military life laying mines and blowing up forts and bridges. For someone engaged in such destructive activity he was remarkably, even chronically modest. Something of this diffidence, traceable to his illegitimacy and unsettled childhood, can be seen in his statue. Despite it, he was extremely good at his job. Sir John Moore personally asked for his services in Portugal and he covered Moore's famous retreat from Corunna by demolishing the bridge at Benevente under the very hoofs of the French cavalry. (Burgoyne always believed that Napoleon himself was watching the scene from the hill above and, seeing his route checked, rode off to France, leaving the direction of the war to Marshall Soult.) Burgoyne went on to play a key engineering role in the sieges of Badajoz, Cuidad Roderigo, Salamanca, Retiro, Burgos and St Sebastian. It was extremely dangerous work, with a high casualty rate, and he was fortunate to be quite fearless under fire; as the the bullets whined and the shells exploded, he would call out a cheerful warning and ride on, humming a tune.

After Napoleon's defeat, Burgoyne ceased to knock down French bridges and fortifications and instead built them up at home. He advised on the reconstruction of Westminster Bridge and on the laying of the sewage pipes of Dublin and London. When the Duke of Wellington died, he became the cabinet's closest advisor on military matters. At the time of Crimea he expressed strong disapproval of a plan to land the British army on a swampy plain in full view of the Russians. At the age of 72 he was sent out to survey the battlefield and the plan was changed. However, the eventual landing place was little better and caused appalling problems of transport. "Let them hang us all," was Burgoyne's typically self-effacing response, "then they are bound to get the culprit." In the event it was Burgoyne who was blamed by the press for the disastrous inefficiency of the campaign. He was recalled but the solidness of his reputation ensured a quick return to popularity. His final, ceremonial appointment was as the commander of that most venerable fortress of all, the Tower of London.

Burgoyne was completely fit and active until the year before his death. His statue, too, is trim and entirely without extraneous padding; the figure leans slightly forward, ready for action. It is in fact an extremely skilful piece of portraiture. Sir Joseph Boehm was at the height of his powers in the 1870's and 1880's; after the statue of Burgoyne came those of Carlyle (p126), Lawrence (p198), Tyndale (p312) and Wellington (p249), and he was also responsible for the equestrian figure of Lord Robert Napier which follows (p267). Napier surprised Boehm. He was expecting the glorious conqueror who had led his elephants across the mountains of Abyssinia; instead he was confronted with "a small spare man with quiet eyes and a gentle voice" and so he changed his approach. He believed that a sculptor should have an instinctive perception of character; he used to get his subjects to relax and talk until their inner being emerged and he would then study its essential visual characteristics. Burgoyne must have revealed his innate modesty as well as his vitality; perhaps Boehm got him reminiscing about the Crimea.

Boehm was Austro-Hungarian, the son of the director of the Austrian Mint. Elegant, debonair, he settled in London in 1862 at the age of 28 and took British citizenship. Like Baron Marochetti (p56), he was patronised by Royalty – he was artistic tutor to Princess Louise (p65) – and was often regarded with suspicion; some considered his work

Field Marshal Sir John Fox Burgoyne. Born 1782, illegitimate son of lieutenant-general and professional singer. Brought up by 13th Earl of Derby, 1792-8. Entered Royal Engineers, 1798. Fought against French in Malta, Sicily and Egypt, 1800-7. Played leading part in Peninsular War, 1808-14. Commanded garrisons at Chatham and Portsmouth, 1821-31. Chairman of Irish Board of Public Works, 1831-45. Inspector General of Fortifications and chief military advisor to the cabinet, 1845-68. Administered Irish famine relief, 1847. Military juror at the Great Exhibition, 1851. Sent out to Crimea in unofficial capacity and became effective second-in-command, 1853-5; recalled as scapegoat. Constable of Tower of London, 1865-8. Member of National Red Cross Society Committee during Franco-Prussian War, 1870-1. Died 1871, one year after the drowning of his only son at sea.

Left. Statue by Joseph Boehm. Bronze. South west corner of Waterloo Place. Subscribed to by the officers of the Royal Engineers and erected November, 1877. The inscription on the pedestal is from Shakespeare's Coriolanus: "How youngly he began to serve his country, how long continued". Burgoyne was in the army for just short of seventy years, so the quotation was fully justified.

Right. Vanity Fair's 1881 picture of Boehm. The magazine specialised in half realistic, half humorous portraits of prominent members of society. Boehm and Hamo Thornycroft were the two sculptors so honoured.

too clever by half. In fact he had the ability to create light and shade through a depth of modelling that the younger British sculptors like Onslow Ford, Hamo Thornycroft and Alfred Gilbert were just beginning to learn. He was also more socially adaptable than the temperamental Marochetti. *Vanity Fair* (above right) had no doubts about him. "He has produced a marvellous amount of work," it wrote, "and all of it good; for he knows what he means to express and how he means to express it. He has furnished many statues to India and the Colonies. He delights in quadrupeds, and especially in horses, many of which he has modelled, and one of which he rides every morning at daybreak. He is much admired by the Royal Family. His manners are excellent and his companionship altogether pleasant and profitable. He is a very good man of business."

Lord Robert Napier

Robert Napier's most lasting contributions to the India in which he served were the roads, canals and townships which he designed and built. He was an engineer of the first rank and might well be classed with Stephenson and Brunel rather than with Campbell and Roberts. He turned the Himalayan forest hamlet of Darjeeling into one of India's most beautiful hill-stations, blasting a road to the plain seven thousand feet below. His spacious, shady cantonment at Umbala became the model for all future military settlements and he finally achieved what the meanness of the East India Company had denied his namesake, Sir Charles (p256): high, cool and healthy barracks for the ordinary soldiers. He built the three hundred mile Grand Trunk Road from Lahore to Peshawar and dug or repaired many more miles of canal. If Sir John Lawrence (p198) at first complained of his extravagance, he soon came to appreciate the economy of doing things properly.

In private life Napier was a gentle, cultivated man, a student of botany and geology, a skilful painter and a lover of poetry. In battle quite another side of his character emerged; he had, as his obituary in the *Spectator* said, "the daredevil courage of a Beserk". On his very first day in the field, he saved the life of a wounded fellow officer under fire. At the capture of Perho, in China, his field glasses were shot out of his hand, the hilt of his sword was broken by shell fragments, he had three bullet holes in his coat and one in his boot, but he survived unhurt.

As a military engineer his speciality was siege warfare. He was the fourth of London's commemorated soldiers to be present at the siege of Lucknow during the Indian Mutiny. Having won through to the Residency with Outram (p262), his battles were underground. As the besiegers tunnelled under the complex of buildings and laid mines, so Napier's men, guessing their routes or listening for the scrape of pickaxes, dug down and drove them out or exploded their tunnels prematurely. More than forty shafts and countershafts were sunk in this eerie warfare. Napier's excavations also revealed the stores of food concealed in the Residency by Sir Henry Lawrence just before his death, a discovery which transformed the garrison's situation.

It was Napier's expedition to Abyssinia which established him firmly in the nation's imagination. It was an ideal imperial operation: a righteous cause (King Theodore had unjustly imprisoned some British subjects and refused to release them), a swift and technically brilliant campaign (Napier built a port, resevoirs and a railway for his army, travelled four hundred mountainous miles using elephants and stormed Magdala, regarded as the best natural fortress in the world) and a successful outcome (Theodore dead at his own hand, remarkably little bloodshed and the prisoners released). For this Napier received his baronetcy and was feted everywhere. After the death of Sir John Burgoyne (p264) in 1871, he was Britain's senior soldier; had the Russo-Turkish confrontation of 1880 drawn Britain into war, he would have commanded, despite his age.

His statue, a replica of the one erected in Calcutta on his final departure from India, stands therefore as a memorial not only to a brave and rather likeable man, but also to Britain's nineteenth century technological supremacy and to the principle of doing things well. In 1921 it was moved from military Waterloo Place to Queen's Gate, just up the road from the Imperial College of Science and Technology, a transfer which neatly matches the dual balance of Napier's own career.

Field Marshal Robert Cornelis Napier, 1st Baron Napier of Magdala. Born 1810, Colombo, Ceylon, son of army major. Educated as military engineer at Addiscombe and Chatham, 1824-8. Posted to India, 1828. Carried out numerous canal and irrigation works, 1830-40. Reconstructed hill town of Darjeeling, 1838-42. Fought in Sikh Wars, 1845-6 and 1848-9. Chief civil engineer in Punjab, 1846-56; built Great Trunk Road. Indian Mutiny, 1857-9; commanded engineers at siege of Lucknow; overall commander of campaign against mutineers' leaders in Central India. Second-in-command, expedition to China, 1860. C-in-C, Bombay Army, 1865-7. Commanded expedition to Abyssinia; captured fortress of Magdala, 1867-8. Elected Fellow of the Royal Society, 1869. C-in-C, Indian Army, 1870-5. Governor of Gibraltar, 1876-83. Governor of Tower of London, 1886-90. Died 1890.

Statue by Joseph Boehm, completed by Alfred Gilbert. Bronze. North end of Queen's Gate. Cost £5,000. A replica of the statue erected in Calcutta shortly after Napier's final departure from India. Originally erected in the centre of Waterloo Place and unveiled July 8th, 1891, by the Prince of Wales. Moved 1921 to Queen's Gate to make way for the national memorial to Edward VII. The two men had been on excellent terms, so one may take it that Napier yielded with a good grace.

General Gordon

Charles Gordon was a world military figure. He was also a man of deep principle, ascetic, retiring and unworldly. His single-mindedness gave him a mesmeric power, which he used in the service of the good as he conceived it. However, the English military authorities were always made uncomfortable by his eccentric behaviour and he was never put in command of a home fighting force. In the end he was made a sacrifice to England's own ambivalence towards its imperial role. Gladstone's Liberal Government sent him out on a single-handed mission which, given his qualities, was almost bound to lead to his death. In the eyes of the majority of his fellow-countrymen, this only confirmed and heightened his heroic status.

Gordon's great triumphs were won abroad and achieved by sheer force of will. In China he held together the motley collection of peasants and foreign mercenaries that was the Ever Victorious Army, leading them into battle carrying only his cane (the Chinese called it his Wand of Victory) and smoking a cigar. His victory over the anarchic and mercilessly destructive Taipings saved the Manchu dynasty and probably thousands of ordinary Chinese as well. It made him a legend but he refused to profit by it. He craved anonymity in equal measure with military achievement, since it allowed him to pursue what he saw as life's essentials. According to his private, thought-out faith, God lived in each individual. He spent much time helping the poor, the sick and in particular the orphan boys whom he taught and found jobs for, and whom he called his "kings". For ordinary social life, and for women, he had no time. He was a cheerful, active, ascetic who genuinely thought more of heaven than he did of earth. He consistently refused the greater part of the salaries offered him and he subsisted on a diet of raw eggs, stale bread, tea and cigarettes.

In the Sudan he was the absolute ruler of an area twice the size of Britain. However, he could not achieve the same clear cut success in dealing with the slave trade, which he came to see as endemic to Sudanese society. His knowledge of North Africa led to his final mission. Egypt being at that time an English protectorate, he was ordered to bring out from Khartoum, single-handed, the native Egyptian garrison threatened with annihilation at the hands of the Islamic fundamentalist leader known as the Mahdi. However, as might have been expected, he stayed on to fight and so to die. In England the news of his death raised admiration to fever pitch. Many saw him as the hero betrayed. Gladstone, G.O.M. (Grand Old Man), who had delayed so long in sending out a relief expedition, became Gladstone, M.O.G. (Murderer of Gordon). The Government, no doubt partly out of confusion and shame, voted Gordon's family £20,000, and the money for his statue came from this sum. The public collections in his memory were spent, as he would have wished, on Boys' Homes at Gravesend and Cable Street in London's East End.

Hamo Thornycroft (p206) was characteristically thorough in getting to know the man he was sculpting, reading, studying photographs and listening to the differing reports of those who had known him. In appearance Gordon was a short, well-knit man with curly, brown hair and blue-grey eyes that could, as a friend said, look through a millstone. The statue turned out to be well worthy of its subject. Thornycroft successfully caught the thoughtful, solitary pilgrim behind the victorious commander, the man within the myth, direct yet questioning, powerful yet vulnerable.

Major General Sir Charles Gordon. Born 1833, Woolwich, son of Royal Artillery officer. Studied at Royal Military Academy, Woolwich, 1849-52; known for rebelliousness. Joined Royal Engineers, 1852. Fought in Crimea, 1854-6. Fought in China Expedition and remained as member of garrison, 1860-2. Commanded Emperor's "Ever Victorious Army" and defeated Taiping rebellion, 1862-4. Appointed to supervise building of forts along Thames; engaged in works of charity and conducted own free school for boys, 1865-71. Appointed governor of Equatoria, southern Sudan, by Khedive of Egypt, with instructions to suppress slave trade, 1873. Mapped Nile as far as Lake Albert, 1875-6. Governor of entire Sudan; achieved some limitation of movement of slaves by daring personal threats and interventions, 1876-80. Called to Peking and forcefully persuaded Chinese against "idiotic" war with Russia, 1880. Appointed Governor of tiny British island of Mauritius, 1881-2. Report on causes of racial unrest in Basutoland ignored by Government, 1882. Visited Palestine and wrote book on sacred geometry of Bible, 1882-3. Sent to evacuate Egyptian troops from Khartoum, but remained to fight, 1884-5; English relief force dispatched too late. Killed by soldiers of Mahdi, 1885.

Statue by Hamo Thornycroft. Bronze, 10ft 6ins. Victoria Embankment Gardens. Originally erected in the centre of Trafalgar Square, and unveiled October 16th, 1888, by D. Plunkett, First Commissioner of Works, without ceremony due to fear of Socialist demonstrations. Cost £3,000. Wreaths were regularly laid around the statue on January 26th, the anniversary of Gordon's death; the Gordon Boys School, Woking, continued the practice up to the Second World War.

In 1943 the statue was moved to Mentmore to make way for a Lancastrian bomber on show in the Square. After consistent protest, it was brought back to London in 1953 but its former site was already occupied by the fountains built to honour Admirals Beatty, Jellicoe and Cunningham. Fortunately the new, southernmost section of the Embankment Gardens was just then being laid out and the statue was transferred there. The move out of the limelight seems entirely in keeping with the character of the man.

The Duke of Cambridge

George, Duke of Cambridge was Commander-in-Chief of the British army for longer than any other individual in history and at the age of seventy six profoundly resented his removal from office by interfering politicians. He has often been represented as a monster of conservatism but he simply followed a common human pattern. In his thirties and forties he was enlightened and progressive; in his sixties and seventies, however, time left him behind.

The Duke found the sustained sufferings and horrors of the ill-planned Crimean War shattering. He was brave in attack but in the aftermath of battle, with men and comrades dead and dying, he broke down and wept. On medical advice he returned to England and, though his health and nerve recovered, he was not allowed back in the field. As a soldier, then, he had his limitations. However, he had a very clear idea of army solidarity and tradition and he kept personally in touch with innumerable fellow officers scattered throughout the globe. He also understood the importance of the individual regiment and its loyalty to its own sometimes quaint customs and trophies; it was for this reason that he strongly opposed the wholesale amalgamation and renaming of regiments carried out in 1881. He also spent much of his time fighting cuts in expenditure for, compared to other European countries, Britain ran her imperial army as cheaply as possible.

The Duke's emotional nature showed itself in another way, and of this his soldiers thoroughly approved: he married for love, not position. There were those who saw him as the perfect bridegroom for his cousin, the Queen, but young George kept a wary distance. On the very day of Victoria's wedding he met and fell in love with a charming actress, Louisa Fairbrother. She bore him three children and eventually they married; he was buried not at Windsor, but beside her at Kensal Green.

When the Duke died, Edward VII suggested that he should be commemorated by a statue of "a big man on a big horse". The sculptor, chosen by competition, was, appropriately, a former army officer, Captain Adrian Jones. The statue was such a good likeness that it was said to be instantly recognisable from behind. It was erected in Whitehall opposite the Duke's old headquarters, where the guards still wear the scarlet which he fought so hard to preserve against the encroachment of the duller but less conspicuous khaki.

George William Frederick Charles, 2nd Duke of Cambridge. Born 1819, Hanover, son of 1st Duke and grandson of George III. Brought to England by William IV, 1830. Appointed colonel in army, 1837. Served in Gibraltar, in Leeds during industrial disturbances, in Corfu and in Ireland, 1838-52. Inspector General of Cavalry, 1852-4; published important memoranda on state of army, as a result of which the first ever training manoeuvres were held at Chobham. Commanded First Division at Crimea; led troops in storming of heights of Alma but lost nerve after battle of Inkerman and was invalided home, 1854. Appointed Commander-in-Chief of army, 1856. Founded Staff College at Camberley, 1859. Opposed reforms of Liberal Secretaries of War Cardwell, 1868-74, and Childers, 1880-2; fought re-organisation of regiments and introduction of shorter terms of service. Resigned office under pressure, 1895. Died 1904.

Statue by Captain Adrian Jones. Bronze. Centre of Whitehall, opposite Horseguards Parade. Unveiled June 16th, 1907, by King Edward VII. The Duke wears full Field Marshal's uniform with numerous orders and medals.

Captain Jones spent many years as an army vet before becoming a full-time sculptor, so he well understood the anatomy and movement of horses. Those he looked after in India used to win races against those of the Aga Khan. His greatest work is undoubtedly the Quadriga (or four-horsed chariot) which crowns the triumphal arch at Hyde Park Corner; a towering winged figure representing Peace alights on the war-chariot, as the charioteer pulls in the reins. The project was personally encouraged by Edward VII. This immensely dramatic work was given to the nation by Lord Hellingly and erected in 1912; Jones deserves to be better known for it.

Left. Adrian Jones modelling the charioteer for the Quadriga.

Right. Jones and an assistant taking afternoon tea inside the plaster mould of one of the Quadriga's horses.

Lord Wolseley

Fear, in one form or other, is a constant ingredient of human experience. Garnet Wolseley discovered one sure way of lifting himself free of its constrictions: the self surrender of attack. He first discovered the rapture charging the stronghold of the bandit Myat Toon in the Burmese jungle; his rational mind could not analyse or justify the sensation but any other was, he wrote, "like the tinkling of a doorbell compared to the throbbing of Big Ben." In the Crimea, he was hit while digging trenches under fire. One side of his face was completely cut open and as a result he lost the sight of an eye. The doctors sewed his cheek back and one tugged a splinter of stone out of his jaw while the other held his head between his knees. Wolseley remained quite calm. He suffered much greater torture when his wounds prevented him taking part in the storming of Sebastopol two weeks later. War had indeed cast its glamour over him; the strangest thing is that in private life he could not bear the sight of raw meat or pass a butcher's shop without feeling ill.

Wolseley was not only a military ecstatic but also an extremely efficient commander. He showed himself a master of the art of transport through difficult territory, particularly in the North-west Province of Canada. His "Soldiers' Pocket Book", written when he was still a colonel, was adopted as an official manual of procedure throughout the world; it contained information on such diverse topics as surveying, manoeuvring, the cure of snakebite and singing on the march. In the higher reaches of the army there was no one like him. When he returned from his successful war against King Kofi of the Ashanti, which had put an end to a regime based on 120 years of blood-sacrifice, he was hailed as England's "only soldier". On stage George Grossmith made himself up to look like Wolseley as he sang "I am the very model of a modern major-general" in *The Pirates of Penzance*, and "All Sir Garnet" became an expression for the ultimate in organisational efficiency. Predictably, he clashed head on with the Duke of Cambridge (p270), whom he privately referred to as "that great German bumble-bee". Wolseley was contemptuous of drill or manoeuvres which bore no relation to battle conditions. He also supported the total abolition of promotion by purchase, for he had won his way to the top by his own efforts.

He won victory against the rebel Egyptian army at Tel-el-Kebir by a meticulously planned night attack across the desert. His only military failure, though it achieved wonders in its speedy navigation of the Nile, was the expedition sent out to rescue General Gordon (p268) from Khartoum. Gordon's death infinitely depressed him. The two had become friends in the Crimea; they shared a similar kind of Christian fatalism and indifference to death though Wolseley, as he was the first to admit, had none of Gordon's saintliness. As he said, if he had put down the Taiping rebellion, he would have made himself Emperor of China. In fact he would probably have made a bad ruler. The hasty political settlement which he made in the Transvaal after the recall of Sir Bartle Frere (p200) failed to establish a unified, stable system of administration and ignored the feelings of the Boers in a way that was later to prove disastrous.

Fate denied Wolseley the soldier's death he would have preferred. Even as Commander-in-Chief his memory began to fail and he died obscure and in his bed. He had been born forty years too soon, for England had need of commanders of his calibre when she most needed them, during the First World War.

Field Marshal Viscount Garnet Joseph Wolseley. Born 1833, Dublin, son of army major. Gained non-purchase commission in army, posted to Burma, 1852. Fought in Crimea, 1854-6. Posted to India during Indian Mutiny, 1857-59; he was the first soldier to win through to the besieged garrison during Campbell's first relief of Lucknow (p261). Fought in China Expedition, 1860; (he thoroughly disapproved of the looting of the Emperor's Summer Palace and paid for the few works of art which he acquired.) Held senior staff posts in Canada, 1861-71. Returned to England as Assistant Adjutant General, 1871; supported Cardwell's reforms. Led war against Ashanti, 1873-4. Chief administrator in Natal, 1874; Cyprus, 1878; and Zululand and Transvaal, 1879-80. Won victory of Tel-el-Kebir against rebels in Egyptian army, 1882. Commanded Gordon relief force, 1884-5. Commander-in-Chief of Army in succession to the Duke of Cambridge, 1895-9. Died 1913.

Statue by William Goscombe John. Bronze, cast from guns captured on Wolseley's campaigns. Horseguards Parade. Unveiled June 25th, 1920, by the senior Field Marshal, the Duke of Connaught. Cost £4,000.

Goscombe John was a Welshman, born in Cardiff the son of a woodcarver. He lived for a time in Paris before settling permanently in St John's Wood, his romantic style of work remaining unchanged until his death in 1953. He was noted for his ability to portray character.

Earl Roberts

There's a little red-faced man
Which is Bobs
Rides the tallest 'orse 'e can –
Our Bobs.
If it bucks or kicks or rears,
'E can sit for twenty years
With a smile round both 'is ears,
Can't yer, Bobs?

Lord Roberts more than any other figure sums up the ideal of the Victorian fighting man. He was modest, chivalrous and charming, an excellent horseman, huntsman and polo player and his careful planning and daring tactics won wars against savage tribesmen. Like Napier and Wolseley, he was intensely brave; his V.C. won during the Indian Mutiny testified to that. He was a popular commander who did not waste his soldiers' lives in battle and who in peacetime tried to keep them as comfortable – and as sober – as possible; he extended Havelock's work for temperance throughout the Indian army. Like Campbell, he was a long serving veteran, as another verse of Kipling's popular music hall style ballad, written on Roberts' return from Afghanistan as a national hero, testified.

If you stood 'im on 'is 'ead,
Father Bobs,
You could spill a quart of lead
Outa Bobs.
'Es been at it thirty years
An-amassin' souvenirs
In the way o' slugs an' spears,
Ain't yer, Bobs?

And then, at the age of 67, he went on to turn the fortunes of the Boer War. Yet he was a slight, almost delicate figure, bandy-legged, only 5ft 3ins tall, with a high forehead, kind, penetrating gaze and, as his statue shows, the dignity of a fine pair of moustaches.

His horse was almost as famous as he was. Volonel, named after the chief whose tribe Roberts defeated in the forests of Assam, was a spirited Arab grey. He too was small, little bigger than a pony. He accompanied Roberts throughout his great campaign in Afghanistan and later, at the personal insistence of Queen Victoria, was awarded the Kabul to Khandahar Star and the Afghan War Medal with four clasps. Roberts took him back to England and rode him at the head of the colonial contingent in the Diamond Jubilee procession of 1897. His grave at the Chelsea Hospital is no doubt still tended today.

The statue by Harry Bates on Horseguards Parade should be a good likeness of both horse and man, since sittings took place in 1894, when Volonel was still alive. The original work, which G.F. Watts (p188) called the finest equestrian statue of its time, was destined for Calcutta. It had a high, marble pedestal with figures representing War and Victory and reliefs of the soldiers who formed the core of Roberts' mountain troops, the Royal Highlanders, the Gurkhas and the Sikhs. A complete replica was set up in Kelvingrove Park, Glasgow, in 1916. The Horseguards Parade statue was given a smaller and unadorned pedestal in order to match the companion statue of Field Marshal Wolseley (p272) on the other side of the gateway. The authorities had planned to have Goscombe John sculpt both Wolseley and Roberts; however, Roberts' daughter strong-mindedly insisted on a version of the exisiting work which she so much admired.

Field Marshal Frederick Sleigh Roberts, 1st Earl Roberts of Khandahar, Pretoria and Waterford. Born 1832, Cawnpore, India, son of army general. Educated Eton, Sandhurst and Addiscombe. Joined Indian army, 1852; served on North-West Frontier. Took part in siege of Delhi and first relief of Lucknow during Indian Mutiny, 1857-9; awarded V.C. for habitual disregard of danger. Held high staff rank in Indian army, 1863-78, served in Umbeyla, Abyssinia and Assam. Commander, Afghan Field Force, dispatched after destruction of British Embassy in Kabul, 1879-80; defeated Afghanis at Charasia and, after famous three-week march from Kabul with 10,000 troops, at relief of Khandahar. C-in-C, Indian army, 1885-93. Appointed C-in-C, Boer War, and reversed tide of defeat, 1899-1900. Commander-in-Chief of Army, 1901-4. Supported conscription in face of military threat from Germany, and independence of Ulster from Ireland, 1905-14. Died 1914, while visiting Indian contingent at First World War battlefront.

Statue by Harry Bates. Bronze, 11ft 6ins. Horseguards Parade. Unveiled May 30th, 1924, by Field Marshal the Duke of Connaught. Cost £3,800, paid from State funds. Bates' original version was erected in Calcutta in 1898; this is a smaller replica by Henry Poole.

With Hamo Thornycroft, Gilbert and Ford, Harry Bates was a leading member of the New Sculpture movement. Like Goscombe John, he lived for a time in Paris, where he personally engaged Rodin as his teacher. He shared Rodin's view of sculpture as an expression of energy; this can be seen here in the dramatic turning movement of the horse, over which the rider nevertheless has full control.

Sir George White

Few events are more newsworthy than a siege. There is suspense, there is endurance – the British being at their best with their backs to the wall – and there is the final release from tension. Three times during the Boer War, at Ladysmith, at Mafeking and at Kimberley, British forces found themselves shut in by that unexpectedly tough and mobile army of farmers. Sir George White was the garrison commander during the siege of the Natal town of Ladysmith. It lasted 119 days and White refused to surrender, even when recommended to do so by his commander in the field. Though enteric fever claimed an increasing number of British lives, he hung on until the end. The siege was, nevertheless, in some ways a remarkably gentlemanly affair. At the beginning the British medical corps sent the Boers drugs and brandy with which to treat their dysentery cases and on Christmas day the besiegers lobbed in a shell full of Christmas pudding "with the compliments of the season". The relief of Mafeking made Baden Powell (p110) an international hero and, although White did not attain quite the same degree of fame either then or afterwards, the memory of Ladysmith was sufficient to win him a London statue, subscribed to after his death by "comrades and friends in many parts of the Empire".

Prior to Ladysmith, White spent his military career in India, where his chief field of concern was the North-West Frontier. He won the V.C. fighting outside Kabul in the army commanded by Lord Roberts (p274). Later he commanded his own expeditions against the Orakzais of Miranzai and the Shiranis of Zhob, his slim figure leading his men up and down the precipitous mountain slopes as agilely as any tribesman. The perennial question was, where should the boundaries of Empire be set and how could the threat of Russian expansion be contained? White was one of those who believed that Afghanistan should be maintained as a sphere of British influence. However, the whole region was, then as now, inhabited by fiercely independent peoples who had no desire to be dominated by anyone. The result was much extremely difficult fighting which came to figure dramatically in the imaginations of those at home. As Indian Commander-in-Chief, White planned the relief of Chitral and the Tirah campaign which pacified the area around the Khyber Pass, though at great cost of men and money. "The Great Game", as it was called, was played out against a backdrop of stark mountain ranges with extremes of temperature, fanaticism and fierce courage, and it was really unwinnable, though it produced some enduring legends.

White's statue, on the other hand, became ensnared in parochial disputes. The memorial committee, somewhat rashly, commissioned it and had it cast before finding a definite site. They wanted it to be erected at Chelsea Hospital, where White had been Governor, but the Hospital Commissioners refused, saying that they did not want it cluttering up Wren's buildings. Another Chelsea site was proposed: the north end of Royal Avenue, where it would have made an interesting and gracious addition to the King's Road. However, this land was also found to belong to the Hospital and, though the Governor was in favour, the majority of his committee were still opposed – one aggressive group of officers dismissed White as a has-been and criticised his tactics in holding on to Ladysmith. Eventually a less satisfactory site was found in the borough of Marylebone, in centre of Portland Place, which means that the statue is nowadays hemmed in by traffic.

Field Marshal Sir George White. Born 1835, Whitehall, County Antrim. Entered army and posted to India, 1853-4. Fought in Afghan War, 1879-80; awarded V.C. at battle of Charasia. Commanded expeditions in upper Burma, Baluchistan and North-West Frontier, 1885-9. Commander-in-Chief, Indian army, 1893-7; planned Tirah campaign. Quartermaster General at War Office, 1897-9. Sent to take command in Natal during Boer War; besieged in Ladysmith, 1899-1900. Returned to England in poor health. Governor of Gibraltar, 1900-5. Governor of Chelsea Hospital, 1905-12. Died 1912.

Statue by John Tweed. Bronze, 9ft 6ins, on 10ft pedestal. Portland Place. Unveiled December 19th, 1922, by Lord Derby, Secretary of State for War. Every year, on February 28th, the anniversary of the relief of Ladysmith, the Boer War Veterans laid wreaths at the foot of the statue; the custom continued until 1970, when the youngest member of their association was 83.

John Tweed was an energetic Glaswegian who came to London in 1889 to work for Hamo Thornycroft. He later studied in Paris and became a close friend of Rodin and his greatest champion in England. In 1908 he completed Alfred Stevens' Wellington Memorial in St Paul's Cathedral. He was hot-tempered by nature and once refused to finish the bust of a child for Ramsay MacDonald because he disagreed with one of his anti-imperialist speeches on India.

KITCHENER
1850 1916

ERECTED BY PARLIAMENT

Earl Kitchener *and the First World War*

Field Marshal Horatio Herbert Kitchener, 1st Earl Kitchener of Khartoum and of Broome. Born 1850, Listowel, County Kerry, Ireland, son of Indian army officer. Commissioned in Royal Engineers, 1871. Served in French ambulance unit during Franco-Prussian War and went up in observation balloon; severely reprimanded by Duke of Cambridge but forgiven for youthful ambition, 1871. Seconded to Palestine Exploration Fund; surveyed Holy Land and learned Arabic, 1874-7. Second in command of Egyptian cavalry, 1882-5. Worked as unofficial intelligence officer, established contact with General Gordon in Khartoum and sent news of his death back to England, 1884-5. Reformed Egyptian police, 1890-2. Commander-in-chief, Egyptian army; prepared for advance into Sudan, 1892-8. Defeated Islamic fundamentalist forces at battle of Omdurman and recaptured Khartoum, 1898. Chief of Staff to General Roberts in Boer War, revitalised troops' will to win, 1899. Succeeded Roberts as Commander-in-Chief, 1900-2; pursued policy of burning farms and built camps to house Boer women and children. Insisted on moderate peace terms. Commander-in-Chief, Indian army 1902-9; won clash with Lord Curzon (p218), decentralised command and founded Indian staff college. British Consul-general in Egypt, 1911-14. Secretary of State for War, 1914-16; spearheaded World War I recruiting drive. Drowned off Scapa Flow, 1916.

Statue by John Tweed. Bronze, 7ft on 5ft pedestal. Unveiled June 9th, 1926, by Edward, Prince of Wales. Cost £3,000, paid for by State funds. In contrast with the formality of Cambridge and of Wolseley, Kitchener wears undress Field Marshal's uniform.

Kitchener's statue is the last to a great soldier of Empire. He first won outstanding fame in Egypt and the Sudan where he transformed the national army and, after long preparation, broke the power established by the Mahdi. Thus was Gordon avenged (p268). He was sent out with General Roberts (p274) to defeat the Boers. This he achieved by will-power and determination and by methods which have branded him as the inventor of the concentration camp. Tactically, there have been better generals; his strength was in his farsightedness. He was one of the few to anticipate the depth of the struggle with Germany which would, he prophesied, be won by the last million men, not the first. For the first two years of the war, there was no conscription. Service was voluntary and Kitchener was the symbol of that service; he personally led the drive for recruits and the men of England flocked to join "Kitchener's army".

The week by week running of the war was his generals' responsibility, not his. However, it is almost certain that he personally forced Sir John French to keep the first, small British Expeditionary Force in the field, so helping to turn the German onslaught at the crucial battle of the Marne. Had he lived through the stalemate of 1916 to the war's conclusion, he might have been hailed as a leader on a par with Churchill, but in June of that year the warship which was carrying him to Russia was hit by a German mine and the waters off Scapa Flow closed over his head.

His reputation, too, has been submerged by changing attitudes; his bristling moustache and pointing finger, and his slogan "Your country needs you", seem to belong to a past age. He was, however, a man of his time, admired as a strong, successful soldier, tall, aloof, with distant gaze, eyesight and complexion scarred by desert wind and sand. John Tweed, in his third and most personal outdoor London statue, has successfully caught his brooding expression of challenge.

The unveiling of his statue was a major ceremonial occasion. Horseguards Parade was packed with troops and there were thousands of private spectators. Yet the siting of the statue is oddly asymmetrical; unlike Wolseley and Roberts, it has no balancing figure and its position close to the wall on the south side makes it seem more like an afterthought. How unlike a scheme (see overleaf) published in 1909 by an architect named F.W.Speaight and supported by some eminent men, including Hamo Thornycroft and the art critic, M.H. Speilmann. This proposed the complete remodelling of Horseguards and St James's Park along the lines of the Avenue of Heroes in Berlin. Everything is symmetrical. Charles II's original canal is restored and clipped recesses in the hedges await statues of military leaders from King Alfred to Sir John Moore. At the end is the statue of Achilles, brought from Hyde Park, and a ring of equestrian figures; then to left and right are Napier and Havelock from Trafalgar Square and beside each a line of four more standing statues. However, neither this plan nor the one to erect a similar line of heroes along The Mall were ever carried out. There would indeed have been something alien to the national spirit in such an ordered celebration of military might. The scheme would have been even more unacceptable after the First World War, which was fought against just such militarism.

The First World War indeed represents a watershed in commemorative sculpture (see Introduction, p14). An unprecedented number of the nation's people took part in it and its true heroes were the hundreds of thousands of common soldiers killed and wounded in the trenches. Thus there were many memorials but their emphasis swung away from the individual to the collective: the brigade, the division or the corps. Up to that time in London there were few figures celebrating the heroism of the ordinary soldier – there were three on the Guards' Crimea Memorial (p165) and four on Wellington's last commemoration (p249). Now there were more than thirty. Some, like Adrian Jones' St. George commemorating the Cavalry Corps in Hyde Park, were triumphant in style. Others, like Jagger's soldiers and howitzer commemorating the Royal Artillery at Hyde Park Corner, were starkly realistic. The most popular and revered memorial of all, the Whitehall Cenotaph, was an oblong block of white stone, its simplicity saying, perhaps, that the grief of war is beyond expression in images.

This is a book about individual, not collective commemorations. Nevertheless, many of the figures on London's war memorials must have been modelled on actual fighting men. On the City of London Royal Fusiliers Regimental Memorial in Holborn, for example, stands a sergeant who fought throughout the First World War and died of wounds on the last day of the Second. In this book the ordinary soldiers are represented by the poet Robert Graves, who sat as a model for his friend Eric Kennington while he was carving the 24th Division Memorial for Battersea Park. Graves enlisted at the beginning of the war in the Royal Welsh Fusiliers and became a captain. He was severely wounded in the battle of the Somme and was reported dead, but some unseen power pulled him back from the threshold of oblivion. His book *Goodbye To All That* is one of the most revealing accounts of the war, full of humour and pride as well as anger at the frequent mismanagement and futility of the conflict.

Below. A scheme, published in 1909 and rapidly outdated by the First World War, for turning Horseguards Parade and St James's Park into a British Avenue of Heroes along German lines.

Right The memorial to the 24th Division by Eric Kennington in Battersea Park. Three soldiers are cramped together on the narrow plinth in a way that illustrates the claustrophobia of the trenches. However, the fact that they are holding hands also symbolises the intense companionship which grew up in the face of hardship and death.

As a young man Robert Graves was the model for one of the three soldiers and in 1976, while in London, he paid a return visit to the memorial.

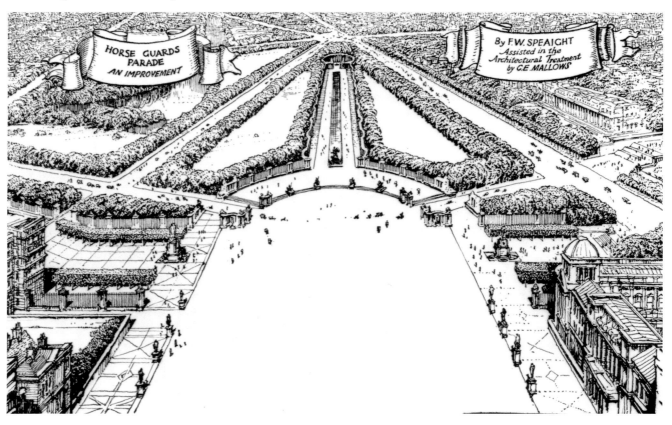

Marshal Foch

The day of the unveiling of Marshal Foch's statue, June 5th, 1930, provided a double reminder of the truth that the bitterest of enemies may later become the closest of friends, for it was on that same day that a statue of General Wolfe was unveiled at Greenwich by the Marquis de Montcalm, the direct descendant of the French general whom Wolfe had defeated at Quebec. Of all the French generals of the First World War, Marshal Foch had the closest ties with Britain. As a leader he was cast in a heroic mould; one fellow officer spoke of the "luminosity which quite spiritualises a face that otherwise would be almost brutal, with its great moustache and protruding jaw." Unfortunately, his military thinking was largely based on the lightning conquest of Alsace by Germany in 1870 and took little account of the subsequent invention of barbed wire and of the machine gun. By 1918, however, his strategy had become more subtle and in that year, backed for the first time by tanks, he led to victory the largest conquering army the world had ever seen.

Nowadays Foch's statue paternally greets all, of whatever nationality, who arrive on the boat train at Victoria station. However, his presence there also has a sombre aspect, for Victoria was the departure point for many of the hundreds of thousands of Englishmen who set out for the mud and gunfire of France, never to return.

Marshal Ferdinand Foch. Born 1851, Tarbes, Hautes-Pyrénées, son of police officer. Suffered humiliation of German occupation as student in Metz, 1871. Commissioned in artillery, 1873. Professor of military history and Commandant of French Staff College, 1895-1900 & 1908-11. Commander of forces in Flanders during Battle of the Marne, 1914. Commander of Northern Army Group until relieved of command after Battle of the Somme, 1915-6. Commander-in-Chief of Allied armies; received German surrender, 1918. Died 1929.

Statue by G. Mallissard. Bronze, 3m 20cm. Grosvenor Gardens, facing Victoria Station. Unveiled June 5th, 1930, by Edward, Prince of Wales. Cost £5,000. A replica of the statue stands in Cassel, between Calais and Lille, where Foch had his Flanders headquarters.

General Wolfe

Major General Sir James Wolfe. Born 1727, Westerham, Kent, son of army general. Received commission in father's regiment 1741. Fought in Flanders and Holland in War of Austrian Succession, 1742-7. Took effective command of Regiment of 20th Foot, aged 22; paid careful and conscientious attention to living conditions of his men. Held regimental commands in Scotland and south of England, 1748-1757. Appointed Quartermaster General on expedition against French at Rochefort, 1757-8; the expedition failed because his daring plan of attack was not carried out. Won approval of George II ("Mad is he?" the King said. "Then I wish he would bite some of my other generals.") Overall commander of expedition to Quebec, 1759. Broke months of stalemate by climbing Heights of Abraham and defeating French army; killed in battle, 1759.

Statue by Tait Mackenzie. Bronze, 9ft on 20ft pedestal. Greenwich Park, beside the Royal Observatory, looking down on Greenwich Hospital and the statue of George II (p40). Paid for by funds raised in Canada and presented by the Canadian people. Unveiled June 5th, 1930, by the Marquis de Montcalm, a descendant of the French commander at Quebec. History has always perceived the bond between Wolfe and Montcalm. Both were outstanding professional soldiers and the Marquis also died shortly after the battle, far from his native land, fighting for what Voltaire called "a few acres of snow".

Wolfe is buried close by the statue in St Alfege's Church. His health was always poor – he survived his campaigns by strength of will rather than physique – and he was no heroic beauty: his long legs, thin body, receding chin and retroussé nose are all faithfully reproduced here.

Stubborn and tenacious, Wolfe stood far above the other, rather feeble English military commanders of his day. He is remembered for the daring attack which won the mastery of Canada. At night, 4,500 men were ferried across the St Lawrence River and scaled a cliff path so narrow and wooded that the French had always disregarded it. By dawn they were drawn up within a mile of the city. By noon Quebec had fallen and Wolfe was dead.

During the river crossing, he is said to have quoted a line from Gray's *Elegy* – "The paths of glory lead but to the grave". These words, mingling triumph and death, set the tone of his heroic appeal to future generations.

Earl Haig

The appallingly destructive nature of the First World War has led to a downgrading of the qualities of its leaders. Field Marshal Haig has been perceived as an inept, callous kind of monster but this is far from the truth. He was a reserved, inarticulate man and a very poor communicator. However, his dispatches show that he was far from indifferent to the fate of his men and after the war he spent all his active time working for their welfare; he refused all personal honours until he was satisfied with their treatment.

Militarily, Haig was an efficient staff officer who took on the responsibilities of an entirely new type and scale of warfare as best he could. As the two immense forces became locked along static lines of mud-filled trenches stretching from Switzerland to the North Sea, Haig, who rightly believed in the all-importance of this Western Front, could see no alternative to a war of attrition in which the first army to exhaust the other would win. His "wearing-out" attacks, conducted by raw, volunteer troops and beset by difficulties of communication, were sometimes rigidly and unimaginatively planned and involved great loss of life. However, until the invention of the tank there seemed no way in which his troops could be mobile enough to consolidate the limited territorial gains which they sometimes made.

Haig's great strength was his quiet, confident self-possession, a marked contrast to the temperamentally unstable Sir John French whom he succeeded as Commander-in-Chief. The picture of him trotting imperturbably along the Menin road to discover the true state of the fighting during the First Battle of Ypres is one that has often been invoked. Because of his lack of eloquence, he got on badly with politicians, in particular Lloyd George, who became Prime Minister in 1916 and would have liked to remove him from command. This he was unable to do, since Haig still had the general confidence of both officers and men. It was largely his determination to win which brought the war to a close in 1918, while those at home believed that it would continue for another one or two years.

As commander of the 1st Army Corps, Haig would ride out every day to visit his forward units and so the horse on which he sits in Whitehall is no anachronism. A.F. Hardiman's design, however, mixed the traditional and the modern in a way that provoked a great deal of controversy. The figure of the Field Marshal is fully representational, while his horse and cloak are stylised and non-realistic. To the professional panel of assessors who awarded Hardiman the commission and to Sir Philip Sassoon, formerly Haig's Military Secretary and now the First Commissioner of Works, the combination was dignified and original. However, Lady Haig disliked the horse intensely; so too did the King and a great number of the general public. "The legs behind cry Forward! and the head in front cries Back!", wrote *Country Life*. "The stance of the hind legs will have, to anyone who has had anything to do with horses, an immediate significance of which the artist may be unaware." In vain did Hardiman explain that it had never occurred to him to study a a real army horse, his purpose being sculpture, not photography. He was obliged to produce three different models, acting throughout with exemplary patience, before the controversy eventually died away.

Other banalities bedevilled the statue's first year of existence. A large advertising poster was erected just behind the Cenotaph promoting Haig's whisky – "Order Haig and don't be Vague". After objections to the juxtaposition, a Dewar's poster was substituted.

Field Marshal Earl Haig. Born 1861, son of whisky distiller. Educated at Clifton, Brasenose and Sandhurst. Played polo for England, 1884. Commissioned in 7th Hussars and served in India, 1885-94. Studied at Camberley Staff College, 1896-8. Fought under Kitchener in Sudan and in Boer War, 1898-1901. On General Staff at War Office; helped Lord Haldane with army reorganisation, 1906-9. Chief of Staff, India, prepared Indian army for participation in European war, which he foresaw, 1909-12. Commander, 1st Army Corps and 1st Army in France, 1914-5. C-in-C, British Forces in France, 1915-8. Founder-President of the British Legion and Chairman of the United Services Fund, 1921-8. Died 1928.

Statue by A.F. Hardiman. Bronze. Whitehall. Unveiled by the Duke of Gloucester on November 10th, 1937, the day before the anniversary of the Armistice (which was signed at the eleventh hour of the eleventh day of the eleventh month). Cost £9,000, paid by the Government, subscriptions to Haig's Memorial Fund being devoted to homes for disabled ex-servicemen.

Lord Trenchard

"Boom" Trenchard, known as the Father of the Royal Air Force, was a man of intensely independent character. As an odd-man-out he was ideally suited to lead the new service that was struggling into independent existence during and after the First World War. His nickname derived from his manner of speech, loud, at times almost inarticulate, explosive and direct. As a young army officer in India he found himself poor and poorly educated. He was also an obsessively keen horseman and polo player; though serving in an infantry regiment, he succeeded in converting his fellow officers to the game. He was badly wounded in the Boer War and fom 1900 he survived – unknown to the R.A.F. – on one lung. The same injury left him half paralysed; in that state, convalescing in Switzerland, he took up bob-sleighing and a dramatic spill on the Cresta run restored him to complete mobility!

He took up flying at the age of 39, just a few months short of the age limit for the newly formed Royal Flying Corps. He owed his initial promotions to his seniority and obvious administrative abilities and he was never a skilled pilot. However, he became the sheet-anchor and inspiration for the aggressive, daring and often costly reconnaissance and bombing sorties of the First World War. He and Field Marshal Haig (p284) had a deep respect for one another. Like Haig, Trenchard has been called an unfeeling monster but this was far from the case; he simply believed in the overriding necessity to win. "It was my job," he wrote, "to prod, cajole, help, comfort and will the pilots on, sometimes to their death. It was not pleasant. They were a new breed of fighting men grappling with unknown forces in the loneliest element of all."

Immediately after the war the R.A.F. proved the worth of its existence policing the scattered desert tribes of the newly formed kingdom of Iraq. The adoption of this policy owed much to T.E. Lawrence, who later found his own haven as a member of the ordinary ranks of the Air Force. He too felt Trenchard's unique personal influence, the hero become hero-worshipper. "The R.A.F. is your single work," he wrote to him privately, "and every one of us, in so far as he is moulded to type, is moulded after your image; it's through your being head and shoulders greater in character than ordinary men that your force, even in childhood, surpasses the immemorial army and navy."

The immense bombing raids of the Second World War had their foundation in Trenchard's philosophy of air attack. However, by the time the war came he was no longer in command. Having fought with great tenacity to raise the efficiency and educational level of the Metropolitan Police Force, he still loomed as a major figure on the national scene. Churchill offered him the position of overall commander of home forces in the event of an invasion. Knowing only too well the labyrinthine nature of civil and military politics, he peremptorily rejected it as unworkable.

Trenchard's statue was erected at the south end of the newly opened section of the Victoria Embankment Gardens, also known as Whitehall Gardens, at the opposite end to General Gordon's. It was decided to concentrate R.A.F. commemorations in this area and a few years later Air Chief Marshal Portal's statue (p288) was placed between them. The figure of Trenchard, with its high collar and sword, seems curiously archaic for the leader of the latest and least ceremonial of the Armed Forces. However, the likeness, the stoic, lined face, the puckered brows and bristling moustache, is good.

Marshal of the Royal Air Force Viscount Hugh Trenchard. Born 1873, Taunton, son of lawyer. Failed army and navy entrance examinations; eventually passed militia exam and posted to India, 1893-9. Fought in Boer War; severely wounded but returned to command irregular cavalry units and carry out special assignments for C-in-C Kitchener, 1899-1902. Assistant commandant of South Nigerian Regiment; successful in control of jungle tribes, 1903-10. Joined Royal Flying Corps; appointed administrator of Central Flying School, Farnborough, 1913-4. Posted to France, 1914. Commander of Royal Flying Corps in France; developed new reconnaissance and bombing methods; 1915-8. Royal Air Force formed; appointed first Chief of Staff but resigned after clashes with Air Minister, Lord Rothermere, 1918; given command of bombing force in France. Returned as Chief of Air Staff with Churchill as Minister, 1919. Built up new service against hostility of army and navy, 1919-29; founded Cadet College and Staff College. Commissioner of Metropolitan Police, 1931-5. Roving ambassador of Air Council; visited bases and improved morale, 1939-45. Died 1958.

Statue by William Macmillan. Bronze. Victoria Embankment Gardens. Unveiled July 19th, 1961, by Prime Minister Harold Macmillan. Cost £7,000.

Lord Portal

"Come with me, reader, for half an hour and see whether hawking is not a beautiful sport. Do you know those crisp October mornings when a bead of dew glitters on every thorn in the pale sunlight, when the air is still and bright and the last wisp of fog is leaving the valley?...Now for the first time you are to see for yourself the speed of the hawk. He passes like a shooting star right across the sky, and is soon almost over the speeding covey. There is a yet grander sight to come, for after a few more mighty strokes his wings shut close and he hurls himself, with truly appalling speed, down through the sunlit air... The eye can scarcely follow it, but the ear can hear the high screams of the bell and the hiss of the hawk's wings as he goes".

So wrote the twenty-eight year old Squadron Leader "Peter" Portal, hawker since childhood, First World War flying ace and chief flying instructor at Cranwell Cadet College, where he kept his own hawk tethered to a post outside his office. Had he not seen hawks in action, he told a colleague, he would not have survived the war, manoeuvring to avoid the superior German fighters as he flew his tiny, open biplane on reconnaissance over enemy lines. He went on to command the Royal Air Force in the war against against Hitler and to oversee the development of Britain's atomic bomb. Thus did one man in a lifetime run the entire gamut of mankind's science of airborne destruction from its earliest, natural beginnings to its technological, nuclear apotheosis.

Portal's article on hawking in the Cranwell magazine was a rare public expression of emotion. He was an intensely private, efficient and undemonstrative man and for that reason his fame is not as great as that of some others of comparable rank. Portal fought the Second World War at his desk in Whitehall; he did not visit his airfields, believing that if he went to one he would have to go to all. However, his close colleagues, who proposed and subscribed to his statue, appreciated his all-round abilities. "Anything you can do," said Sir Arthur Harris, "Peter Portal can do better." Churchill valued him as the calmest and most level headed of the four Chiefs of Staff who with him ran the overall conduct of the war. In 1951, he offered him the position of Minister of Defence but Portal, who felt that he had done more than his public duty, turned him down at once and did not even tell his wife and family what had happened.

Oscar Nemon (p290) visited Portal several times shortly before his death for sittings. Born in Yugoslavia, Nemon worked in Vienna and Brussels and in his youth sculpted Freud (p168). Shortly before the outbreak of the Second World War, he came to Britain to fulfil various commissions; he married and stayed. He sculpted a number of world leaders, including Churchill, Eisenhower and Macmillan. (Figures of Sir Winston and Lady Churchill still await casting and erection in Kensington Gardens.)

Nemon believed that the exact details of dress are not what the eye perceives in a living man and that in a sculpture they distract from the essential character. Here, though the overall stance is defiant, Portal's body remains an outline impression. All the attention is concentrated in the face, the prominent nose, the firm lines around the mouth and the upward, expectant gaze. With dramatic effect, the statue's gaze seems to be following the flight, not of a falcon, but of the golden eagle which surmounts the R.A.F Memorial next to the river; so did the station commanders of the World Wars watch anxiously for the return of their planes.

Marshal of the Royal Air Force Viscount Portal of Hungerford. Born 1893, son of country gentleman. Joined Royal Engineers and became motor-bicycle dispatch rider in France, 1914. Seconded to Royal Flying Corps, 1915. Served as air pilot, specialising in observation, range-finding and night bombing, 1915-8. Chief Flying Instructor, Cranwell Cadet College, 1918-22. Worked at Air Ministry in various advisory and administrative posts; helped Trenchard (p286) during R.A.F.'s struggle for independent survival, 1922-5, 1930-33, and 1937-9. Squadron Commander, specialising in accurate bombing, 1927-9. Officer Commanding British forces in Aden; conducted air campaign on behalf of Yemeni tribesmen, 1933-5. Commander-in-chief, Bomber Command; instigated bombing of Berlin, 1940. Chief of Air Staff, head of R.A.F. and member of Chief of Staffs' Committee, 1940-6. Controller of Atomic Energy, 1946-51. President of M.C.C., 1958-9. Chairman of British Aircraft Corporation, 1960-4. Died 1971.

Statue by Oscar Nemon. Bronze, 9ft on 6ft pedestal. Victoria Embankment Gardens, in front of Ministry of Defence. Unveiled 21st May, 1975, by Harold Macmillan. Cost £20,000.

Above. The golden eagle on the R.A.F. Memorial, sculpted by William Reid Dick, towards which Portal directs his gaze.

Lord Montgomery

"Monty" ended his life as a self-appointed sage of the atomic age, flying privately to Moscow and Peking to confer with Krushchev and Mao Tse-Tung and to present his clear-cut solutions to world problems. The roots of this self-confidence lay in the same Victorian Christianity that inspired Gordon and Roberts, coupled with the fact that he was arguably England's greatest soldier of genius since Wellington. His father was a benign Anglican bishop; his mother brought him up on strict principles. He read his Bible daily and placed his faith in the Lord Mighty in Battles. On the other hand he was a rebel, highly unconventional and critical of both superiors and inferiors. He saw things in black and white, simplifying situations down to their essentials. Fortunately for the opponents of Fascist tyranny, he was almost always right.

To him the military philosophy of the First World War was stupid and wasteful. After the war, as a staff officer and lecturer, he set out a new approach involving minute reconnaissance and deception of the enemy, with the minimum of casualties. He also wanted senior officers to explain to the troops in the field exactly what they were doing and why. All these ideas were put into practice when, during the Second World War, he was sent out to command the Eighth Army on the only land front remaining after Dunkirk. Rommel was advancing across North Africa, the Allied forces were demoralised. The transformation which Montgomery achieved in a few short weeks was little short of miraculous. He announced his battle plan which which would trap Rommel in a surprise encirclement; it would, he said with characteristically straightforward arrogance, be the turning point of the war and one of the decisive battles of history. And so it was. Within ten months the Axis powers had been driven out of Africa and the Allies were about to invade Sicily.

During the campaign he kept in close, personal touch with all his troops, who knew him simply as "Monty". Travelling to the front in a tank, he changed his general's hat for a more comfortable soldier's beret. He wore it ever afterwards, despite official criticism, and festooned it with the badges of the various units serving under him. This was partly vanity but also a practical recognition of the value of personal and identifiable leadership. The beret became his hallmark and his statue in Whitehall wears it today, together with a comparatively modest pair of badges.

Field Marshal Viscount Montgomery of Alamein. Born 1887, Kennington, South London, son of Anglican clergyman. Commissioned in army and served in India, 1909-13. Served in France, 1914-8; severely wounded in lung. Instructor, Camberley Staff College, 1926-31. Married Mrs Betty Carver, widowed artist, 1927. Served in Palestine, Egypt and India. Death of wife increased loneliness and dedication to profession, 1937. Commanded 3rd Division in France, 1939-40. Commanded 12th Corps, England, 1940-2. Posted to Cairo to take command of 8th Army; won battle of El Alamein. Took major part in recovery of whole of North Africa and Sicily, 1942-3. Commanded "D-Day" landings in Normandy, 1944; his insistence on having double the proposed number of troops was crucial in their success. C-in-C of all British forces in Allied advance across France and Germany, 1944-5; openly critical of overall command of General Eisenhower. Chief of Imperial General Staff, 1946-8. Helped to set up NATO alliance, insisting on membership of West Germany and becoming deputy C-in-C NATO forces in Paris, 1948-58. Retired to Isington Mill, Hampshire, 1958; made private diplomatic visits to China, Russia, South Africa and many other countries. Died 1976.

Statue by Oscar Nemon. Bronze, 10ft. Raleigh Green, Whitehall. Unveiled June 6th, 1980, by Queen Elizabeth the Queen Mother. Cost £30,000.

Below. The sculptor (left) studies the cardboard model erected to test the look of the site.

Earl Alexander

Alexander, like Wellington, was an Irish aristocrat. Both soldiers combined coolness and cheerfulness but whereas the Duke's detachment made him hard like steel, Alexander's gave him a chivalric softness; he always seemed relaxed, happy simply to excel in his chosen profession. From 1914 onwards he was an outstanding leader. As Kipling wrote in his history of the Irish Guards, "He had the gift of handling the men in the lines to which they most readily responded. At the worst crises he was both inventive and cordial and, on such occasions as they all strove together in the gates of death, would somehow contrive to dress the affair in high comedy." An example of the latter was the occasion when he took out a party to capture a German officer and, since there was snow on the ground, dressed them all in white night-dresses and underwear requisitioned from the local village. He genuinely enjoyed the First World War and, strange as such sentiments may seem now, was sorry when it was over. "We were," he said, "fit, tough, screwed up with patriotism and desire for glory. It was a terrific adventure." He liked and admired the Germans as worthy enemies and in Latvia in 1919 found himself commanding the German Balts against the Russians; some of the veterans of that army later became his foes in North Africa and Italy.

At the beginning of the Second World War Alexander was one of the most highly regarded officers in the army, marked out for great things. In fact he began by overseeing two major retreats. At Dunkirk he was given a last minute appointment and succeeded in bringing home more British troops than anyone had believed possible. In Burma, too, he refused to be deflected from his purpose of getting out and saving lives. His great strength was his ability to appreciate the characters and abilities of his fellow commanders and to work with them harmoniously. The partnership between Alexander and Montgomery (p290) in North Africa in 1942 was one of the most fortunate in British military history. Perhaps no other overall commander would have given the arrogant and demanding Monty the freedom to do exactly as he wanted, with such crucial success. He accepted his plan for El Alamein, gave him the troops and stores he needed and deflected Churchill's impatience to begin sooner than he thought advisable. So it is fitting that the statues of the two men should have been erected so close to each other in time.

Alexander won his own victories at Tunis, Salerno and in northern Italy. By the end, it seems, he had had enough of fighting. As he said in 1946 to the delegates to the First General Assembly of the United Nations gathered in the Albert Hall, "We are a nation who hate and detest war and no one hates it more than we soldiers who have seen at first hand the misery and degradation which it brings." But," he added, "at a time of great crisis some of man's noblest qualities emerge: bravery, enterprise, discipline, self-sacrifice and comradeship."

Alexander's statue stands just in front of the Guards' Chapel, where one can still feel that spirit of care and dedication to which he contributed his own particular qualities. James Butler, its sculptor, studied old newsreel film in search of some revealing aspect of his subject's appearance. During the Italian campaign he would often wear an old, battered flying jacket which gave him a slightly rakish air. He also had a characteristic way of standing. The two together gave Butler the sculptural mass he required and also conveyed the appropriate mixture of elegance and dynamism.

Field Marshal Earl Alexander of Tunis. Born 1891, London, son of the 4th Earl of Caledon. Brought up on family estate in County Tyrone, Northern Ireland. Commissioned in Irish Guards, 1911. Fought in First World War, rising to rank of Lt.Col., 1914-8. Commanded Baltic Landeswar against Russians in Latvia, 1919-20. Served in Turkey, England and Indian North-west Frontier, 1922-38. Appointed Major General commanding 1st Division in France, 1939. Led rearguard in evacuation of Dunkirk, 1940. Commanded retreat from Burma, 1942. C-in-C, Middle East; supported General Montgomery at El Alamein, 1942. Overall commander of campaigns in Sicily and Italy, 1943-5. Governor General of Canada, 1946-52. Minister of Defence, 1952-4. Died 1969.

Statue by James Butler. Bronze, 10ft on 3ft 6ins pedestal. Guards' Headquarters, Birdcage Walk. Unveiled May 9th, 1985, by H.M. Queen Elizabeth. Cost £30,000.

The erection of the statue marked the completion of the 22 year project to rebuild the London headquarters of the five regiments of Footguards. Alexander was Colonel of the Irish Guards from 1946 to 1969.

Earl Mountbatten

"Dickie" Mountbatten was Queen Victoria's great grandson and a nephew of the Czar of Russia. His lifelong ambition was straightforward: to work his way through the ranks of the Royal Navy and become First Sea Lord, the office held by his father before public feeling against his German origins forced him to resign in 1914. He reached this goal in 1955, having in the meantime held much greater military and political offices. However, it was his master-image and it is appropriate that his statue, in naval uniform, looks across to the old Admiralty building on the north side of Horseguards Parade.

From there Mountbatten can continue to watch the ceremonial displays which he loved with an intensity bordering on obsession. His position as Colonel of the Life-Guards brought him the privilege of riding behind the Queen at the Trooping of the Colour; he would practise for weeks beforehand, dressed in high boots and burnished helmet, riding his charger around the lanes near his Hampshire estate and chatting to the local farmers.

As with Montgomery (p290), the common touch was one of his greatest gifts. The crew of the destroyer H.M.S. Kelly, which he commanded in swashbuckling style until she was sunk off Crete, were devoted to him and reunion dinners continued until his death. In South East Asia he transformed military morale by establishing personal contact with all his units, large and small. After a formal parade, he would get on a soapbox and call his troops to gather round, joking with them, sometimes scurrilously, and taking them into his confidence, promising better things. By improving confidence, by successfully combating malaria and by fighting on during the monsoon with full air support, he was able to inflict on the Japanese their first defeat of the entire war.

As the last Viceroy of India, it was Mountbatten's task to dismember the torso of the British Empire. Historians will always dispute whether he forced through independence too quickly. He certainly charmed both Gandhi and Nehru, though he could not unfreeze Jinnah's determination to establish a separate Muslim state.

Mountbatten read little and disliked solitude; he was essentially a man of action. Franta Belsky, the Czech-born sculptor of his statue, wished to represent a heroic moment of action frozen in time. The Admiral is on the point of raising his binoculars, as he looks towards far horizons. What does he see – the trail of a German U-boat or the inevitable political movements of his times? He was that paradox, the aristocrat with socialist convictions. After the Second World War, he saw the growth of the new, nationalist movements in South East Asia and he did what he could to help their emergence. In England he was accused in some quarters of being a communist sympathiser. And when, at Gandhi's funeral, he sat on the ground in his governor general's uniform, the sense of shock was extreme. Paradoxically again, as an aristocrat it was all the more possible for him to act as he did and to ride out the criticism.

In his last years he grew appalled at the prospect of nuclear war and campaigned strongly for multilateral disarmament. In a romantic gesture, Belsky planned to include the metal of an enemy gun in the casting of his statue but Mountbatten's family claimed him as a man of peace and disapproved, so rejecting a tradition of triumph which had begun with Wellington. One wonders, indeed, how and for what the next generation of military men after Mountbatten's will be commemorated?

Admiral of the Fleet Earl Mountbatten of Burma. Born 1900, Windsor, second son of Prince Louis of Battenberg. Began career in navy as midshipman, 1916. Married Edwina Ashley, American banking heiress, 1922. Promoted Captain, commanded H.M.S. Kelly and 5th destroyer flotilla in action in English Channel and Atlantic, in Norwegian campaign and in Battle of Crete, 1939-41. As Chief of Combined Operations, was one of the inner circle of service chiefs directing the Second World War, 1941-3. Supreme Allied Commander, South East Asia, 1943-6. Viceroy and afterwards Governor general of India, 1947-8. Returned to naval career as Flag Officer, 1948. Became First Sea Lord, 1955. Chief of Defence Staff, in command of all three armed services, 1959-65. Died 1979, assassinated by the I.R.A.

Statue by Franta Belsky. Bronze, 9 ft on 5ft pedestal. Foreign Office Green, looking towards Horseguards Parade. Unveiled November 2nd, 1983, by H.M. the Queen. Overall cost £100,000, more than half of which came in individual donations of less than £10.

CHAPTER 7
EXPLORATION AND RELIGION

Having completed the major categories of commemoration – royalty and philanthropy, arts and sciences, politics and warfare – two more, minor divisions remain, each containing half a dozen or more statues. These are the explorers and the religious leaders, celebrated from the 1860's onwards. The composition of both groups reflects the dramatic, expansive nature of the last few hundred years of human history. Sir Walter Raleigh was chief among the Elizabethans who pioneered the British move westwards and Captain John Smith ensured the survival of the first permanent North American settlement. Captain Cook, shown opposite, was the first man to chart with certainty the southern waters of the world and his voyages led to the establishment of the British colony of Australia. Two heroic voyagers, however, ended their lives marooned by polar ice and snow; the deep admiration felt for Sir John Franklin and for Captain Scott highlights the British fascination with death in the pursuit of duty.

So too does the commemoration of three religious martyrs – Becket, Tyndale and More. Their fate illustrates the turbulent relationship between Christianity and power politics in earlier centuries. Yet the English are not a "professionally" devout people; their spirituality is as much practical as devotional. Over the last two hundred years faith and social betterment have marched together. The very first man to be given a statue in the cause of religion was the portly, extrovert newspaper proprietor who founded the Sunday School movement, and John Wesley and William and Catherine Booth also took the gospel to the poorest in the land.

It seems appropriate that the pioneers of external, geographical space should share a chapter with those of inner, spiritual and moral space, as during Britain's colonial period missionary zeal and the quest for new lands were closely identified. David Livingstone, who passionately believed that commerce and Christianity would together be the salvation of Africa, exemplifies this state of mind and his statue on the Royal Geographical Society building is included here. (However, more traditional religious ikons, such as the St Paul on the replaced Cross in St Paul's Churchyard or the golden Buddha in the Pagoda of Peace in Battersea Park, are not included.) One wonders which religious leaders will in future grace the streets of this increasingly cosmopolitan capital. We end with St Volodymyr; in 988 he inaugurated Russian Orthodox Christianity and in 1988 his exiled Ukrainian compatriots commemorated him in Holland Park.

Sir John Franklin

The search for a sea-way linking the Atlantic and the Pacific via the ice-fields of northern Canada, the so-called North West Passage, was a preoccupation of English explorers from the time of Drake onwards. In fact the passage barely exists and certainly offers no possibilities as a trade route. Whether or not the religious, dependable and cheerful Franklin was the first to discover it has always been controversial but it makes little difference to his position as a hero.

The mysterious disappearance of his expedition led to numerous attempts to discover its fate. However, it was only the passionate persistence of his widow, Jane, which eventually resulted in the finding of one of the ships and a log of the expedition. Over the years further traces were recovered. It seems that, after surviving one Arctic winter, the vessels became locked in a terrible ice-crunch generated by the meeting of three great channels. Franklin and various others died and, after another winter, the rest abandoned ship, only to leave their bones scattered across King William Land. Then in the 1980's the original graves of two of the seamen were located. Their bodies, perfectly preserved in the ice, showed concentrations of lead far above the normal; the expedition's food had been stored in primitive metal tins soldered with lead.

Sir John's expedition also passed into folk history and inspired many poems and ballads. Of all London's nineteenth century statues, it seems that the ordinary people found his the most interesting. Crowds of ragged working folk would gather around the pedestal to hear one of their number recount the story of "Lord" Franklin and his tragic death.

Sir John Franklin. Born 1786, Spilsby, Lincolnshire, twelfth son of shopkeeper. Joined navy, fought in Battle of Trafalgar and in British-American War, 1800-15. Went on first Arctic expeditions, 1818-22; travelled 5,500 miles mapping northern Canada. Expedition to Garry Island, 1825-7. Lieutenant Governor of Van Dieman's Land penal colony, 1836-43; improved lot of convicts, despite opposition from local society and from Colonial Secretary, Lord Derby (p190). Leader of expedition to discover North West Passage, 1845. Died June 11th, 1847.

Statue by Matthew Noble. Bronze, 8ft 4ins. Waterloo Place. Unveiled November 15th, 1866, in the presence of Sir John Packington, First Sea Lord, and Sir Roderick Murchisson, President of the Royal Geographical Society. Cost £1,950. Franklin is informing his crew of the discovery of the North West Passage.

Below. The beautiful, bronze plaque on the front of the pedestal shows Franklin's funeral service being conducted by Captain Crozier, his fellow commander.

Captain Cook

"A world Venice with the sea for streets" – so Prince Arthur of Connaught described the British Empire as he unveiled the statue of Captain James Cook at the east end of the Mall. Given the picturesque image, then Cook played a key part in laying down the thoroughfares and establishing the boundaries of that city, for his three great voyages gave the known world substantially the shape it has today.

At the time it seemed that Cook was more important for what he did *not* find. The Royal Society first sent him to Tahiti to observe the transit of Venus but it proved impossible to get the accurate timings that would have established the distance between the Earth and the Sun. His co-sponsors, the Admiralty, were in search of the fabled Great Southern Continent – Terra Australis Incognita – vast, temperate, fertile, teeming with inhabitants and ripe for trade. Cook proved conclusively that it did not exist, pushing the southern boundaries of the world's oceans into the regions of perpetual ice and, on his second voyage, coming within seventy miles of Antarctica. Subordinate to this quest, Cook also circumnavigated New Zealand for the first time and, almost as an afterthought, sailed up the unexplored eastern coast of Australia. He landed for a few days at Botany Bay (which he first called Sting-Ray Bay) and again for a few weeks at the mouth of the Endeavour River for ship repairs. Finally, as a ritual gesture, he planted the English flag at the north eastern extremity of the continent and left, never to return.

The belief that Cook was the discoverer of Australia is therefore somewhat exaggerated. The Portuguese and then the Dutch had been active on the eastern side of the country for the previous two hundred years. The first Englishman to land there was William Dampier, who visited the western and southern coast in 1688 and 1699 and planned to establish a colony next to Dutch New Holland. Cook, on the other hand, was generally unimpressed with what he saw, finding the western coast dry and barren. It was really the urging of Sir Joseph Banks, the wealthy naturalist who accompanied Cook on his first voyage, and the loss of America as a place for transporting convicts which led to the establishing of a penal colony close to Botany Bay in 1788 and laid the rough, repressive foundations of the present-day country. Young nations, however, need their heroes. With the gold rush of the 1850's Australia, now fully British, finally cast aside its penal status and soon afterwards the cult of Captain Cook began to gather momentum. As a labourer's son who had risen through the ranks of the navy by ability and diligence, he was the ideal embodiment of rugged Australian virtues. The first plans for a public statue of him were put forward in the 1860's; these finally bore fruit in 1879 when Thomas Woolner's gigantic thirteen and a half foot figure was erected in Hyde Park, Sydney, having been displayed in London's Waterloo Place prior to shipment.

The statue in the Mall also owes its genesis to the Australian search for roots. Sir Joseph Carruthers, Premier of New South Wales from 1904-8, was, like Cook, a self-made man, and was his most vigorous world-wide promoter. In 1908, after a visit to England, Carruthers wrote to *The Times* bewailing the lack of a memorial in London. The British Empire League took up his plea and George, Prince of Wales (who as a midshipman had once attended a celebration picnic at Cook's supposed landing site in Botany Bay) became Chairman of the Memorial Committee. The sculptor chosen was Thomas Brock, who was then working on the figures for the Victoria Memorial (p70).

Captain James Cook. Born 1728, Marton-in-Cleveland, Yorkshire, son of farm labourer. Employed in coal trade around English coast, 1747-55. Joined Navy as ordinary seaman, 1755. Master on H.M.S. Pembroke, 1757-8; successfully charted St Lawrence River for English fleet and was present at fall of Quebec. Continued surveys of Canadian coast, 1758-68; work commended by the Royal Society. First Pacific Voyage, 1768-71; charted North and South Islands of New Zealand for the first time, sailed along east coast of Australia and landed at Botany Bay. Second Pacific Voyage, 1772-5; circumnavigated entire southern latitudes and became first European to enter Antarctic Circle. Third Pacific Voyage, 1776-9; explored Bering Straits but failed to find North-west Passage. Killed by Hawaiian islanders at Kealakekua Bay, 1779.

See also frontispiece to chapter, p296. Statue by Thomas Brock. Bronze. East end of The Mall. Unveiled July 7th, 1914, by Prince Arthur of Connaught. Cost £3,000.

Sir Aston Webb's original plans for the re-designing of the Mall envisaged lines of statues representing the colonies along the avenue, though these were subsequently placed on the various gates around the Memorial. Cook's place at the Mall's western end is therefore quite appropriate. There were various suggestions that it might become a kind of gallery of statues of great men, but in the event Cook's was the only free-standing figure erected there.

If Cook's status as a founder of empire has been somewhat exaggerated, there can be no doubt about his genius as a navigator. His achievement in accurately charting the entire 2,400 mile-long New Zealand coastline in his tiny vessel has been described as awesome. Appropriately, his statue looks towards the figure representing navigation in a niche on the left side of Admiralty Arch. As ship's commander, Cook was supremely in control. He kept his men fit and occupied and entirely free from scurvy through the frequent consumption of dried soup and sauerkraut. His greatest failing was his shortness of temper. The people of the South Seas whom he encountered generally liked and respected him, and on one occasion at least treated him as a mythological hero-god, but he could never tolerate their habit of pilfering objects from his expeditions. By their standards this was no crime, since the ordinary people held property in common, but Cook punished the thieves harshly and took hostages, sometimes by force. An incident of this kind led to his murder in Hawaii. It was a sad end to an outstanding life and a bad augury for relations between white and aboriginal peoples.

Captain Scott

Captain Scott's statue in Waterloo Place is a unique kind of commemoration, a special act of love, for it was sculpted by his widow, Kathleen. They married when he was forty, an impoverished navy captain with an international reputation as an explorer, for whom life in general had been a hard struggle in a difficult world. She was twenty nine, fresh from life in bohemian Paris as a student of sculpture. He feared that he would be too set in his ways for her free, vital spirit but he was the man for whom she had been keeping herself. They had one son, Peter – named after Peter Pan, J.M. Barrie being their close friend – who grew up to become one of the world's leading naturalists. Not long after their marriage, the opportunity for a second British expedition to Antarctica arose and Scott answered the challenge. Between their first falling in love and their last farewells on the shores of New Zealand, they had only three years together.

Scott was not a conscious hero. Exploration was his skill and patriotism and a sense of duty high among his motivations. However, the "race" for the South Pole which developed between his party and the Norwegian Amundsen, the bad luck which continually dogged him, and the discovery of his last camp, together with his journals and final letters, ensured his place as a legend. Some words from that journal are inscribed on the pedestal of the statue: "Had we lived I should have had a tale to tell of the hardihood, endurance and courage of my companions which would have stirred the heart of every Englishman. These notes and our dead bodies must tell the tale." The names of his fellow explorers, Wilson, Bowen, Evans, and Oates who deliberately walked out into the night when his weakness was delaying the party, are also inscribed there.

Scott's statue is unusual in another way: it was erected during the First World War. So too was Florence Nightingale's, but very rarely are statues erected while a major war is in progress. This demonstrates the deep impression made by his journey. His struggle against extreme cold, hunger and blizzards seemed to mirror the conflict in hand; his devotion to duty and his dignity in the face of death were an example to many as they set out for the uncertainties of battle.

Kathleen Scott became a well respected and successful artist. The secret of portraiture, she maintained, lay in emphasis, in the careful exaggeration of certain features to bring out the inner personality. In sculpting the husband with whom she had lived so briefly she focused on the active smile which would sometimes illuminate his round, determined face, the same smile which can be seen on newsreel films of his departure for Antarctica. She specialised in portrait busts and sculpted a number of famous men; George V, George VI, Asquith, Lloyd George, Bernard Shaw and T.E. Lawrence were among those who sat for her and her bust of Lord Northcliffe is on St Dunstan's Church in Fleet Street. Her sitters often became her friends. Given Herbert Asquith's antipathy to women in politics (see pp 210 & 220), it is surprising to learn that she became his close confidante, particularly during his last year as Prime Minister in 1916; to her he revealed his deep disillusionment with life. George V, during a sitting in 1935, laid bare his dislike of public statues (see p76). He offered to give her a hundred pounds if she would break up a certain statue he disliked – her journal does not say which. She would be fined twenty five pounds, the King explained, but she would make a profit of seventy five pounds on the transaction. She accepted – but nothing, it seems, came of it.

Captain Robert Falcon Scott. Born 1868, Devonport, son of brewer. Joined Navy, 1880. Promoted lieutenant, 1889; specialised in steam and torpedo warfare. Bankruptcy and death of father, 1894-7. Proposed as leader of National Antarctic Expedition by Sir Clements Markham, President of the National Geographical Society, 1899. Led expedition, 1901-4; carried out valuable scientific work and reached to within 500 miles of South Pole. Married Kathleen Bruce, sculptress, 1908. Led second Antarctic expedition, 1910-11; reached South Pole 17th January, 1911, to find that the Norwegian Amundsen had arrived five weeks earlier. Delayed by blizzards on return journey and died from exposure and malnutrition in tent only eleven miles from depot.

Statue by Kathleen Scott. Bronze. Waterloo Place. Unveiled November 5th, 1915, by A.J. Balfour, First Lord of the Admiralty. The funds for the statue were raised by a special appeal among officers of the navy. Scott is dressed as for the Antarctic and carries a ski-stick; he gazes into the distance across the snowy wastes. A marble replica was erected in Christchurch, New Zealand.

Below. Kathleen Scott, photographed around the time of her marriage.

ROBERT FALCON SCOTT
CAPTAIN ROYAL NAVY

David Livingstone

There are two statues in alcoves on the Royal Geographical Society building in Kensington Gore. One of them is of the Antarctic explorer Ernest Shackleton and faces onto Exhibition Road; it is by C. Sergeant Jagger and was erected in 1932. It was felt by many people that Shackleton was as deserving of a memorial as Captain Scott (p302) and their two statues are in fact rather similar. On the front of the building is the better-known statue of David Livingstone. Though not a free-standing figure, it is included here partly because its striding, determined pose catches the eye of so many people and partly because Livingstone is a key figure in the pantheon of British heroes. More than anyone, he brought together the two seemingly disparate themes of this chapter. He began as a missionary and ended as an explorer, though he was always both; he believed passionately that European commerce and Christianity would together open up, unify and reform Africa.

Livingstone travelled thousands of miles through territory largely unknown to Europeans. He had a genuine love of Africans and he usually preferred their company to that of white men. He was a difficult travelling companion, temperamental, almost pathologically over-optimistic and intolerant of others' weaknesses. On his two, brief returns to England, he was received as a national hero. Yet, as he lay dying in the swamps of Bangweolo, his life must have seemed to him a complete failure. None of the schemes which he had initiated had taken root, he had not converted a single African and in his travels around Lake Tanganyika he had had to depend for his life on the very Arab slavers whose trade he had set out to destroy. Nevertheless in that very year, stimulated by the reports which he had given to H.M. Stanley, an embassy led by Sir Bartle Frere (p200) succeeded in persuading the Sultan of Zanzibar to close his all-important slave markets, so spelling an end to slavery in East Africa. Within twenty one years Nyasaland and Uganda were British Protectorates and the British Empire in Africa was fully under way. What idealism it possessed, what genuine desire to understand and care for its native peoples, may be traced back to the example of that strange and paradoxical man, David Livingstone.

David Livingstone. Born 1813, Blantyre, Lanarkshire, son of mill-worker. Began working twelve hour day in mill, aged 10, 1823; educated himself in spare time. Trained with London Missionary Society and qualified as doctor, 1837-40. Sailed for southern Africa, 1840. Established various missionary settlements, moving northwards through present-day Botswana; crossed Kalahari Desert and reached Lake Ngami and Zambesi River, 1841-52. Sent wife and children back to Scotland and explored entire Zambesi from west to east coast, 1853-6; found Victoria Falls. Returned to England and was received as hero; spoke widely on "Commerce and Christianity", 1857-8. Appointed leader of government expedition; explored eastern Zambesi, Shire River and Lake Nyasa by steamboat, 1857-63. Returned to England, 1864-5. Went alone to wild territory around Lake Nyasa in order to work against slave-trade and discover source of Nile, 1866-73; suffered extreme ill-health and failed in both aims. Famous meeting with Stanley at Ujiji, 1871. Died 1873.

Right. Statue by T.B. Huxley-Jones. Bronze, 8ft 6ins. Royal Geographical Society, Kensington Gore. Unveiled October 23rd, 1953, by Mr Oliver Lyttelton, Secretary of State for the Colonies. Livingstone's body, miraculously brought back to England, lay in state at the Royal Geographical Society before being buried in Westminster Abbey. Funds collected by the Society were used to set up and care for a memorial at the site of his death in Chitambo's Village; when this was taken over by the Northern Rhodesian government, the balance of the fund, together with a donation by Lord Catto of Cairncatto, were used to pay for the present statue.

Left. There have been several commemorations of Livingstone, both in Britain and Africa. A 12 ft statue by Sir William Reid Dick (p77) was commissioned by the Federated Caledonian Society of South Africa and erected close by the Victoria Falls in 1934. Here Reid Dick surveys the plaster model in his studio. (This was at No 16, Maida Vale, and was originally built by Alfred Gilbert (pp75 & 96).) On the left is his statue of the Indian Viceroy, Lord Willingdon.

LIVINGSTONE

Sir Walter Raleigh

Explorer, soldier and administrator, hermetist and poet, Sir Walter Raleigh deserves commemoration on many counts. During his ten years as Queen Elizabeth's favourite he was the foremost man in the kingdom. When Elizabeth died, rumour would have made him king. His presence was altogether too threatening for James I, who imprisoned him perpetually in the Tower on a trumped up charge.

How then is Raleigh best classified? For the purposes of this book the problem is solved by the circumstances surrounding his statue. For just as Captain Cook (p300) presides magisterially over the beginnings of Australia, so Raleigh, gallant, enterprising, puffing on his Virginian tobacco (he once wagered the Queen that he could weigh its smoke and won by balancing the ashes against an equal quantity of unsmoked plant) looms large in the North American imagination. In 1956 the Commission for the celebration of the 350th anniversary of the first permanent North American settlement came from Virginia to London and found no memorial of their discoverer and founder. Their report of this lack was taken up by Colonel John Dodge, Chairman of The Ends of the Earth Club, an Anglo-American dining association, and, assisted by the English Speaking Union, the funds for a statue were raised.

Strictly speaking Raleigh neither discovered or established British North America, though he financed the former and showed the way for the latter by his vision and example. "To seek new worlds, for gold, for praise, for glory," always fascinated him. It was America, rather than the Orient, which drew him and during the 1580's he invested £40,000 (a sum which nowadays would amount to millions) in organising expeditions to its northern coasts. The Queen craved his company and feared for his life too much to allow him to leave England personally. However, it was at his instigation that landings were made on Roanoke Island, off the present day coast of North Carolina, at the mouth of Albermarle Sound. His explorers called the land Virginia, a happy blend of its Indian name Wingandacoa and the Virgin Queen's own title, for which compliment Raleigh was awarded his knighthood. Moreover, on one of the return journeys some Spanish ships were very satisfactorily plundered, so recovering a good part of the original investment.

In 1595, no longer the Queen's favourite, Raleigh himself sailed further south and explored Guiana. He found it a paradise and envisaged the building up of a British Empire which would rival that of Spain. In this he was far ahead of his time. In fact all his foreign ventures ended unsuccessfully; none of his North American settlements survived and his last, make-or-break journey to Guiana in 1617 failed to find gold and so led to his execution in Old Palace Yard. The honour of ensuring the survival of the first British North American settlement belongs instead to a certain Captain John Smith, whose statue in the City (p308), erected two years after Raleigh's, makes an interesting companion piece.

Raleigh was never King of Virginia, as he had hoped to be, and a great human opportunity was lost. As a colonist, he was exceptional in insisting on friendly relations with local tribespeople; if his instructions forbidding violence had been obeyed, his second Virginian expedition might well have have survived. He likewise saw little difference between the maidens of Guiana, for all their simple nakedness, and the beauties of the English court; they too were human beings and he ordered his men to show them an equal respect.

Sir Walter Raleigh. Born 1552, Hayes Barton, Devon, son of gentleman landowner. Joined Inns of Court, 1574. Military captain in Ireland, 1580-1. Queen Elisabeth's principal favourite, 1582-92; appointed Lord Lieutenant of Cornwall and granted various important and profitable monopolies. Financed expeditions to North America, 1584, 5 & 7: the first laid claim to "Virginia"; the second settled but left after repeated clashes with the Indians; and the village established by the third was later found deserted for causes unknown. Imprisoned briefly in the Tower for affair with Elizabeth's Lady-in-waiting Elisabeth Throckmorton, whom he afterwards married, 1592. Commanded expedition to Guiana, 1595. Sentenced to death for treason and imprisoned in the Tower, 1603-16; tutored James's elder son Henry and wrote A History of the World. Released to search for gold in Guiana, 1616; son killed by Spaniards. Executed 1618.

Statue by William Macmillan. Bronze, life-size. Raleigh Green, Whitehall. Unveiled October 28th, 1959, by John Hay Whitney, United States Ambassador. Even after 350 years, Raleigh was still a controversial figure; the secretary of the National Society of Non-Smokers attended the unveiling and distributed pamphlets entitled "don't make an ash of yourself". The day was drizzling and muddy, which provoked references to the famous cloak which Raleigh laid before the feet of Queen Elizabeth and which Macmillan has draped over the statue's left shoulder.

The figure of "that great Lucifer" looks well in the dark. That background is appropriate for one whose melancholy matched his pride and who, with the astronomer Thomas Harriot, the poet Christopher Marlowe and the "Wizard Earl" of Northumberland, was one of the group of free-thinkers nicknamed by Shakespeare "The School of Night".

Captain John Smith

Surrounded on three sides by office blocks, a tough, intrepid looking man, bearded and booted, stands in St Mary-le-Bow Churchyard, his hand on his sword. He bears the commonest name in England and looks like some kind of Elizabethan sailor. He is little known, but John Smith, President of Virginia and Admiral of New England, to give him the grandest of his titles, deserves to stand with Drake or Raleigh (p306) as an explorer and adventurer.

The events of his early years were so much larger than life that his own accounts of them were often doubted; however, their substance is now regarded as true. In search of adventure he became a soldier in Europe and, for his bravery during the Dutch revolt against the Spanish, Maurice of Nassau rewarded him with a fortune. In Transylvania he defeated three Turkish champions with lance, scimitar and battle-axe in a specially staged single combat. He was imprisoned in a Constantinople harem, from which he escaped across Russia to England. Later he rescued an English girl who had been a fellow slave of the Turks from a Moroccan castle. He was a close friend of Raleigh, Hakluyt and Henry, Prince of Wales. His mistresses were many and invariably blond; they ranged from the Lady Camallata, niece of the Governor of Rostov, and the exquisite and intelligent Frances, Duchess of Lennox and Richmond, to other, less distinguished ladies whose names are unknown to history.

The first permanent English settlement in North America owed its first two crucial winters of survival to Smith's toughness and natural leadership. He was the ideal pioneer, far ahead of his fellows in his understanding of survival and defence and in his ability to communicate with the local Indian tribes. He learned their language and won their trust and co-operation through a combination of presence, friendliness, threat and bluff. The most famous story Smith told was how the eleven year old Princess Pocahontas (see p78) leapt forward to save him from execution at the hands of her father Powhatan – though it is possible that the Chief was only submitting him to a ceremony of ritual adoption.

America inspired him and he tried to inspire others on its behalf. "So vast are the forests of the New World, so broad and swift are her rivers, so towering her mountains and so great her riches," he wrote in one of his highly popular accounts, "that one who has cast anchor in her bays and lived in her wilderness is tempted to exaggerate her glories. But man is dwarfed by this virgin land, and the mind of the explorer is numbed; so one speaks the truth as best one is able." His truths were, however, sometimes unpalatable to London speculators out for a quick profit. There was no gold in Virginia, he reported, though there was timber and furs, and what the settlements required was slow, hard building and planting.

It was just as well that Smith missed returning to Virginia with the strict Puritan Pilgrim Fathers, for they would have found each other intolerable. Self-confident to the point of arrogance, a man who enjoyed life to the full, Smith was no saint, though our picture opposite haloes him in one of the windows of the church of St Mary-le-Bow. In the early 1600's that church heard many sermons supporting the colonisation of the New World as a pious and Christian venture. But fine words and good intentions were not enough to establish a footing on a new and unknown continent. What was required was the curiosity, the experience and the ruthlessness which John Smith possessed in such full measure.

Captain John Smith. Born 1580, near Willoughby, Lincolnshire, son of farmer. Fought in French and Dutch armies as mercenary, 1596-1600. Fought against Turks under Prince Sigismund Bathory of Hungary, 1601-5. Captured and sold as slave; escaped to England across Russia, 1601-5. Member of London Company expedition to Virginia, 1607; became natural leader of Jamestown settlement, despite much dissension. Elected President of settlement, 1608. Was badly hurt in accidental explosion and returned to London, 1609; wrote extremely successful books on New World and worked to promote further expeditions. Mapped American coast from Nova Scotia to Rhode Island on voyage of exploration, trade and fishery, 1614. Leader of fully equipped expedition to settle New England, 1615; turned back by storm. Appointed Admiral of New England by James II but failed to raise further funds, 1617. Advised Pilgrim Fathers but failed to accompany them as military leader due to clash of temperaments, 1618-19. Continued to publish maps, books, pamphlets and autobiography, The True Travels, Adventures and Observations of Captain John Smith, *1620-30. Died 1631.*

Statue by John Charles Rennick, a replica of the one in Richmond, Virginia by William Couper. Bronze. Churchyard of St Mary-le-Bow, Cheapside. Unveiled October 31st, 1960, by Queen Elizabeth the Queen Mother. Presented by the Jamestown Foundation of the Commonwealth of Virginia.

Robert Raikes

Robert Raikes. Born 1736, Gloucester, son of printer and owner of Gloucester Journal. Took over father's business, 1761. Founded first Sunday School in Gloucester, 1780. Published accounts of schools in Gloucester Journal and these were reprinted in the London press, 1783-4. Spread of movement throughout Midlands, 1783-5. Sunday School Council set up in London by William Fox, 1785. Movement won support of Anglican bishops, 1786. Presented to George III and Queen Charlotte at Windsor, 1787. Sunday Schools introduced into Wales, 1789, and later into Scotland, Ireland and the United States. Retired from business, 1802. Founding of Sunday School Union with organisation of paid teachers, 1803. Died 1811.

Statue by Thomas Brock. Bronze. Victoria Embankment Gardens. Unveiled July, 1880. According to the inscription, the statue was paid for by "contributions from teachers and scholars of Sunday Schools in Great Britain."

In the eighteenth century no less than two hundred offences carried the death penalty. The age of the offender was immaterial; in 1789 boys of twelve and fourteen were condemned to execution at the Old Bailey. A child picking a pocket or stealing a hen might be given the milder alternative of prison or transportation but this only completed the process of brutalization begun by poverty and by the working conditions in the factories of the Industrial Revolution.

Robert Raikes, the owner of one of the country's most important provincial newspapers and a frequent compassionate visitor to Gloucester Castle Gaol, saw the situation and was appalled. As a well-to-do businessman and prominent citizen of Gloucester, he did not question the structure of the social order or the severity of the penal code. He was no revolutionary. However, he differed from many of his contemporaries in believing that the "lower orders", uncouth, unwashed and ignorant, were nevertheless capable of improvement. He looked at the swarming crowds of children released from work on Sundays and saw how easily they might turn to crime. And so he took an alternative, the Sunday School, which existed already in a small way up and down the country, and by determined patronage and publicity turned it into a national movement.

Together with the Rev Thomas Stock, a local clergyman, Raikes founded his first Sunday School in Sooty Alley, a slum near Gloucester gaol inhabited by chimney-sweeps. More schools followed. The curriculum was morality, church attendance, cleanliness, reading and simple spelling based on Scripture. Raikes paid the teachers and encouraged the most ragged and disorderly children to attend. His manner was confident, authoritarian and generally benevolent. He was a clever teacher himself; wishing to demonstrate the invisible power of goodness, he produced a magnet. "They see the magnet draw the Needle without touching it," he wrote. "Thus, I tell them, I wish to draw them to the paths of duty and thus lead them to Heaven and Happiness." Once magnetised, one needle could attract another and "upon this idea those children are now endeavouring to bring other children to meet me at the Church, and you would be diverted to see with what a group I am surrounded every morning at seven o'clock prayers at the Cathedral, especially upon a Sunday; at which time I give Books, or Combs, or other encouragements."

Raikes accounts of his work were taken up by the press in other parts of the country and were widely imitated. Within six years it was reported that there were over 200,000 children in Sunday Schools; Queen Charlotte herself (p44) expressed the wish that she might follow the example of other well-born ladies of Windsor and become a teacher. In 1832, the year of the Great Reform Bill, it was estimated that no less than one and a quarter million children were preparing for life in Victorian England by attending Sunday School. Clearly, Raikes' movement was playing a highly significant part in underpinning the moral and social cohesion of the nation.

At the behest of the Sunday School Union, Sir Thomas Brock provided a lively yet respectful centenary portrait. Raikes was a plump, fashionable, eighteenth century gentleman, his brown wig sporting a double row of curls; Fanny Burney, visiting Gloucester, remarked on his "overflowing of successful spirits and delighted vanity". Brock, however, has curbed the paunch and the curls and has given Raikes a more serious look appropriate to the founding father of a national institution.

William Tyndale

In 1884 the British and Foreign Bible Society celebrated its anniversary day by unveiling a statue of the great translator, William Tyndale. For eighty years the Society had dedicated itself to the task of supplying good, cheap, vernacular bibles to every quarter of the globe – to India and Africa, to Gaelic Scotland and Wales, even to the Catholic strongholds of France and Italy – in an operation as comprehensive and as self-confident as the acquisition of Empire itself. By 1900 it would have translated the bible into over 300 languages, from Ainu, the aboriginal language of northern Japan, to Yahagan, spoken in Tierra del Fuego.

Tyndale was a young cleric, a contemporary of Martin Luther and as revolutionary in his views. At that time the production of a public version of the bible in English was a highly dangerous undertaking, as the only version permitted by the Church was in Latin and the right to read and interpret it was guarded by her scholars. However, Tyndale was disillusioned with the ignorance and worldliness of churchmen. "If God spare my life," he said to a priest of his native Gloucestershire, "I will cause a boy that driveth the plough shall know more of the Scripture than thou dost." Finding no support in England for his proposed translation, he left for the Continent and found a haven in Antwerp with certain well-disposed merchants. Printing facilities were also more easily available and his bibles were smuggled into England in their thousands. He was not above a bit of sharp practice in a good cause. In 1529, a merchant named Packington came to Antwerp as an agent for the Bishop of London; he had been given a large sum of money to buy up Tyndale's bibles and so suppress them. Being a secret sympathiser, Packington went straight to Tyndale and explained the plan; he handed over a moderate number of copies and used the bishop's money to produce a new edition.

In the end Tyndale was betrayed, arrested by the authorities of the Holy Roman Empire and condemned for heresy; he was strangled and his body burned. His last words were, "Lord, open the King of England's eyes". In those times of dramatic change his prayer was soon answered; within a few years Henry VIII, encouraged by Thomas Cromwell and by Cranmer, had ordered that bibles in English should be placed in every parish church.

In honouring Tyndale the British and Foreign Bible Society was returning to its roots. The King James Authorised Version is one of England's glories. It is not generally realised that, like most other subsequent translations, it was largely based on Tyndale; sometimes the two versions follow each other word for word. Its images and cadences have entered the fibre of the language, yet many of those sentences, monumental as eternity yet ever fresh and alive, were written by one poor fugitive working under threat of death.

Sir Joseph Boehm based his statue on a portrait which now hangs above the high table at Hertford College, Oxford. There the translator wears nondescript black clothes and a skull cap, a garb as unrewarding for a grand, commemorative statue as the "tight trousers" of a later age. Boehm has therefore given him the academic robes to which he was entitled but which he is unlikely to have worn for his great work. He has also augmented the beard, softened the lines of strain around the eyes and shielded the great, domed forehead. His statue is exceptionally skilful and impressive but it says more, perhaps, about the gravity of its sponsors than about the pioneering courage of William Tyndale.

William Tyndale. Born 1490/95, Gloucestershire, son of yeoman farmer. Educated at Oxford and ordained priest, 1508-15. Decided to translate Bible, 1523; proposals rejected by Bishop of London. Left England for Germany and Netherlands, 1524. Translated and printed New Testament, 1525-6. Translation of first five books of Old Testament lost in shipwreck; re-translated them with help of Coverdale, 1530. Conducted bitter written debate with Sir Thomas More (p323) over Church orthodoxy and authority, 1529-31. Refused Henry VIII's request to return to England, 1531. Betrayed and imprisoned in Netherlands State Prison at Vilvorde, 1535. Condemned for heresy and executed, 1536.

Statue by Joseph Boehm. Bronze, 11ft on 11ft 10ins pedestal of Portland stone; 2 tons 6cwt. Victoria Embankment Gardens. Unveiled May 7th, 1884, by the 82 year-old Lord Shaftesbury (p96) as President of the British and Foreign Bible Society; the ceremony began with prayers and concluded with a blessing. Cost, £2,400; a plaque on the pedestal records the institutions which contributed more than £100, including Oxford and Cambridge Universities and the Y.M.C.A. Tyndale is pointing towards one of his bibles; it rests on a printing press which Boehm copied exactly from a sixteenth century example in the Antwerp Museum.

John Wesley

John Wesley was the father of the Methodist movement. He came from a strong Anglican background and he both studied and taught at Oxford University. He was ordained, yet his religious life only took fire after a second conversion, in which he abandoned himself entirely to faith in God and God's love of man in Jesus. Now freed from doubt and defying social convention, untiringly active, he began preaching at large, frequently in the open air. He built up a network of Methodist societies, gaining the loyalty of the artisans, traders, miners and farm labourers for whom the eighteenth century Church of England showed little concern. He travelled the length and breadth of Great Britain and Ireland, covering, it is said, a quarter of a million miles, most of it on horseback.

Above all, Wesley wished to save souls. He certainly believed in heaven and hell; as a child he had been narrowly rescued from a fire at his father's vicarage and he always described himself as "a brand saved from burning". But he also wished to improve the earthly health, self-respect and literacy of his congregations and so he opened dispensaries and published cheap books on secular subjects. By his leadership and organisation he created a movement which later became the bedrock of working and lower middle class Christianity. Despite his unconventional approach, he was always a neat figure, in jacket, cravat, bands, and black cassock or long, flowing gown. His sermons were measured and reasonable, yet they had an extraordinary effect; in the early years violent seizures and dramatic conversions were common. He often had to face hostility organised by his religious opponents but he had a mesmeric way with trouble-makers. Once an assailant rushed up to him with arm raised to strike but could only stroke his head, saying in amazement, "What soft hair he has!" The statue outside the City Road Chapel successfully catches both the impeccable appearance, the hair disarmingly curled, and the impassioned reasonableness.

Its sculptor, John Adams Acton, was one of the most prolific and vigorous of Victorian portrait sculptors. He studied with John Gibson (p180) in Rome and was a friend of Gladstone (p204). Though not a Methodist himself, he carried out a number of commissions for them and was known as "the Wesleyan sculptor". He made the beautiful memorial tablet to John Wesley and his brother Charles for Westminster Abbey and several busts of leading figures for the interior of the City Road Chapel. His wife's journals tell a most extraordinary story about this particular commission. It was to be unveiled exactly a hundred years after Wesley's death and it seems that he was given only a month to produce it, an impossibly short time for such a complex operation. However, being an extremely fast worker, he completed the full sized plaster figure in time. He tinted it to look like bronze and dispatched it, keeping the deception a complete secret. The only dangerous moment came when the drapery was drawn back and caught on the outstretched arm. Immediately afterwards the figure was boarded up to prevent damage and it was later removed for casting, so that what we see today is of course the completed bronze!

London now has a second statue of Wesley, copied from an early nineteenth century original and unveiled in St Paul's Churchyard in 1988 (see chapter 10, p356). The sculptors of both figures made use of one of the best contemporary likenesses, the bust carved from life by the enterprising 22-year-old Enoch Wood in 1781, a version of which may be seen in the Methodist Museum in City Road.

John Wesley. Born 1703, Epworth, Lincolnshire, son of Anglican parson. Educated Charterhouse and Oxford. Ordained priest, 1725. Elected Fellow of Lincoln College, 1726. Became leader of small group of high-minded, young Oxford men nicknamed "methodists", 1729. Went on unsuccessful mission to colony of Georgia, 1735-7. Influenced by Moravians and by religious Societies of artisans in City of London; converted to salvation by faith, 1738. Preached first open-air sermon near Bristol to three thousand people, 1739. Formed first Methodist Societies, 1739. Began itinerant preaching with tour of South Wales, 1741. Held first Methodist Conference, 1744. Published best-selling book of practical remedies, Primitive Physic, 1747. Married Mrs Molly Nazeille, 1751; breakdown of marriage, 1755. Ordained own ministers for Methodist Societies in North America, so causing official break with Church of England, 1784. Died 1791.

Statue by John Adams Acton. Bronze. Outside Wesley's Chapel, City Road, also called the Mother Church of Methodism. Unveiled March 3rd, 1891, by Rev Dr W.F. Moulton, President of the Wesleyan Conference (and himself the subject of one of Adams Acton's busts inside the Chapel). From 1779 Wesley lived in a house next door to the Chapel, which is now a museum.

Below. The sculptor John Adams Acton in relaxed, artistic mood.

THE WORLD IS MY PARISH.

ERECTED WITH FUNDS COLLECTED
BY THE CHILDREN OF METHODISM

Cardinal Newman

"Who could resist the charm of that spiritual apparition, gliding in the dim afternoon light through the aisles of St Mary's, rising into the pulpit and then, in the most entrancing of voices, breaking the silence with words and thoughts that were a religious music – subtle, sweet, mournful? I seem to hear him still."

So wrote Matthew Arnold of his Oxford days, when Newman was vicar of the University Church and one of the luminaries of the "Oxford Movement", an influential group of Anglicans who wished to deepen the spirituality of their church within a framework of traditional rites and practices. Newman's search for the roots of his religion led him in the end to Rome, an apostasy which shocked many of his fellow countrymen to the core. However, by the time of his death forty five years later, his distinction and obvious integrity had earned him general forgiveness. Victorians of all denominations loved to sing his hymns, *Lead, Kindly Light* and *Praise to the Holiest in the Height*. He had done more than anyone to persuade the average Englishman, his mind still transfixed by gunpowder, treason and plot, that a Catholic priest could also be an admirable human being.

Newman died in 1890, when the great age of commemoration was at its height, and a public statue was clearly in order. His Memorial Committee decided on Oxford and the Oxford City Council, awed perhaps by the presence of the Duke of Norfolk as the Committee's chairman, gave permission for the statue to be erected in the centre of Broad Street, opposite Trinity College. The result was a storm of protest. A petition was organised by the Regius Professor of Divinity and signed by over a thousand objectors; the site, it was pointed out, was only yards away from the spot where Cranmer, Latimer and Ridley had been martyred by the Catholic Queen Mary. In fact, many distinguished Oxford men had subscribed to the memorial; the more sober objection was that Oxford, unlike London, had (and still has) no outdoor public statues and would hardly wish to begin with one of Newman. Faced with such opposition, the committee withdrew and turned its attentions elsewhere. Birmingham, Newman's home throughout his Catholic ministry, was suggested but in the end London was chosen as befitting the national figure that he had become.

The resulting statue was considered a good likeness of the introspective, ascetic churchman. As *The Times* wrote, "The sad and ironical expression of the mouth is exceedingly characteristic and seems to express the idea conveyed in the inscription written by the Cardinal for his tomb: Ex umbris et imaginibus in veritate." That epitaph – "from shadows and imaginations into the truth" – could be read "from shadowy statues..." Newman hated ostentation and only accepted his cardinal's hat to enhance the reputation of English Catholicism; no doubt he would have viewed his commemoration in in the same light. Moreover, layers of unexorcised grime have since deepened the statue's shade. Once again the fate of the image is entirely appropriate to the man, as the following story illustrates. Newman was once standing at the back of St Paul's Cathedral in his ancient, threadbare coat listening to the singing; an officious verger offered him a seat and, when he declined it, turned him out of the building as a tramp.

As a religious thinker Newman is still relevant today. He believed, for example, in the slow, collective evolution of the Church's understanding of God and the Second Vatican Council has often been referred to as "Newman's Council".

Cardinal John Henry Newman. Born 1801, London, son of banker. Experienced first conversion, 1816. Entered Trinity College, Oxford, 1816. Elected fellow of Oriel College, 1822. Ordained in Church of England, 1824. Vicar of University Church and leading member of Oxford Movement, 1828-43. Entered Church of Rome, 1845. Established Oratory in Birmingham, conducting pastoral work among poor of city, 1847. Published The Idea of a University, *1852. Rector of Dublin Catholic University, 1854-58. Autobiography,* Apologia Pro Vita Sua, *published and well received, 1864. Elected Cardinal, 1879. Died 1890.*

Statue by Leon-Joseph Chavalliaud, for Farmer and Brindlay Ltd. Campanella marble under canopy of Portland stone. Outside Brompton Oratory, Brompton Road. Unveiled July 15th, 1896, by the Duke of Norfolk, England's premier lay Catholic.

William Booth

"General" William Booth was England's most dynamic religious figure since John Wesley (p314). Energetic, moody, unsophisticated, he took up the conversion of the outcast and underprivileged where Wesley had left it seventy years earlier, employing an irresistible mixture of head-on confrontation with the world and clever adaptation to its methods. The one-man mission which he began in the slums of Whitechapel, preaching in dance halls and outside pubs, became the Salvation Army. By 1900, five and a half million people in forty seven countries were attending its services.

Booth's youthful apprenticeship to a pawnbroker brought him into intimate contact with the precarious misery of the poor. He experienced a religious conversion and became a Methodist lay preacher and minister. However, he was far too radical for the various churches for whom he worked. Methodism had by that time acquired a patina of respectability and the young Booth was inclined to put the most disreputable paupers in the best pews. So he decided to go his own way, despite the insecurity that involved for himself and his family. Mile End Waste, in the East End, was the place where he launched his first important, independent work; it is now marked by his bust and a replica of the statue at Denmark Hill.

There he gathered round him a small band of helpers to whom the ordinary pub-goer could relate: men like Jimmy Glover, former potboy and alcoholic, John Allen, the sixteen stone Poplar navvy who became the strictest of Sunday observers, and Peter Monk, the converted Irish prize fighter who was his much needed bodyguard. His eldest son Bramwell provided the steady organising ability the father lacked. At first the movement grew slowly. The adopion of the name Salvation Army was the result of a casual conversation but, together with the new uniform and the use of brass band music, it triggered a dramatic expansion. Success sometimes brought a correspondingly intense hostility and during the 1880's the respectable towns of Worthing and Basingstoke were all but reduced to mob law by the violent protests organised against the Army's parades.

Booth was no intellectual and he undoubtedly believed in the devil and in hell for the unconverted. But he also understood that the brutal conditions in which the poor of England lived led them to sin. At least, he said with bitter irony, we should treat the poor as well as we do our cab horses, who have both food and employment. From this came the Army's many social projects, the cheap food shops, the hostels and the East End match factory whose workers no longer died from "fossy jaw" (see p205).

Booth continued with his labours until the age of 83. He is said to have travelled five million miles and preached sixty thousand sermons. His tall, spare figure with its pronounced, Jewish features and flowing beard became internationally famous. He took tea with kings – Haakon of Norway, Gustav of Sweden and Edward VII – and he opened the United States Senate with a prayer. In his latter years chronic indigestion and insomnia made him short-tempered and a hard taskmaster to his immediate associates. His poverty, like Gandhi's (p236), was maintained in meticulous detail. Three of his children seceded completely from the autocratic rule which he still exercised over the Army. Perhaps he missed Catherine's wise encouragement and restraint. Or perhaps, like Job, a part of him was angry with God that, despite everything he had done, the misery of humankind continued unabated.

William Booth. Born 1829, Nottingham, son of builder. Apprenticed to pawnbroker after bankruptcy of father, 1842. Experienced religious conversion, 1844. Became methodist lay preacher, 1846. Engagement and marriage to Catherine Mumford, 1852-5. Minister in Methodist New Connexion, 1852-61. Resigned and began independent evangelistic work, 1861. Started East London Christian Mission, 1865. Movement renamed Salvation Army with Booth as General, 1878. Great expansion of Army in Britain and abroad in the teeth of opposition, 1878-90. Published In Darkest England And The Way Out *, best-selling appeal for social improvement, 1890; organised housing, emigration and legal aid schemes for poor. Began numerous overseas tours and received hero's welcome in America, 1895-6. Continued extensive tours of Britain by motor-car, 1904. Began worsening blindness, 1908. Died 1912.*

Statue by George Edward Wade. Bronze.
William Booth Training College,
Champion Park, Denmark Hill. Erected
1929.

When Booth died, his son Bramwell
launched a memorial appeal to build and
fund a Salvation Army training college.
The statues of William and Catherine
Booth set the seal on its completion in
1929, the centenary year of their births. A
fibre glass replica of William's statue was
erected in the Mile End Road, near the
junction with Cambridge Heath Road, in
1979.

Catherine Booth

William's wife Catherine was no less remarkable a person than her husband and she shared in every aspect of his work. Their deeply happy marriage was a meeting of opposites: he unsophisticated, energetic and moody, she also deeply religious but gentle and well educated; she provided him with much of his intellectual consistency. In her youth she was a semi-invalid; however, she fought off ill health to raise eight remarkable children. She died twenty two years before William and he no doubt missed her judicious and critical sympathy – she once remarked that the Pope could only think himself infallible because he was an old bachelor. She had four rules for a happy marriage: have no secrets, share your money, argue out all your differences but not in front of the children.

Catherine Booth always believed most strongly that women had the same right to preach as men and she backed her views with lengthy theological arguments. The Salvation Army was indeed one of the very first organisations in Britain to practice strict equality of the sexes. However, her own shyness held her back until she was thirty one. Then, one Sunday, she made her way to William's Methodist pulpit in Gateshead and he announced to his surprised congregation that his wife would be giving the sermon that evening. She acquitted herself well and from that time on played an ever increasing public role. She too became a travelling preacher, an unprecedented step for a woman of her time.

The secret of her strength, she believed, was her willingness to risk everything for God. In Gateshead she visited the poor women of the slums and encouraged them to come to church. Once she encountered a violent and drunken husband but, hearing his life history, stayed to pray with him and receive his pledge of future temperance. She continued to be even more uncompromising than William in her insistence on the evils of alchohol. She also roundly opposed blood-sports and the destructive nature of war.

The height of her influence came in 1885 when, together with William and Bramwell, she played a crucial role in W.T. Stead's campaign to expose teenage abduction and prostitution. This flourished in Victorian times but was almost completely hushed up. Speaking to thousands at a London meeting, she told the true story of a merchant who had paid for a young girl to be lured away from Sunday School and found himself confronted with his own daughter. She wrote to Queen Victoria and to Gladstone presenting her case. The facts assembled by the campaigners shamed Parliament into passing new measures to suppress the trade and raise the age of consent to sixteen.

Nothing characterises the Salvation Army more clearly than its brass band music. This became a part of their message from 1878 onwards, when the Fry family of Salisbury offered their services as bodyguards and, incidentally, as musicians. In our photograph a group of student bandsmen and women from the William Booth Training College are paying Catherine a lighthearted, latter day tribute. She loved music and used to give piano lessons in the early years of her marriage before the piano was sold to raise cash. She thoroughly approved the adaptation of cheerful, popular melodies which brought such success. William was at first doubtful when he heard *Champagne Charlie is My Name* rendered as *Bless His Name, He Sets me Free* but he conceded, saying, "Why should the devil have all the best tunes?" Catherine had her own version of the famous remark: "I contend that the devil has no right to a single note".

Catherine Booth. Born 1829, Derbyshire, daughter of coach builder and preacher. Ill with spinal trouble and tuberculosis, 1843-7. Religious childhood culminated in experience of conversion, 1844. Joined Methodist New Connexion, 1850. Engagement and marriage to William Booth, 1852-5. Delivered first sermon in William's church in Gateshead, 1860. Moved to London, conducted services in West End, 1865. Conducted evangelistic rallies in South Coast towns, 1869-76. Played key part in campaign for Criminal Law Amendment Act against teenage prostitution, 1885. Made extensive lecture tours of South and Midlands, 1886-7. Fell ill with cancer, 1888. Died 1890.

Statue by George Edward Wade. Bronze. William Booth Training College, Denmark Hill. Erected 1929.

G.E. Wade was also responsible for the figure of Queen Alexandra at the London Hospital (p72) – an appropriate link since, to mark the Queen's death, a Salvation Army band played in the courtyard of Buckingham Palace, the first non-military band ever to perform there.

Thomas More

Saint Thomas More

Sir Thomas More. Born 1477/8, London, son of a lawyer. Called to the Bar, 1496. Member of network of Renaissance scholars which included Erasmus and John Colet (p102). Published Utopia, a vision of a just and stable commonwealth, 1516. Member of King's Council, 1517. Became Lord Chancellor after fall of Wolsey, 1529-32; conducted campaign against dissenters, including Tyndale (p312). Avoided supporting Henry VIII's plan to divorce Catherine of Aragon and extend royal control of the Church; resigned, 1532. Refused to sign compulsory oath assenting to divorce and Royal Supremacy and was imprisoned in the Tower, 1534. Tried for treason and executed, 1535. Beatified by Pope Leo XIII, 1886. Canonised by Pope Pius XI, 1935.

Statue by L. Cubitt Bevis. Bronze, gilded. Cheyne Walk, outside Chelsea Old Church, where More is buried. Unveiled July 21st, 1969, by Dr Henry King, Speaker of the House of Commons, as More had once been.

Thomas More is, like Thomas Carlyle (p126), a *genius loci* of Chelsea and it was Chelsea's residents who organised the appeal for his statue. He lived there in the days of his prosperity, his garden running down to the river, surrounded by his children, step-children and grandchildren. He worshipped in the church by which the statue now stands; even at the height of his power, he used to sing in the choir dressed in a simple surplice – "God's body," exclaimed the Duke of Norfolk, "my Lord Chancellor a parish clerk?" He kept a family jester, one Henry Patenson. His own role at Henry VIII's court had at first been that of a jester; the King enjoyed his wit and the two men were genuinely fond of each other. However, Henry was mistaken in his belief that More would make an amenable Chancellor. In the end he became one of those who would not yield to the movement of power as it swung first one way and then the other in mid-sixteenth century England, and who paid the ultimate penalty.

As a martyred "prisoner of conscience" More is well known. However, many would be surprised to learn that he is also a saint of the Roman Church; Pius XI conferred the title on him in 1935 with the intention of strengthening English Catholicism. The unveiling of the Chelsea statue was, however, very much an ecumenical affair. Present were Dr Ramsay, Archbishop of Canterbury (second left), Cardinal Heenan, Catholic Primate of England, (to his left), and Rev A.C. Neil, Moderator of the Free Church Federal Council. The sculptor, Cubitt Bevis, is in the centre and on his right is the Mayor of Chelsea.

Saint Thomas Becket

London has only one commemorative statue in a modern, non-representational style. Becket's mediaeval shrine at Canterbury was sheathed in plates of pure gold and encrusted with jewels; some of the gems, as Erasmus observed on his famous visit with John Colet (see p102), were as big as goose's eggs. That was the mediaeval spirit. The modern age remembers him in a completely different way, as outside St Paul's Cathedral, close to his birthplace in Cheapside, a skeleton of bronze lays bare the tenacity of his will and delineates the sufferings of his fallen body.

The career of Thomas Becket (or Thomas of London, as he was generally known) bears an uncanny similarity to that of Thomas More (p323). Both men were the companions and chief servants of powerful kings and both lost their lives maintaining the authority of the existing religious order. But whereas More had to wait four centuries for his canonisation, Becket became a saint within three years of his death, after an extraordinary series of paranormal healings had taken place in his name. These are mentioned in passing in the history books and perhaps they embarrass modern historians. Whatever their explanation – supernatural intervention or collective faith, pious invention or convenient coincidence – they illuminate their age to perfection. One cannot imagine the same events taking place after More's death three hundred and sixty five years later. They drew thousand upon thousands of penitents to Canterbury and established the newly rebuilt cathedral as one of the greatest centres of pilgrimage of the Middle Ages. Henry VIII, doubtless struck by the similarity mentioned above, destroyed Becket's shrine and unsuccessfully tried to expunge all mention of him from the historical records.

Without the miracles, Becket would not have been an obvious candidate for sainthood. An efficient and ambitious Chancellor, he was very much the second man in the kingdom; he collected taxes and judged lawsuits, he made war and he negotiated peace. He liked to conduct affairs in style. There is a description of him setting out on a mission to Paris in 1158 with several hundred finely dressed knights, clerks, soldiers and squires. Horses and caravans bore gifts of silks, furs and beer, gold and silver plate, and Becket's own private chapel and room. Accompanied by staghounds and hawks, the whole party marched along, singing as they went in the English style.

Despite this outward display, Becket's own personal life remained simple, as he followed the monastic pattern which he had learned as a member of Archbishop Theobald's household. (From the time of his continental exile, he even wore a verminous hair-shirt next to his skin.) He was therefore probably more at home as a churchman than as a politician, yet in both roles he continued to pursue his aims with the same stubborn energy and assertiveness.

The murder of the Archbishop at his own high altar is one of those events which have a firm and abiding hold on the national imagination. It was carried out by four senior barons acting on King Henry's indirect and intemperate instructions. They pursued him into his own cathedral and cut him down as he was about to say vespers. He challenged them openly and made no attempt to avoid his fate. One of them split open his head and there, as an eyewitness described it with all the symbolic intensity of the mediaeval imagination, "The blood whitening with brain and the brain reddening with blood dyed the floor with the white of the lily and the red of the rose, colours of the Virgin and the Mother, colours of the life and death of the martyr

Thomas Becket. Born 1118, London, son of merchant. Clerk and auditor to sheriffs of London, 1140-3. Joined household of Archbishop of Canterbury, 1143. Chancellor to King Henry II and Archdeacon of Canterbury, 1154-62. Made Archbishop of Canterbury, 1162; resigned as Chancellor and quarrelled with King over respective positions of Church and State, especially over right of clerics to be tried exclusively in Church courts. Tried and condemned for feudal disobedience, 1164; fled country. Lived in exile in France, 1164-70. Briefly reconciled with Henry II and returned to England, 1170; excommunicated King's followers. Murdered in Canterbury Cathedral, 1170. Canonised, 1173.

Statue by Edward Bainbridge Copnall. Bronze. St Paul's Churchyard, south side of Cathedral. Unveiled March 30th, 1973, the 800th anniversary of Becket's canonisation, by Mr Frederick Cleary, Chairman of Corporation of London Open Spaces Committee. Cost £2,000, purchased by the Corporation.

Copnall was an extremely versatile sculptor. The nude figure of Aspiration on Marks and Spencer's in Edgware Road is his, as is the 20ft aluminium stag in Stag Place, Victoria.

and confessor."

That night a monk, in a dream, saw Becket approach the high altar, beautiful and dazzling in his vestments. "I was dead," he said, "but I have risen again." Two days later the miracles began. The wife of a Sussex knight was cured of blindness on making a vow to Thomas. Scores of others followed. Robert, Prior of St Frideswide in Oxford, recovered from a painful disease of the leg after praying at his tomb. Odo of Falaise recovered the sight of his right eye after weeping for him. A cow was restored to life and a horse rescued from a pit on invocation of his name. Henry II was obliged to acknowledge his part in the murder and make an abject penance; kneeling before the new shrine, he was scourged by the monks of Canterbury. Within days his forgiveness was signalled by the news that the King of Scotland had been captured and the rebellion in the north ended.

Saint Volodymyr

The year 1988 saw the commemoration of a thousand years of Christianity in Russia. The celebrations focused attention on a period little known to outsiders, at whose heart stands the half-historical, half-legendary figure of Volodymyr, prince and saint, bright sun of the people of Rus' and the founder of their faith. According to the *Primary Chronicle*, written by the monk Nestor in the twelfth century, Volodymyr was, prior to his conversion, a lustful and warlike man; he kept eight hundred concubines and performed human sacrifices to pagan deities. Then, wishing to find a better way of life by which to unify his people, he sent out envoys to study the various monotheistic religions which surrounded him. He disliked the Muslim prohibitions concerning wine and pork and he had little use for the Jews' God, since He had scattered his people in exile. His envoys found the worship of the Latin churches dull and ugly but when they came to Byzantium, with its rich vestments and singing and incense, they did not know whether they were in heaven or on earth. So Volodymyr accepted baptism into the Orthodox Church and required all the inhabitants of his capital, Kiev, to come one morning to the river Dneiper and do likewise, on pain of his severe displeasure.

A study of the further, scanty historical evidence reveals a somewhat different picture. Christianity was already present in Kiev in Volodymyr's time. In fact his grandmother Olha had been baptised in Constantinople and his brother Yaropolk, whom he had had murdered on his way to the throne, was brought up a Christian. Nevertheless, Volodymyr's own change of heart and full-scale conversion of his people must have been the essential historical turning point. It prepared the way for the extraordinary transformation which occurred in Kiev during the reign of his son Yaroslav, when churches were built on a monumental scale and Christian art and ritual became the centre of the nation's soul.

But who exactly were the people of Rus'? Turkic, Finno-Ugrian and Slavonic, ruled (probably) by a dynasty of Vikings, they were quite different from the Moscow based Russians of later times. Kiev is now the capital of the Ukraine, a region larger than France within the U.S.S.R., and it is the fate of the Ukraine which underlies the erection of Volodymyr's statue in Holland Park. In 1685 its church was made subordinate to the Patriarchy in Moscow and in 1709 it lost its political independence to Peter the Great. Nevertheless, Ukrainian Orthodoxy continued to maintain an independent existence until the 1930's when it was all but wiped out at the hands of Stalin. During and after the Second World War thousands of Ukrainians suffered that exile which Volodymyr had found so distasteful when experienced by the Jews. Some of these were members of the Western Ukraine's Catholic Uniate Church, which is a part of Rome but uses the traditional Byzantine rite and whose leaders and clergy were arrested and imprisoned in 1945.

There are now about thirty five thousand Ukrainians in the United Kingdom, with their own churches and social organisations. They have taken the millennium as an opportunity to draw attention to the origins of Russian Christianity in their country and to highlight the persecutions which their churches have suffered. More than half of all functioning Orthodox church buildings in the U.S.S.R. are found in the Ukraine and if the present Russian government wishes to extend religious freedom, then it will have to take account of the spirit of Volodymyr as it lives on both abroad and on its own home soil.

Volodymyr the Great, Prince of Rus'. Born 960, Kiev, son of prince Sviatoslav and his housekeeper Malusha. Brought up as a pagan by his uncle, Dobrynia. Allied with Varangians and had brother Yaropolk murdered. Became ruler of Kievan Rus', 980. Conquered Cherven cities of Poland, 981, and northern tribes, 982 & 4. Decided to unify country under one religion; was baptised and married sister of Byzantine Emperor Basil II. Ordered inhabitants of Kiev to be baptised, 988. Abolished capital punishment and founded schools. Appointed sons as viceroys. Died 1015. Canonised by Kievan Church, c.1200-50.

Statue by Leonid Molodozhanyn (Leo Mol). Bronze. Corner of Holland Park and Holland Park Avenue, in front of the premises of the Sophia Society, a Ukrainian religious and social centre. Unveiled May 29th, 1988.

Leo Mol is a sculptor with an international reputation who lives in Canada; another statue of St Volodymyr by him was unveiled the same year in Rome.

Below. The guests of honour at the unveiling were Metropolitan Mstyslav Skrypnyk, Head of the Ukrainian Autocephalous Orthodox Church, who is standing left of centre, and, second on the right, Cardinal Myroslav Lubachivsky, Head of the Ukrainian Catholic Church.

CHAPTER 8

THE MAKING OF A BRONZE

This chapter charts the progress of one of London's most recent commemorations, the statue of Clement Attlee which was unveiled outside Limehouse Library on November 30th, 1988. It was commissioned in 1985-6 by the Greater London Council as part of a series commemorating the heroes of Socialism. These included the statue of Fenner Brockway (p226), the bust of Nelson Mandela which stands again by the Festival Hall, after its burning by arsonists, and a memorial to the Spanish Civil War International Brigade also on the South Bank. A public competition was held for the Attlee commission. It was won by the thirty three year old Frank Forster, who submitted drawings and a quarter-size plaster maquette.

The career of a portrait sculptor nowadays is not an easy one. Forster had the advantage of being trained, like so many of the leading nineteenth century sculptors, at the City and Guilds School, Kennington. There representational drawing and the life class were kept alive at a time – the late 60's and 70's – when art education was moving more and more into abstraction and free expression. His other works include busts, medals, a racehorse for an Arab sheikh and four large figures representing the seasons for Buscot Park, Farringdon. He is also not above turning his hand to carpentry and roof-mending when there are no sculptural commissions to hand. He is, fortunately, a relaxed and good-natured artist and so was not distracted by the presence of a photographer at the various stages of this work.

His first task was to study the nature of his subject. Clement Attlee was Prime Minister of the Labour Government which between 1945 and 1951 laid the foundation of the Welfare State. He was in some ways an unlikely Labour leader, middle-class, respectable, a conservative in everything but politics. He became a socialist through his experiences as a youth leader in the East End of London. He had a passionate belief in social equality, tempered by considerable intelligence and common sense. He was extremely successful in reconciling the different strands within his party and in harmonising the more tempestuous abilities of men like Bevin, Bevan and Morrison. During the Second World War, his quiet efficiency was the perfect complement to Churchill's dynamism. His style was short and crisp. However, his inner personality was hard to fathom. Forster consulted a collection of impressions written by those who had known him; all seemed to agree that he was difficult to know. He was a shy man, a poor conversationalist, except on the subject of cricket, and averse to publicity. However his modesty, dedication and efficiency were universally recognised and Forster therefore decided to create a figure

Clement Attlee, 1st Earl Attlee. Born 1883, son of solicitor. Educated at Haileybury and Oxford. Practised as barrister, 1906-9. Managed Haileybury House, boys' settlement in Limehouse, 1907. Became Socialist, 1907. Lecturer at Ruskin College and London School of Economics, 1911-3. Served in First World War, becoming major, 1914-9. Mayor of Stepney, 1919-20. M.P. for Limehouse, 1922-50. Member of Simon Commission on future of India, 1927-30. Postmaster General, 1930. Became deputy leader of Labour Party after many leading figures lost their seats in general election, 1931. Became leader of Labour Party, 1935. Member of War Cabinet as Lord Privy Seal, 1940-2. Deputy Prime Minister, 1942-5. Prime Minister, 1945-51; introduced National Health and National Insurance, State housing and nationalisation of major industries. Gave independence to India. Leader of Opposition, 1951-5. Died 1967.

Above right. While working on his statue, Forster was given the loan of a large collection of photographs by Clement Attlee's son, the second Earl Attlee, which helped to focus his impressions. The photograph opposite, in which Attlee is speaking from the steps of 10 Downing Street, came the closest to his conception.

Below right. The agony of the artist. These two versions of the full sized clay figure are separated by a number of months and various revisions; the overall height has been increased to a foot above life size and the pose has been made more lively – the left hand has moved from pocket to lapel and the right hand, unfinished in the first picture, is closer to the body.

close to everyday life, expressing Attlee's military background and precise, unheroic style of leadership.

Forster's studio is a large, airy room above a church meeting hall in Griggs Walk, off Tower Bridge Road. There he worked amid the usual paraphenalia of tools, sacks, bins and the detritus of discarded workings. He began his full sized figure in clay, considering it to be the most creative initial medium, producing the most subtle and varied effects. On the other hand, the conversion of a clay figure into one

Left. The sculptor at work on the full sized clay figure. On an easel at the back is a selection of photographic images of the subject. A trunk and pair of legs suspended from a pulley and a ghostly torso, both dressed in the sculptor's oldest suit, keep him informed of the outline of the human body. Since clay is soft and malleable, this is the stage where most of the creative work is done. The figure is built up around a strong internal skeleton made of wire and pieces of wood and metal – anything that will serve to give it stability. The clay is added piece by piece and shaped and smoothed out by hand or knife. Clay must be kept damp or it will crack, so the end of every working day is spent spraying the figure and covering it with a plastic sheet.

Right. The clay figure is not rigid enough to be transported to the foundry or used as the basis of a mould capable of taking molten metal. It must therefore be converted, section by section, into its equivalent in plaster. First the clay figure is divided into sections by the insertion of thin strips of metal called shims. These can be seen running down the left side of the figure and up the inside of the legs. The back of the figure has also been split laterally into four.

Then the clay figure is covered with a layer of plaster. Here the sculptor, in arctic gear, has been pelting it with a snowstorm of wet pieces, this being the only way to ensure that the plaster fully penetrates the interstices of the clay. Afterwards the shims are extracted and the result looks like a great, shapeless snowman.

of bronze is an immensely long affair; someone unfamiliar with the process would have little or no idea of its complexity. First comes the two-fold process of converting the malleable clay into its tougher equivalent in plaster. At the foundry this forms the basis of a version in hardened sand or wax, from which the final bronze emerges. The essence of the process is reflective, impressing image on substance by means of an externally applied pattern, or mould. It is an age-old technique. Early man made open moulds of stone into which he poured the molten metal for his spear and arrow heads. The Ancient Greeks and Romans brought bronze sculpture to a peak of achievement and the methods they used were probably little different from the classical techniques used today. Here, in the conversion of the clay figure to plaster, we see how the original material is lost and how it is the inverted mirror-memory which keeps the key, holding the labour of months in suspension before re-embodying it.

Left. The inside surface of the plaster now holds the reverse image of the statue. The clay has served its purpose and must be removed. The sculptor loosens it by forcing water through the gaps made by the removal of the shims, then lifts off the uppermost back section and prises out the clay which once made up the head and shoulders. He then washes down the surface and the new outline is revealed.

The picture shows clearly the external skeleton of metal rods which has been built up to support the new figure, particularly the front part, the single "mother" mould. One by one the four back sections are removed and cleaned out, leaving the mother mould standing on its own.

Right. In places the outline of the mould is so sharp that the concave surface appears convex. It is difficult to realise that you are actually looking *into* this stilly dreaming countenance.

Above left. Now the new plaster figure is built up. The mother mould is laid prone on the floor. Behind it, the internal skeleton of the clay figure hangs useless, its weird improvisation revealed.

Below left. The sections of the back take their place beside it. All the inner surfaces have been coated with soap to create separation and then filled with the layer of plaster which will form the new figure. The metal bars which will provide the basis of its internal skeleton are lying inside.

Right. The complete figure has been built up again around the internal skeleton. The external layer of plaster which formed the mould is being chipped off, revealing the man below. Here the process is half-completed. The new figure will be smoothed down and re-worked and will then be ready to be taken to the foundry.

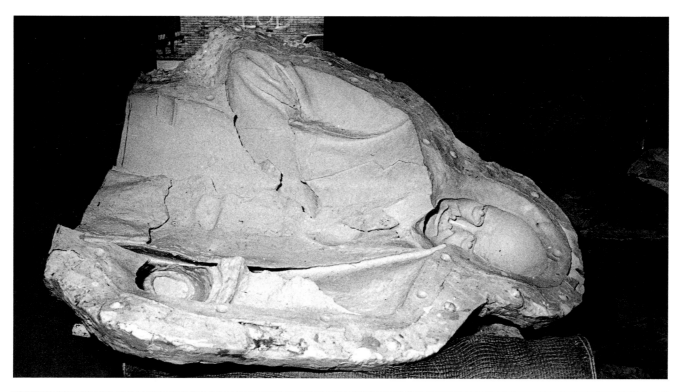

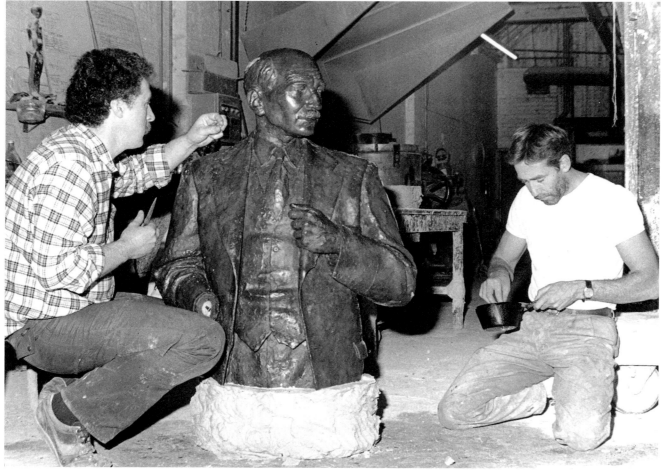

After arriving at the foundry, the plaster figure is first divided into sections, top and bottom, back and front, with ribs of plaster. The right hand and its paper are also, throughout, treated as a separate section. The figure is then given a covering of clay and an outer jacket of plaster. When hard, the jacket is removed, section by section, and the clay dug out. The sections are then replaced, the result being that the figure and the mould are now separated by a gap of about an inch. Molten rubber is poured in through holes in the mould. After this has hardened, the outer sections are again removed; they now form the pieces of what is called the rubber mould. They are given an inner coating of wax three sixteenths to a quarter of an inch thick. Inside them are spread the snake-like tubes of wax which will establish the internal pathways for the molten bronze when it is poured in; these end in a cup at top or bottom which will receive the metal. The mould is then assembled into two halves, upper and lower, and a mixture of liquid plaster and brick dust called grog is poured in through a hole in the top; this forms a core figure which underlies the wax.

Above left. The rubber mould is then removed. A discarded section is shown here.

Below left. The wax figure now shines free and can be worked. This is the last possible occasion for adjustments and improvements.

Right. Nails are hammered through the wax into the core figure to keep their alignment constant. Then the two sections are "invested", that is to say covered with a layer of grog and ludo (a special type of heat-resistant clay) and a jacket of plaster and sacking. Here we see the investing of the legs well advanced.

The scene now shifts to the foundry, the A & A Bronze Company, who have their premises in a former dog-biscuit factory in Fawe Street, Limehouse, in London's East End. The large, warehouse-like buildings are ideal for artistic activities and some of the rooms are rented out as studios. Sculptures of all kind stand around in different stages of completion: bronze maquettes of a soldier by Jagger, huge, loping hares by Barry Flanagan and the huge plaster model head from Nicholas Kostmanis' 32ft high statue of Archbishop Makarios.

Two principal methods of casting are employed today, both traditional: sand and lost wax. Sand casting is generally used for the larger sections such as torso and trunk; beds of chemically hardened sand form the mould into which the molten bronze is poured. The lost wax method produces a more refined, subtle finish and is generally used for heads, hands and other more intricate sections. However, since this is the technique exclusively employed at A & A, the whole of the Attlee statue was cast in this way.

However, much water flowed under the bridge between the completion of the plaster figure in December, 1987, and its delivery to the foundry in September, 1988. Statues, as this book has shown, are highly charged tokens of human achievement, imbued with the ideas and emotions of those who commission them. Others, however, only see them as expensive luxuries. As public objects, they can also

Above left. The sections are then placed in a kiln and baked, in order to harden them up for the pouring. The wax evaporates away, so that all that now remains of the figure is the impression on the inner surface of the grog and ludo mould.

Right. Now comes the most crucial moment. A few seconds will make or unmake the entire process of production. The bronze is heated in a crucible and poured into the entrance previously formed by the wax cup. The molten metal flows down the thicker tubes (or "runners") and all around between the mould and the core. The air and the gas from the bronze are driven up and out through the thinner tubes (or "risers").

Below left. The sections of the mould are left to cool overnight and are then "broken out". The covering is chipped away with an axe and brushed off with a steel brush to reveal the bronze beneath. If all has gone well, this is one of the sculptor's greatest moments of triumph. In this case the casting has been successful. There is still a lot of work to do: there are roughnesses on the bronze and ridges where the metal has broken a short way through the contours of the mould, which will all be dealt with in due course. In the meantime the surfaces and interior of the statue are completely cleaned with a high pressure hose.

Left. Once the roughnesses on the bronze have been smoothed away to satisfaction, the sections are welded together. Head and breast are reunited with legs and trunk; here one can see how the bronze has been rubbed bright along the line of the join. The right hand and paper, too intricate to be treated as part of the main figure, are also welded on. Holding the torch is Henry "Ab" Abercrombie, one of the two partners in charge of A & A.

The surface of the bronze is then thoroughly cleaned. This makes it shine like the morning sun but, unfortunately, it is impossible to erect it in that state. Bronze inevitably discolours in the open air, due to a natural reaction with the gases of the atmosphere; whether the discoloration inclines to green or black depends on the air's chemical composition. No way has been found to stop this process. Matthew Cotes Wyatt attempted to do so with his statue of George III in Cockspur Street (p48). At the unveiling it was reported to be "of a gorgeous gold colour, varnished to resist the effects of the weather"; however, the brightness clearly did not last. Bronze statues are therefore always given a unified, dark brown patina; this corresponds to the probable discoloration and can be renewed after erection. In this case Forster used a compound called liver of sulphate.

Right. The sculptor then built his own modest, 3ft 6ins pedestal of brick and stone mouldings, in keeping with the nature of the site and with Attlee's character. Already welded to its base, the statue was craned in and bolted down. It is interesting to note that from 1912 to 1914 Attlee lived in Norway Place, seen to the rear of the picture.

become the helpless pawns of bureaucratic intrigue and controversy. The statue of Attlee was no exception. We have seen the vicissitudes suffered by those of Charles I, James II, George IV, Pitt, Peel, Brunel and Campbell. In this case the problems centred on the site and on the cost of erection. The G.L.C. had planned to erect it on the corner of Mile End Road and Burdett Road, in front of a small park which they had just laid out. They had paid the sculptor for his work but had omitted the final £3,500 required for the pedestal and the final installation.

Before they could make the final payment, the G.L.C. was abolished. Responsibility for the statue was then transferred to the Borough of Tower Hamlets. It had just passed under Liberal control

and refused to devote any of its arts' budget to erecting the statue of a former Labour Prime Minister. In addition, it was on the point of splitting administratively into seven and it was not clear which of the new "neighbourhoods" would inherit the figure. (A similar problem arises over Gladstone's East End statue (p204); Bow neighbourhood wish to re-erect it in Tredegar Square but they own only the statesman's northern, right-hand half.) Attlee's closest personal links were with Limehouse, since he had been their M.P. for forty years. Wapping neighbourhood therefore adopted the statue and looked for sites; however, they were not prepared to contribute the whole £3,500 required, though it was indeed a small sum to pay for a full sized bronze statue. London Transport showed interest but in the end declined to erect it near Tower Hill on the grounds that it would be a political act. Finally the stalemate was spotted by a sharp-eyed investigative journalist named Claire Hargreaves. Her article in the *Daily Telegraph* broke the log-jam. It was read by a Leeds businessman, Mr M.P. Frankel, whose father, Dan Frankel, had, like Attlee, once been Mayor of Stepney and had served as M.P. for Mile End from 1935 to 1945. Mr Frankel promised to donate the money required in memory of his father, who had died earlier in the year, and of his mother, who had been a member of Stepney Borough Council and also Attlee's secretary in 1919-20. This happy gift brought additional funds from borough and neighbourhood, and Frank Foster, now sure that he would not be left with a homeless and extremely heavy bronze on his hands, dispatched the plaster figure for casting.

A splendid opening ceremony and reception were arranged by Mr Ian Ogilvie, Director of Wapping's Library Services. To the exhibition inside the library the Attlee Foundation contributed a series of photographs, beginning with the earnest young man seated among the orphan boys of Limehouse and ending with the bent, retired statesman long-sightedly scanning the world's affairs in his newspaper. As the great, red tarpaulin was pulled away from the statue, there was a gasp of genuine appreciation from the crowd; there, finished to perfection, was the leader in middle life, human, modest and determined.

The Chairman and Elected members of Wapping Neighbourhood Standing Committee request the pleasure of your company

at the official unveiling of a statue of Clement Attlee — the Rt. Hon. Earl Attlee KG, OM, CH, FRS (1883 – 1967) by the Rt. Hon. Lord Wilson of Rievaulx KG, OBE, FRS

outside Limehouse Library, 638 Commercial Road, London, E14 at 11.00am on Wednesday 30th November, 1988.

Reception to follow

WAPPING
neighbourhood

RSVP Ian Orton
Chief Executive Wapping Neighbourhood
Limehouse Town Hall
646 Commercial Road
E14 7HA
Tel: 01-987 9200

Statue by Frank Forster. Bronze, 6ft 8ins (the plaster figure was 6ft 10ins but 2ins were lost in the casting). Outside Limehouse Library, Commercial Road. Unveiled November 30th, 1988, by Lord Wilson of Rievaulx. Cost £24,000.

The former Prime Minister, making one of his rare public appearances, spoke of the social revolution which Attlee had carried out and a number of political luminaries, past and present, were in attendance.

CHAPTER 9
VANISHED STATUES

Though a death was the proximate cause of almost every statue in this book, the preceding chapters have not dwelt much on human mortality. As we look up at these heroic figures, we do not think first of death. Those portrayed are no longer with us. However, their fame survives them; they have attained the earthly immortality of good and great deeds. The keenest sense of the transitoriness of man and his works comes when we look back at the statues which once graced the capital but now are gone – lost, destroyed, put away or banished for ever. The destructive agencies have been neglect, urban development and changing aesthetic taste, rather than war or revolution. And since what follows is a substantially complete catalogue, we may take comfort in the fact that the losses have been comparatively few.

"Imperial Caesar, dead and turned to clay, Might stop a hole to keep the wind away." Free-standing statues of Julius and Augustus

Below right and below. Statue of G. F. Handel by Louis-Francois Roubiliac. Marble. Erected 1738, in Vauxhall Gardens. Removed c.1800 and acquired c.1840 by Novello's music company, who kept it in the hallway of their offices in Wardour Street. It is now in the Victoria and Albert Museum. Handel is playing a lyre carved with the head of the sun-god Apollo; he is also wearing a loose-fitting robe, slippers and night-cap. Roubiliac employed the same wit when he placed the fatal molehill under the hooves of his equestrian William III at Bristol, an effect later copied by John Bacon in St James's Square (see pp46-7).

Above right. Statue of Charles II by an unknown Italian sculptor, altered by Jasper Latham. Stone. Erected 1677 in the Stocks Market by Sir Thomas Vyner. It is said that Vyner bought the statue through his agent in Italy. It had been ordered by the Polish ambassador as a representation of the Polish King John Sobieski overcoming the Turks; however, the ambassador had found himself unable to meet the bill. Vyner commissioned Latham to recarve the head of the rider and alter the recumbent figure of the Turk to that of Oliver Cromwell. It was taken down in 1738 to make way for the building of the Mansion House on the site of the Stocks Market. It spent forty years in an inn yard in Aldersgate and in 1779 was re-erected at Newby Hall, Ripon, by a descendant of Vyner.

Vyner understood his merry monarch well. In 1674 he entertained him to a sumptuous dinner at the Guildhall. As the King got up to leave, Vyner seized hold of his arm and begged him to come back and finish the second bottle of wine. "He who is drunk is as great as a king," Charles replied and returned to the table.

Caesar, Mark Anthony and Pompey the Great used to stand in Lincoln's Inn gardens; they were erected between 1672 and 1675 and were almost certainly removed in 1776, in a much mutilated state. Moreover, because of their greater age and number, it is the statues of England's rulers which figure most frequently among those which have vanished. Many kings and queens stood in the niches on London's ancient gates, on Temple Bar and on the Royal Exchange; however, not being free-standing, they do not come within the compass of this book. An equestrian statue of Charles II (see previous page) used to stand on a high pedestal in the City's principal shopping-place, the Stocks Market. We have already mentioned George I's golden horses (p38-9), George IV's unpopular national memorial (pp50-1), the Licensed Victuallers' tight-trousered Prince Albert, now in Berkshire (p60), and Doulton's terra-cotta Queen Victoria (p66). A somewhat clumsy equestrian statue of George III by Beaupré and Wilton stood in Berkeley Square from 1766 to 1827 but has not survived. A very early statue of Queen Victoria was erected in 1840 in Victoria Square by the first Marquis of Westminster; it was taken down a few years later, the design, a figure underneath a globe, being much disliked. Henry Price's 1904, nine foot high, bronze figure of Victoria is no longer at the Royal Military Academy, Woolwich, having been kidnapped by a rival group of Sandhurst cadets.

A statue of great wit and distinction used to stand in Vauxhall Gardens, the fashionable public pleasure gardens on the south bank of the Thames (see p344-5). Erected in 1738, it was of the composer Handel, whose music was often performed there. But the Gardens fell

Statue of the Duke of Cumberland by Henry Cheere. Lead. Erected November 4th, 1770, in Cavendish Square, by Lieutenant General William Strode, "In Gratitude for His Private Kindness, In Honour of His Publick Virtue". It was removed "for repairs" in 1868 by the 5th Duke of Portland and, against the wishes of the residents, melted down.

This is the statue which called down the wrath of Sir Joshua Reynolds (see pp42 & 140); he did not consider its modern dress worthy of the dignity of sculpture.

Statue of Robert Milligan by Richard Westmacott. Bronze. Erected c.1810 in front of the West India Docks by the directors and proprietors. It was thus a very early outdoor commemoration for a commoner, contemporary with that of the Fifth Duke of Bedford (p148). In 1943 the statue was removed from the top of the central pier of the gateway in order to allow the passage of aeroplanes imported as deck cargo from America. The photograph shows it in store at the Museum of Docklands.

into decline and Handel now bides out his time in a silent corridor of the Victoria and Albert Museum.

London's earliest outdoor statue of a soldier was that of the pistol-toting "Butcher" Duke of Cumberland, who defeated the Scots at the Battle of Culloden. It held its place in Cavendish Square for less than a hundred years. London's only statue of a businessman pure and simple, that of Robert Milligan who built the West India Docks, has also, at the time of writing, failed to hold its place, though it will probably be re-erected as part of the current Docklands development. A stone statue of Dick Whittington – or rather of Sir Richard Whittington, Lord Mayor and a leading member of the Mercers' Company – used to sit listening to the sound of Bow Bells outside the Mercers' almshouses on Highgate Hill. Whittington died in 1423 but the statue was erected in the philanthropic tradition in

1822. It was recently taken down, together with the almshouses, to make way for the the widening of the Archway Road; it was, apparently, an undistinguished work but one wonders what was done with it.

The weightiest of all departures was that made by the Duke of Wellington from the triumphal arch at Hyde Park Corner (pp 246-7). The forty ton statue was always controversial. Having decided in 1883 to remove it, the authorities had great difficulty in finding a site and there was talk of melting it down. Eventually the statue was taken to the outskirts of Aldershot, where it stands on a wooded hill close by the garrison church. It seems very much at home there and might well become a place of pilgrimage for future, history conscious generations. The sylvan spaciousness seems to absorb some of its military bombast, the green below it is a perfect place for picnics and the proximity of the church reminds one of the sacrifice made

Statue of the Duke of Wellington by Matthew Cotes Wyatt (see pp246-7). Bronze, from captured enemy canon; 30ft, 40 tons. First erected September 29th, 1846, on top of the triumphal arch at Hyde Park Corner. Cost £30,000. During the 1880's the arch was resited and in 1883 the authorities took the opportunity to remove the statue. After a great deal of controversy, it was claimed by the army and re-erected on Round Hill, Aldershot.

by the many brave soldiers who fought under Wellington's command.

Pilgrimages might also be made by the art conscious to Liphook, Hampshire, to see the statue of Sir Hugh Rose, 1st Baron Strathnairn, by Edward Onslow Ford (see p94). This vivid and unstuffy portrait of one of the military heroes of the Indian Mutiny was first erected in Knightsbridge in 1895 and was taken down in 1931. It suffered at the hands of the general disillusionment about monuments of Empire prevalent in the 1930's and 40's; as one official of the Ministry of Works wrote to another, "The view is perhaps permissible that it would be most unfortunate for one of London's lost but unlamented statues to be re-erected." In 1964, after its availability had been advertised in the *Times*, it was given a new home at Foley Manor.

A statue of a brave, but in this case foolhardy, soldier was unveiled by the Prince of Wales at the Royal Military Academy, Woolwich, in 1883. It was of Louis Bonaparte, the Crown Prince Imperial of France, who fought in the British army during the Zulu War. He was killed leading a patrol skirmish and his death was felt to be a particularly futile and tragic waste. His nine foot, bronze statue once stood at the north end of the Academy Green, but is no longer known of at Woolwich.

Another brave man who made a strong impression on his contemporaries was Henry Fawcett, radical Liberal M.P. and Postmaster General. He was made blind by a shooting accident at the age of twenty-five. Despite it, he led as normal a life as possible; relying on touch and memory, he continued to fish, ride and even ice-skate. He

Statue of Sir Hugh Rose, 1st Baron Strathnairn by Edward Onslow Ford. Bronze, from gun-metal presented by the Indian Government. First unveiled June 19th, 1895, at the junction of Knightsbridge and Brompton Road. Cost £3,500. Removed in 1931 for the building of an Underground station and for reasons of traffic and placed, as shown in the photograph, in Westminster Council's store in Chelsea. Purchased in 1964 by Mr Vernon Northcott, of Foley Manor, Liphook, Hampshire, and re-erected near a public footpath through his estate.

Below. The crowning glory of the original work was the ceremonial plume of ostrich feathers on top of the helmet. This was wisely removed while the statue was in store but was reinstated after the move to Liphook.

was straightforward, genial and gallant. He was a particular champion of the rights of the Indian native population and was known in Parliament as "the member for India". As Postmaster General he introduced parcel post, postal orders and the postal savings bank. His statue, entirely of Doulton terra-cotta, had a certain spiritual charm. However by 1955, the year of its destruction, its style must have seemed completely outdated and his virtues had no doubt been similarly forgotten.

London once had an outdoor monument to poetry, the art in which the British have most excelled. Unfortunately the donor died before the arrangements for its care had been finalised and as a result the authorities always regarded it as a regrettable nuisance. To no avail did Hamo Thornycroft complain that the fountains had not been connected up. In the 1900's not even the Metropolitan Drinking Fountain and Cattle Trough Association would take responsibility for its welfare. It was apparently damaged by bombs during the Second World War – though not seriously – and afterwards it was not felt worth spending the £2,000 necessary to repair it.

Far Left. The Poets' Fountain or Poetry Memorial by William and Hamo Thornycroft. The central, marble figures are of Shakespeare, Chaucer and, out of sight, Milton. The bronze figures below represent Comedy, History and Tragedy, and above is the gilded bronze figure of Fame. Inaugurated July 9th, 1875, at the junction of Hamilton Place and Park Lane (Marble Arch can be seen in the distance in this early photograph). Cost £5,000, the gift of Mrs Maria Mangin Brown, a private resident of Mayfair.

Left. Statue of Henry Fawcett by George Tinworth. Terra-cotta. Unveiled June 7th, 1893, in Vauxhall Park, close by Fawcett's house. The gift of Sir Henry Doulton, the proprietor of the Doulton Pottery Manufactory on the Albert Embankment (see p66). The figures visible on the panels are, in the front Courage, and on the side Sympathy flanked by Good News and Bad News (both conveyed by letter). On the reverse were the Post Office, Truth, India and Justice. The statue was taken down and destroyed in 1955.

Fawcett was also given a memorial fountain in the Victoria Embankment Gardens.

Below. Fame descending from The Poetry Memorial, during its demolition in 1947.

CHAPTER 10

THE PRESENT OF THE PAST

The year 1988 was London's commemorative *annus mirabilis*. Between May and November no less than five new outdoor statues were unveiled, making it the capital's most productive year ever. (The previous best was 1882, when there were four.) Has this marked some significant turning point, after four comparatively modest decades? If so, what are the factors involved: a new prosperity, a new sense of national pride or a deeper appreciation of the past? What is the evidence of the statues?

The first to be unveiled was of Saint Volodymyr, the founding father of Christianity in Russia. This statue (described in chapter 7, p326-7) was erected by the Ukrainian community and so was the fruit of Britain's internationalism and of the role which she has played as a haven for the persecuted minorities of the world. The statue of Clement Attlee was the subject of chapter 8. Originally commissioned by the Greater London Council, it must on the whole be seen as a political enterprise undertaken by that Socialist "state-within-a-state". However, it also restored the balance of history; London had a prominent outdoor statue of his contemporary, Winston Churchill, but none of the man who led the social transformation of Britain after the Second World War.

The erection of a statue of John Wilkes, the eighteenth century champion of free speech and the rights of the citizen, also restored the commemorative balance. Along with figures like Tom Paine and the Levellers, Wilkes belongs to the egalitarian party of protest rather than the royalist, loyalist tradition. Between 1763 and 1774, the cry in the streets of London was "Wilkes and Liberty!" It accompanied riots and strikes and stimulated the birth of political demonstrations and political journalism. If Wilkes had been an unscrupulous demagogue, he might have led a revolution; as it was, he remained a fair-minded and somewhat philosophic City alderman and magistrate. (He was also an uninhibited womaniser, in his youth an enthusiastic member of Sir Francis Dashwood's so-called "Hell-Fire Club".)

Quite by chance, the statue of John Wilkes was unveiled on the same day as that of Lord Dowding, who led R.A.F. Fighter Command during the Battle of Britain. That battle still exercises a great hold over the national imagination, more perhaps than any other event of the recent past. It took place in full view, in the skies above the South Coast and the English Channel, and it saved Britain from almost certain invasion. "The Few" who fought it numbered 2,900 in all, from fourteen different nationalities, and 1,000 of them were killed or wounded.

It was Dowding's foresight and determination which laid the basis

John Wilkes. Born 1725, Clerkenwell, son of distiller. Received university education and married rich wife. Developed interest in philosophy; elected Fellow of the Royal Society, 1749. Elected M.P., 1757. Attacked Lord Bute and weakness of George II's treaty with French; imprisoned in Tower on General Warrant but released, 1763. General Warrants declared illegal by judges and parliament, 1765-6. Imprisonment for seditious libel led to riots, 1768. Alderman of City of London, 1769-97. Exclusion from parliament led to widespread public political meetings of protest, 1769. Lord Mayor of London, 1774. Supported cause of American colonists. Introduced Bill for the Just and Equal Representation of the People of England, 1776. Defended Bank of England during Gordon Riots, 1780. Died 1797.

Statue of John Wilkes by James Butler. Bronze, 8ft 6ins on 4ft pedestal. Corner of Fetter Lane and New Fetter Lane. Unveiled October 31st, 1988, by Dr James Cope. Cost £35,000.

The statue was the brainchild of Dr Cope, a medical adviser to City Companies and, like Wilkes himself, an alderman for the Ward of Farringdon Without for more than twenty years. Becoming increasingly fascinated by Wilkes' place in history, he began his project in 1980; he raised funds principally from the livery companies and Fleet Street newspapers and from the City Corporation. In the photograph he is standing on the left, with James Butler, the sculptor, on his right.

Wilkes was a fit, impressive but unhandsome man. Butler studied the bust by Roubiliac and all the available portraits but found them somewhat contradictory. The most consistent feature was his squint, so this is almost certainly the only cross-eyed statue in London.

of the victory. Yet he was always something of an outsider in the service. Nicknamed "Stuffy" by his colleagues, he was personally unaggressive, unimpressed by class distinctions and outwardly unhumorous. Astonishingly, he was removed from significant command almost immediately after the Battle of Britain. He was also never commemorated after the War. To the 600 or so members of the Battle of Britain Fighters' Association, this always seemed a great injustice. Their view, put bluntly by their chairman, Air Chief Marshal Sir Christopher Foxley-Norris, at the unveiling of the statue, was this: that, without Dowding, all the statues in London would now be German. (The Allies, one may note, destroyed a number of German military statues after the Second World War.) They began their project in earnest in 1983 and at first met with official discouragement. However, they eventually won the support of the Planning Committee of Westminster City Council, who own the ground outside St Clement Dane's Church. They commissioned the statue and raised the necessary funds. As it was being craned into place, a cockney bystander was heard to remark, "And about bloody time too!"

The fifth statue was put up to mark another religious anniversary –

Air Chief Marshal Hugh Dowding, first Baron Dowding. Born 1882, Moffat, Dumfreisshire, son of schoolmaster. Joined Royal Garrison Artillery, 1901. Served in India, 1904-10. Studied at Camberley Staff College; learned to fly, 1912-3. Joined Royal Flying Corps; held commands in England and France, 1914-8. Joined new, permanent Royal Air Force; served in Kenya, Britain, Iraq and Palestine, 1919-30. Member of Air Council for Supply and Research, 1930-5. Commander-in-Chief, Fighter Command, 1936-40; built up and conserved force of fast, manoeuvrable monoplanes, Hurricanes and Spitfires, together with centralised control system equipped with radar and radio. Led Battle of Britain, July 10th - October 31st, 1940. His book on R.A.F policy, war and philosophy suppressed by Churchill, 1941. Retired, 1942; devoted himself to spiritualism and theosophy. Died 1970.

Statue by Faith Winter. Bronze, 9ft. Outside St Clement Danes, the Church of the R.A.F., at the east end of the Strand. Unveiled October 31st, 1988, by Queen Elizabeth the Queen Mother.
Cost (including plaques and pedestal) £41,600. Unlike the statue of Attlee (chapter 8), this figure was modelled directly in plaster. The deliberately unheroic pose is, according to those who knew Dowding, extremely lifelike.

not quite a millennium but a more modest two hundred and fifty years, for it was in 1738 that John Wesley first experienced the joy of complete surrender to Christ. His conversion took place in Nettleton Court, Aldersgate, now the site of the London Museum. The decision to mark the anniversary by a new statue was implemented by the Aldersgate Trustees, a group with a special responsibility for Methodist history and for memorials in the City. (They were also responsible for the great flame-shaped bronze scroll inscribed with Wesley's own account of his conversion which stands by the London Museum.) Unlike the Victorian statue in City Road (p314), this figure represents his actual height of five foot one; it is strange to stand beside it and imagine so much spiritual vitality pouring from so diminutive a form.

Its situation links it with one of London's most highly profiled redevelopments, that of Paternoster Square just to the north of St Paul's Cathedral. The Prince of Wales has had much to say about it and his views have won wide public support. At the time of writing, Arup Associates, the development's architects, intend to integrate the Wesley statue in their plan by placing it at the centre of an arcade or in a pedestrian garden or thoroughfare. Indeed, what better way could there be of establishing a human scale and linking the present and the past than by a historical figure erected at a less than imperial height? If the commemorative revival is to continue, then the quest to make public spaces more attractive and evocative must become increasingly important. Arup intend to make full use of their site's sculptural possibilities, noting in their master plan that early editions of Shakespeare's plays were printed there in the seventeenth century.

None of the five statues erected in 1988, then, commemorated a figure belonging to the immediate past. If for some there has been a recent increase in national self-confidence, there is also continuing evidence of a wider view of history in which previous imbalances are corrected. Two of the statues represent a return to the religious roots of culture, one, that of St Volodymyr, by a community in exile,

John Wesley. For biography, see p314.

Statue cast by lost wax process from a marble figure begun by Samuel Manning the Elder and finished by his son, Samuel, in 1839 (the original is now in Westminster Central Hall). Like Adams Acton (p314), Manning used the bust carved from the life by Enoch Wood as a model. Bronze, 5ft 1in (life size). Erected temporarily in St Paul's Churchyard. Unveiled September 17th, 1988, by the Rev Dr Richard Jones, President of the Methodist Conference. Cost £33,000, subscribed by private Methodist trusts.

This statue, like many others in this book, was cast by Morris Singer Ltd., at their workshops in Basingstoke. Singer's have been casting statues for over a hundred years and have the longest continuous tradition of any foundry in Britain. (Of the many foundries which operated during the great age of commemoration, only the one at Thames Ditton, latterly A.B. Burton Ltd., was of comparable importance; it ceased trading in 1939.) The company began as J.W. Singer and started casting statues in the 1880's at their workshops in Frome. It was there that Lord Robert Napier (p267), the Duke of Devonshire (p213), Captain Scott (p303), Mackennal's Edward VII (p74) and Thornycroft's Cromwell (p208), Gladstone (p206) and John Colet (p103) were first embodied in bronze. The most complex and protracted operation of those years was the casting of Boadicea (p68). In 1927 J.W. Singer joined up with a previous offshoot, the Morris Art Bronze Foundry (who cast William and Catherine Booth (p319-21)), and established themselves in Lambeth as Morris Singer. There they cast the statues of Earl Haig (p285), Sir Joshua Reynolds (p141), President Roosevelt (p233), and William Macmillan's George VI (p79), Raleigh (p307), Trenchard (p287) and Coram (p115). In 1967 they moved out of London once again, to Basingstoke. There they were responsible for the gilded statue of Sir Thomas More (p322) and Oscar Nemon's Freud (p169), and they continued to do a great deal of work for Henry Moore and Barbara Hepworth. As well as the recent statue of Wesley, they also cast the new replica of John Foley's statue of Faraday introduced on pp362-3.

the other very much on home ground – for if one could put the clock back two hundred and fifty years or so one would see John Wesley attending evensong at· St Paul's on the very day of his conversion. This sense of a locality as a palimpsest, with the layers of its past superimposed and waiting to be invoked, offers a great opportunity for the imaginative placing of statues and must be a theme for the future. An excellent existing example is the traditional figure of the Roman Emperor Trajan which stands beside the largest surviving portion of the original wall of Roman London. Beside it, inscribed on a new stone wall, are words from London's oldest lettered monument, that to the procurator Julius Alpinus Classicanus, who between 61 and 65 A.D. restored harmony to the country after Boudicca's revolt (see p68). So as the crowds hurry to and from Tower Hill Underground station, their city's two thousand year old presence is suddenly revealed to them in tangible form.

Another example of enlightened positioning is the presence of two mediaeval crutched (or "crossed") friars in the narrow road near Fenchurch Street station which bears their name. When in 1984 the sculptor Michael Black was commissioned to provide figures for the new Commercial Union Assurance building, he found that between 1200 and 1420 the indigent and charitable friars had occupied a house on that site, by the eastern gate of the city. He also based his two

Statue of the Emperor Trajan in the classical manner, probably by an unknown late eighteenth century Italian sculptor. Bronze. Trinity Place, below Tower Hill Underground Station.

The statue was discovered in a Southampton scrapyard by the Rev "Doc" Clayton, the founder of Toc H. It was erected on its present site in 1980, through the Tower Hill Improvement Trust.

Below. Statues of two crutched friars by Michael Black. Swedish red granite with heads, hands and feet of off-white, Bardiglio marble, 6ft. Outside the former Commercial Union Assurance building, Crutched Friars, off Fenchurch Street. Erected 1985. Cost £30,000.

moving figures on Herman Hesse's fictional characters Narziss and Goldmundt, the one representing thoughtful contemplation and the other active engagement in the world. Their presence in this book is perhaps somewhat marginal; however, they win a place by their beauty and the way in which they illustrate the theme of locality and the ever increasing recovery of the past.

Through the studies of archaeologists, archivists and historians, we now know more about our history than ever before; as the Mexican poet Octavio Paz put it, the past has become the present. However, the greater part of life is still lived far from that timeless continuum. Square, flat glass surfaces are very much the architectural style and the pace of change demands impermanent structures which do not invite commemorative figures in their vicinity. Caught in a blizzard of new construction, we seem barely in charge of our own destiny. All this is reflected in one of London's most unusual recent statues. It is by Sir Eduardo Paolozzi and, though erected primarily as a work of art, it is the only occasion on which a sculptor has commemorated himself. Sectioned out by the logic of its design, it shows the artist in a society which favours material over spiritual values. The

figure holds a "strange machine" rather like a tennis racquet and, unlike all the previous bearers of sceptres, swords and speeches, seems uncertain what to do with it. If London's streets have a commemorative anti-hero, then this is he. Nevertheless at the end of 1988, our *annus mirabilis*, Paolozzi was awarded a knighthood, so giving an official recognition to his vision.

There is no such uncertainty in the wide, sweeping forehand executed by Fred Perry's statue at Wimbledon. It was put up in 1984 by the All England Tennis Club to commemorate the fiftieth anniversary of the first of his three consecutive victories in the Men's Championship. It introduced a new category of commemoration, being London's only outdoor figure of a sportsman.

Of course the most glaring imbalance revealed by a comprehensive head-count of statues is the almost complete absence of the ordinary citizen. Apart from the soldiers represented on war memorials (see pp165, 249 & 280), such figures barely exist. Yet the common man outnumbers the hero by hundreds of thousands to one and it is on his intelligence and integrity that civilisation ultimately depends. So it refreshing to see that three excellent statues of passengers were recently commissioned by British Rail and erected on Brixton railway station. They are universally well-liked and up to the time of writing have never been vandalised. The subjects were volunteers; one enlisted on the station platform and the two others in a local community centre. The Public Arts Development Trust played an important part in organising the project and one hopes that it will be the first of many.

Right. Statues of Peter Lloyd (above left), Joy Battick (above right) and Karen Heistermann (below) by Kevin Atherton. Bronze. Brixton Railway Station. Unveiled June 30th, 1986, by Sir Hugh Casson (see Foreword, p6); the statue of Joy Battick was specially craned in for the occasion and lowered 40ft to the accompaniment of a steel band.

Below left. Self-portrait by Eduardo Paolozzi, entitled *The Artist as Hephaistos*. Bronze. Outside 34-6 High Holborn. Erected 1987. Commissioned by the London and Bristol Development PLC, who then owned the building.

Below right. Statue of Fred Perry by David Wynne. Bronze, 4ft 6ins. All England Tennis Club, Wimbledon, opposite the entrance to the Members Enclosure and visible from the main, Doherty entrance gates. Unveiled May 20th, 1984, by the Duke of Kent.

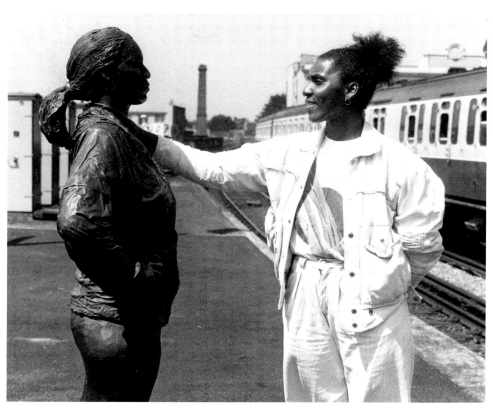

1988 was, as we said at the beginning of this chapter, a remarkable year for London's statues and 1989 provided no abatement. Its first month saw the unveiling of a statue to General Eisenhower in Grosvenor Square, a commemoration which continued the tradition of gifts from abroad. Eisenhower presided with remarkable bonhomie over the later stages of the war against Hitler and over one of the most difficult and intolerant periods of American history. He was an extremely popular public figure. Some found him inconsistent and rambling but he had a deep, instinctive knowledge of what measure of peace and unity were possible.

A book like this can have no final ending. Though the writing is done and the presses roll, the story continues, as men continue to submit their heroes to the mysterious alchemy of stone and bronze. (One may note that the name Eisenhower means, in German, "hewer of metal", Ike's family having left that country in the 1730's, seeking the freedom to practice their strict Protestant faith.) In May 1989, other currents of commemoration are due to make contact with their earth, as the Institute of Electrical Engineers unveil their statue of the father of their profession, Michael Faraday, outside their headquarters in Savoy Place. Faraday was perhaps the greatest

General Dwight D. Eisenhower. Born 1890, Denison, Texas, son of mechanic. Graduated from West Point and joined U.S. Army, 1915. Commander of Allied Forces In North Africa, 1942-3. Supreme Allied Commander, Europe, 1943-5. Chief of Staff, American Army, 1945-48. President of Columbia University, 1948-50. First Military Commander of NATO, 1950-2. President of the United States, 1952-6 & 1956-60; ended Korean War, began construction of interstate highway system and signed into law Civil Rights Act. Died 1969.

Statue by Robert Dean. Bronze, 10ft on 6ft pedestal of Portland stone. Grosvenor Square. Eisenhower had his headquarters in the Square during the Second World War, and it is now the location both of the American Embassy and of the memorials to President Roosevelt (p232) and the pilots of the American Eagle Squadrons.

The presentation originated with Charles H. Price, the American Ambassador in London from 1983 to 1989, and his wife Carol Ann. They noticed that there was no statue of the former Allied Commander in London and, being distinguished citizens of Kansas City in whose locality Eisenhower grew up, they arranged the raising of funds among their friends and business associates there.

Left. The statue was unveiled on January 23rd, 1989, by Margaret Thatcher and Ambassador Charles H. Price, seen here standing on the left. Robert Dean, who sculpted and cast the statue in Florence, is seated second from the left in the front row.

experimental scientist of the nineteenth century. His discovery that an electric current could be produced from a magnetic field led to the development of the dynamo, the generator, the electric motor and the transformer. Like Wesley's recent statue, Faraday's is a bronze cast of an earlier work, in this case the marble figure by John Foley (p186) at the Royal Institution.

By the middle of 1989, therefore, seven new statues will have been raised in the twelve months following that of St Volodymyr (p326). Seven is, of course, a magical number and refers, among other things, to the seven celestial lights: the sun and moon and the five planets visible to the naked eye. Since the art of bronze casting was once regarded with a kind of numinous awe and since our commemorative pageant has been so much greater than the sum of its parts, one might look to see whether the metaphors of astrological magic, ancient and modern, can help us to follow its progress. Our story began with Jupiter and Saturn: with kingship and authority, with jovial generosity yet also, demonstrated in the concerns of our philanthropists, with an awareness of limitation, old age and death. The first statues graced the dignified and self-contained world of city square, hospital and almshouse. But just as the discovery of Uranus in 1781 broke the mould of the heavens, so the growth of political consciousness, the French Revolution and the terrible confrontation with Napoleon changed English society and radically enriched the nature of its commemorations. They celebrated political idealism and independence, with Cartwright and Fox. They soared to the sky, with the Duke of York and Nelson on their columns and Wellington on his arch.

The discovery of Neptune in mid-century heralded that extraordinary period when the world was substantially controlled and governed from Whitehall and from the Home Countries of England, and when so many improvements to human life were made. Here was a suitable companion star for a maritime empire held together by the bonds of self-sacrifice and religion. The images of its heroes, springing up richly robed in the streets of the capital, reinforced those bonds, and over half of London's outdoor statues were erected during this time. The country also found its own Sun-centre, in the much commemorated Great Exhibition, perhaps, in the home-clad figure of Sir Robert Peel or the primrose-garlanded Spring hero, Disraeli. Of the other lights, Mars was much in evidence; so too was Mercury, in all the eloquently gesturing statesmen. Venus seemed much neglected but re-appeared in the many allegorical figures, bare-breasted Asia, for example, whose chilly clays cost John Foley his health (p62), or Gladstone's Courage, moulded more happily by Hamo Thornycroft (p206).

The discovery of Pluto in 1930 accompanied a descent into an underworld of comparative poverty and a continuing loss of national self-confidence. With the many statues of foreigners or from abroad, the Moon's reflected light replaced that of the Sun. In some ways that situation is still with us. However, new wealth has been found in the depths and the Moon's tides are recovering ever greater areas of the past. In the darkness, are our heroes and demi-gods re-assembling and making their presences felt, asking for a rebirth of character in a confused and confusing world? To divine new trends is like searching for a new planet. What should one say? Man continues to need heroes of substance, peace-makers and those who will protect the torn fabric of the Earth. One day, no doubt, they too will be given their statues.

CHAPTER 11
WHERE TO WALK

After looking into the long and varied history of London's statues, the time comes to breathe the fresh air of the present and take to the streets. The best tours go where it is pleasant to walk and where a satisfying number of figures can be seen without too much trekking along traffic-laden streets. Fortunately there are many statues concentrated in the administrative and ceremonial heart of the city around Whitehall and St James's, together with the one garden and parkland area which has always allowed them unrestricted access, the Victoria Embankment Gardens.

Our first walk therefore begins at St Clement Dane's Church at the east end of the Strand, where we find Dr Johnson, Gladstone and one of London's newest commemorations, Lord Dowding. From here, a short descent to the river finds us at the top end of the Embankment Gardens. A host of worthies awaits us. As well as the free-standing figures shown on the map, notice the bust of Sir Arthur Sullivan by William Goscombe John, with the beautiful weeping figure beneath it, which stands at the beginning of the second garden. Likewise the tiny, exquisite memorial to the Imperial Camel Corps, near to Robert Burns, is not to be missed; it shows a soldier riding a camel and was sculpted by a member of the Corps, Major Cecil Brown.

At the southern end of this first itinerary, in the lea of the Houses of Parliament, is the statue of Mrs Pankhurst. You may wish to break here and make the journey back up Whitehall later, as this is a longish walk and there is a great deal to take in. Also in the Victoria Tower Gardens is *The Burghers of Calais* by Auguste Rodin, who had such a great influence on British sculptors of the late nineteenth and early twentieth centuries. At Calais this sculpture commemorates the burghers' personal and perilous surrender of the city to Edward III in 1347, but the London version was acquired simply as a work of art. At the end of the same gardens is the curious Buxton Anti-Slavery Fountain (see p57).

Parliament Square is the political heart of affairs, with six British Prime Ministers, one President of the U.S.A. and one Prime Minister of South Africa. As you proceed up Whitehall, keeping to the right of Horseguards, you pass the Cenotaph and two equestrian Field Marshals. It is interesting to compare their mounts; one was sculpted in the 1900's by a former army vet, the other thirty years later by an artist aiming for abstract rather than representational truth. At the top of Whitehall is the horseman who has been riding the streets longer than any other, King Charles I.

It is worth making a short detour from Trafalgar Square to see the "pigtail and pump-handle" statue of George III. Along the north

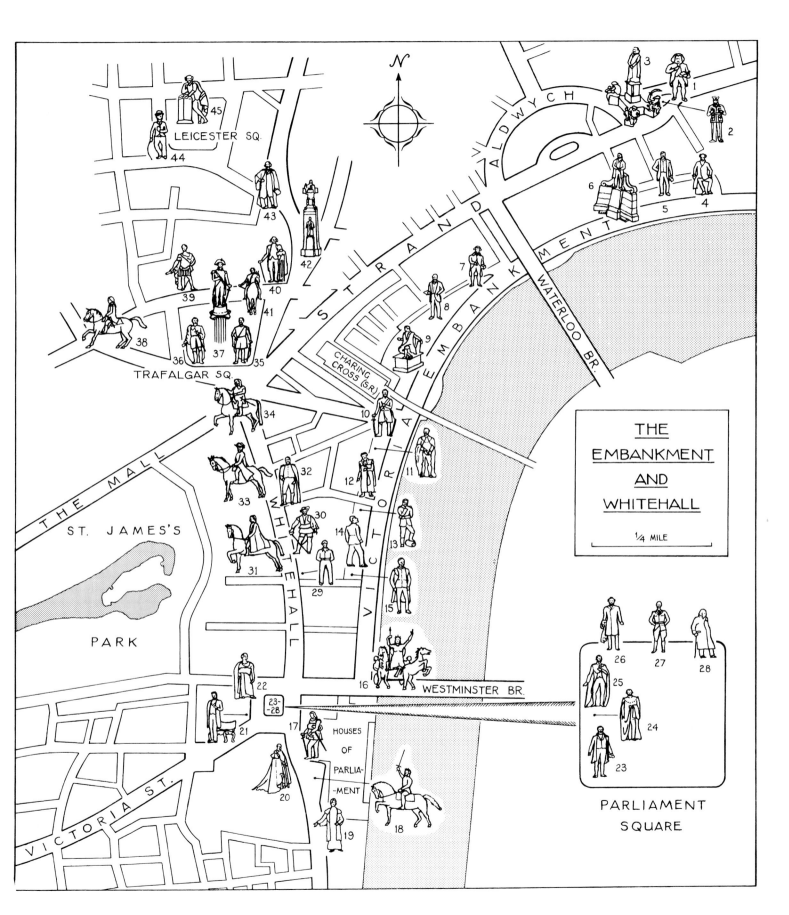

N

ALDWYCH

3

1

2

6

5

4

LEICESTER SQ.

45

44

43

42

S T R A N D

7

8

9

CHARING CROSS (SR)

39

40

41

36 37 35

TRAFALGAR SQ.

V I C T O R I A   E M B A N K M E N T

WATERLOO BR.

34

10

THE
EMBANKMENT
AND
WHITEHALL

¼ MILE

32

33

12 11

30

14 13

29

15

THE MALL

ST. JAMES'S

W H I T E H A L L

V I C T O R I A

26

27

28

31

PARK

25

24

23

16

WESTMINSTER BR.

PARLIAMENT
SQUARE

22

23-
28

21

17

HOUSES

OF

PARLIA-

-MENT

18

20

VICTORIA ST.

19

wall of the Square's central area notice the three naval busts of Admirals Jellicoe, Beatty and Cunningham; the famous fountains are also a part of their memorial. The walk ends in London's theatreland, with appropriately sited statues of Irving, Shakespeare and Charlie Chaplin.

The next walk centres around St James's Park and the architectural grandeur of The Mall (see p70). Begin at Admiralty Arch, which was designed to set off The Mall's perspective from its eastern end. Notice Thomas Brock's stone figures of Navigation and Gunnery on its sides; both are incongruously represented by women. Immediately to the left, next to the former Admiralty building, is the statue of the great navigator, Captain Cook. Then turn down to Horseguards Parade, once the functioning headquarters of the army and still its ceremonial heart. It has only three statues of military commanders but their bronze is always kept in tip-top condition.

From Birdcage Walk make a short detour to check whether the statue of Queen Anne has been wandering from its pedestal. After viewing Field Marshal Alexander at the Guards' London Headquarters, it is preferable to walk back and cross the foot-bridge over the lake in St James's Park. This avoids some of the traffic and also provides the correct approach up The Mall to the Victoria Memorial. Cross over to the central island and inspect the various figures; in a good light the overall impression is stunning. Sundays are the best days as the whole of The Mall is then closed to traffic.

Retrace your steps and make a detour up Marlborough Road to see the Alexandra Memorial set in its wall. Then find the steps leading up to Carlton House Terrace; at the top stands the statue of George VI. Half-way along the Terrace is the Duke of York's majestic column. Waterloo Place contains a variety of figures: a king, two explorers, two field marshals and a viceroy of India. It also extends across Pall Mall to include the Guards' Crimea Memorial and the statues of Sidney Herbert and Florence Nightingale. Then turn left off Regent Street down Charles II Street and find the classical equestrian statue of William III whose silhouette graces the back cover of this book.

There are other groupings, though not on such a concentrated scale. To the west of St Paul's Cathedral we find Queen Anne and the countries of her dominion (p32), to the south the modern representation of St Thomas Becket (p324) and to the north the more recent of the two figures of John Wesley (p356). Further to the north, outside the Post Office Headquarters in King Edward St, we find Sir Rowland Hill (p94). A longish walk down Cheapside passes Bow Churchyard and the statue of Captain John Smith (p308) and reaches the Royal Exchange. In front of it is the Duke of Wellington, seated on his dignified charger (p244) and behind and to the left is the banker George Peabody, seated in his well-upholstered chair (p92). In the same lane is Michael Black's granite herm of Reuter, the Baron of international news. Down Cornhill, outside St Michael's Church, is Richard Goulden's memorial of the First World War (see p106).

Bloomsbury also has its quota. A walk here might begin with Sir Francis Bacon at Gray's Inn (p162) or, preferably, with Mrs MacDonald in Lincoln's Inn Fields (p106). Then proceed to Fenner Brockway in Red Lion Square (p226), Charles James Fox in Bloomsbury Square (p174) and his fellow Whig, the Duke of Bedford, in Russell Square (p148). Cross Southampton Row to find Queen Charlotte in her own Queen Square (p44) and Captain Coram in Brunswick Square, behind

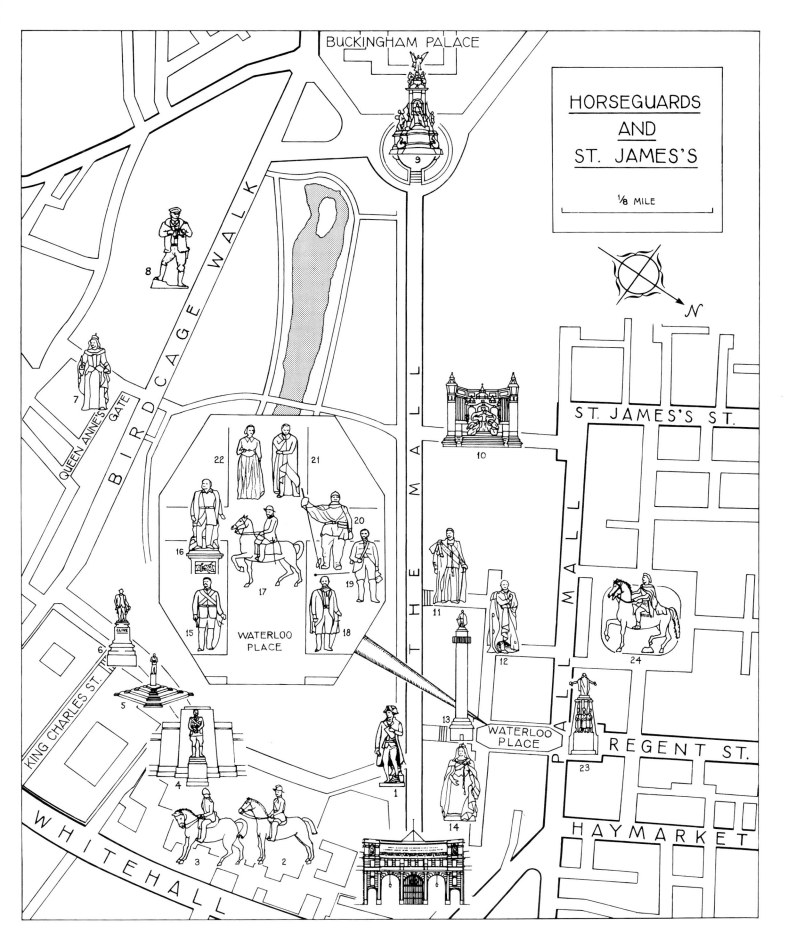

BUCKINGHAM PALACE

HORSEGUARDS
AND
ST. JAMES'S

⅛ MILE

N

BIRDCAGE WALK

QUEEN ANNE'S GATE

ST. JAMES'S ST.

THE MALL

WATERLOO PLACE

PALL MALL

WATERLOO PLACE

REGENT ST.

KING CHARLES ST.

WHITEHALL

HAYMARKET

his children's playgound (p114). Further steps northwards and westwards would find Major Cartwright in Cartwright Gardens (p176) and Gandhi, meditating in Tavistock Square (p234). Last comes Robert Stephenson (p158) outside Euston station.

Picadilly Circus, with Eros (p96), Golden Square, with George II (p41), Hanover Square, with William Pitt (p172) and Cavendish Square, with Lord George Bentinck (p182), lie more or less on a straight line crossing Regent Street and Oxford Street. Cavendish Square also has Epstein's beautiful Madonna and Child on the wall of a convent on the north side. Portland Place continues on northwards; in the centre of the carriageway are Quintin Hogg (p104) and Sir George White (p276) and at the top the Duke of Kent (p88), though not, as history determined, the Shakespeare National Memorial (see p120).

The third most varied and attractive tour, however, involves Kensington Gardens and the area to the south. There Queen Victoria was brought up and there Prince Albert left his most permanent architectural mark on his adopted country. The walk begins with the statue of Victoria at her coronation, sculpted by her daughter Princess Louise, and continues round the corner of the Palace gardens to the German statue of William III in its plumed hat. Then go south-east and pay your respects to Lord Napier at Queen's Gate. Behind the Albert Hall is the Memorial to the Great Exhibition with its statue of Prince Albert who planned it all. At the corner of Kensington Gore and Exhibition Road is the Royal Geographical Society; in niches on its northern and eastern sides are statues of the explorers Livingstone and Shackleton. Across the Gore the Albert Memorial dominates the scene. Inspect as much as you can of its elaborate symbolic detail, though at the time of writing it is scheduled for major rebuilding.

Proceeding northwards through the Gardens, you will find G.F. Watts' greatest sculptural creation, the horse and rider *Physical Energy*, at a main junction of paths. To the north is the obelisk erected in memory of John Hanning Speke who did what Livingstone failed to do, discovering the source of the Nile in 1860. Down to the right towards the Serpentine, at his fairy-tale landing place, is the Prince of Immortals, Peter Pan. The journey ends with water and the statue of Dr Jenner among the pools and fountains.

Over two thirds of London's free-standing statues have been mentioned so far in these itineraries. The rest are somewhat more isolated. A very few are situated at the periphery of the city, spread out around the points of the compass, from Edward VII at Tooting (p72) in the south, Sir Sydney Waterlow at Highgate (p100) in the north, John Colet at Hammersmith (p102) in the west and Gladstone at Bow (p204) in the east. The East End has three more statues, all of local denizens: Richard Green (p90), William Booth (p318, caption) and Clement Attlee (pp328-43). Despite its traffic, Hyde Park Corner, together with Apsley House (which is open to the public and contains some interesting sculptural items) should be viewed as a shrine to the Duke of Wellington; here are Achilles (pp241-3) and Joseph Boehm's equestrian statue guarded by its soldiers (p249). The arch itself was once home to another highly prominent statue of Wellington (pp246-7 & 348) but now bears the magnificent Quadriga (see p270). Close by is Lord Byron (p124). St Thomas's Hospital has four statues – one of Sir Robert Clayton (p82), two of Edward VI (p36) and a minor Florence Nightingale (p165). Guy's has two – Thomas Guy (p84) and

1. Queen Victoria (p65).
2. William III (p71).
3. Field Marshal Lord Napier of Magdala (p266).
4. Prince Albert, The Great Exhibition Memorial (p58).
5. David Livingstone (p304).
6. Sir Ernest Shackleton (see p304)
7. The Albert Memorial (p62).
8. Physical Energy (see p188).
9. Peter Pan (p136).
10. Dr Edward Jenner (p152).

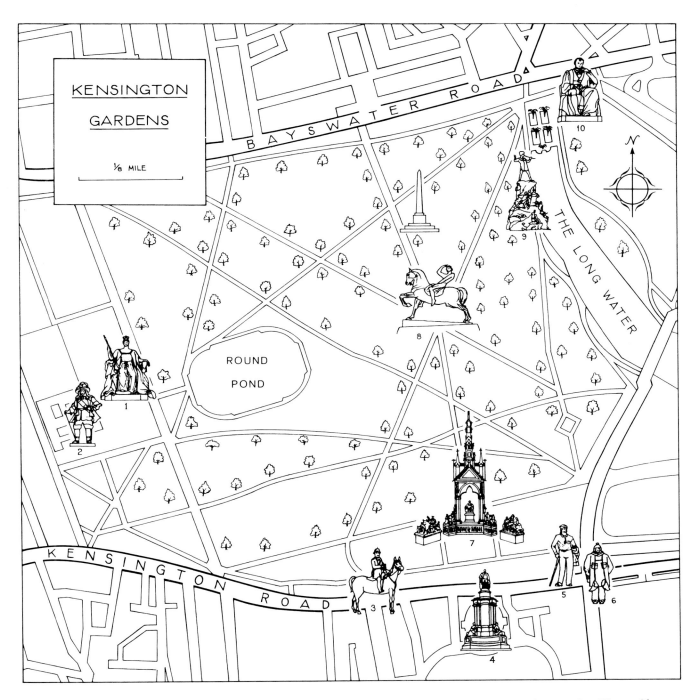

Lord Nuffield (p108). There are four at Chelsea – Sir Hans Sloane (p146), Thomas Carlyle (p126) and Sir Thomas More (p322), all of whom lived in the borough, and a contemporaneous statue of Charles II, who founded Chelsea Hospital (p26). Greenwich has George II (p40), William IV (p54) and General Wolfe (p283), all on or near the Prime Meridian.

To walk about ones *civitas* and appreciate the memorials to the figures of its past is an essential part of civilised life. Through this great company of statues, we in London have an outstanding opportunity to attune ourselves to the achievements of our country and its position in world culture. Let us take this opportunity together.

APPENDIX

By the Statue of King Charles at Charing Cross
by
Lionel Johnson

Sombre and rich the skies:
Great glooms and starry plains
Gently the night wind sighs:
Else a vast silence reigns

The splendid silence clings
Around me: and around
The saddest of all kings
Crowned and again discrowned.

Comely and calm he rides
Hard by his own Whitehall:
Only the night wind glides:
No crowds, nor rebels, brawl

Gone too his Court: and yet
The stars his courtiers are:
Stars in their stations set
And every wandering star.

Alone he rides, alone,
The fair and fatal king:
Dark night is all his own,
The strange and solemn thing.

Which are more full of fate:
The stars; or those sad eyes?
Which are more still and great:
Those brows; or the dark skies?

Although his whole heart yearns
In passionate tragedy:
Never was face so stern
With sweet austerity.

Vanquished in life, his death
By beauty made amends:
The passing of his breath
Won his defeated ends.

Brief life, and hapless? Nay:
Through death, life grew sublime.
Speak after sentence? Yea:
And to the end of time.

Armoured he rides, his head
Bare to the stars of doom:
He triumphs now, the dead,
Beholding London's gloom.

Our wearier spirit faints,
Vexed in the world's employ.
His soul was of the saints:
And art to him was joy.

King, tried in fires of woe!
Men hunger for thy grace:
And through the night I go
Loving thy mournful face.

Yet when the city sleeps;
When all the cries are still:
The stars and heavenly deeps
Work out a perfect will.

Bibliography, Sources and Photographic Acknowledgements

Source material relating directly to the statues is given here. So too are the single biographical sources consulted for less prominent figures. In the case of major historical figures, it would be inappropriate to rely on the point of view of one biographer. To cite all those consulted would be tedious, to cite one would be invidious, so none are given unless directly quoted in the text.

The book's three photographers have in principle divided their work according to chapter. The name of the photographer is given at the beginning of each chapter and any addition or exception is indicated in the notes below.

Common abbreviations used:
PRO Work: Public Record Office, Kew, Office of Works files
T: *The Times*
ILN: *Illustrated London News*
AJ: *Art Journal*
RCHME: Royal Commission on the Historical Monuments of England
GLRO: Greater London Record Office

All publications took place in London unless otherwise stated

Principal General Works

Susan Beattie, *The New Sculpture*. New Haven & London, 1983
Arthur Byron, *London Statues*. 1981.
The Dictionary of National Biography. 1882-1981.
Richard Dorment, *Alfred Gilbert*. New Haven & London, 1985.
Lord Edward Gleichen, *London's Open-Air Statuary*. 1928.
M. Dorothy George, *Catalogue of Political and Personal Satires Preserved in the Department of Prints and Drawings of the British Museum*. 1954.
Rupert Gunnis, *Dictionary of British Sculptors, 1660-1854*. 1951.
London County Council and Greater London Council, *The Survey of London* (42 vols). 1900-1986.
Elfrida Manning, *Marble and Bronze: The Life and Art of Hamo Thornycroft*. 1982.
Benedict Read, *Victorian Sculpture*. New Haven & London, 1982.
Osbert Sitwell, *The People's Album of London Statues*. 1928.
Mark Stocker, *Royalist and Realist: The Life and Work of Sir Joseph Edgar Boehm*. Garland Publishing, New York & London, 1988.
Margaret Whinney, *Sculpture in Britain, 1530-1830*. 1964.
Alison Yarrington, *The Commemoration of the Hero, 1800-1846*. Garland Publishing, New York & London, 1987.

Introduction

Wyatt's proposed design for George III memorial: *Gentleman's Magazine*, vol 92(i) (1822), p269, reproduced by Bodleian Library from Per 22863 e. 193. Memorial advertisement: Royal Academy Ms, Misc/Wyatt 13 (1823), reproduced by Royal Academy. Flaxman: Yarrington, p57-9. Value of money: B.R. Mitchell, *Abstract of Historical Statisics* (Cambridge, 1962) pp468-75, and Central Statistical Office, leaflet (Oct., 1988). Cato: Plutarch, *Parallel Lives*, quoted in Philip Feyl, *The Classical Monument*, (New York, 1972) p52. Havelock: *Havelock's Humble Petition* in

Punch, Vol 40 (1861i), p228. Peabody statue: AJ, 1869, p289. Embankment engraving, *The Graphic*, author's collection. Suez cartoon: Osbert Lancaster, cover, *The Year of the Comet* (1957). Richard Coeur de Lion, frontispiece photograph: B.B.C. Hulton Picture Library.

Chapter 1: Royalty
Photographer: Caroline Irwin.

Introduction. "Alfred". Aleck Abrahams, *The Oldest London Statue, 1395-1921*, in *Notes and Queries*, 12th series, vol 9 (Aug. 13th, 1921) p122-3. Sir Robert Cooke, *The Palace of Westminster* (1987), pp32-3.

Charles I. D.G.Denoon, *The Statue of King Charles I at Charing Cross*, in *London and Middlesex Archaeological Transactions*, vol 6 (1927-31) pp461-486, *The Survey of London*, vol 37, The Parish of St Paul, Covent Garden (1970), pp125-6, and R.M. Ball, *On the Statue of King Charles at Charing Cross*, in *Antiquaries Journal*, vol 69 part I (1987) pp97-101. Background: Roy Strong, *Van Dyck: Charles I on Horseback*, (1972) chap 3. Le Sueur: Whinney, pp35-7. Neo-Jacobin ceremonies: PRO Work 20/10-11. Photos: Cartoon and street scene, reproduced by RCHME; Le Sueur and World Wars, reproduced by Bodleian Library from Denoon, above, Soc.9a Lond 8ve.681.

Charles II. Soho Square. *The Survey of London*, Vol 33, The Parish of St Anne, Soho, (1966), pp51-3. Exile: Frederick Goodall, *Reminiscences* (1902) p285. Return: T, Feb. 19, 1938, 9b. Photograph by Paul Barkshire, reproduced by permission of RHCME. Chelsea Hospital. Statue: Whinney, p55 and n. p249. D.B. Green, *Grinling Gibbons, his Work as Carver and Statuary*. (1964) pp54-7. Martin Lister, *A Journey to Paris in the Year 1698* (1679 ed), pp26-8. Roman dress: M.Simpkins, *The Roman Army from Caesar to Trajan*, Osprey Men-at-Arms series (1974). Royal Oak: Thomas Blount, *Boscabel* (1786 edition), pp40-2 & 62-4. Quellin: Whinney, pp53-7.

James II. PRO Work 20/51, 133, 242 & 270. Engraving of Privy Gardens: reproduced by GLRO, Prints and Maps.

Anne. St Paul's. *Special Committee on Statues, Monuments and Other Memorials in the City of London, Report* (1947). Garth's satire: see Dr Johnson's English Poets, vol 10. Photo of originals reproduced by Guildhall Library. Queen Anne's Gate. Erection: *The Survey of London*, Vol 10, St Margaret's, Westminster, Pt I, (1926) pp101-4, 122 & plate 77. Move: *Gentleman's Magazine*, vol 84 (1814) p238. Damage and restoration: PRO Work 20/99, 114 & 238. Unbricking photo: *The Architect's Journal*, May 8, 1947.

Edward VI. Edward and St Thomas's: W.K.Jordan, *Edward VI and the Threshold of Power* (1970), esp. chap 7, The Rise of the Secular Charitable Impulse. Scheemakers: Virtue, in Walpole Society, vol 22, pp108-9 & 116, Whinney, pp92-7, Gunnis, p341-3. Position of statues: Cameron (see Thomas Guy, chap 2, below), pp38-9.

George I. Timothy Shaw, *The Golden Horse of Leicester Square*, in *Country Life*, Dec 5th, 1968, pp1532-3. Canons: C.H. Collins Baker and M.I. Baker, *The Life and Circumstances of James Brydges, Duke of Chandos* (1949) and Alexander Pope, *Epistle to*

Richard Boyle, Earl of Burlington, line 120. Van Nost and Carpenter: Sheila O'Connell, *The Nosts, a Revision of Family History* in *The Burlington Magazine,* Dec. 1987, pp802-6. Engraving and cartoon reproduced by the Local History Library, Victoria.

George II. Greenwich. Hasted's *History of Kent,* enlarged edition (1886) by H.H.Drake, p72 & note, and P.S.Newell, *A Royal Foundation, Greenwich Hospital,* p66-70. Vandalism: letter to Newell from Hospital Estate Office, March 9th, 1966. Golden Square. Repairs and pre-repairs photo: PRO Work 20/283.

George III and Queen Caroline. Bacon and Somerset House: Ann Cox-Johnson, *John Bacon R.A.,* St Marylebone Society Publications, no 4 (1961). Joshua Reynolds, Discourse 10 (1797 edition), lines 386-9. Charlotte's life and portraits: Olwen Hedley, *Queen Caroline* (1975). Supposed ugliness: J.H.Plumb, *The Four Georges* (1956), p105. Controversy over statue's identity: Francis Draper, *Queen Anne or Queen Charlotte?,* in *Home Counties Magazine,* vol 13 (1911) pp142-5. Gleichen, pp 178-9. Numerous local newspaper cuttings c.1960 in PRO Work 20/119 & 282. George's illness: Dr Richard Hunter and Dr Ida Macalpine, *The "Insanity" of George III; a Classic case of Pophyria,* in British Medical Journal, Jan. 8th, 1966, pp65-71, and *George III and the Madness Business* (1969). Portrait of Charlotte reproduced by The Royal Collection, St James's Palace.

William III. Earliest statue proposals: Narcissus Luttral, *A Brief Historical Relation of State Affairs* (1872 edition) vol 4, p316 (Dec. 9th, 1697), & Vol 5, p154 (March 9th, 1702). City's rejection: *Daily Journal,* Oct. 22 & 23, 1731. Bacon and St James's Square: Ann Cox-Johnson, see George III, above, and Arthur Dasent, *History of St James's Square* (1895) pp51-61.

George III's National Memorial. J.M.Robinson, *The Wyatts, An Architectural Dynasty* (1979), pp173-184. Subscriptions, based on R.A. Ms., see Introduction, above. Sabotage, court case and unveiling: T, Aug. 9th, 1836, 4b.

George IV. National Memorial. Advertisement: reproduced by GLRO, Prints and Maps. Demolition: ILN, February 5th, 1845, reproduced by Bodleian Library from above, Per 170 b.6. Cartoon: British Museum, Department of Prints and Drawings, reproduced from George 15850. Trafalgar Square. PRO Work 20/27. Chantrey: John Holland, *Memorials of Sir Francis Chantrey, R.A., Sculptor.* (1851). Engraving, AJ, 1850, p45, reproduced by Bodleian Library from above, Per 170 c.3.

William IV. T, Oct. 17th, 4f, & Dec. 19th, 3a, 1844, & Jan. 8th, 5c, & 9th, 5c, & Feb 1st, 5e, 1845. Move: PRO Work 20/98 & 246. Print of City site and photo of move reproduced by Guildhall Library.

Richard I. Life: John Gillingham, *Richard The Lion Heart* (1978). Statue: PRO Work 20/28.

Albert. Great Exhibition Memorial. *The Survey of London,* vol 38, The Museums Area of South Kensington and Westminster, (1975) esp. pp133-136. Viewing pit: painting by A.C.Stannus, reproduced by Victoria and Albert Museum. Unveiling: T, June 11th, 1863, 11c-f. Licensed Victuallers' Association. Unveiling: ILN, Aug. 20th, 1864, engraving reproduced by Bodleian Library from above, N.2288.b.6. Subsequent history: Licensed Victuallers' National Homes, private communication. Holborn. ILN, Jan. 4th, 1869. Kensington Memorial. Stephen Bayley, *The Albert Memorial* (1981). Statue's unboarding: T, March 13, 1876, p8. Engraving by T.A. Prior from painting by G.A. Andrews, reproduced by Kensington Public Library.

Queen Victoria. Elisabeth Darby, *Statues of Queen Victoria and Prince Albert, A Study in Commemorative Portrait Statuary, 1837-1924.* Courtauld Institute, Unpublished Thesis, 1983.

Kensington Gardens. Princess Louise: Jehanne Wake, *Princess Louise, Queen Victoria's Unconventional Daughter* (1988) (pp302-3 has a picture of the statue's unveiling). Blackfriars Bridge. Unveiling: T, July 22nd, 1896, p9. Mall Memorial. Construction and unveiling: PRO Work 20/19-21. *Pall Mall Gazette,* Aug. 23rd, 1904. T, May 15th, 1911, 8a-b, 16th, 7b-f, 17th, 11f & 12a-d; photo reproduced by GLRO Library.

Boadicea. Graham Webster, *Boudica, the British Revolt against Rome, A.D.60.* (1978). Statue: Manning, pp 38-41 & 56-7. Costs: Gleichen, p98. Photo: from ILN, 18th Feb. 1961, p271, supplied by Photo Source. Engraving of Thornycroft: *The Graphic* vol 50 (Nov. 3rd, 1894) p526, reproduced by Bodleian Library from above, N.2288 b.8.

William III, Kensington Gardens. PRO Work 20/60. *Evening News,* Nov 6th, 1907, quoted in *Notes and Queries,* 10th series, vol 10 (1908), p493.

Edward VII. Tooting Broadway. *Wandsworth Borough News,* Nov. 3rd, 1911 & July 26th, 1912. National Memorial. PRO Work 20/63.

Alexandra. London Hospital. Life and Hospital: David Duff, *Alexandra* (1980) pp147-50 and Georgina Battiscombe, *Queen Alexandra* (1969) pp257-8. Unveiling: T, July 11th, 1908, 12c. Memorial. PRO, Work 20/178 and Dorment, pp304-24.

George V. History and first model: Sir Charles Stuart, *Memorial to a King* (1954), photo reproduced by Bodleian Library from above. Controversy over canopy: T, Jan. 12th, 1939, 10f etc., to March 31st, 15e. Photograph of unveiling: *The Sphere,* Vol 191 (Nov. 1st, 1947) p129, reproduced by Bodleian Library from above, N.2288 b.34.

George VI. T, Feb. 22nd, 1955, 6d. Statue of Prince Imperial: *The Graphic,* Jan. 20th, 1883, pp53 & 55.

Chapter 2: Philanthropy and Education.

Photographer: Richard Cheatle

Sir Robert Clayton. Life: Benjamin Golding, *A Historical Account of St Thomas's Hospital, Southwark* (1819) pp91 & 108-10, and Benjamin Orridge, *The Citizens of London* (1867) pp145-51. Jeffries: Seward, *Anecdotes of Distinguished Persons* (5th edition, 1804) vol 2, pp141-2. Dryden: Absolom and Achitophel, Part 2, (1682), lines 280-5. Sir John Moore's statue: Wren Society Publications, vol 11, p77.

Thomas Guy. S. Wilks and G.J.Bettany, *A Biographical History of Guy's Hospital* (1892) pp1-73 & 94-5 and H.C.Cameron, *Mr Guy's Hospital* (1954), pp7-34, 68 & 70.

James Hulbert. Fishmongers' Company Archives, document "The New Erected Almshouses" and personal communications. Photograph by Paul Barkshire.

Robert Aske. J.R.Meredith, *The Foundation and Early History of Aske's Hospital at Hoxton* (Birmingham, 1964) pp5-23 and L.E. Ingarfield and M.B. Alexander, *Haberdashers' Aske's Boys' School, A Short History* (1985), pp1-5 & 13-5. Stowe's *Survey of London,* ed. Strype (1720), pp212-3.

The Duke of Kent. Life: Roger Fulford, *The Royal Dukes* (1933) pp161-204. Charities: Rev Erskine Neale, *Life of the Duke of Kent* (1850), pp230-6. Owen: Robert Owen, *The Life of Robert Owen by Himself* (1857), vol 1, pp193-200 & 223-9, & Appendix Q. Meeting for statue: *Gentlemen's Magazine,* Vol 90 (1820i), p464.

Richard Green. Life and statue: ILN May 19th, 1866. Incident with firemen and photograph, *Daily Mirror,* Oct. 5th, 1967.

George Peabody. Anon, *Lord Shaftesbury and George Peabody, The Story of Two Great Public Benefactors* (W.R.Chambers, Ltd., undated) especially pp124-6. AJ, 1869, p289. Beattie, pp201-3.

Engraving of unveiling: *Appleton's Journal of Popular Literature, Science and Art*, July 31st, 1869, copy kindly supplied by The Peabody Trust.

Sir Rowland Hill. Eleanor C. Smyth, *Sir Rowland Hill, The Story of a Great Reformer* (1907), especially pp300-1. Read, pp292-4.

Lord Shaftesbury Memorial. *Survey of London*, Vol 31 (Parish of St James, Westminster, Part II), (1963), pp101-10. Dorment, pp100-3 & 108-15. Restoration: Royal Academy, Friends' Magazine no 11 (Summer, 1986). Photos: Gilbert, reproduced by National Portrait Gallery; Shaftesbury, copied by Bodleian library from original kindly supplied by the Shaftesbury Society; frozen memorial, supplied by Photo Source.

Sir Sydney Waterlow. Life and statue: George Smalley, *The Life of Sir Sydney H. Waterlow, Bart.* (1909). Photograph by David Nabarro.

John Colet. Life: Kalyan K. Chatterjee, *In Praise of Learning, John Colet and Literary Humanism* (New Delhi, 1974), especially pp85-92. St Paul's School, personal communications. Close-up photograph by Philip Ward-Jackson, reproduced by permission of the Courtauld Institute.

Quintin Hogg. Ethel M. Wood, *The Polytechnic and Its Founder, Quintin Hogg* (932), especially pp292-4. Unveiling: T, Nov. 26th, 1906, 10b. Photograph by Philip Ward-Jackson, reproduced by permission of the Courtauld Institute.

Margaret MacDonald. J. Ramsay MacDonald, *Margaret Ethel MacDonald*, (1912). Lucy Herbert, *Mrs Margaret MacDonald* (1924). Goulden: Major M.R.R. Goulden, private communications and photograph.

Nuffield. Robert Jackson, *The Nuffield Story* (1964), especially pp236-7. Benefactions: P.W.S. Andrews & Elisabeth Brunner, *Lord Nuffield*, (Oxford, 1955), pp259-336.

Baden-Powell. Life: Eileen K. Wade, *The Chief* (1975) and Michael Rosenthal, *The Character Factory* (1986). Statue: Donald Potter, personal communications and photographs.

Captain Coram. Ruth K. McClure, *Coram's Children* (New Haven and London, 1981).

Chapter 3: The Arts
Photographer: Caroline Irwin

Palladio and Inigo Jones. M.I.Webb, *Michael Rysbrack, Sculptor* (1954) pp101-12. Chiswick House photograph by Paul Barkshire.

William Shakespeare. Tom Taylor, *Leicester Square, Its Associations and Worthies* (1874) pp478-484. Stratford Reference Library. Correspondence held at Library, especially from Rupert Gunnis. Photo: Guildhall Library. Dover statue: AJ, 1881, p328-9. Proposed National Memorial: *Notes and Queries*, 10th series, vol 10, p211 (Sept 12th, 1908).

J.S. Mill. Appearance of statue: G.Shaw Lefevre, *Statues and Monuments in London*, in *Nineteenth Century*, Jan. 1884, pp28-48. Woolner photo: Ashmolean Library, Oxford.

Lord Byron. Life: Jonathan Boulting, personal communications. PRO Work 20/47. Belt trial: Read pp66-7 & ILN, Vol 81 (1882ii) p517, engraving reproduced by Bodleian Library.

Thomas Carlyle. Carlyle and Boehm: Stocker, pp217-9. Unveiling: ILN, Vol 81 (Nov. 4th, 1882), pp465-6.

Robert Burns. Edwin Muir: quotation from *The Burns Myth*, in W. Montgomerie ed., *New Judgements: Robert Burns* (Glasgow, 1947) pp5-12. ILN, Vol 85 (Aug. 9th, 1884), p126. Photo: Hulton Picture Library.

Sarah Siddons. Unveiling: T, June 15th, 12e. Col Siddons Young: *Bayswater Chronicle*, June 19th, 1897.

Sir John Everett Millais. J.G.Millais, *Life: The Life and Letters of Sir John Everett Millais* (1899). Brock: J.A.Sankey, *London's Forgotten Sculptor*, in ILN, Christmas 1985, pp61-4.

Peter Pan. J.M. Barrie, *The Little White Bird* (1902), pp141-226; map reproduced by Bodleian Library from above, 2561 e. 1325. Roger Lancelyn Green, *Fifty Years of Peter Pan* (1954), p120. Henrietta Llewellyn-Davies, private communication.

Dr Johnson. Penningtons: Curator of Johnson's House, Gough Square, private communications.

Sir Henry Irving. Nature of art: Edward Gordon Craig, *Henry Irving* (1930). Unveiling: T, July 16th, 13d & Dec. 6th, 13d.

Sir Joshua Reynolds. Alfred Drury: Mrs Enid Drury, private communications. Progress of statue: Royal Academy Annual Reports. 1916, p6 and App 13, 1917, p6, 1925, p26, 1926, p10, 1929, p19, 1931, p23, 1932, p23. Photograph by Philip Ward-Jackson, reproduced by permission of the Courtauld Institute.

Charlie Chaplin. Sir Charles Chaplin, *My Autobiography*, (1966) p154. GLRO Library, press cuttings under 45:Chap. Royal Fine Arts Commission: Sir David Piper, personal communication. Tommy Steel photo: Press Association.

Chapter 4: Science and Medicine
Photographer: Richard Cheatle

Introduction. Freud quotation: *The Question of a Weltangschaung?* in *New Introductory Lectures On Psycho-Analysis*, The Complete Works ed. J. Strachey, Vol 22, p174.

Sir Hans Sloane. Life: E.StJ. Brooks, *Sir Hans Sloane, the Great Collector, and his Circle*, (1954). M.I. Webb, *Michael Rysbrack, Sculptor* (1954) p70. Photograph by Caroline Irwin.

The Duke of Bedford. Life: Christopher Trent, *The Russells* (1966) and Georgiana Blakiston, *Woburn and the Russells* (1980). Engraving by Shepherd, reproduced by GLRO Prints and Maps. Other photos reproduced by permission of the Courtauld Institute, seasons photographed by Philip Ward-Jackson.

Edward Jenner. Arthur Calder Marshall, *A Colossal Bronze*, in *The Listener*, Jan. 8th, 1953. Sites: PRO, Work 20/33.

Dr Bentley Todd. Life: L.S. Beale, *On Medical Progress, In Memoriam R.B.Todd* (1870).

Sir James McGrigor. Life: Richard L. Blanco, *Wellington's Surgeon General, Sir James McGrigor* (Duke University Press, 1974).

Sir Hugh Myddleton. Life: J.W. Gough, *Sir Hugh Myddleton, Entrepreneur and Engineer* (1964). Gladstone and unveiling: T, July 28th, 1862, 6c. John Thomas: ILN, Vol 41, pp231-2 (Aug. 30th, 1862). Thomas and Peto: Read, pp143-6. Photograph by Paul Barkshire.

Robert Stephenson and I.K. Brunel: PRO Work 20/253.

Sir Francis Bacon. Life and vision: J.G. Crowther, *Francis Bacon, The First Statesman of Science* (1960). Grays Inn Gardens: Christian Teale, *New Glimpses of Francis Bacon*, in *Home Counties Magazine*, Vol 14 (1912) pp220-8.

Florence Nightingale. PRO Work 20/67. St Thomas's statue: Hospital archivist, personal communication.

Edith Cavell. Life: Rowland Ryder, *Edith Cavell* (1975). PRO Work 20/126.

Freud. *Hampstead and Highgate Express*, Sept. 20th & Oct. 9th, 1970. Unveiling photograph by Nigel Sutton.

Chapter 5: Politics.

Photographer: Philip Ward-Jackson, photographs reproducd by permission of the Courtauld Institute. Colour photographs by Richard Cheatle.

Introduction. Cartoon: reproduced by British Museum, Department of Prints and Drawings, from George 9863.

William Pitt. Angerstein: Hugh Cockerell, *Lloyds of London, a Portrait* (1984) pp127-9. Progress of fund: Cobbett's *Annual Register*, Vol 2 (1803), pp1012-1024, and *Gentleman's Magazine*, vol 85(ii) (Sept, 1815) pp196-7, & vol 89(i) (March, 1819) p271. Westmacott statue: PRO, Work 20/291. Erection: Holland, pp 301-2. Unveiling: T, Aug. 23rd, 1831, 3b.

Charles James Fox. Nicholas Penny, *The Whig Cult of Fox in Early Nineteenth Century Sculpture*, in *Past and Present*, Vol 70 (1976) pp94-105. Cartoon: reproduced by British Museum, Department of Prints and Drawings, from George 7902.

Major John Cartwright. Life: John W. Osborne, *John Cartwright* (1972). Naval temple: John Cartwright, *The Trident or the National Policy of Naval Celebration* (1802). See also Nicholas Penny, *"Amor Publicus Posuit": Mounuments for the People and of the People*, in *Burlington Magazine*, vol 129 (Dec. 1987), pp 795-7. Statue: F.D. Cartwright, *The Life and Correspondence of Major Cartwright* (1826) vol 2, pp290-8.

George Canning. Statue's sculptor: T, Jan. 19th, 3a, Feb. 21st, 2d & March 31st, 1828. Erection: PRO, TI/4029, & T, May 4th, 1832, 3a. Criticism: *Observer*, quoted in T, May 21st, 2e. Move: AJ, 1867, p213. Canning portrait reproduced by National Portrait Gallery.

William Huskisson. Life: C.R.Fay, *Huskisson and His Age* (1951). Statue: Lady Eastlake (ed.), *Life of John Gibson, R.A., Sculptor* (1870), pp112ff and Joseph Ineichen, *The Intruder & The Hunt is Over*, in *Lloyd's Log*, Sept. 1975, pp18-19 and March 1976, pp16-17. "Boredom", Sitwell, op. cit. For a photograph of Gibson's first statue of Huskisson, see T. Matthews, *The Biography of John Gibson, R.A., Sculptor, Rome,* (1911) p80. Gibson also did a third, bronze figure for the outside of Liverpool Customs House. Photograph by Paul Berkshire.

Lord George Bentinck. Life: Michael Seth-Smith, *Lord Paramount of the Turf* (1971). Subscribers: T, Jan. 20th, 1849, 3a.

Richard Cobden: Jean Scott Rogers, *How Cobden came to Camden Town*, in *Camden History Society Review*, no 9 (1981), pp20-22.

Sir Robert Peel. Cheapside. T, Oct. 10th, 1850, 5d; April 6th, 6d, Oct. 12th, 6f, & 15th, 9b, & Nov. 14th, 10e, 1853; May 3rd, 1855, 12d. AJ, 1851, pp203 & 222. Moves: *City Press*, June 6th, 1974. Marochetti statue and Noble, Parliament Square: PRO Work 20/31. Hansard, 3rd series, vol 192 (May 11th-June 25th, 1868) pp2138-2149 and AJ, 1868, p160.

Sidney Herbert. Foley and engraving: AJ, 1849, p49, reproduced by Bodleian Library from Per 170 c.3.

Lord Holland. Life: Leslie Mitchell, *Holland House* (London, 1980). Erection: T, Dec. 1st, 1871, 6d. Watts: Read, pp276-86 and Richard Jeffries, Watts Gallery, Compton, personal communications. Photograph of *Physical Energy*: printed by kind permission of Watts Gallery.

Lord Derby. Life: W.D.Jones, *Lord Derby and Victorian Conservatism* (Oxford, 1956). *Art Journal* 1874, p254. Unveiling: T, July 13th, 10a. Plaques: Gleichen, p35. Noble photo: reproduced by Tate Gallery from Archive 795.9.

Palmerston. Life: Jasper Ridley, *Lord Palmerston* (1970). Woolner: Amy Woolner, *Thomas Woolner, His Life in Art and Letters* (1917), esp. p280. Verdict: AJ, 1876, p94.

Disraeli. Shrewsbury Column: Punch, vol 7 (Sept, 1844) p138, reproduced by Bodleian library from above, N.2706 d.10; I am most grateful to Ms. Frankie Morris for drawing my attention to this cartoon. G.J. Shaw Lefevre, as in J.S. Mill, chap 3, above. Unveiling: T, April 20th, 1883, 11a, & ILN, April 28th, 1883, reproduced by Bodleian Library from latter, N.2288 b.6. Primrose Day photo: reproduced by RCHME.

Lord Lawrence. Life: Sir Charles Aitcheson, *Lord Lawrence* (Oxford, 1892). Pen and sword: Robert Cust, quoted in Aitcheson, pp45-6, & n1. See also Gleichen, pp24-5, who does not accept the story, and Stocker, pp124-8.

Sir Bartle Frere. Life: John Martineau, *The Life of Sir Bartle Frere* (1895). Unveiling and plaque: T, June 6th, 12e.

W.E.Forster. Life: T. Wemyss Reid, *Life of the Rt. Hon. W.E. Forster* (1888).

W.E. Gladstone. Bow. Unveiling: T, Aug. 10th, 1881, 12a. Bryant and May Fountain: J.T. Page in *Notes and Queries*, 10th series, vol 9 (1908) p1. 1898 photo: Local History Library, Bancroft Road. Strand. Thornycroft and quotation from Gosse: Manning, pp137-40; the Thornycroft photograph was originally in her collection. That and the statue photograh by James Austin are reproduced by courtesy of the Courtauld Institute.

Oliver Cromwell. Lord Rosebery, *Oliver Cromwell, a Eulogy and an Appreciation* (1900). Hansard, 4th series, vol 33 (1895), p1168, vol 34 (1895), pp1181-94, p1270-1, pp1342-1361 & p1546, vol 70 (1899), p515 & pp810-2, & vol 77 (1895), pp749-60. PRO, Work 20/100 & 115. Manning p129. Charles II photo: anonymous scaffolder, 1987.

Sir Wilfrid Lawson. Life and statue: *Sir Wilfrid Lawson, A Memoir*, ed. George Russell (1909). Unveiling: T, July 21st, 1909, 10b.

The Duke of Devonshire. Life and likenesses: Henry Leach, *The Duke of Devonshire* (1904).

Colonel Bevington. Life: obituary in *Southward and Bermondsey Recorder and South London Gazette*, April 20th, 1907, p5. Statue and unveiling photograph: as above, March 24th, 1911, p5, reproduced by Newspaper Library, Colindale.

Sir Robert Clive. PRO, Work 20/61 & 107.

Lord Curzon. Life: Family's view of statue: PRO, Work 20/181.

Emmeline Pankhurst. PRO, Work 20/188. David Mitchell, *The Fighting Pankhursts* (1967) pp208-9. Unveiling: T, March 7th, 1930, 13a and Dame Ethel Smythe, *Female Pipings in Eden* (1933) pp272-81.

Winston Churchill. Ivor Roberts-Jones, personal communications. Balzac photo by Steichen, contretype B. Jarret, courtesy Rodin Museum, Paris (Ref:Ph 226). Hawk photograph by Richard Cheatle, courtesy British Museum.

Fenner Brockway. Life: Fenner Brockway, *Towards Tomorrow* (1977). Statue: Ian Walters, personal communications and *Morning Star*, July 31st, 1985. Photograph by Steve King.

Abraham Lincoln. Life and likenesses: Lord Longford, *Abraham Lincoln* (1974). Statues: PRO Work 20/10 and *Manchester Guardian*, May 6th, 1919, & Feb. 3rd, 1968. Manchester photograph by James Austin, reproduced by permission of the Courtauld Institute.

George Washington. Mythography and statue: Garry Wills, *George Washington and the Enlightenment* (1985) esp. pp 220-40. John.S. Hallam, *Houdon's Washington in Richmond: Some New Observations*, in *American Art Journal*, Nov 1978, pp72-80.

F.D. Roosevelt. Sir Campbell Stuart, *Britain's Tribute to Franklin Roosevelt,* (1947). Booth photo from above, supplied by Photo Source.

Mahatma Gandhi. *Hampstead and Highgate Express*, May 17th & 24th, 1968.

Smuts. Life: *Dictionary of South African Biography*, vol 1 (Cape Town, 1968), pp737-758. PRO Work 20/222 & 284. Unveiling photograph: ILN, Nov. 11th, 1956, supplied by Photo Source.

Simon Bolivar. Life: J.B.Trend, *Bolivar and the Independence of Spanish America* (1946). The Venezuelan Embassy and Dr Malcolm Deas, personal communications.

Chapter 6: The Armed Forces

Photographer: Philip Ward-Jackson, photographs reproduced by permission of the Courtauld Institute. Colour photographs by Richard Cheatle.

Wellington. Greenwich proposal: Yarrington, pp197-9. Wallpapers etc.: Lord Gerald Wellesléy and John Steepman, *The Iconography of the 1st Duke of Wellington* (1935), pix. Achilles. Westmacott's reaction: letter to James Elmes, Oct 25, 1822, Royal Academy, Jupp Vol 6, p154. Cartoon: reproduced by British Museum, Department of Prints and Drawings, from George 14383. Wyatt, Marble Arch. John Physick, *The Banishment of the Bronze Duke*, in *Country Life*, Oct. 27th, 1966, and *The Wellington Monument* (1970). Wyatt's studio: ILN vol 9 (1846ii) pp21-2, reproduced by Bodleian Library from above, N.2288 b.6. Woolwich. Photo: Press Association.

The Duke of York. Life: Alfred Burne, *The Noble Duke of York* (1949). Jests and protests: George, vol 11, p694 & fig 17283, and *The New Monthly Magazine* et al, quoted in J.T. Page, *The East London Advertiser*, Oct. 17th, p6. Unveiling: T, April 14th, 1834, 4e. Heights: Gleichen, p26 & DOE fact sheet. Costs: PRO Work 20/5/1/154, 156 & 274. Cleaning photo: *Evening Standard*, Jan. 1961, reproduced by RCHME.

Nelson. Read, pp87-90. Yarrington, chaps 3 & 5. Rodney Mace, *Trafalgar Square, Emblem of Empire* (1967), pp23-110 & 134-232. Bailey carving: picture reproduced by Royal Institute of British Architects. Erection: ILN, Nov. 1843, reproduced by Bodleian Library from above, N.2288 b.6. Landseer: Punch, 1867(i), p255. 1987 clean-up photos: Press Association.

Sir Charles Napier. Life and sketch: Rosamond Lawrence, *Charles Napier, Friend and Fighter* (1952). Unveiling: T, November 27th, 1856, 4d. Verdict: AJ, 1862, p98.

Sir Henry Havelock. Life: Leonard Cooper, *Havelock* (1957) and J.C.Pollock, *The Way To Glory, Havelock of Lucknow* (1957) esp. prologue. Behnes: AJ, 1864, pp83-4.

Sir Colin Campbell. Life: Lt. Gen. Lawrence Shadwell, *The Life of Sir Colin Campbell, Lord Clyde* (Edinburgh, 1881). Appearance: ILN, vol 20 (1868i) pp59 & 76. Resemblance to statue: "T.F.D." in *Notes and Queries*, 10th series, Vol 10, p494. Move of pedestal: PRO Work 20/38.

Sir James Outram. Lionel Trotter, *The Bayard of India* (1909) esp. testimonials, pp215-6.

Sir John Burgoyne. Life: Sir Francis Head, *Field Marshal Sir John Burgoyne* (1872). Boehme: Stocker, op. cit., and *Vanity Fair*, Vol 25 (Jan. 22nd, 1881) p51 and facing, portrait reproduced by Bodleian Library from above.

Lord Robert Napier. DNB & *In Memoriam Field Marshal Lord Napier of Magdala* (1890).

General Gordon. Memorials: T, June 2nd, 8c & Nov. 13th, 9f, 1885. Statue funds: Hansard, vol 245 (1885), p1037. Thornycroft: Manning, p102. Move: PRO Work 20/215.

The Duke of Cambridge. Life: Giles St Aubyn, *The Royal George* (1963). Jones: Captain Adrian Jones, *Memoirs of a Soldier Artist* (1933), photos reproduced by Bodleian Library from above,

170 e.54.

Wolseley. Life: Joseph Lehmann, *All Sir Garnet* (1964). Roberts. Life: W.H. Hannah, *Bobs, Kipling's General* (1972). Statue: PRO Work 20/136 & Beattie pp219-221. Volonel: Stella Walker, *Historic Horses in Bronze and Stone*, in *Country Life*, vol 140ii (1966), pp1302-6.

Sir George White. Gerald Sharp, *The Seige of Ladysmith* (1976). Sites controversy: PRO Work 20/145. Tweed: Lendal Tweed, *John Tweed, A Memoir* (1936).

Kitchener and the First World War. Unveiling: T, June 10th, 11a & 20. Scheme: F.W.Speaight, *Horseguards' Parade, A Suggested Improvement by a Citizen of London* (1909), map reproduced by Guildhall Library from above, FOPam 705. London War Memorials: Byron, pp354-71. Graves: Ruth Manion & Beryl Graves, private communications, and photograph by Paul Joyce.

Marshal Foch. Life: Basil Liddell Hart, *Foch, the Man of Orleans* (1931). PRO Work 20/193.

General Wolfe. PRO Work 20/172. Unveiling: T, June 6th, 1930, 11a-b & 20. Photograph by Caroline Irwin.

Haig. Earl Haig, *Memories of the Field Marshal*, in *Stand To!*, the journal of the Western Front Association, No. 21, Dec. 1987 (including eye-witness account of the unveiling). Statue controversy: *Country Life*, Vol 82 (Nov 20th, 1937) pp509-11. Cost: PRO Work 20/185-6.

Trenchard. Life: Andrew Boyle, *Trenchard* (1962). PRO Work 20/272.

Portal. Life: Denis Richards, *Portal of Hungerford* (1977). Nemon: F. Nemon-Stewart, personal communication.

Montgomery. Photograph of model: T, June 1st, 1980, 2f. Unveiling: T, 7th, 14c.

Alexander. Life: Nigel Nicolson, *Alex* (1973). Statue: T, May 10th, 1985, 3d, and James Butler, personal communications.

Mountbatten. Press cuttings, Local History Library, Victoria.

Chapter 7: Exploration and Religion

Photographer: Richard Cheatle

Sir John Franklin. Life: G.F.Lamb, *Franklin, Happy Voyager* (1956). Unveiling: T, Nov. 16th, 1866, 10a. Popular appeal of statue: G. Shaw Lefevre, see J.S. Mill, chap 3, above.

Captain Cook. Mythography and statues: Jillian Robertson, *The Captain Cook Myth* (London and Australia, 1981). The Mall, Darby, p410. Unveiling: T, July 8th, 1914, 10f, PRO Work 20/79. Photo: GLRO Library.

Captain Scott. Kathleen Scott: Lady Kennet (Kathleen, Lady Scott) *Self-Portrait of an Artist* (London, 1947) esp. George V story, p302 and *Homage, A Book of Sculpture by Kathleen Scott*, with commentary by Stephen Gwynn (1938). Photograph from Elspeth Huxley, *Scott of the Antarctic* (1977), reproduced by the Bodleian Library from above, 2036 d.95, and printed by kind permission of Lord Kennet.

David Livingstone. Geographical Journal, 1954, pp15-20. Photo of Reid Dick studio: reproduced by Tate Gallery from Archive 8110.

Sir Walter Raleigh. PRO Work 20/268-9. Unveiling: T, Oct 29th, 1959, 8g.

Captain John Smith. Life: Paul Lewis, *That Great Rogue* (1966).

Robert Raikes. Life: Frank Booth, *Robert Raikes of Gloucester* (1980).

William Tyndale. Life: C.H. William, *William Tyndale* (1969). T, Jan. 24th, 5f, & May 8th, 4d, 1884. Photograph by Philip

Ward-Jackson, reproduced by permission of the Courtauld Institute.

John Wesley. Adams-Acton: A.M.W. Stirling, *Victorian Sidelights: From the Papers of the Late Mrs Adams-Acton* (1954). Photo of A-A reproduced from above by Bodleian Library.

Cardinal Newman. Statue in Oxford: T, 1892, Jan. 8th, 8f, 12th, 8b, 27th, 7a, Feb. 3rd, 5f, 4th, 12a, & 27th. In London: T, July 16th, 1896, 12c.

William and Catherine Booth. Lives: Richard Collier, *General Next to God*, (1965) and Geoffrey Hawks, *God's Special Army* (1980). William compared to Job: *Dictionary of National Biography*, entry by Harold Begbie.

St. Thomas More. Unveiling: T, July 22nd, 1969, 8d, 22 & 24, and photo: Press Association.

St Thomas Becket. Unveiling: March 31st, 1973, p3.

St Volodvmyr. *Ukraine: A Concise Encyclopaedia*, ed Kubijovyc (Toronto, 1963), pp581-92. J.R. Hawrych, Chairman, Ukrainian Millenium Committee, personal communications and photo of unveiling. Photograph of statue by Caroline Irwin.

Chapter 8: The Making of a Bronze

Photographer: Caroline Irwin.

Downing Street photograph reproduced by kind permission of Earl and Countess Attlee. First photograph of modelling by Heidi Larsen.

Chapter 9: Vanished Statues

Charles II, Stocks Market. Sir William Treolar, *A Statue With A Strange Story*, in *The Graphic*, Nov. 11th, 1916. Engraving reproduced by GLRO, Prints and Maps.

Lincoln's Inn Romans: E. Hatton, *A New View of London* (1708), pp799 etc. & Librarian, Lincoln's Inn, personal communications.

Handel. Gleichen, p227. Engraving of Vauxhall Gardens reproduced by GLRO, Prints and Maps. Photograph: Victoria and Albert Museum.

Duke of Cumberland. Gleichen, p226-7. Engraving reproduced by GLRO, Prints and Maps.

Milligan. Gleichen, p202. Photograph by Maria Busco.

Wellington. See chap 6, above. Photograph by David Collett.

Strathnairn. PRO Work 20/164 and Beattie, pp218-9. Store photo: T, from Oct. 22nd, 1964. Close-up photograph by Susan Beattie.

Fawcett. Gleichen, p170. Photo: GLRO Library.

Poetry Fountain. PRO Work 20/249. Photo: Victoria and Albert Museum. Dismantling photo: ILN, from Feb 12th, 1949.

Chapter 10: The Present of the Past

John Wilkes. Life: Dr James Cope, personal communications and Audrey Williamson, *Wilkes, a Friend to Liberty* (1974). Statue: Dr James Cope and James Butler, personal communications. Photo: *The Times*.

Lord Dowding. Wing Commander N.W.P. Hancock, Secretary and Treasurer, Battle of Britain Fighter Association, and Faith Winter, personal communications. Photographs by Caroline Irwin.

John Wesley. Martin Ludlow, Aldersgate Trustees, personal communications. Photos by Paul Harrington, *Methodist Recorder*. Morris Singer Ltd: Duncan James, personal communications.

Trajan. Photo by Richard Cheatle. Crutched Friars. Michael Black, personal communications. Photo by Thea Musgrave.

Paolozzi. National Portrait Gallery exhibition, 1988. Photo by Courtauld Institute. Perry. Photo by Micky White.

Brixton Passengers. Public Arts Development Trust, personal communications. Photographs by Edward Woodman.

Eisenhower. Unveiling brochure. Photographs by Ilkay Mehmet, *Daily Telegraph*.

Faraday. D. Steward, Manager, Building Services, Institute of Electrical Engineers, personal communications.

Chapter 11: Where To Walk

Maps by Ralph Coward.

INDEX